COMPLETE
YEAR

Weekly Learning Activities

Thinking Kids™
Carson-Dellosa Publishing LLC
Greensboro, North Carolina

Thinking Kids™
Carson-Dellosa Publishing LLC
P.O. Box 35665
Greensboro, NC 27425 USA

Printed in the USA • All rights reserved.   ISBN 978-1-4838-0195-7
01-153147784

Table of Contents

Table of Contents

Table of Contents

The *Complete Year* series has been designed by educators to provide an entire school year's worth of practice pages, teaching suggestions, and multi-sensory activities to support your child's learning at home. Handy organizers are included to help students and parents stay on track and to let you see at a glance the important skills for each quarter and each week of the academic year.

A variety of resources are included to help you provide high-quality learning experiences during this important year of your child's development.

Suggested Calendar (Page 7)

Use this recommended timetable to plan learning activities for your child during all 36 weeks of the school year.

A Guide to School Skills for Fifth Grade: Reading and Language Arts, Math, Science, Social Studies (Page 8)

Refer to this useful guide for information about what your child will be learning this school year, what to expect from your fifth grader, and how to help your child develop skills in each subject area.

Quarter Introductions (Pages 14, 108, 202, 296)

Four brief introductions outline the skills covered in practice pages for each nine-week grading period of the school year. In addition, they include a variety of ideas for multi-sensory learning activities in each subject area. These active, hands-on projects are fun for parents and children to do together and emphasize real-world applications for school skills.

Weekly Skill Summaries (Example: Page 17)

Thirty-six handy charts precede the practice pages for each week and give a snapshot of the skills covered. In addition, they provide ideas for fun, multi-sensory learning activities for each subject area.

Practice Pages (Example: Page 18)

Nine practice pages are provided each week for a total of over 300 skill-building activities to help your child succeed this year.

Quarter Check-Ups (Pages 107, 201, 295, 389)

Four informal assessment pages allow students to do a quick self-check of the important skills emphasized during the previous nine weeks. Parents can use these pages to see at a glance the skills their children have mastered.

Suggested *Complete Year* Calendar*

First Quarter: Weeks 1–9
(First nine-week grading period of the school year, usually August–October)

Second Quarter: Weeks 10–18
(Second nine-week grading period of the school year, usually October–December)

Third Quarter: Weeks 19–27
(Third nine-week grading period of the school year, usually January–March)

Fourth Quarter: Weeks 28–36
(Fourth nine-week grading period of the school year, usually April–June)

During Each Nine-Week Quarter:

- Read the **Quarter Introduction** to get an overview of the skills and subject areas emphasized. Choose several multi-sensory learning activities you plan to do with your child this quarter.

- Each week, glance at the **Weekly Skill Summary** to see targeted skills. Make a quick plan for the practice pages and multi-sensory learning activities your child will complete.

- Choose **Practice Pages** that emphasize skills your child needs to work on. Each page should take 10 minutes or less to complete.

- Ask your child to check the boxes on the **Quarter Check-Up** to show what skills he or she has mastered. Praise your child's progress and take note of what he or she still needs to work on.

* This calendar provides a schedule for using *Complete Year* during a typical nine-month academic calendar. If your child attends a year-round school or a school with a different schedule, you can easily adapt this calendar by counting the weeks your child attends school and dividing by four.

A Guide to School Skills for Fifth Grade

This guide provides background information about the skills and subject areas that are important for success in fifth grade. Tips are provided for helping your child develop in each curricular area.

Complete Year supports skills included in the Grade 5 Common Core State Standards for English Language Arts and Mathematics, which have been adopted by most U.S. states. A complete guide to these standards may be found at www.corestandards.org.

In addition, activities in *Complete Year* support the study of science and social studies topics appropriate for fifth grade.

 Reading and Language Arts

Reading

Teach reading through books that fit your child's abilities and interests. Use a variety of books from a bookstore or library. You will find book suggestions throughout *Complete Year*, and an extended list on page 394. The suggested books are age-appropriate and of the highest quality, but you are also encouraged to choose other literature that may better suit your child's interests and abilities. Reading a wide variety of literature, including fantasy, adventure, biography, and poetry, is highly recommended. There is so much great literature for children available today. Find the latest titles and instill the joy of reading in your child.

- Independent Reading and Reading Aloud
  Set aside 15 to 30 minutes each day for your child to read silently. Let him or her choose which book to read. Silent reading time should be a time to read for pleasure. Do not evaluate your child at this time. On the other hand, do not avoid talking about the book. Also, read books aloud to your child that are at a higher level than his or her independent reading level. This will spark interest in various topics and motivate him or her to improve. Read-aloud time is very special and can continue even after your child is reading independently. Some parents continue reading aloud well into the middle school years.

- Reading Comprehension
  Read to and with your child every day. Build a love of reading through positive experiences with books. A child who loves reading will be a more successful reader. The goal of reading is to acquire meaning from text. After reading a book, ask your child a variety of questions to test comprehension, such as "Explain what the character meant by ..." or "Make a time line of events in the story." Ask questions related to context clues to test your child's comprehension of information that is not overtly given and must be inferred.

Language Skills

Language skills should be taught in real contexts and in all subject areas. Whenever possible, integrate your teaching of grammar, handwriting, and writing skills into other areas of the curriculum, such as science or social studies. Ask your child to write on a science topic he or she is currently investigating or to answer a question in writing about a historical event.

- Vocabulary Development
  Your child will work with figurative language, including metaphors, similes, personification, and analogies in his or her writing. This use of figurative language will help your child learn to write more interesting pieces. Additionally, your child will continue to study antonyms, homonyms, and synonyms and expand his or her knowledge of correct word usage.

- Grammar and Usage
  This year, your child will work with parts of speech (nouns, pronouns, verbs, adjectives, adverbs, prepositions, conjunctions, and interjections), sentence structure (types of sentences, complete sentences, and subject-verb agreement), and punctuation. Help your child develop these skills by closely examining sentences from a favorite book, pointing out capital letters, punctuation marks, subject-verb agreement, and other features. Avoid emphasizing too many skills at once. If your child's writing shows several types of language errors, choose just one or two to emphasize during rewriting.

- Spelling

  Spelling is applicable to all areas of study, so work to integrate it into all areas of the curriculum. As your child encounters new terms in social studies, science, and math, add them to a list. The most effective technique for retaining accurate spelling is to use the words in context. Each week, engage your child in a writing activity using new spelling words. Steady exposure to words through reading will also improve your child's ability to spell.

Writing

Create opportunities to get your child writing. The more often your child writes, the more fluent he or she will become. Engage your child in meaningful writing activities each week. Use a writing lesson as an opportunity to stress a newly learned grammatical skill. While the focus of some writing activities will be correctness, others will encourage fluency. Devote some time each week to writing, whether it be creative writing or writing in other areas of the curriculum. The writing process is ongoing but generally includes these steps:

- Prewriting

  The writer brainstorms ideas, gathers, and organizes information.

- Drafting

  The writer composes or writes a rough draft using prewriting ideas. He or she should not worry about mistakes at this stage. The emphasis here is on fluency, not accuracy. The writer dates the drafts and keeps them in a writing folder.

- Revising

  The writer rereads the draft, checking to see that it is fluent, interesting and stays on topic. Then, he or she reads the rough draft to another person to gather feedback on word choice, fluency, clarity, and interest. The writer makes changes as needed.

- Editing
  The writer proofreads, then edits, the revised piece of writing for proper spelling, capitalization, and grammar.

- Publishing
  The writer copies the corrected proof and prepares to present it.

Speaking and Listening

Good speaking and listening skills are essential to school success. By paying careful attention to what is being said, your child will not only learn more but will develop the skill of being a good conversationalist as well. Make sure to provide ample opportunities for your child to listen to songs, poetry, and stories.

Math

The fifth-grade math curriculum is filled with activities and exercises designed to help your child comprehend the logic behind math operations. Your child will review the fundamental concepts of place value, addition, subtraction, multiplication, and division, and will learn to apply these concepts to rounding, estimation, geometry, graphing, tangrams, fractions, and decimals. Your child will also learn how to work with numbers in different bases, such as base ten. Whatever the topic, look for opportunities to relate math to your child's own world. Show your child the practical applications of mathematics.

- Place Value
  Learning place value will help your child conceptualize large numbers and will lead to greater understanding of addition, subtraction, multiplication, and division. This year, your child will learn place value of increasingly larger numbers, up to the trillions place. He or she will also use place value understanding to round decimals.

- Multiplication and Division
  Fifth graders should be increasingly fluent in multiplying whole numbers, as well as dividing whole numbers with up to four-digit dividends and two-digit divisors. This year, your child will also be expected to multiply and divide by decimal numbers.

- Fractions and Decimals

  Fractions and decimals can both be described as parts of a whole. In the fifth grade, your child will continue working with fractions. He or she will add and subtract fractions with unlike denominators, including mixed numbers; solve word problems involving fractions in real-life situations; and multiply fractions and whole numbers by fractions. Fifth grade students will also be expected to read, write, and compare decimals to thousandths, as well as add, subtract, multiply, and divide decimals to hundredths.

- Measurement

  This year, measurement concepts will focus on using customary and metric units. Students will learn to compare and convert measurements in length, weight, capacity, and temperature. This is also connected with geometry as they learn how to measure the area, volume, and perimeter of different geometric shapes.

- Graphing

  Graphs can display information about two variables and can be prevalent in all areas of education—reading, math, social studies, and science. This year, your child become familiar with graphs, working to organize and interpret data from several types of graphs, including charts, bar graphs, picture graphs, circle graphs, and line graphs. He or she will also be able to locate points on a grid and plot ordered pairs.

 Science

Fifth-grade science covers a wide range of topics. This year, your child may learn about the plant and animal kingdoms, as well as living organisms that do not belong to either of these categories. Your child may also investigate earth science, specifically various landforms, bodies of water, and climate. Finally, your child may study physical science, conducting experiments to explore the concepts of force, motion, and work.

Encourage your child to follow the science learning cycle whenever he or she has a question related to science or when exploring a new idea. First, begin with a question. For example, "What will happen if I leave this half-eaten apple on the counter?" State a possible hypothesis, then follow up the question with an exploration that involves observation, play, experimentation, debate, and other methods of inquiry. Encourage your child to use descriptive language, measure when appropriate, and keep a journal of observations. Next, propose explanations and solutions for the initial question. An explanation may prove or disprove the earlier hypothesis. This is a time of writing, talking, and evaluating. After this step, you may need to return to the second step of the cycle, exploring the topic further.

Then, apply the knowledge to real life. Ask, "Where have you seen this happen before? What will you do differently because of the experiment?" This step may also spark a new question that will begin the cycle again.

 Social Studies

In the fifth grade, your child may explore American history in-depth, including culture, geography and economics from the time of Columbus through the Civil War. Other topics of study may include physical features, natural resources, regions, famous Americans, and the nation's capital. Seek a variety of resources to teach social studies, such as textbooks, posters, videos, films, magazines, books, audio clips, computer software, and reference books. Check your area for historians, archaeologists, geographers, inventors, and politicians who might be available to speak with your child.

First Quarter Introduction

Fifth grade is a time of transition for your child, as he or she prepares to enter middle school or junior high school. This year should challenge your child, as well as ready him or her with knowledge and skills needed in the school years ahead. During the first weeks of school, utilize the opportunity to acquaint your child with the new material and what is expected of him or her in the upcoming year.

First Quarter Skills

Practice pages in this book for Weeks 1–9 will help your child improve the following skills.

Reading and Language Arts

- Write and identify figurative language, including metaphors, similes, and personification
- Complete word analogies
- Understand common idioms and expressions
- Find main ideas and details in text and use them to take notes and write summaries
- Make an outline of main ideas and details
- Read nonfiction texts, then compare and contrast information
- Use conjunctions to combine words and sentences
- Punctuate interjections using commas and exclamation points
- Use commas in examples of direct address
- Identify homophones that are frequently confused
- Read text and understand its mood or tone
- Understand differing points of view in text
- Write events in chronological order
- Write a true story, or personal narrative
- Describe fictional characters and write fictional stories
- Understand cause and effect
- Identify prepositions and use them correctly in writing

Math

- Round numbers to the nearest hundred thousand
- Identify place values in numbers to the trillions place
- Use the four operations symbols (+, −, x, ÷) to write equations
  - Write and solve equations
  - Multiply by one-, two-, and three-digit numbers
    - Divide by one- and two-digit divisors
    - Solve division problems with and without remainders

Multi-Sensory Learning Activities

Try these fun activities for enhancing your child's learning and development during the first quarter of the school year. Be sure to choose activities that include speaking, listening, touching, and active movement.

 Reading and Language Arts

Challenge your child to write a fictional story that personifies a backpack, a pair of smelly gym shoes, or another inanimate object.

Write incomplete analogies for your child to complete. For example, write, "Gas is to car as _____ is to person." Your child might complete the analogy with "food."

 Math

Take turns with your child describing numbers for each of you to write. For example, say, "Write a number with 3 in the hundred thousands place." Check the numbers you write and read each one aloud.

Have your child read *How Much Is a Million?* by David Schwartz. Make flash cards by writing large numbers in numeral form on one side and in words on the reverse side. Use the cards to quiz your child on reading and writing numbers.

Read the following challenge to your child, one clue at a time. Allow your child time to think before reading the next clue. Repeat the clues if necessary. Have your child solve for the mystery number: "The mystery number has five digits. No numeral is repeated. The first digit is an odd number, and it is five times as much as the last digit. The second digit is two times the third digit. The fourth digit multiplied by 8 is 0. The sum of the digits is 15. Can you name the mystery number?" The correct answer is 56,301.

Social Studies

Have your child read "Paul Revere's Ride," a poem by Henry Wadsworth Longfellow. Discuss the events of the battles at Lexington and Concord. Then, have your child find Lexington and Concord on a current map of Massachusetts.

First Quarter Introduction, cont.

Have your child read about some of the natural wonders found in the United States. Have your child choose one natural wonder to write about in a poem.

 Science

Have your child read about a famous cave or group of caves, such as Lascaux Cave, Carlsbad Caverns, or Mammoth Cave. Encourage your child to learn about the features that make the cave(s) unique. Then, have your child write a travelogue presentation on that cave, including pictures.

Have your child read about the major rivers of the world. Have him or her locate the following rivers on a map or globe: Nile, Amazon, Niger, Mississippi, Missouri, Yangtze, Yenisei, Congo, Huang He, Lena, Mekong, Amur, Mackenzie, Ob, and Volga.

 Seasonal Fun

Have your child collect three large leaves from the same tree, making note of the color of the leaves. Tear the leaves into very small pieces and put them into a small jar. Add enough rubbing alcohol to the jar to cover the leaves. Using a plastic knife or spoon, carefully chop and grind the leaves in the alcohol. Have your child cover the jar very loosely with plastic wrap or aluminum foil. Place the jar carefully into a shallow tray containing one inch of hot water. Keep the jar in the water for at least 30 minutes until the alcohol has become colored (the darker the better).

Twirl the jar gently about every five minutes, replacing the hot water if it cools off. Then, have your child cut a long thin strip of coffee filter paper. Remove the jar from the water and uncover. Place a strip of filter paper into the jar so that one end is in the alcohol. Bend the other end over the top of the jar and secure it with tape. The alcohol will travel up the paper, bringing the colors with it. After 30–90 minutes, the colors will travel different distances up the paper as the alcohol evaporates. What colors can your child see on the paper? Are they the same as the colors of the leaf originally?

Week 1 Skills

Subject	Skill	Multi-Sensory Learning Activities
Reading and Language Arts	Write and identify figurative language, including metaphors, similes, and personification.	• Complete Practice Pages 18–20. • Read *Hang Tough, Paul Mather* by Alfred Slote. Ask your child to reread chapters 7 and 8, then write similes and metaphors to describe Paul's pitching.
	Complete word analogies.	• Complete Practice Page 21. • Challenge your child to write analogies using one of these groups of four words: **nests, squirrels, people, homes; listening, seeing, eyes, ears; hands, fingers, toes, feet.**
Math	Identify place values in numbers to the billions place.	• Complete Practice Pages 22, 23, and 24. • Search for very large numbers in news articles, in almanacs, or at www.census.gov. Challenge your child to read each number aloud. Do not use the word **and**. For example, the number **900,016,047,245** is read as: "nine hundred billion, sixteen million, forty-seven thousand, two hundred forty-five."
	Round numbers to the nearest hundred thousand.	• Complete Practice Pages 24 and 25. • Give your child some large numbers. Can he or she use mental math to round them to any place value (ones, tens, hundreds, thousands, ten thousands, hundred thousands)?

Similes and Metaphors in Poetry

Many poems use similes and metaphors to create a more interesting description of what the poem is about.

Read the following poems and underline any similes or metaphors you see.

Flint

An emerald is as green as grass,
A ruby red as blood;
A sapphire shines as blue as heaven;
A flint lies in the mud.

A diamond is a brilliant stone,
    To catch the world's desire;
An opal holds a fiery spark;
    But a flint holds fire.

    —Christina Rossetti

The Night Is a Big Black Cat

The night is a big black cat
The moon is her topaz eye,
The stars are the mice she hunts at night,
In the field of the sultry sky.

    —G. Orr Clark

Now, write your own poem, using at least one simile and one metaphor.

_____

_____

_____

_____

_____

_____

_____

_____

_____

_____

Like...a Simile!

Underline the two being compared in each sentence. On the blank, write if the comparison is a **simile** or a **metaphor**. Remember, a simile uses **like** or **as**; a metaphor does not.

1. Angel was as mean as a wild bull. _____

2. Toni and Mattie were like toast and jam. _____

3. Mr. Ashby expected the students to be as busy as beavers. _____

4. The pin was a masterpiece in Mattie's mind. _____

5. The park's peacefulness was a friend to Mattie. _____

6. The words came as slow as molasses into Mattie's mind. _____

7. Mrs. Stamps's apartment was like a museum. _____

8. Mrs. Benson was as happy as a lark when Mattie won the contest.

_____

9. Mr. Phillip's smile was a glowing beam to Mattie and Mrs. Benson.

_____

10. Mattie ran like the wind to get her money. _____

11. Angel's mean words cut through Charlene like glass. _____

12. Mr. Bacon was a fairy godmother to Mattie. _____

13. The gingko tree's leaves were like fans. _____

Complete the following similes.

1. Matt was as artistic as _____

2. Hannibal's teeth were like _____

3. Toni's mind worked fast like _____

4. Mattie was as sad as _____

5. Mrs. Stamps was like _____

Personification

Sometimes, writers use descriptions like: The fire engine **screamed** as it rushed down the street. The sun **crawled** slowly across the sky. We know that fire engines do not really scream, and the sun does not really crawl. Writers use descriptions like these to make their writing more interesting and vivid. When a writer gives an object or animal human qualities, it is called **personification**.

For each object below, write a sentence using personification. The first one has been done for you.

1. the barn door

   The old, rusty barn door groaned loudly when I pushed it open.

2. the rain

   _____

3. the pickup truck

   _____

4. the radiator

   _____

5. the leaves

   _____

6. the television

   _____

7. the kite

   _____

8. the river

   _____

Analogies

An **analogy** is a way of comparing objects to show how they relate.

Example: Nose is to smell as tongue is to taste.

Write the correct word on the blank to fill in the missing part of each analogy. The first one has been done for you.

1. <u>Scissors</u> are to paper as saw is to wood.   fold   (scissors)   thin

2. Man is to boy as woman is to_____.   mother   girl   lady

3. _____ is to cellar as sky is to ground.   down   attic   up

4. Rag is to dust as_____ is to sweep.   floor   straw   broom

5. Freezer is to cold as stove is to _____.   cook   hot   recipe

6. Car is to _____ as book is to bookshelf.   ride   gas   garage

7. Window is to_____as car is to metal.   glass   clear   house

8. Eyes are to seeing as feet are to _____.   legs   walking   shoes

9. Gas is to car as _____ is to lamp.   electricity   plug   cord

10. Refrigerator is to food as_____is to clothes.   fold   material   closet

11. Floor is to down as ceiling is to_____ .   high   over   up

12. Pillow is to soft as rock is to _____.   dirt   hard   hurt

13. Carpenter is to house as poet is to _____.   verse   novel   writing

14. Lamp is to light as clock is to_____ .   time   hands   numbers

15. _____ is to hand as sole is to foot.   wrist   finger   palm

Place Value

The place value of a digit or numeral is shown by where it is in the number. In the number **1,234**, 1 has the place value of thousands, 2 is hundreds, 3 is tens and 4 is ones.

Example: 1,250,000,000

Read: One billion, two hundred fifty million

Write: 1,250,000,000

Billions			**Millions**			**Thousands**			**Ones**		
h	t	o	h	t	o	h	t	o	h	t	o
		1,	2	5	0,	0	0	0,	0	0	0

Read the words. Then write the numbers.

twenty million, three hundred four thousand _____

five thousand, four hundred twenty-three _____

one hundred fifty billion, eight million,
one thousand, five hundred _____

sixty billion, seven hundred million,
one hundred thousand, three hundred twelve _____

four hundred million, fifteen thousand,
seven hundred one _____

six hundred ninety-nine million, four thousand,
nine hundred forty-two _____

Here's a game to play with a partner.

Write a ten-digit number using each digit, 0 to 9, only once. Do not show the number to your partner. Give clues like: "There is a five in the hundreds place." The clues can be given in any order. See if your partner can write the same number you have written.

Place Value

Draw a line to connect each number to its correct written form.

1. 791,000   Three hundred fifty thousand

2. 350,000   Seventeen million, five hundred thousand

3. 17,500,000   Seven hundred ninety-one thousand

4. 3,500,000   Seventy thousand, nine hundred ten

5. 70,910   Three million, five hundred thousand

6. 35,500,000   Seventeen billion, five hundred thousand

7. 17,000,500,000   Thirty-five million, five hundred thousand

Look carefully at this number: **2,071,463,548**. Write the numeral for each of the following places.

8. _____ ten thousands

9. _____ millions

10. _____ hundreds

11. _____ billions

12. _____ hundred thousands

13. _____ ten millions

14. _____ one thousands

15. _____ hundred millions

Rounding

Follow these steps to round numbers to a given place.

Example: Round 35,634 to the nearest thousand.

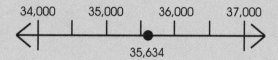

a. Locate and highlight the place to which the number is to be rounded.	▶ Highlight the digit in the thousands place: 3**5**,634.
b. Look at the digit to the right of the designated place. If the number is 5 or greater, round the highlighted number up. If the number is 4 or less, round the highlighted number down by keeping the digit the same.	▶ Six is greater than 5, so round the highlighted number up.
c. Rewrite the original number with the amended digit in the highlighted place and change all of the digits to the right to zeros.	▶ The rounded number is 36,000.

Example: Round 782 to the nearest 10.

▶ Highlight the digit in the tens place: 7**8**2.

▶ Two is four or less, so round down by keeping the tens digit the same: 782.

▶ The rounded number is 780.

Round each number to the given place.

nearest 10:   1. 855 _____   2. 333 _____

nearest 100:   3. 725 _____   4. 2,348 _____

nearest 1,000:   5. 4,317 _____   6. 8,650 _____

nearest 10,000:   7. 25,199 _____   8. 529,740 _____

nearest 100,000:   9. 496,225 _____   10. 97,008 _____

Number-Line Rounding

Label the endpoints. Plot the given number. Circle the closer endpoint. The first three have been done for you.

1.

   Round 87 to the nearest ten.

2.

   Round 1,322 to the nearest hundred.

3.

   Round 1,475 to the nearest ten.

4.

   Round 8,274 to the nearest ten.

5.

   Round 8,274 to the nearest hundred.

6.

   Round 1,452 to the nearest thousand.

7.

   Round 1,452 to the nearest ten.

8.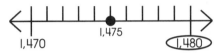

   Round 6,937 to the nearest thousand.

9.

   Round 8,485 to the nearest thousand.

10.

    Round 25,683 to the nearest ten thousand.

Millions Mysteries

Follow the clues to fill in the mystery numbers.

1. Use the numbers 3 to 9. Each is used only once.
2. The ones, tens and hundreds are odd numbers.
3. The hundred thousands, ten thousands and thousands are in backwards counting order.
4. There are 3 times as many hundreds as ones.
5. There are 2 times as many hundred thousands as millions.

1. Use the numbers 2 to 8. Each is used only once.
2. The hundreds, tens and ones are in counting order.
3. The sum of the ones, tens and hundreds is 9.
4. There are 2 times as many ten thousands as tens.
5. There are 2 times as many thousands as ones.
6. The sum of the millions, hundred thousands and ten thousands is 18.

Week 2 Skills

Subject	Skill	Multi-Sensory Learning Activities
Reading and Language Arts	Complete word analogies.	• Complete Practice Pages 28–30. • When solving analogies, first think of a sentence that describes the relationship between the given words. For item #9 on page 28, say, "Humans are covered in skin." Then, think of a word that will complete the same sentence for the second pair: "Fish are covered in **scales**."
Math	Understand common idioms and expressions.	• Complete Practice Page 31. • Have fun with your child thinking of common sayings and idioms such as "hit the road," "piece of cake," or "missed the boat." Ask your child to choose one and draw two pictures: one to illustrate the idiom's literal meaning and another to illustrate its figurative meaning.
	Identify place values in numbers to the trillions place.	• Complete Practice Pages 32–36. • Challenge your child to write the number that comes just before one trillion. Can he or she read the number out loud and write the number in expanded notation (following the model on page 34)?

Sing Is to Song as...

Complete each phrase.

1. Glue is to sticking as pencil is to _____.

2. Son is to mother as daughter is to _____.

3. Country is to continent as city is to _____.

4. 5 is to 15 as 4 is to _____.

5. Garage is to car as library is to _____.

6. Victoria is to lake as Pacific is to _____.

7. Hot is to steam as cold is to _____.

8. Weak is to strong as good is to _____.

9. Skin is to human as _____ are to fish.

10. 2 is to bicycle as 3 is to_____.

11. Clipper is to sail as _____ is to paddle.

12. Drama is to act as ballet is to _____.

13. *Adiós* is to Spanish as *au revoir* is to _____.

14. Pilot is to aircraft as nurse is to _____.

15. Damascus is to Syria as Tokyo is to _____.

16. Moo is to herd as _____ is to flock.

17. Lion is to pride as wolf is to _____.

18. Racket is to tennis as club is to _____.

Synonym and Antonym Analogies

Analogies are a way of comparing items to show how they are related. Analogies can show different types of relationships. Two relationships analogies might show are synonyms or antonyms.

Examples:

> **Antonyms:** hot is to cold as happy is to sad

> **Synonyms:** happy is to glad as run is to jog

You can write an analogy this way:

> slow:fast::up:down

You read it this way:

> slow is to fast as up is to down

Write **S** for synonym or **A** for antonym in the blanks in front of each analogy. Then complete the analogies by choosing a word from the box.

life	run	comforter	fail	photograph
above	feline	play	drape	different

_____ 1. dog:canine::cat: _____

_____ 2. coat:parka::curtain: _____

_____ 3. asleep:awake::work: _____

_____ 4. ground:sky::below: _____

_____ 5. freeze:thaw::stroll: _____

_____ 6. dangerous:treacherous::picture: _____

_____ 7. ancient:old::bedspread: _____

_____ 8. win:lose::succeed: _____

_____ 9. manmade:artificial::unique: _____

_____ 10. wealthy:poor::death: _____

Part/Whole and Cause/Effect Analogies

Other types of analogies are part to whole and cause and effect.

Example:

Part to whole: fingers:hand::toes:foot

Cause and effect: rain:flood::matches:fire

Write **P** for part to whole or **C** for cause and effect in the blanks in front of each analogy. Then, complete the analogies by choosing a word from the box.

tree	bike	punishment	stomachache
beach	laugh	fingers	hawk
pencil	blizzard		

_____ 1. hair:head::fingernails: _____

_____ 2. germ:infection::misbehavior: _____

_____ 3. fall:injury::overeating: _____

_____ 4. keyboard:computer::wheels: _____

_____ 5. tongue:shoe::sand: _____

_____ 6. practice:win::joke: _____

_____ 7. read:learn::snow: _____

_____ 8. pouch:kangaroo::beak: _____

_____ 9. leaf:plant::bark: _____

_____ 10. ink:pen::lead: _____

Up a Tree

Match these expressions with their meanings.

_____ all the personality of wallpaper paste   a. without question

_____ a piece of my mind   b. consider clearly

_____ running amok   c. becoming wild

_____ beyond a shadow of a doubt   d. gather up great quantities

_____ think straight   e. a very bland disposition

_____ ace in the hole   f. strong opinion

_____ shop like a bear about to hibernate   g. from a bad situation to a worse one

_____ out of the frying pan and into the fire   h. special advantage

Write two sentences using the above expressions.

Example: When my teacher asked me to give the answer, I couldn't think straight.

1. _____

2. _____

Place Value

Place value is the position of a digit in a number. A digit's place in a number shows its value. Numbers left of the decimal point represent whole numbers. Numbers right of the decimal point represent a part, or fraction, of a whole number. These parts are broken down into tenths, hundredths, thousandths, and so on.

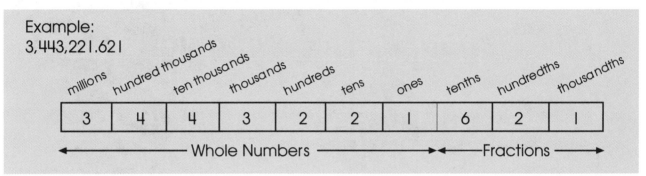

Example:
3,443,221.621

Write the following number words as numbers.

1. Three million, forty-four thousand, six hundred twenty-one

   _____

2. One million, seventy-seven _____

3. Nine million, six hundred thousand, one hundred two _____

4. Twenty-nine million, one hundred three thousand and nine tenths

   _____

5. One million, one hundred thousand, one hundred seventy-one and
   thirteen hundredths _____

In each box, write the corresponding number for each place value.

    1. 4,822,000.00   ☐ hundreds

    2. 55,907,003.00   ☐ thousands

    3. 190,641,225.07   ☐ hundred thousands

    4. 247,308,211.59   ☐ tenths

    5. 7,594,097.33   ☐ millions

    6. 201,480,110.01   ☐ hundred thousands

    7. 42,367,109,074.25   ☐ hundredths

Place Value

The chart below shows the place value of each number.

trillions			billions			millions			thousands			ones		
h	t	o	h	t	o	h	t	o	h	t	o	h	t	o
		2		1	4	0	9	0	0	6	8	0	3	5	0

Word form: two trillion, one hundred forty billion, nine hundred million, six hundred eighty thousand, three hundred fifty

Draw a line to the correct value of each underlined digit. The first one is done for you.

6<u>4</u>3,000   2 hundred million

<u>1</u>3,294,125   9 billion

<u>6</u>78,446   40 thousand

389,<u>2</u>76   2 thousand

1<u>9</u>,000,089,965   2 billion

78,<u>7</u>64   1 hundred thousand

61<u>2</u>,689   9 thousand

<u>2</u>98,154,370   70 thousand

8<u>9</u>,256   10 million

1,<u>3</u>70   30 million

853,6<u>7</u>2,175   7 hundred

<u>2</u>,842,751,360   3 hundred

<u>1</u>63,456   2 hundred

4<u>3</u>8,276,587   6 hundred thousand

Expanded Notation

Expanded notation is writing out the value of each digit in a number.

Example:
8,920,077 = 8,000,000 + 900,000 + 20,000 + 70 + 7

Word form: Eight million, nine hundred twenty thousand, seventy-seven

Write the following numbers using expanded notation.

1. 20,769,033 _____

_____

2. 1,183,541,029 _____

_____

3. 776,003,091 _____

_____

4. 5,920,100,808 _____

_____

5. 14,141,543,760 _____

_____

Write the following numbers.

1. 700,000 + 900 + 60 + 7 _____

2. 35,000,000 + 600,000 + 400 + 40 + 2 _____

3. 12,000,000 + 700,000 + 60,000 + 4,000 + 10 + 4 _____

4. 80,000,000,000 + 8,000,000,000 + 400,000,000 + 80,000,000 + 10,000 + 400 + 30

_____

5. 4,000,000,000 + 16,000,000 + 30 + 2 _____

Place Value

Read and solve.

1. Write the number 2,058,763 in words. _____

_____

2. Write the following in numerals: eight billion, two hundred thirty-seven million, eighty-five thousand, three hundred four.

_____

3. In the number 9,876,543,210 . . .

which digit is in the hundred thousands place? _____

which digit is in the ones place? _____

in what place is the 9? _____

4. Add.

3,259 + 32,769 + 305 = _____

8,759,233 + 3,410 + 655,200 = _____

5. Round . . .

84,239 to the nearest ten. _____

7,857,355 to the nearest ten thousand. _____

6. Estimate the sum.

34,396   ⟶

+ 5,875   + _____

Place Value Games

1. Choose any 2-digit number. Multiply the tens digit by 5. Add 7. Now, double this number. Add the ones digit of the original number. Now subtract 14. The answer is the original number.

2. Choose any 3-digit number. Multiply the hundreds digit by 2. Add 3. Now, multiply by 5. Add 7. Add the tens digit. Multiply by 2. Add 3. Multiply by 5. Add the ones digit. Now, subtract 235. The answer is the original number.

3. Fold a sheet of paper so that there are 16 squares and each crease can fold either way. Number the squares from 1 to 16 as shown in the diagram below. Now, fold the paper into a one-by-one square any way you like. Using scissors, trim the four edges so that there are sixteen separate squares. Without flipping any of the squares, lay them out on a desk or table. Add the numbers facing upward. Their total is 68.

1	2	3	4
5	6	7	8
9	10	11	12
13	14	15	16

4. One week (Sunday through Saturday) there is a birthday party every day. No two children are invited to the same party. Find out the day that each child attends a party.

   Hint: Use a chart with days of the week across and children s names down the side.

   a. Lisa and Pat don t go to a party on a Friday or a Saturday.

   b. Pat and Alice don t go on a Tuesday, but Sandy does.

   c. Jennifer goes to a party on Wednesday.

   d. Jim goes to a party the day after Jennifer.

   e. Lisa goes to a party the day before Pat.

   f. Paul goes to a party on a Saturday.

Week 3 Skills

Subject	Skill	Multi-Sensory Learning Activities
Reading and Language Arts	Find main ideas and details in text and use them to take notes and write summaries.	• Complete Practice Pages 38–40. • The paragraphs on page 38 refer to the book *The Lion, the Witch, and the Wardrobe* by C. S. Lewis. Choose 10 pages from that book. Challenge your child to take notes on those pages and write a summary. What is the main idea of the summary your child wrote?
	Make an outline of main ideas and details.	• Complete Practice Pages 41 and 42. • Go to the library and help your child pick out a biography of a famous person. Encourage your child to check out other related books at the same time. Teach your child to take notes on the main ideas of the biography and to organize this information in an outline.
Math	Use the four operations symbols (**+, −, x, ÷**) to write equations.	• Complete Practice Pages 43–46. • Give your child clues and ask him or her to solve the riddle and tell you the correct number. For example, say, "What pair of numbers has a sum of 9 and a quotient of 2?" The correct answer would be 6 and 3.
Bonus: Social Studies		• Have your child read about the three branches of government. Have your child complete a chart of the three branches, including the titles of the leaders and their duties.

What's the Idea?

Circle the sentence that best expresses the main idea of each paragraph.

1. Edmund began to question whether or not the lion in the Queen's courtyard was alive. The large creature looked as if it were about to pounce on a dwarf. But it did not move. Then Edmund noticed the snow on the lion's head and back. Only a statue would be covered like that!

   • The statue is snow-covered.
   • Edmund wonders if the lion is alive.
   • The lion is ready to jump.

2. The resting party of children and beavers heard the sound of jingling bells. Mr. Beaver dashed out of his hiding place and soon called the others to join him. He could hardly contain himself with excitement. Father Christmas is here!

   • Mr. Beaver is a brave animal.   • The group hears a jingling sound.
   • Father Christmas has come to Narnia.

3. Poor Edmund! Because he came to the Queen, he expected her to reward him gratefully with Turkish delight. After all, he had traveled so far and had suffered miserably in the cold. When the Queen finally commanded that he receive food and drink, the cruel dwarf brought Edmund a bowl of water and a hunk of dry bread.

   • Edmund is not rewarded as he expects.   • Edmund receives bread
   • The young boy suffered from the cold.   and water.

4. Peter knew he must rescue Susan from the wolf. When the wolf charged, Susan climbed up a nearby tree. The wolf's snapping and snarling mouth was inches away. When Peter looked more closely, he realized that his sister was about to faint. Rushing in with his sword, Peter slashed at the beast.

   • Peter kills the wolf.   • The wolf snarls at Susan.
   • Peter realizes he must save his sister.

Choose one of the following sentences as your main idea and write a paragraph.

1. The Queen demands that Edmund be returned to her.
2. Aslan's army loses the Queen and her dwarf.
3. Father Christmas gives gifts to the beavers and the three children.

_____

_____

_____

Taking Notes: Egyptian Mummies

Taking notes is the process of writing important points to remember, such as taking notes from material prepared by your teacher or from what is discussed in class or from an article you read. Taking notes is useful when preparing for a test or when writing a report. When taking notes, follow these steps:

1. Read the article carefully.
2. Select one or two important points from each paragraph.
3. Write your notes in your own words.
4. Reread your notes to be sure you understand what you have written.
5. Abbreviate words to save time.

Read about Egyptian mummies. Select one or two important points from each paragraph. Write your notes in your own words.

After the Egyptians discovered that bodies buried in the hot, dry sand of the desert became mummified, they began searching for ways to improve the mummification process. The use of natron became a vital part of embalming.

Natron is a type of white powdery salt found in oases throughout Egypt. An oasis is a place in the desert where underground water rises to the surface. This water contains many types of salts, including table salt. It also contains natron. As the water evaporates in the hot sun of the desert, the salts are left behind. Natron was collected for use in the mummification process.

The body was dried in natron for up to 40 days. The natron caused the body to shrink and the skin to become leathery. For thousands of years, natron was a vital ingredient in preserving the bodies of kings, queens and other wealthy Egyptian citizens.

Sample notes:

Paragraph 1 _Bodies buried in hot dry sand became mummified._

Natron is vital for embalming.

Paragraph 2 _____

_____

Paragraph 3 _____

_____

Summarizing

A **summary** includes the main points from an article, book or speech.

Example:

Tomb robbing was an important business in ancient Egypt. Often entire families participated in the plunder of tombs. These robbers may have been laborers, officials, tomb architects or guards, but they all probably had one thing in common. They were involved in the building or designing of the tomb or they wouldn't have had the knowledge necessary to successfully rob the burial sites. Not only did tomb robbing ensure a rich life for the robbers but it also enabled them to be buried with many riches themselves.

Summary:

Tomb robbing occurred in ancient Egypt. The robbers stole riches to use in their present lives or in their burials. Tomb robbers usually had some part in the building or design of the tomb. This allowed them to find the burial rooms where the treasures were stored.

Read about life in ancient Egypt. Then write a three- to five-sentence summary.

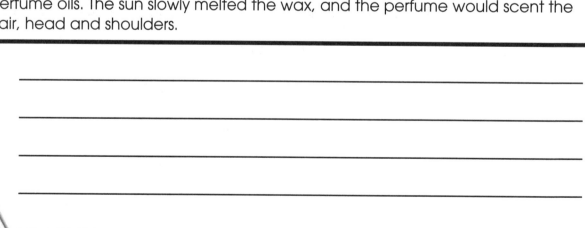

Egyptologists have learned much about the pyramids and mummies of ancient Egypt from the items left by grave robbers.

Women of ancient Egypt wore makeup to enhance their features. Dark colored minerals called *kohl* were used as eyeliner and eye shadow. Men also wore eyeliner. Women used another mineral called *ocher* on their cheeks and lips to redden them. Henna, a plant which produces an orange dye, tinted the fingernails, the palms of their hands and the soles of their feet.

Perfume was also important in ancient Egypt. Small cones made of wax were worn on top of the head. These cones contained perfume oils. The sun slowly melted the wax, and the perfume would scent the hair, head and shoulders.

_____

_____

_____

_____

_____

Outlining

Outlining is a way to organize information before you write an essay or informational paragraph. Outlining helps you understand the information you read.

This sample form will help you get started. When outlining, you can add more main points, more smaller points and/or more examples.

Title
I. First Main Idea
   A. A smaller idea
      1. An example
      2. An example
   B. Another smaller idea
II. Second Main Idea
   A. A smaller idea
   B. Another smaller idea
      1. An example
      2. An example
III. Third Main Idea
   A. A smaller idea
   B. A smaller idea

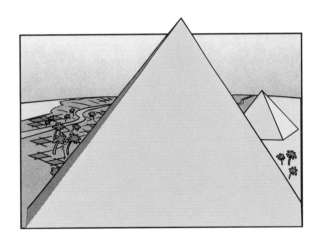

Read about building pyramids. Then, complete the outline on the next page.

> The process of building pyramids began as a way to honor a king or queen. Since the Egyptians believed in an afterlife, they thought it only fitting for their kings and queens to have elaborate burial tombs filled with treasures to enjoy in the afterlife. Thus, the idea of the pyramid was born.
>
> At first, pyramids were not built as they are known today. In the early stages of the Egyptian dynasty, kings were entombed in a mastaba. Mastabas were tombs made of mud-dried bricks. They formed a rectangular tomb with angled sides and a flat roof.
>
> Later, as the Egyptian kingdom became more powerful, kings felt they needed grander tombs. The step pyramid was developed. These pyramids were made of stone rather than mud and were much taller. A large mastaba was built on the ground. Then, four more mastabas (each smaller than the previous) were stacked on top.
>
> Finally, the pyramids took the shape that is familiar today. They were constructed with a flat bottom and four slanting sides which ascended to a final point. One of the tallest is over 400 feet high. These pyramids were also built of stone and were finished with an exterior of white limestone.

Outlining: Egyptian Pyramids

Complete the outline. Then answer the question.

_____
(title)

I. Mastabas

   A. _____

   B. _____

   C. _____

II. Step pyramids

   A. _____

   B. _____

   C. _____

III. Pyramids

   A. _____

   B. _____

   C. _____

What do you find is the most interesting aspect about the pyramids of ancient Egypt? Why?

_____

_____

_____

Trial and Error

Use trial and error to complete each diagram so all the equations work.

Example:

$$\underline{}6\underline{},\ \underline{}7\ \begin{cases} + \to \underline{\ 13\ } \\ \times \to \underline{\ 42\ } \end{cases}$$

$$\underline{},\ \underline{}4\ \begin{cases} + \to \underline{} \\ \times \to \underline{\ 28\ } \end{cases}$$

$$\underline{}4\underline{},\ \underline{}\ \begin{cases} + \to \underline{\ 12\ } \\ \times \to \underline{} \end{cases}$$

$$\underline{},\ \underline{}\ \begin{cases} + \to \underline{\ 8\ } \\ \times \to \underline{\ 16\ } \end{cases}$$

$$\underline{}7\underline{},\ \underline{}\ \begin{cases} + \to \underline{\ 7\ } \\ \times \to \underline{} \end{cases}$$

$$\underline{},\ \underline{}\ \begin{cases} + \to \underline{\ 15\ } \\ \times \to \underline{\ 56\ } \end{cases}$$

$$\underline{},\ \underline{}9\ \begin{cases} + \to \underline{\ 17\ } \\ \times \to \underline{} \end{cases}$$

$$\underline{},\ \underline{}9\ \begin{cases} + \to \underline{} \\ \times \to \underline{\ 54\ } \end{cases}$$

$$\underline{},\ \underline{}16\ \begin{cases} + \to \underline{\ 31\ } \\ \times \to \underline{} \end{cases}$$

$$\underline{},\ \underline{}\ \begin{cases} + \to \underline{\ 11\ } \\ \times \to \underline{\ 10\ } \end{cases}$$

$$\underline{},\ \underline{}\ \begin{cases} + \to \underline{\ 101\ } \\ \times \to \underline{\ 100\ } \end{cases}$$

Missing Signs

Fill in the circles with +, –, x, or ÷ to make the problem true.

3 ◯ 3 ◯ 3 ⟶ 9

3 ◯ 3 ◯ 3 ⟶ 3

3 ◯ 3 ◯ 3 ⟶ 2

3 ◯ 3 ◯ 3 ⟶ 4

3 ◯ 3 ◯ 3 ⟶ 12

3 ◯ 3 ◯ 3 ⟶ 18

3 ◯ 3 ◯ 3 ⟶ 3

3 ◯ 3 ◯ 3 ⟶ 6

3 ◯ 3 ◯ 3 ⟶ 0

3 ◯ 3 ◯ 3 ⟶ 27

5 ◯ 5 ◯ 5 ⟶ 50

5 ◯ 5 ◯ 5 ⟶ 5

5 ◯ 5 ◯ 5 ⟶ 30

5 ◯ 5 ◯ 5 ⟶ 2

5 ◯ 5 ◯ 5 ⟶ 15

5 ◯ 5 ◯ 5 ⟶ 20

5 ◯ 5 ◯ 5 ⟶ 6

5 ◯ 5 ◯ 5 ⟶ 125

5 ◯ 5 ◯ 5 ⟶ 0

5 ◯ 5 ◯ 5 ⟶ 5

A Number Challenge

Fill in the blanks to make each problem true. To check your work, start at the left and do each operation in order to get the given answer.

1. __ + __ − __ = 2

2. __ − __ ÷ __ = 3

3. __ + __ ÷ __ = 4

4. __ × __ − __ = 5

5. __ − __ × __ = 6

6. __ × __ ÷ __ = 3

7. __ ÷ __ + __ = 4

8. __ ÷ __ − __ = 5

9. __ ÷ __ × __ = 6

10. __ × __ + __ = 7

11. __ ÷ __ + __ = 12

12. __ ÷ __ − __ = 15

13. __ ÷ __ × __ = 20

14. __ × __ ÷ __ = 8

15. __ + __ × __ = 24

Equations

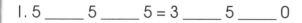

Write the correct operation signs in the blanks to make accurate equations.

1. 5 _____ 5 _____ 5 = 3 _____ 5 _____ 0

2. (50 _____ 0) _____ 2 = 25 _____ 2 _____ 2

3. 2 _____ 2 _____ 2 _____ 2 = 2 _____ 2 _____ 4

4. (4 _____ 5) _____ 5 _____ 5 = 2 _____ 3 _____ 5

5. (25 _____ 5) _____ 2 _____ 3 = 3 _____ 6 _____ 2 _____ 5

6. (125 _____ 7) _____ 2 _____ 3 = 100 _____ 2 _____ 4 _____ 70 _____ 10

7. (100 _____ 10) _____ 5 _____ 10 = 10 _____ 5 _____ 100 _____ 10

8. 35 _____ 35 _____ 5 _____ 2 = 5 _____ 3 _____ 2 _____ 5

9. (60 _____ 2) _____ 3 = 3 _____ 3 _____ 3 _____ 0 _____ 15 _____ (5 _____ 15)

10. (120 _____ 4) _____ 7 _____ 3 = (7 _____ 7) _____ (2 _____ 5)

11. (91 _____ 3 _____ 6) _____ 3 = 2 _____ 5 _____ 1 _____ 3 _____ (2 _____ 5)

12. (16 _____ 4) _____ 8 = 5 _____ 5 _____ (2 _____ 3) _____ 6

13. 0 _____ 5 _____ 15 _____ 4 = 3 _____ 3 _____ 3 _____ 8

14. 16 _____ 3 _____ 12 _____ (2 _____ 20) = (2 _____ 2) _____ 6 _____ 10 _____ (2 _____ 7)

15. 21 _____ (3 _____ 3) _____ 3 _____ 1 = 3 _____ 1 _____ 2 _____ 20

Week 4 Skills

Subject	Skill	Multi-Sensory Learning Activities
Reading and Language Arts	Read nonfiction texts, then compare and contrast information.	• Complete Practice Pages 48–51. • Have your child choose two books to compare. Have him or her draw a line down the middle of a page and write the name of one book at the top of each column. Ask your child to list what he or she liked and disliked about each book.
Math	Write and solve equations.	• Complete Practice Pages 52 and 53. • Ask your child to think about a real-life situation involving numbers and write an equation based on those numbers. For example, if he or she and 20 classmates buy lunch five days a week and spend about $4 each day, how much does is the total spent each week?
	Practice multiplication facts.	• Complete Practice Page 54. • Give your child a page of 50 multiplication problems, up to **12 x 12**. Time your child to see how fast he or she can accurately complete the problems.
	Multiply by one- and two-digit numbers.	• Complete Practice Pages 55 and 56. • Give your child a series of multiplication problems to estimate, then solve. Have your child check his or her work if the answer and estimate are not close.

What's the Difference?

One day, David and Donald were discussing alligators. David insisted that alligators and crocodiles were the same animal but that people called them by different names. Donald insisted, however, that the two animals were entirely different reptiles. Kim walked up just in time to save the boys from further squabbling. Kim, who had lived in Florida for ten years, could settle this one.

She told David that alligators and crocodiles are separate reptiles. She told them that although they are similar looking and are both called crocodilians, they are very different. Both have a long, low, cigar-shaped body, short legs and a long, powerful tail to help them swim. But most crocodiles have a pointed snout instead of a round one like the alligator's. She also pointed out that while both have tough hides, long snouts and sharp teeth to grasp their prey, the crocodile is only about two-thirds as heavy as an American alligator of the same length and can therefore move much more quickly. David and Donald were impressed with Kim's knowledge.

Kim also told the boys another way to tell the two reptiles apart. She said that both have an extra long lower fourth tooth. This tooth fits into a pit in the alligator's upper jaw, while in the crocodile, it fits into a groove in the side of the upper jaw and shows when the crocodile's mouth is closed. David and Donald thanked Kim for the information, looked at each other sheepishly and walked away laughing.

Match:

crocodile   fourth tooth shows when mouth is shut
                     round snout
                     called crocodilian
alligator   fourth tooth is in a pocket in upper jaw
                     pointed snout

Write three ways alligators and crocodiles are alike and three ways they are different.

Alike	Different
_____	_____
_____	_____
_____	_____

Name two other animals that are sometimes thought to be the same.

_____   _____

Comprehension: The *Lusitania*

The *Lusitania* was a British passenger steamship. It became famous when it was torpedoed and sunk by the Germans during World War I. On May 7, 1915, the *Lusitania* was traveling off the coast of Ireland when a German submarine fired on it without warning. The ship stood no chance of surviving the attack and sunk in an astonishing 20 minutes. 1,198 people perished, of whom 128 were American citizens. At the time the ship was torpedoed, the United States was not yet involved in the war. Public opinion over the attack put pressure on President Woodrow Wilson to declare war on Germany. The Germans proclaimed that the *Lusitania* was carrying weapons for the use of the allies.

This claim was later proven to be true. President Wilson demanded that the German government apologize for the sinking and make amends. Germany did not accept responsibility but did promise to avoid sinking any more passenger ships without first giving a warning.

Answer these questions about the *Lusitania*.

1. What does **proclaimed** mean?_____

2. What does **perished** mean?_____

3. What does **amends** mean?_____

4. What does **allies** mean?_____

5. If the *Lusitania* was carrying arms, do you think the Germans had a right to sink it? Why or why not?

_____

_____

_____

_____

Comprehension: The *Titanic*

The British passenger ship, *Titanic*, debuted in the spring of 1912. It was billed as an unsinkable ship due to its construction. It had 16 watertight compartments that would hold the ship afloat even in the event that four of the compartments were damaged.

But on the evening of April 14, 1912, during *Titanic*'s first voyage, its design proved unworthy. Just before midnight, *Titanic* struck an iceberg, which punctured 5 of the 16 compartments. The ship sunk in a little under 3 hours. Approximately 1,513 of the over 2,220 people onboard died. Most of these people died because there weren't enough lifeboats to accommodate everyone onboard. These people were left floating in the water. Many died from exposure, since the Atlantic Ocean was near freezing in temperature. It was one of the worst ocean disasters in history.

Because of the investigations that followed the *Titanic* disaster, the passenger ship industry instituted many reforms. It is now required that there is ample lifeboat space for all passengers and crew. An international ice patrol and full-time radio coverage were also instituted to prevent such disasters in the future.

Answer these questions about the *Titanic*.

1. How did most of the 1,513 people onboard the *Titanic* die?_____

2. Why did this "unsinkable" ship sink?_____

_____

3. What changes have been made in ship safety as a result of the *Titanic* tragedy?

_____

_____

4. There have been many attempts to rescue artifacts from the *Titanic*. But many families of the dead wish the site to be left alone, as it is the final resting place of their relatives. They feel burial sites should not be disrupted. Do you agree or disagree? Why?

_____

_____

_____

Venn Diagram: *Lusitania* and *Titanic*

A **Venn diagram** is used to chart information that shows similarities and differences between two things.

Example:

Dogs	Both	Cats
bark	good pets	one size
dependent	can live inside or outside	kill mice
large and small breeds	have fur	can use litterbox
protect the home	four legs	independent

Complete the Venn diagram for the *Lusitania* and the *Titanic*.

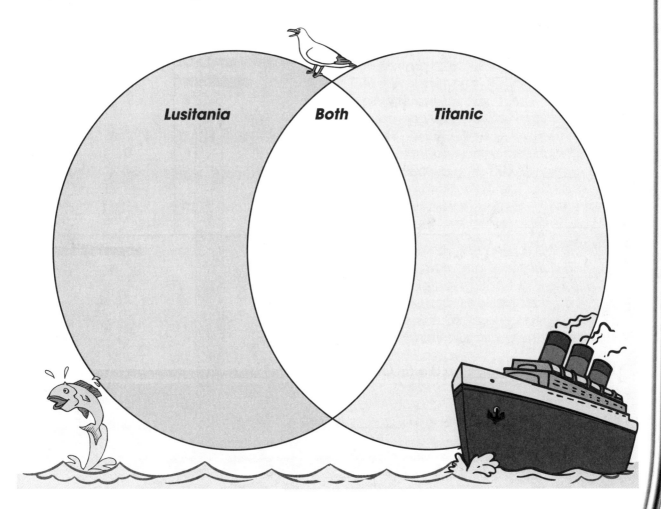

Equations

In an **equation**, the value on the left of the equal sign must equal the value on the right. Remember the order of operations: solve from left to right, multiply or divide numbers before adding or subtracting and do the operation inside parentheses first. Write the correct operation signs in the blanks to make accurate equations.

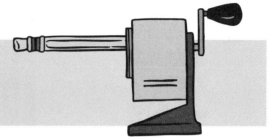

Example: 6 + 4 − 2 = 4 x 2

         10 − 2 =   8
             8   =   8

Write the correct operation signs in the blanks to make accurate equations.

1. (25 _____ 25) _____ 2 = 100 _____ 75

2. (76 _____ 24) _____ 3 = 150 _____ 2

3. 140 _____ 2 _____ 10 = 500 _____ 50 _____ 150

4. 2,100 _____ 2,000 _____ 60 = 80 _____ 2

5. 80 _____ 8 _____ 4 = 160 _____ 160 _____ 160

6. (55 _____ 100) _____ 11 = (1,000 _____ 2) _____ 4

7. 137 _____ 81 _____ 52 = 3 _____ 90

8. 3,000 _____ 10 _____ 10 = (600 _____ 300) _____ 30

9. (720 _____ 20) _____ 4 = 37 _____ 5

10. (457 _____ 43) _____ 500 = (21 _____ 40) x 0

COMPLETE YEAR GRADE 5

Equations

Solve the equations on another sheet of paper.
Write your answers here.

1. $5 + 64 =$

2. $(3 \times 4) \div 3 =$

3. $(32 \div 8) + 3 =$

4. $(40 \div 8) \times 2 =$

5. $6 + (8 \times 3) =$

6. $14 + 12 - 6 =$

7. $(2 \times 9) + 4 =$

8. $(8 \times 8) + 6 =$

9. $6 + (6 \div 6) =$

10. $45 \div (5 \times 3) =$

11. $9 + 7 - 10 =$

12. $(15 \times 2) \div 3 =$

13. $(3 \times 7) - 1 =$

14. $(18 \div 9) \times 8 =$

15. $(36 \div 9) + 8 =$

16. $(21 \div 7) + 6 =$

17. $7 + 8 - 8 =$

18. $9 + 6 - 12 =$

19. $12 + 7 - 8 =$

20. $(56 \div 8) + 4 =$

21. $(64 \div 8) + 5 =$

22. $14 + (2 \times 8) =$

23. $(7 + 9) \div 2 =$

24. $(15 \div 3) \times 2 =$

25. $(5 + 3) \times 3 =$

26. $15 - 7 + 3 =$

27. $(3 + 7) \times (10 - 2) =$

28. $6 + (8 \div 2) =$

29. $3 \times (5 + 6) =$

30. $15 + (3 \times 2) =$

31. $14 - (8 - 2) - 1 =$

32. $16 - (10 - 4) =$

33. $(14 + 6) \div 5 =$

34. $(3 + 2) \times (4 + 6) =$

35. $12 \times (3 + 2) =$

36. $6 \times (4 + 5) =$

37. $3 + (6 \times 2) + 5 =$

38. $8 + (4 \times 5) =$

39. $(6 \times 8) + 2 =$

40. $30 + (16 \times 2) =$

41. $3 \times (9 + 2) =$

42. $52 - (5 + 3) =$

43. $(64 \div 8) \times 3 =$

44. $25 - (3 + 8) =$

45. $21 \div (3 + 4) =$

Timed Multiplication

1 x 1	9 x 3	4 x 10	8 x 3	2 x 10	5 x 7	7 x 4	12 x 3
10 x 3	12 x 9	10 x 5	4 x 9	7 x 5	11 x 2	6 x 6	3 x 2
5 x 8	10 x 4	9 x 4	3 x 3	5 x 9	9 x 6	8 x 5	6 x 7
4 x 8	11 x 3	12 x 5	1 x 4	7 x 7	10 x 6	2 x 7	4 x 7
3 x 4	6 x 8	9 x 5	5 x 10	11 x 9	3 x 5	10 x 7	1 x 5
2 x 6	8 x 7	9 x 2	4 x 6	9 x 8	8 x 8	7 x 9	4 x 5
10 x 8	3 x 6	6 x 10	11 x 6	9 x 7	2 x 5	12 x 10	7 x 10

COMPLETE YEAR GRADE 5

Multiplication (One-Digit Multiplier)

Example A (no regrouping)	234 x 2 — 468	**Step 1** Multiply ones. 2 x 4 = 8 **Step 2** Multiply tens. 2 x 3 = 6 **Step 3** Multiply hundreds. 2 x 2 = 4

Example B (regrouping)	2 1 563 x 4 — 2,252	**Step 1** Multiply ones. 4 x 3 = 12 ones = 1 ten 2 ones. Carry the 1. **Step 2** Multiply tens. 4 x 6 + 1 = 25 tens = 2 hundreds 5 tens. Carry the 2. **Step 3** Multiply hundreds. 4 x 5 + 2 = 22 hundreds = 2 thousands 2 hundreds.

Example C (regrouping and zeros)	7 5 7,086 x 9 — 63,774	**Step 1** Multiply ones. 9 x 6 = 54 ones = 5 tens 4 ones. Carry the 5. **Step 2** Multiply tens. 9 x 8 + 5 = 77 tens = 7 hundreds 7 tens. Carry the 7. **Step 3** Multiply hundreds. 9 x 0 + 7 = 7 hundreds. **Step 4** Multiply thousands. 9 x 7 = 63 thousands = 6 ten-thousands 3 thousands.

Multiply.

1.   323
    x   8

2.   1,132
    x   2

3.   789
    x   5

4.   4,008
    x   7

5.   2,580
    x   3

6.   888
    x   6

7.   4,234
    x   4

8.   589
    x   9

9.   3,211
    x   3

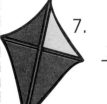

Multiplication

Multiply the following numbers. Be sure to keep the numbers aligned and place a 0 in the ones place when multiplying by the tens digit.

Example:	Correct	Incorrect
	55	55
	x 15	x 15
	275	275
	550	55
	825	330

1. 12
    x 6

2. 44
    x 9

3. 27
    x 7

4. 92
    x 6

5. 85
    x 9

6. 78
    x 24

7. 32
    x 17

8. 19
    x 46

9. 63
    x 12

10. 38
    x 77

11. 125
    x 6

12. 641
    x 25

13. 713
    x 47

14. 586
    x 45

15. 294
    x 79

16. 20 x 4 x 7 = _____

17. 9 x 5 x 11 = _____

18. 16 x 2 x 2 = _____

19. 7 x 6 x 3 = _____

20. 33 x 11 x 3 = _____

21. 2 x 8 x 10 = _____

Week 5 Skills

Subject	Skill	Multi-Sensory Learning Activities
Reading and Language Arts	Use conjunctions to combine words and sentences.	• Complete Practice Pages 58–61. • Have your child write a fiction or nonfiction story about a favorite mammal. Ask your child to circle every sentence that includes a conjunction.
	Punctuate interjections using commas and exclamation points.	• Complete Practice Page 62. • Write a series of sentences with interjections, leaving off the punctuation. For example, write, "Wow did you see that" or "Please I have asked you twenty times to stop cracking your knuckles." Ask your child to punctuate the sentences correctly and circle the interjections.
	Use commas in examples of direct address.	• Complete Practice Page 63. • Dictate a series of commands to your child, including his or her first name (for example, say, "Anna, clean your room"). Ask your child to write the command, then check to ensure that he or she added a comma as needed.
Math	Multiply by one- and two-digit numbers.	• Complete Practice Pages 64–66. • Show your child how to measure his or her pulse at the wrist or neck. Have him or her count the number of beats for 15 seconds, then multiply that number by 4 to get his or her pulse rate for one minute.

Conjunctions

The conjunctions **and**, **or**, **but** and **nor** can be used to make a compound subject, a compound predicate or a compound sentence.

Examples:
Compound subject: My friend **and** I will go to the mall.
Compound predicate: We ran **and** jumped in gym class.
Compound sentence: I am a talented violinist, **but** my father is better.

Write two sentences of your own in each section.

Compound subject:

1. _____

_____

2. _____

_____

Compound predicate:

1. _____

_____

2. _____

_____

Compound sentence:

1. _____

_____

2. _____

_____

Conjunctions

A conjunction joins words, groups of words or entire sentences. The most common conjunctions are **and**, **or**, **but**.

Examples:
*Christian Huygens **and** Jean Cassini made discoveries about Saturn.* (joins subjects)

*The Italian astronomer Galileo first saw Saturn's rings through a telescope, **but** the rings weren't very clear.* (joins sentences)

*He discovered the rings in the early 1600s **and** thought they were large satellites.* (joins predicates)

Add a conjunction to each sentence below.

1. Did you know that Saturn takes about 29 $\frac{1}{2}$ Earth-years to orbit the Sun, _____ are you still looking up that fact?

2. Saturn _____ Earth have very different day lengths.

3. Earth's day is about 24 hours, _____ Saturn's is only about 10 $\frac{1}{2}$ hours.

4. Saturn has 23 satellites that have been discovered, _____ Earth has only one.

5. Saturn's natural satellites all have different names, _____ Earth's satellite is just called "the Moon."

6. Saturn has many rings that surround it, _____ Earth has none.

Add a conjunction to each phrase below that describes Saturn.

1. beautiful _____ majestic

2. far away, _____ gigantic

3. larger than Earth, _____ lighter in comparison

4. shorter days than Earth _____ faster rotation

5. atmosphere of mostly hydrogen _____ helium

6. beautiful rings _____ not the only planet with them

Conjuctions

A conjunction joins words or groups of words in a sentence. The most commonly used conjunctions are **and**, **but** and **or**.

Examples: My brother **and** I each want to win the trophy.
Tonight, it will rain **or** sleet.
I wanted to go to the party, **but** I got sick.

Circle the conjunctions.

1. Dolphins and whales are mammals.

2. They must rise to the surface of the water to breathe, or they will die.

3. Dolphins resemble fish, but they are not fish.

4. Sightseeing boats are often entertained by groups of dolphins or whales.

5. Whales appear to effortlessly leap out of the water and execute flips.

6. Both whale and dolphin babies are born alive.

7. The babies are called calves and are born in the water, but must breathe air within a few minutes of birth.

8. Sometimes an entire pod of whales will help a mother and calf reach the surface to breathe.

9. Scientists and marine biologists have long been intrigued by these ocean animals.

10. Whales and dolphins do not seem to be afraid of humans or boats.

Write six sentences using conjunctions.

11. _____

12. _____

13. _____

14. _____

15. _____

16. _____

Writing: Conjunctions

Too many short sentences make writing seem choppy. Short sentences can be combined to make writing flow better. Words used to combine sentences are called **conjunctions**.

Examples: but, before, after, because, when, or, so, and

Use **or**, **but**, **before**, **after**, **because**, **when**, **and** or **so** to combine each pair of sentences. The first one has been done for you.

1. I was wearing my winter coat. I started to shiver.

   I was wearing my winter coat, but I started to shiver.

2. Animals all need water. They may perish without it.

   _____

3. The sun came out. The ice began to thaw.

   _____

4. The sun came out. The day was still chilly.

   _____

5. Will the flowers perish? Will they thrive?

   _____

6. The bear came closer. We began to feel threatened.

   _____

7. Winning was a challenge. Our team didn't have much experience.

   _____

8. Winning was a challenge. Our team was up to it.

   _____

Write three sentences of your own. Use a conjunction in each sentence.

_____

_____

_____

Interjections

An **interjection** that shows strong feeling is followed by an exclamation point. The next word begins with a capital letter.
Example: Quiet! He's not finished yet.

An **interjection** that shows mild feeling is followed by a comma. The next word is not capitalized.
Example: Oh, is that correct?

Rewrite the sentences to show strong feeling. Punctuate and capitalize properly.

1. hurrah we won the game.

_____

2. whew that was a close one.

_____

Rewrite the sentences on the lines. Punctuate and capitalize properly.

1. yes you may go to the movies.

_____

2. well we're glad you're finally here.

_____

Rewrite the sentences below correctly.

1. hush you don't want to upset her.

_____

2. well we're glad you came to the meeting.

_____

3. quiet you'll wake up everyone.

_____

COMPLETE YEAR GRADE 5

Interjections and Direct Address

Strong interjections, which show great feeling, are followed by exclamation points.

Mild interjections, such as **now**, **well** and **yes**, are set apart by commas.

A comma or commas are used to set apart the name of a person being directly spoken to, or addressed, in a sentence. This is called **direct address**.

Examples:
Ugh! That soup is horrible. (strong interjection)
No, I haven't finished my homework yet. (mild interjection)
Sue, please hand me the pencil. (direct address)
Thank you, Jean, for your contribution. (direct address)

Add commas and exclamation points where they are needed in the following sentences.

1. Yes we will finish the science project soon.

2. Wow I forgot that it must be completed by Friday.

3. Oh I forgot that the materials for the experiment are at home.

4. Jim bring the microscope to the science lab.

5. Now Leonard it's your turn to work on the experiment.

6. Will the research for the project be completed soon Amy?

7. No Mrs. Clarke it will take at least another week.

8. Yikes That was a scary experiment you did Mark.

Add commas and exclamation points where they are needed in the following sentences. In the blank, write the letter of the reason each punctuation mark is used. Some have two answers.

A. Interjection   **B.** Direct Address

1. _____ Lewis will you attempt this experiment on air pressure?

2. _____ No I need to work on my electricity project Sam.

3. _____ I need some help Mr. Johnson with my electrical circuit.

4. _____ The science lab is too crowded to set up the project Ms. Chang.

5. _____ Cool I would love to use the other lab.

6. _____ Yes I'll try to set up the project in that room Sarah.

7. _____ Well that solved my problem.

Multiplication

Multiplication is a process of quick addition of a number a certain number of times.

Example: $3 \times 15 = 45$ is the same as adding 15 three times. $15 + 15 + 15 = 45$

Multiply.

$\begin{array}{r} 32 \\ \times\ 3 \\ \hline \end{array}$ $\begin{array}{r} 48 \\ \times\ 7 \\ \hline \end{array}$ $\begin{array}{r} 26 \\ \times\ 5 \\ \hline \end{array}$ $\begin{array}{r} 19 \\ \times\ 6 \\ \hline \end{array}$ $\begin{array}{r} 63 \\ \times\ 2 \\ \hline \end{array}$

$\begin{array}{r} 251 \\ \times\ 4 \\ \hline \end{array}$ $\begin{array}{r} 523 \\ \times\ 8 \\ \hline \end{array}$ $\begin{array}{r} 915 \\ \times\ 3 \\ \hline \end{array}$ $\begin{array}{r} 431 \\ \times\ 7 \\ \hline \end{array}$ $\begin{array}{r} 275 \\ \times\ 3 \\ \hline \end{array}$

$\begin{array}{r} 412 \\ \times\ 21 \\ \hline \end{array}$ $\begin{array}{r} 643 \\ \times\ 17 \\ \hline \end{array}$ $\begin{array}{r} 526 \\ \times\ 22 \\ \hline \end{array}$ $\begin{array}{r} 742 \\ \times\ 35 \\ \hline \end{array}$

$\begin{array}{r} 256 \\ \times\ 74 \\ \hline \end{array}$ $\begin{array}{r} 874 \\ \times\ 15 \\ \hline \end{array}$ $\begin{array}{r} 372 \\ \times\ 45 \\ \hline \end{array}$ $\begin{array}{r} 951 \\ \times\ 34 \\ \hline \end{array}$

Cathy is on the cross country team. She runs 3 miles every day of the year except on her birthday. How many miles does she run each year?

_____

Multiplication

Multiply.

1. 649
    x   8

2. 858
    x   7

3. 7,642
    x   5

4. 8,219
    x   3

5. 5,238
    x   6

6. 8,249
    x   4

7. 6,518
    x   7

8. 8,943
    x   9

9. 3,268
    x   5

10. 4,637
     x   8

11. 5,387
     x   4

12. 8,264
     x   9

13. 4,875
     x   7

14. 5,689
     x   8

15. 9,243
     x   4

16. 8,540
     x   6

17. 3,726
     x   5

18. 83,243
     x   6

19. 74,254
     x   7

20. 62,435
     x   9

21. 73,643
     x   8

22. 51,476
     x   4

23. 73,629
     x   5

24. 87,642
     x   7

25. 25,624
     x   4

26. 98,215
     x   6

27. 41,826
     x   9

28. 53,214
     x   8

29. 83,265
     x   4

30. 65,429
     x   5

31. 46,254
     x   7

32. 91,242
     x   8

33. 73,263
     x   6

34. 35,584
     x   2

35. 79,267
     x   2

Multiplying With Zeros

Multiply the following numbers. If a number ends with zero, you can eliminate it while calculating the rest of the answer. Then count how many zeros you took off and add them to your answer.

Example:	550	Take off 2 zeros	500	Take off 2 zeros
	x 50		x 5	
	27,500	Add on 2 zeros	2,500	Add on 2 zeros

1. 300
    x   6

2. 400
    x   7

3. 620
    x   5

4. 290
    x   7

5. 142
    x 20

6. 505
    x 50

7. 340
    x 70

8. 600
    x 60

9.   550
     x 380

10.   290
      x 150

11. 2,040
    x 360

12. 8,800
    x 200

13. Bruce traveled 600 miles each day of a 10-day trip.
    How far did he go during the entire trip? _____

14. 30 children each sold items for the school fund-raiser.
    Each child earned $100 for the school.
    How much money did the school collect? _____

15. 10 x 40 x 2 = _____

16. 30 x 30 x 10 = _____

17. 100 x 60 x 10 = _____

18. 500 x 11 x 2 = _____

19. 9 x 10 x 10 = _____

20. 7,000 x 20 x 10 = _____

Week 6 Skills

Subject	Skill	Multi-Sensory Learning Activities
Reading and Language Arts	Identify homophones that are frequently confused.	• Complete Practice Pages 68 and 71. • Play a game of "Memory Match" using homophones. Cut a piece of paper into at least 20 squares. Write one homophone per card, then turn them upside down. Take turns flipping two cards at once. If you find a homophone pair, you must use each word correctly in a sentence before collecting the pair and taking another turn. The player who collects the most pairs is the winner.
Math	Multiply by two- and three-digit numbers.	• Complete Practice Pages 72–76. • Help your child design a project that requires shopping for large quantities of different products, such as setting up a lemonade stand or planning a family picnic. Have your child determine the price and quantity of each item needed for the project. Using multiplication and addition, have your child estimate, then figure the actual cost of the project.
Bonus: Science		• Ask your child to name natural and artificial sources of light, such as fireflies, lightning, the sun, light bulbs, candles, and fireworks. Using old magazines and newspapers, have your child make a poster of the forms of light energy.

Homophones

Homophones are words that sound alike but have different spellings and meanings.

Write the correct homophone in the blank.

__Their__ house is around the corner from us. (their, there)

1. We couldn't decide _____ to visit Boston or St. Louis. (weather, whether)

2. We chose to visit Boston, the _____ of Massachusetts. (capital, capitol)

3. We drove _____ the city in _____ days. (to, too, two)

4. Our _____ was over interstate highways. (route, root)

5. We _____ many signs along the way. (read, red)

6. My brothers couldn't hide _____ excitement. (their, there)

7. We found that _____ an exciting city. (its, it's)

8. It was interesting to _____ the accent of the people. (hear, here)

9. Many people related interesting _____ about the city's history. (tales, tails)

10. We appreciated the _____ and quiet of the parks. (peace, piece)

11. We walked up and down _____ of houses in the historic district. (rows, rose)

12. I wore a _____ in one of my shoes from _____ much walking. (whole, hole) (so, sew)

13. Luckily, this caused me _____ _____. (know, no) (pain, pane)

14. I had to have the _____ of the shoe repaired. (soul, sole)

Who's and Whose

Who's is a contraction for **who is**.

Whose is a possessive pronoun.

Examples:
   Who's going to come?
   Whose shirt is this?

To know which word to use, substitute the words "who is." If the sentence makes sense, use **who's**.

Write the correct words to complete these sentences.

_____ 1. Do you know who's/whose invited to the party?

_____ 2. I don't even know who's/whose house it will be at.

_____ 3. Who's/Whose towel is on the floor?

_____ 4. Who's/Whose going to drive us?

_____ 5. Who's/Whose ice cream is melting?

_____ 6. I'm the person who's/whose gloves are lost.

_____ 7. Who's/Whose in your group?

_____ 8. Who's/Whose group is first?

_____ 9. Can you tell who's/whose at the door?

_____ 10. Who's/Whose friend are you?

_____ 11. Who's/Whose cooking tonight?

_____ 12. Who's/Whose cooking do you like best?

Their, There, and They're

Their is a possessive pronoun meaning "belonging to them."

There is an adverb that indicates place.

They're is a contraction for **they are**.

Examples:

Ron and Sue took **their** dog to the park.
They like to go **there** on Sunday afternoon.
They're probably going back next Sunday, too.

Write the correct words to complete these sentences.

_____ 1. All the students should bring their/there/they're books to class.

_____ 2. I've never been to France, but I hope to travel their/there/they're someday.

_____ 3. We studied how dolphins care for their/there/they're young.

_____ 4. My parents are going on vacation next week, and their/there/they're taking my sister.

_____ 5. Their/There/They're was a lot of food at the party.

_____ 6. My favorite baseball team lost their/there/they're star pitcher this year.

_____ 7. Those peaches look good, but their/there/they're not ripe yet.

_____ 8. The book is right their/there/they're on the table.

Principal and Principle

Principal means main, leader or chief, or a sum of money that earns interest.

Examples:
> The high school **principal** earned interest on the **principal** in his savings account.
> The **principal** reason for his savings account was to save for retirement.

Principle means a truth, law or a moral outlook that governs the way someone behaves.

Example:
> Einstein discovered some fundamental **principles** of science.
> Stealing is against her **principles**.

Write **principle** or **principal** in the blanks to complete these sentences correctly. The first one has been done for you.

principle 1. A (principle/principal) of biology is "the survival of the fittest."

_____ 2. She was a person of strong (principles/principals).

_____ 3. The (principles/principals) sat together at the district conference.

_____ 4. How much of the total in my savings account is (principle/principal)?

_____ 5. His hay fever was the (principle/principal) reason for his sneezing.

_____ 6. It's not the facts that upset me, it's the (principles/principals) of the case.

_____ 7. The jury heard only the (principle/principal) facts.

_____ 8. Our school (principle/principal) is strict but fair.

_____ 9. Spend the interest, but don't touch the (principle/principal).

_____ 10. Helping others is a guiding (principle/principal) of the homeless shelter.

_____ 11. In (principle/principal), we agree; on the facts, we do not.

_____ 12. The (principle/principal) course at dinner was leg of lamb.

_____ 13. Some mathematical (principles/principals) are difficult to understand.

_____ 14. The baby was the (principle/principal) reason for his happiness.

Multiplication (Two-Digit Multiplier)

Example A
(no regrouping)

```
    21
x   44
    84
+  840
   924
```

Step 1 Multiply by ones.
4 x 1 = 4
4 x 2 = 8

Step 2 Multiply by tens.
Add zero in the ones column.
4 x 1 = 4
4 x 2 = 8

Step 3 Add.
84 + 840 = 924

Example B
(regrouping)

```
      67
x     58
     536
+  3,350
   3,886
```

Step 1 Multiply by ones.
8 x 7 = 56 (Carry the 5.)
8 x 6 + 5 = 53

Step 2 Multiply by tens.
Add zero in the ones column.
5 x 7 = 35 (Carry the 3.)
5 x 6 + 3 = 33

Step 3 Add.
536 + 3,350 = 3,886

Multiply.

1.
```
    43
x   33
```

2.
```
    55
x   46
```

3.
```
    78
x   68
```

4.
```
    39
x   27
```

5.
```
    21
x   87
```

6.
```
    77
x   24
```

7.
```
    44
x   16
```

8.
```
    80
x   71
```

9.
```
    65
x   49
```

COMPLETE YEAR GRADE 5

Multiplication Maze

These multiplication problems have already been done, but some of them are wrong. Check each problem. Connect the problems with correct answers to make a path for Zerpo to get back to his ship. Then, correct each wrong answer.

$$\begin{array}{r} 863 \\ \times\ \ 24 \\ \hline 21,712 \end{array}$$

$$\begin{array}{r} 904 \\ \times\ \ 93 \\ \hline 85,072 \end{array}$$

$$\begin{array}{r} 6,520 \\ \times\ \ \ 74 \\ \hline 582,480 \end{array}$$

$$\begin{array}{r} 199 \\ \times\ \ 98 \\ \hline 19,502 \end{array}$$

$$\begin{array}{r} 663 \\ \times\ \ 54 \\ \hline 53,802 \end{array}$$

$$\begin{array}{r} 392 \\ \times\ \ 28 \\ \hline 11,976 \end{array}$$

$$\begin{array}{r} 485 \\ \times\ \ 53 \\ \hline 24,605 \end{array}$$

$$\begin{array}{r} 925 \\ \times\ \ 68 \\ \hline 62,900 \end{array}$$

$$\begin{array}{r} 566 \\ \times\ \ 74 \\ \hline 35,884 \end{array}$$

$$\begin{array}{r} 2,576 \\ \times\ \ \ 92 \\ \hline 236,992 \end{array}$$

$$\begin{array}{r} 466 \\ \times\ \ 18 \\ \hline 8,388 \end{array}$$

$$\begin{array}{r} 4,516 \\ \times\ \ \ 22 \\ \hline 98,352 \end{array}$$

$$\begin{array}{r} 1,530 \\ \times\ \ \ 93 \\ \hline 152,290 \end{array}$$

$$\begin{array}{r} 5,563 \\ \times\ \ \ 35 \\ \hline 194,705 \end{array}$$

$$\begin{array}{r} 719 \\ \times\ \ 82 \\ \hline 69,958 \end{array}$$

$$\begin{array}{r} 239 \\ \times\ \ 15 \\ \hline 4,585 \end{array}$$

$$\begin{array}{r} 534 \\ \times\ \ 34 \\ \hline 28,156 \end{array}$$

$$\begin{array}{r} 329 \\ \times\ \ 16 \\ \hline 5,624 \end{array}$$

$$\begin{array}{r} 1,344 \\ \times\ \ \ 49 \\ \hline 65,856 \end{array}$$

$$\begin{array}{r} 671 \\ \times\ \ 68 \\ \hline 45,628 \end{array}$$

$$\begin{array}{r} 793 \\ \times\ \ 81 \\ \hline 64,233 \end{array}$$

$$\begin{array}{r} 861 \\ \times\ \ 57 \\ \hline 50,077 \end{array}$$

$$\begin{array}{r} 651 \\ \times\ \ 83 \\ \hline 34,738 \end{array}$$

$$\begin{array}{r} 1,524 \\ \times\ \ \ 43 \\ \hline 64,532 \end{array}$$

$$\begin{array}{r} 819 \\ \times\ \ 76 \\ \hline 52,244 \end{array}$$

$$\begin{array}{r} 2,316 \\ \times\ \ \ 27 \\ \hline 62,532 \end{array}$$

$$\begin{array}{r} 4,110 \\ \times\ \ \ 28 \\ \hline 125,080 \end{array}$$

Multiplication

certain to keep the proper place value when multiplying by tens and hundreds.

Examples:

```
   143          250
 x 262        x 150
   286          000
   858        1 250
   286          250
 37,466       37,500
```

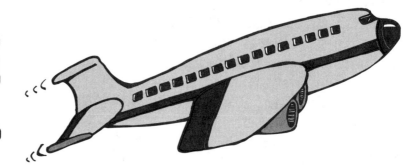

Multiply

```
  701          621          348          597
 x308         x538         x200         x424
```

```
  537          416          682          180
 x189         x727         x472         x340
```

```
  878          267          893          907
 x638         x196         x214         x428
```

An airplane flies 720 trips a year between the cities of Chicago and Columbus. Each trip is 375 miles. How many miles does the airplane fly each year?

_____

Multiplication

Solve.

1. 467
    x 35

2. 538
    x 47

3. 393
    x 82

4. 304
    x 529

5. 246
    x 824

6. 146
    x 532

7. 308
    x 236

8. 326
    x 92

9. 735
    x 45

10. 268
    x 39

11. 486
    x 513

12. 314
    x 249

Puzzling Cross Number

Solve the multiplication problems below. Write the answers in the puzzle.

Across

1.	462	5.	234	7.	926
	x 212		x 101		x 815

Down

2.	634	3.	208	4.	672
	x 755		x 422		x 833

8.	624	11.	832
	x 783		x 458

6.	547	9.	926
	x 900		x 950

13.	336	14.	801
	x 817		x 101

10.	698	12.	111
	x 741		x 111

Week 7 Skills

Subject	Skill	Multi-Sensory Learning Activities
Reading and Language Arts	Read text and understand its mood or tone.	• Complete Practice Page 78. • Provide a list of subject/signal word pairs that indicate the tone of a quotation (e.g., "Mother yelled") and have your child complete the imagined quotations. For example, your child may finish the above sentence as "Mother yelled, 'I told you to clean your room!'"
	Understand differing points of view in text.	• Complete Practice Pages 78 and 80. • Read *Shiloh* by Phyllis Reynolds Naylor. From what or whose point of view is the story written? Discuss why the author chose to tell the story from that perspective.
Math	Practice division facts.	• Complete Practice Page 81. • Give your child a page of 50 division problems, up to $144 \div 12$. Remind your child to think of known multiplication facts to help solve unknown division facts. Time your child to see how fast he or she can accurately complete the problems.
	Divide by one- and two-digit divisors.	• Complete Practice Pages 82–86. • Use small objects to help your child visualize division problems as repeated subtraction. For example, start with 28 counters. Take away a group of four counters seven times to show that 28 can be divided into seven groups of four.

How's It Said?

Circle the word which best describes the mood or tone of the person speaking.

1. When Winnie's grandmother heard the little melody in the woods, she said, "That's it! That's the elf music I told you about."

           resentful   eager   anxious

2. Winnie spied on Jesse in the woods and watched as he drank from the spring. When he saw her, Jesse cried, "What're you doing here?"

           bored   hopeless   surprised

3. When Jesse told her not to drink from the spring, Winnie questioned, "Why not? It's mine, anyway, if it's in the wood."

           stubborn   reluctant   worried

4. Winnie cried when she realized she was being kidnapped. Seeing this, Mae exclaimed, "Please don't cry, child! We're not bad people, truly we're not."

           angry   reluctant   dismayed

5. When Winnie was calmed, everyone relaxed. Jesse began to explain the family's story. "We're friends, we really are. But you got to help us."

           confident   happy   pleading

6. Miles recalled how his family reacted when he didn't age. "My wife, she left me. She went away and she took the children with her."

           stern   sad   stubborn

What might you say if . . .

1. . . . you were angry at your parents for not letting you go outside?

_____

_____

2. . . . you were hopelessly unprepared for your spelling test?

_____

_____

Writing: Different Points of View

A **fact** is a statement that can be proved. An **opinion** is what someone thinks or believes.

Write **F** if the statement is a fact or **O** if it is an opinion.

1. _____ The amusement park near our town just opened last summer.

2. _____ It's the best one in our state.

3. _____ It has a roller coaster that's 300 feet high.

4. _____ You're a chicken if you don't go on it.

OPINION

FACT

Think about the last movie or TV show you saw. Write one fact and one opinion about it.

Fact: _____

Opinion: _____

In a story, a **point of view** is how one character feels about an event and reacts to it.

Different points of view show how characters feel about the same situation.

What if you were at the mall with a friend and saw a CD you really wanted on sale? You didn't bring enough money, so you borrowed five dollars from your friend to buy the CD. Then you lost the money in the store!

Write a sentence describing what happened from the point of view of each person named below. Explain how each person felt.

Yourself _____

_____

Your friend _____

_____

The store clerk who watched you look for the money _____

_____

The person who found the money _____

_____

Writing: Point of View

People often have different opinions about the same thing. This is because each of us has a different "point of view." **Point of view** is the attitude someone has about a particular topic as a result of his or her personal experience or knowledge.

Read the topic sentence below about the outcome of a basketball game. Then write two short paragraphs, one from the point of view of a player for the Reds and one from the point of view of a player for the Cowboys. Be sure to give each person's opinion of the outcome of the game.

Topic Sentence: In the last second of the basketball game between the Reds and the Cowboys, the Reds scored and won the game.

Terry, a player for the Reds . . . _____

_____

_____

Chris, a player for the Cowboys . . . _____

_____

_____

Here's a different situation. Read the topic sentence, and then write three short paragraphs from the points of view of Katie, her dad and her brother.

Topic Sentence: Katie's dog had chewed up another one of her father's shoes.

Katie . . . _____

_____

Katie's father . . . _____

_____

Katie's brother Mark, who would rather have a cat . . . _____

_____

Division Facts

Solve.

3)24	9)81	8)40	4)4	9)90	8)56	6)24
7)14	7)49	5)20	6)36	9)72	4)16	3)27
8)64	9)36	5)25	9)45	2)18	4)24	8)8
3)9	2)14	6)54	7)21	8)32	5)30	1)6
2)4	9)81	6)30	4)8	5)50	5)15	2)20
1)10	7)7	2)16	3)15	7)49	1)4	9)63
8)16	2)12	8)72	3)30	9)63	3)18	7)56
9)9	7)63	2)8	8)80	7)28	6)12	3)6
7)42	3)12	7)35	9)27	6)42	5)10	5)45
2)10	9)54	4)20	8)48	9)18	6)6	2)6

Division in Three Ways

The equation $12 \div 3$ can also be written as $3\overline{)12}$ or $\frac{12}{3}$.

Write each equation in the three forms.
The first one has been done for you.

1. $12 \div 3 = \quad 3\overline{)12} \quad = \quad \frac{12}{3}$

2. $24 \div 8 = \quad 8\overline{)} \quad = \quad \frac{}{8}$

3. $56 \div \underline{} = \quad 8\overline{)56} \quad = \quad \frac{56}{}$

4. $\underline{} \div 9 = \quad \overline{)63} \quad = \quad \frac{63}{}$

5. $\underline{} \div \underline{} = \quad \overline{)} \quad = \quad \frac{42}{6}$

6. $15 \div 5 = \quad 5\overline{)} \quad = \quad \frac{15}{}$

7. $42 \div 7 = \quad \overline{)42} \quad = \quad \frac{42}{}$

8. $72 \div \underline{} = \quad 9\overline{)} \quad = \quad \frac{}{9}$

Solve.

9. $20\overline{)440}$

10. $440 \div 20 = \underline{}$

11. $\frac{440}{20} = $

12. $12\overline{)780}$

13. $650 \div 13 = \underline{}$

14. $\frac{720}{15} = $

Multiplication's Opposite

Use the multiplication problem to help solve the division problems.

Example:
$6 \times 7 = 42$
$42 \div 7 = 6$
$42 \div 6 = 7$

1. $4 \times 8 = 32$
    $32 \div \underline{\hspace{1cm}} = 4$
    $32 \div \underline{\hspace{1cm}} = 8$

2. $9 \times 9 = 81$
    $81 \div 9 = \underline{\hspace{1cm}}$

3. $7 \times 8 = 56$
    $\underline{\hspace{1cm}} \div 8 = 7$
    $56 \div \underline{\hspace{1cm}} = 8$

4. $22 \times 12 = 264$
    $\underline{\hspace{1cm}} \div 12 = 22$
    $264 \div 22 = \underline{\hspace{1cm}}$

5. $37 \times 19 = 703$
    $\underline{\hspace{1cm}} \div 37 = 19$
    $703 \div 19 = \underline{\hspace{1cm}}$

Solve the following problems and write two related division problems for each.

6. $22 \times 17 = \underline{\hspace{2cm}}$

7. $45 \times 29 = \underline{\hspace{2cm}}$

8. $19 \times 82 = \underline{\hspace{2cm}}$

9. $671 \times 63 = \underline{\hspace{2cm}}$

10. $663 \times 54 = \underline{\hspace{2cm}}$

11. $719 \times 73 = \underline{\hspace{2cm}}$

Zeros in the Quotient

Zero holds a place in the quotient.

Example:

$$\begin{array}{r} 1 \\ 5\overline{)545} \\ -5 \\ \hline 04 \end{array}$$

Five goes into 4 zero times.

$$\begin{array}{r} 10 \\ 5\overline{)545} \\ -5 \\ \hline 45 \end{array}$$

Five goes into 45 nine times.

$$\begin{array}{r} 109 \\ 5\overline{)545} \\ -5 \\ \hline 45 \\ -45 \\ \hline 0 \end{array}$$

1. $4\overline{)420}$

2. $6\overline{)636}$

3. $9\overline{)963}$

4. $9\overline{)945}$

5. $9\overline{)963}$

6. $8\overline{)816}$

7. $3\overline{)312}$

8. $3\overline{)9,021}$

9. $7\overline{)1,386}$

Division

Solve.

1. 9$\overline{)3,654}$

2. 8$\overline{)835}$

3. 6$\overline{)618}$

Estimate.

4. 36$\overline{)660}$

5. 23$\overline{)4,280}$

6. 158 ÷ 21

Solve.

7. 24$\overline{)228}$

8. 1298 ÷ 37

9. $\dfrac{703}{41}$

10. What is the cost for 1 golf ball?

_____

On Sale
Today Only
One dozen golf balls
Only $3.36

Division Review

Divide.

1. 32) 6,543

2. 69) 112,346

3. 9) 876

4. How many hours are in 255 minutes?

5. How many weeks are there in 90 days?

6. Find the missing length.

    | area = 153 m² | 9m |

7. 17x = 272

    x = _____

8. Write the remainder as a fraction.

    27) 6,925

9. A chicken farm produced 7,256 eggs each day. How many egg cartons are needed each day? (A carton holds one dozen eggs.)

Week 8 Skills

Subject	Skill	Multi-Sensory Learning Activities
Reading and Language Arts	Write events in chronological order.	• Complete Practice Page 88. • Read *Hang Tough, Paul Mather* by Alfred Slote. Have your child rate the excitement of each chapter as **dull**, **somewhat interesting**, **interesting**, **getting tense**, or **exciting**. Have your child plot the chapter ratings on a line graph in chronological order to see a plot profile.
	Write a true story, or personal narrative.	• Complete Practice Pages 89 and 90. • Have your child write a narrative about a personal experience, describing the events in sequential order. Let your child choose whether to write in the first person or in the third person.
	Describe fictional characters and write fictional stories.	• Complete Practice Pages 91–92. • Read *The Trumpet of the Swan* by E. B. White. Discuss the character of Sam. Work with your child to complete a character web for Sam Beaver.
Math	Solve division problems with and without remainders.	• Complete Practice Pages 93–96. • Give your child 10–15 division problems with remainders to solve. Have your child check his or her answers using multiplication.

Writing: Sequencing

When writing paragraphs, it is important to write events in the correct order. Think about what happens first, next, later and last.

The following sentences tell about Chandra's day, but they are all mixed up.

Read each sentence and number them in the order in which they happened.

____ She arrived at school and went to her locker to get her books.

____ After dinner, she did the dishes, then read a book for a while.

____ Chandra brushed her teeth and put on her pajamas.

____ She rode the bus home, then she fixed herself a snack.

____ She ate breakfast and went out to wait for the bus.

____ Chandra woke up and picked out her clothes for school.

____ She met her friend Sarah on the way to the cafeteria.

____ She worked on homework and watched TV until her mom called her for dinner.

Write a short paragraph about what you did today. Use words like **first**, **next**, **then**, **later** and **finally** to indicate the order in which you did things.

_____

_____

_____

_____

_____

_____

_____

_____

Personal Narratives

A **personal narrative** tells about a person's own experiences.

Read the example of a personal narrative. Write your answers in complete sentences.

My Worst Year

When I look back on that year, I can hardly believe that one person could have such terrible luck for a whole year. But then again, I should have realized that if things could begin to go wrong in January, it didn't bode well for the rest of the year.

It was the night of January 26. One of my best friends was celebrating her birthday at the local roller-skating rink, and I had been invited. The evening began well enough with pizza and laughs. I admit I have never been a cracker jack roller skater, but I could hold my own. After a few minutes of skating, I decided to exit the rink for a cold soda.

Unfortunately, I did not notice the trailing ribbons of carpet which wrapped around the wheel of my skate, yanking my left leg from under me. My leg was broken. It wasn't just broken in one place but in four places! At the hospital, the doctor set the bone and put a cast on my leg. Three months later, I felt like a new person.

Sadly, the happiness wasn't meant to last. Five short months after the final cast was removed, I fell and broke the same leg again. Not only did it rebreak but it broke in the same four places! We found out later that it hadn't healed correctly. Three months later, it was early December and the end of a year I did not wish to repeat.

1. List the sequence of events in this personal narrative.

_____

_____

_____

_____

2. From reading the personal narrative, what do you think were the author's feelings toward the events that occurred?

_____

_____

Personal Narratives

A **narrative** is a spoken or written account of an actual event. A **personal narrative** tells about your own experience. It can be written about any event in your life and may be serious or comical.

When writing a personal narrative, remember to use correct sentence structure and punctuation. Include important dates, sights, sounds, smells, tastes and feelings to give your reader a clear picture of the event.

Write a personal narrative about an event in your life that was funny.

_____

_____

_____

_____

_____

_____

_____

_____

_____

_____

_____

_____

_____

_____

Describing Characters

When you write a story, your characters must seem like real people. You need to let your reader know not only how they look but how they act and how they feel. You could just tell the reader that a character is friendly, scared or angry, but your story will be more interesting if you show these feelings by the characters' actions.

Example:
Character: A frightened child
Adjectives and adverbs: red-haired, freckled, scared, lost, worried
Simile: as frightened as a mouse cornered by a cat
Action: He peeked between his fingers, but his mother was nowhere in sight.

It started like this. . . .

Write adjectives, adverbs, similes and/or metaphors that tell how each character feels. Then write a sentence that shows how the character feels.

1. an angry woman
   Adjectives and adverbs: _____

   Metaphor or simile: _____

   Sentence: _____

2. a disappointed man
   Adjectives and adverbs: _____

   Metaphor or simile: _____

   Sentence: _____

3. a hungry child
   Adjectives and adverbs: _____

   Metaphor or simile: _____

   Sentence: _____

4. a tired boy
   Adjectives and adverbs: _____

   Metaphor or simile: _____

   Sentence: _____

Writing Fiction

Use descriptive writing to complete each story. Write at least five sentences.

1. It was a cold, wintry morning in January. Snow had fallen steadily for 4 days. I was staring out my bedroom window when I saw the bedraggled dog staggering through the snow.

_____

_____

_____

_____

_____

2. Mindy was home Saturday studying for a big science test. Report cards were due next Friday, and the test on Monday would be on the report card. Mindy needed to do well on the test to get an A in Science. The phone rang. It was her best friend, Jenny.

_____

_____

_____

_____

_____

3. Martin works every weekend delivering newspapers. He wakes up at 5:30 A.M. and begins his route at 6:00 A.M. He delivers 150 newspapers on his bike. He enjoys his weekend job because he is working toward a goal.

_____

_____

_____

_____

_____

Division

The remainder in a division problem must always be less than the divisor.

Example:

```
        244 r 23
26 ) 6,367
     5 2
     116
     104
      127
      104
       23
```

Divide.

53) 1,220   37) 1,528   83) 6,270   26) 3,618

14) 389   29) 2,645   60) 8,010   57) 5,406

35) 2,546   43) 492   83) 4,608   19) 185

The Oregon Trail is 2,197 miles long. How long would it take a covered wagon traveling 20 miles a day to complete the trip?

_____

Dividing with Zeros

Sometimes you have a remainder in division problems. You can add a decimal point and zeros to the dividend and keep dividing until you have the answer.

Example:

```
           49
     25 ⌐1,241
         1 00
          241
          225
           16
```

```
          49.64
    25 ⌐1,241.00
        1 00
         241
         225
         160
         150
         100
         100
           0
```

Solve the following problems.

1. 2⌐2.5

2. 4⌐115

3. 12⌐738

4. 8⌐586

5. 25⌐3,415

6. Susie's grandparents sent her a check for $130 to share with her 7 brothers and sisters. How much will each of the 8 children get if the money is divided evenly? _____

7. A vendor had 396 balloons to sell and 16 workers. How many balloons should each worker sell in order to sell out? _____

8. Eight of the workers turned in a total of $753. How much did each worker collect if he/she sold the same number of items? _____

9. A total of 744 tickets were collected from 15 amusement ride operators on the first day of the fair. If each ride required one ticket per person, and they each collected the same number of tickets, how many people rode each ride? _____

   Do you think that was possible? Why? _____

   _____

10. Five people were hired to clean up the area after the fair closed. They turned in a bill for 26 hours of labor. How many hours did each person work? _____

Artifact Facts

Help the archaeologist find the artifact. First, solve the division problems. Then, connect the quotients in numerical order, starting at 795, to make his path.

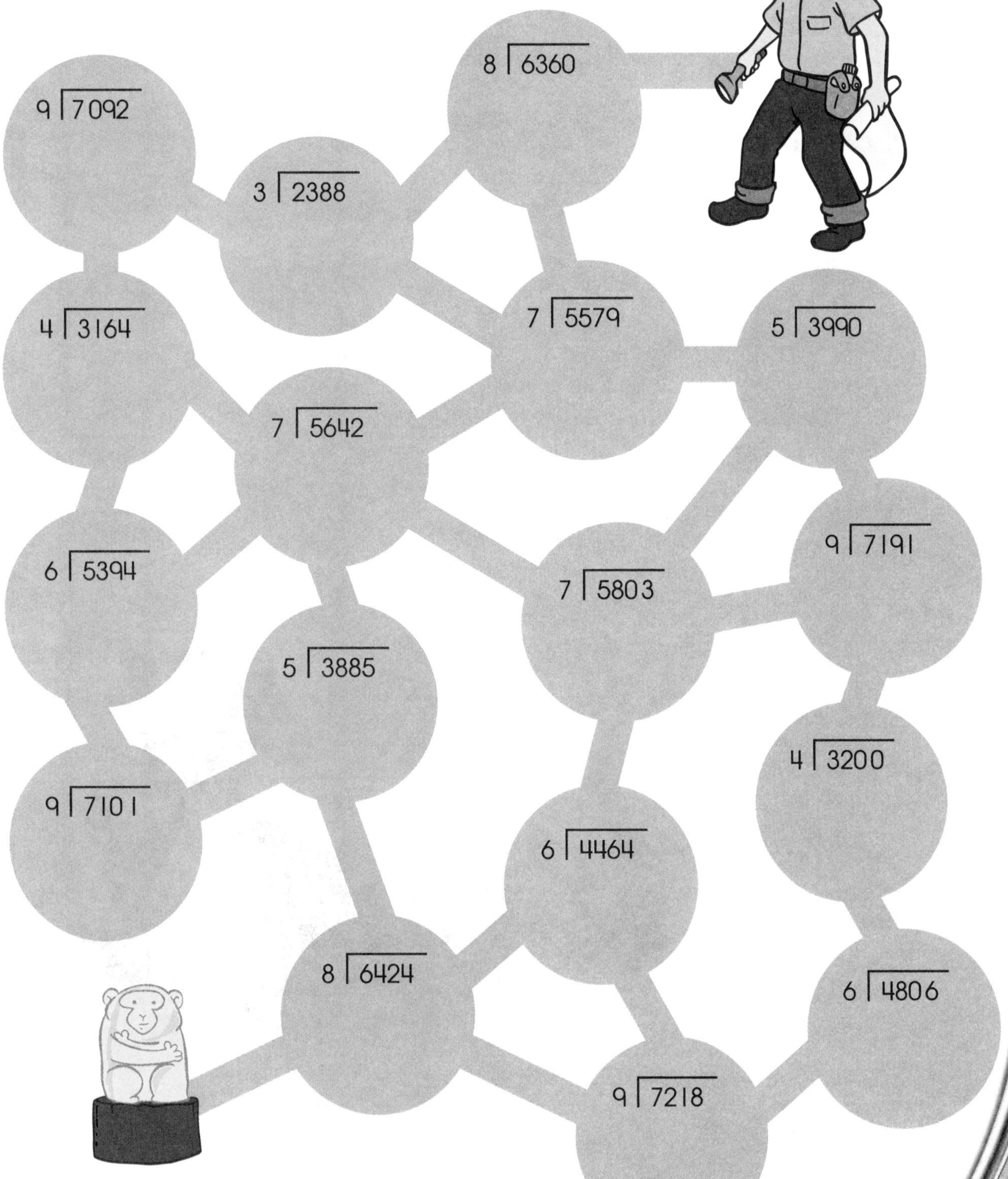

$8\overline{)6360}$

$9\overline{)7092}$

$3\overline{)2388}$

$4\overline{)3164}$

$7\overline{)5579}$

$5\overline{)3990}$

$7\overline{)5642}$

$6\overline{)5394}$

$9\overline{)7191}$

$7\overline{)5803}$

$5\overline{)3885}$

$9\overline{)7101}$

$4\overline{)3200}$

$6\overline{)4464}$

$8\overline{)6424}$

$6\overline{)4806}$

$9\overline{)7218}$

Wisconsin's Nickname

What is Wisconsin known as? To find out, solve the division problems below. Then, find the answers at the bottom of the page and write the corresponding letter on the line above the answer.

T. 14⟌1218   E. 23⟌1633   S. 53⟌2756

A. 38⟌1596   A. 61⟌5185   E. 18⟌1764

T. 22⟌1628   R. 40⟌2520   D. 55⟌4400

G. 31⟌1364   B. 12⟌780

___ ___ ___ ___ ___ ___   ___ ___ ___ ___ ___
65   85   80   44   71   63   52   74   42   87   98

Week 9 Skills

Subject	Skill	Multi-Sensory Learning Activities
Reading and Language Arts	Understand cause and effect.	• Complete Practice Pages 98–100. • Read *The Cay* by Theodore Taylor. Have your child name three things that happened in the story and the effects or causes of those events.
	Identify prepositions and use them correctly in writing.	• Complete Practice Pages 101 and 102. • Play a game like "Simon Says." Direct your child with commands containing prepositional phrases. If you say "Simon says," your child must repeat the prepositional phrase and perform the action. For example, you say, "Simon says put your hand on the table." Your child says, "on the table," and then puts his or her hand on the table.
Math	Solve division problems with and without remainders.	• Complete Practice Pages 103–106. • Using division, have your child find the price per item for things sold in groups. Use real items and real prices, if possible.
Bonus: Social Studies		• Have your child read about Parliament's "Intolerable Acts." Have your child think about the struggle between the British and the American colonists in terms of cause and effect. Have your child write a cause and effect statement about the "Intolerable Acts."

Because...

The sentences below are about the book *Tuck Everlasting* by Natalie Babbitt.

Remember:

The **cause** is the reason for the action or **why** something happened. The **effect** is the result of the action or **what** actually happened.

Underline the causes.

1. Because she knew her face so well, Mae didn't need a mirror.

2. Because the Tucks had drunk water from the spring, they could not age.

3. Mae went into town because her two boys were returning home.

4. The Tucks kidnapped Winnie because she had discovered the spring.

5. Because Miles and Winnie brought no fish home for breakfast, the Tucks had flapjacks instead.

Circle the effects.

1. The Tuck boys never worked in the same place for long because their employers would become suspicious.

2. Because the stranger wished to obtain the property in the woods, he offered to return Winnie to her parents.

3. Because the stranger planned to sell the secret, Mae clubbed him.

4. The constable couldn't charge the Tucks with kidnapping because Winnie declared that she had gone with them of her own free will.

5. Winnie's grandmother ordered her to enter the house soon, because the heat was intense that day.

What Do You Think?

Read each sentence. Write two sentences explaining what could have caused each event to happen.

1. The bird ceased its singing in the forest.

    a. _____

    b. _____

2. Tim came home crying. His backpack was open.

    a. _____

    b. _____

3. Five hundred people laughed at Lana as she stood in the bright light.

    a. _____

    b. _____

4. The saddled horse galloped onto the track without a jockey.

    a. _____

    b. _____

5. Pam sat soaking wet on the bench with her friends.

    a. _____

    b. _____

6. Martin stared with mouth agape at his teacher, Mr. Lancaster.

    a. _____

    b. _____

Cause and Effect

A **cause** is an event or reason which has an effect on something else.

Example:

> The heavy rains produced flooding in Chicago.
> Heavy rains were the **cause** of the flooding in Chicago.

An **effect** is an event that results from a cause.

Example:

> Flooding in Chicago was due to the heavy rains.
> Flooding was the **effect** caused by the heavy rains.

Read the paragraphs. Complete the charts by writing the missing cause (reason) or effect (result).

Club-footed toads are small toads that live in the rainforests of Central and South America. Because they give off a poisonous substance on their skins, other animals cannot eat them.

Cause: **Effect:**

They give off a poisonous substance.   _____

Civets (siv its) are weasel-like animals. The best known of the civets is the mongoose, which eats rats and snakes. For this reason, it is welcome around homes in its native India.

Cause: **Effect:**

_____   It is welcome around homes in its native India.

Bluebirds can be found in most areas of the United States. Like other members of the thrush family of birds, young bluebirds have speckled breasts. This makes them difficult to see and helps them hide from their enemies. The Pilgrims called them "blue robins" because they are much like the English robin. They are the same size and have the same red breast and friendly song as the English robin.

Cause: **Effect:**

Young bluebirds have speckled breasts.   _____

_____   The Pilgrims called them "blue robins."

Prepositions

A **preposition** is a word that comes before a noun or pronoun and shows the relationship of that noun or pronoun to other words in the sentence.

The **object of a preposition** is a noun or pronoun that follows a preposition and completes its meaning. A **prepositional phase** includes a preposition and the object(s) of the preposition.

Examples:

The girl **with red hair** spoke first.
With is the preposition.
Hair is the object of the preposition.
With red hair is a prepositional phase.

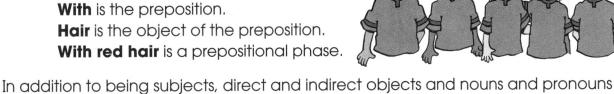

In addition to being subjects, direct and indirect objects and nouns and pronouns can also be objects of prepositions.

Prepositions						
across	behind	from	near	over	to	on
by	through	in	around	off	with	of
after	before	for	between	beyond	at	into

Underline the prepositional phrases in these sentences. Circle the prepositions.

The first sentence has been done for you.

1. The name ⟨of⟩ our street is Redsail Court.

2. We have lived in our house for three years.

3. In our family, we eat a lot of hamburgers.

4. We like hamburgers on toasted buns with mustard.

5. Sometimes we eat in the living room in front of the TV.

6. In the summer, we have picnics in the backyard.

7. The ants crawl into our food and into our clothes.

8. Behind our house is a park with swings.

9. Kids from the neighborhood walk through our yard to the park.

10. Sometimes they cut across Mom's garden and stomp on her beans.

11. Mom says we need a tall fence without a gate.

12. With a fence around our yard, we could get a dog!

Preposition, Adverb, or Verb?

Don't confuse prepositions with adverbs or with phrases made of **to** plus a verb.

Examples: All the students went **to** the zoo. (preposition)
We really wanted **to** go. (verb part)
We started getting excited **before** the trip. (preposition)
Have you gone to the zoo **before**? (adverb)

Identify each **bold** word as a preposition, adverb or verb part.

1. It was incredible how they had trained the animals **to** move like that! _____

2. A monkey followed me **to** the concession stand. _____

3. A beautiful dove flew **around** the audience. _____

4. A seal tossed a ball **around** to show off. _____

5. We took pictures of the walrus **before** the show. _____

6. I had never seen a walrus up close **before**. _____

7. The walrus waddled beyond the stage over **to** the audience. _____

8. My friends were brave, and they decided **to** stay and pet him. _____

9. David asked us, "Who wants **to** see the Dolphin Show at 2:00?" _____

10. The whale catapulted **to** the top and grabbed the fish. _____

11. The monkeys would have liked **to** swing through the trees. _____

12. I looked **up** when I heard the parrot talk. _____

13. I noticed a pigeon flying **around**. _____

14. The elephants came **near**. _____

15. The pigeon carried the message **to** its destination. _____

16. The chimpanzees shouted **across** the water. _____

Checking Division

Answers in division problems can be checked by multiplying.

Example:

```
        481 r 17        Check:        481
  33)15,890                          x  33
      13 2                           1 443
       2 69                          14 43
       2 64                         15,873
         50                   +         17      Add the
         33                        15,890       remainder
         17
```

Divide and check your answers.

61)2,736 Check:	73)86,143 Check:
59)9,390 Check:	43)77,141 Check:
33)82,050 Check:	93)84,039 Check:

Denny has a baseball card collection. He has 13,789 cards. He wants to put the cards in a scrapbook that holds 15 cards on a page. How many pages does Denny need in his scrapbook? _____

Octopus Crossword

Solve the division problems. Write the remainders in word form to complete the puzzle.

Across

3. 23)1313 4. 41)3501

7. 18)1733 8. 35)2706

10. 64)4618 12. 51)4746

13. 70)5881 14. 32)2132

Down

1. 45)2389 2. 60)3786 3. 28)1076

4. 33)1360 5. 55)3533 6. 72)6128

9. 84)7494 11. 16)1497 12. 22)1088

Division Word Problems

In the example below, 368 is being divided by 4. 4 won't divide into 3, so move over one position and divide 4 into 36. 4 goes into 36 nine times. Then multiply 4 x 9 to get 36. Subtract 36 from 36. The answer is 0, less than the divisor, so 9 is the right number. Now bring down the 8, divide 4 into it and repeat the process.

Example:

$$
\begin{array}{r}
9 \\
4\overline{)368} \\
\underline{36} \\
0
\end{array}
\qquad
\begin{array}{r}
92 \\
4\overline{)368} \\
\underline{36} \\
08 \\
\underline{8} \\
0
\end{array}
$$

To check your division, multiply 4 x 92 = 368.

Solve the following division problems. (For some problems, you will also need to add or subtract.)

1. Kristy helped the kindergarten teacher put a total of 192 crayons into 8 boxes. How many crayons did they put into each box? _____

2. The scout troop has to finish a 12-mile hike in 3 hours. How many miles an hour will they have to walk? _____

3. At her slumber party, Shelly had 4 friends and 25 pieces of candy. If she kept 5 pieces and divided the rest among her friends, how many pieces did each friend get? _____

4. Kenny's book has 147 pages. He wants to read the same number of pages each day and finish reading the book in 7 days. How many pages should he read each day? _____

5. Brian and 2 friends are going to share 27 marbles. How many will each person get? _____

6. To help the school, 5 parents agreed to sell 485 tickets for a raffle. How many tickets will each person have to sell to do his or her part? _____

7. Tim is going to weed his neighbor's garden for $3 an hour. How many hours does he have to work to make $72? _____

Mr. Quotient's Class Divides

Mr. Quotient's class was studying division. Help them solve the following problems.

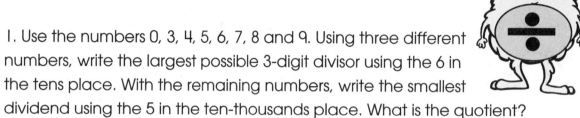

1. Use the numbers 0, 3, 4, 5, 6, 7, 8 and 9. Using three different numbers, write the largest possible 3-digit divisor using the 6 in the tens place. With the remaining numbers, write the smallest dividend using the 5 in the ten-thousands place. What is the quotient?

_____

2. There were 3,192 people in attendance at the football game. There were 45 bleacher rows in the stadium. If 84 people could sit in each bleacher row, did everyone have a seat?

_____

3. There were 1,848 candy bars available for the candy sale. There were 154 students ready to sell them. To keep sales equal, how many candy bars should be put in each salesperson's box?

_____

4. Marathon Mike worked 7,272 problems in 36 weeks. How many did he average each week?

_____

5. Mr. Quotient's class collected a total of 972 leaves for a science project. There were 27 students in the class. What was the average number each student collected?

_____

6. Shanna wrote 144 Spanish vocabulary words during the months of April and May. How many words, on average, did she write each week during those months?

_____

Extension: 96,785,642 ÷ 24 ÷ 35 ÷ 3 = _____

First Quarter Check-Up

Reading and Language Arts

❑ I can write and identify figurative language, including metaphors, similes, and personification.

❑ I can complete word analogies.

❑ I can understand common idioms and expressions.

❑ I can find main ideas and details in text and use them to take notes and write summaries.

❑ I can make an outline of main ideas and details.

❑ I can read nonfiction texts, then compare and contrast information.

❑ I can use conjunctions to combine words and sentences.

❑ I can punctuate interjections using commas and exclamation points.

❑ I can use commas in examples of direct address.

❑ I can identify homophones that are frequently confused.

❑ I can read text and understand its mood or tone.

❑ I understand differing points of view in text.

❑ I can write events in chronological order.

❑ I can write a true story, or personal narrative.

❑ I can describe fictional characters and write fictional stories.

❑ I can understand cause and effect.

❑ I can identify prepositions and use them correctly in writing.

Math

❑ I can round numbers to the nearest hundred thousand.

❑ I can identify place values in numbers to the trillions place.

❑ I can use the four operations symbols (+, -, x, ÷) to write equations.

❑ I can write and solve equations.

❑ I can multiply by one-, two-, and three-digit numbers.

❑ I can divide by one- and two-digit divisors.

❑ I can solve division problems with and without remainders.

Final Project

Write a short story about a math superhero. The story should contain figurative language, such as similes, metaphors, idioms, and analogies. Be sure to include math equations as part of your story using all four operations symbols.

Second Quarter Introduction

During the second quarter of the school year, many children are settled into routines at home and at school. Make sure your family's routines include time for playing, eating and talking together, and reading aloud. Supporting your child's learning and development will build his or her confidence in all areas.

Second Quarter Skills

Practice pages in this book for Weeks 10–18 will help your child improve the following skills.

Reading and Language Arts

- Use prepositional phrases correctly in writing
- Plan an original story
- Use verbs, including helping verbs and linking verbs, correctly in writing
- Understand verbs that are frequently confused
- Understand present, past, and future verb tenses
- Understand that many multisyllabic words are formed from Greek and Latin roots, prefixes, and suffixes
- Understand the meanings of common prefixes and suffixes
- Use quotation marks correctly in writing
- Use italics for titles of books, newspapers, and other publications
- Distinguish between facts and opinions
- Find the main idea of a text
- Write a book report
- Use irregular verb forms correctly in writing
- Write an opinion and support it with reasons

Math

- Use multiplication and division to solve word problems
- Understand and compare decimal numbers
- Add, subtract, multiply, and divide decimal numbers, including money amounts
- Divide decimals by one- and two-digit whole numbers
- Divide decimals by decimals
- Compare and convert decimals and fractions
- Understand equivalent fractions
- Reduce fractions to their lowest terms
  - Convert fractions to mixed numbers and vice-versa

Multi-Sensory Learning Activities

Try these fun activities for enhancing your child's learning and development during the second quarter of the school year. Be sure to choose activities that include speaking, listening, touching, and active movement.

 Reading and Language Arts

Write several complete sentences on long strips of paper. Cut each sentence into two or three parts: cut between the complete subject and complete predicate, and separate any prepositional phrases from the rest of the sentence. Mix up the parts. Have your child arrange the sentence parts to make sensible sentences.

Send your child a text message or e-mail that includes several incorrect shifts in verb tense (for example, write, "How were you? I hoping you are well. Would you have liked tacos for dinner?"). Let your child correct the message and send it back to you.

Discuss a current topic of debate with your child. Then, have your child write his or her opinion on the issue, citing facts as evidence or examples that substantiate his or her viewpoint.

 **Math**

Raid the pantry with your child and pick out at least six food packages. Ask your child to read the capacity of each item aloud and line them up in order, from the least to the greatest capacity.

Ask your child to research prices for 10 party supplies and write them in a list, aligning the decimal points. What is the total price for all the party supplies? How much would the sales tax be for the purchase?

Have your child convert his or her height and the height of other family members to decimals. For example, 5 feet 8 inches equals 5.66 feet. What is the difference between each family member's height and a ceiling that is 8 feet tall?

Second Quarter Introduction, cont.

 **Science**

The three main parts of a plant are the stem, leaves, and roots. The roots have several jobs. Have your child read about roots in an encyclopedia or other resource book. Have your child list three important functions of a plant's roots.

Help your child plant a variety of seeds and label them carefully. Have your child observe and care for the plants daily, then predict which seeds will sprout first. Have your child record his or her observations and analysis.

 Social Studies

Play a game in which you give clues about a famous American and your child tries to guess who it is. Say one clue at a time, giving your child the chance to look in an encyclopedia or other resource to narrow the search. For a variation, have your child research a famous American and write his or her own riddle for you to guess. Here is a sample riddle to get you started: "As the daughter of Quaker abolitionists, she often spoke against slavery. She was a good friend of Elizabeth Cady Stanton. The Nineteenth Amendment to the Constitution was passed 14 years after her death. She helped form the National Woman Suffrage Association. She was the first woman to be pictured on a U.S. coin." Answer: Susan B. Anthony.

 Seasonal Fun

Encourage your child to make holiday-themed scarves to give as gifts for friends and family members. Let your child pick out fleece material for the scarf from your local fabric store. Purchase $\frac{1}{4}$-yard of material per scarf. Then, at home, have your child lay the material on a flat surface and trim with scissors to make it even on all sides, if necessary. Have your child put the material around his or her neck to determine how long each scarf should be. Have your child cut the scarves to the desired lengths, then begin making tassels on the ends. With a ruler and pencil, have your child measure and mark 4-inch slits, $\frac{1}{2}$-inch wide on one end of the scarf. Then, repeat on the opposite end. Have your child cut the slits along the pencil marks on both ends to complete the scarf. There should be a total of 18 tassels on each end of the scarf.

Week 10 Skills

Subject	Skill	Multi-Sensory Learning Activities
Reading and Language Arts	Use prepositional phrases correctly in writing.	• Complete Practice Pages 112–115. • Have your child write directions for someone else to follow. Each sentence should contain a preposition, and the directions should lead to a hidden prize. Have your child give the directions to another person to follow.
	Plan an original story.	• Complete Practice Page 116. • Write an intriguing sentence, such as, "Elliot ran into the house, slamming the door behind him." Ask your child to reflect on the sentence for a few minutes, then write a story based on the sentence.
Math	Use multiplication and division to solve word problems.	• Complete Practice Pages 117–120. • Encourage your child to relate his or her real-life situations to multiplication or division. For example, if your child mows three lawns a week at $20 per lawn, how much money will he or she make in four weeks?
Bonus: Science		• Brainstorm a list of mammals that live in forests and jungles. Have your child read about different forest mammals, then look at pictures to identify them and note the characteristics of each.

Prepositional Phrases

A **prepositional phrase** is a group of words that begins with a preposition and ends with a noun or pronoun. It can act as an adjective or adverb.
Examples: Pineapple is also grown **outside of Hawaii**. (adverb)
The sandwiches **with the peanut butter** were the best ones. (adjective)
We ate the peanut butter sandwiches **at night**. (adverb)

Underline the prepositional phrase in each sentence.

1. Peanuts are enjoyed around the world.

2. Peanuts are native to South America.

3. Peanut pods develop beneath the ground.

4. The pegs, which are the pod stems, push their way under the soil.

5. Peanuts are part of the legume family.

6. Most peanuts are grown in Africa and Asia.

Tell whether each prepositional phrase acts as an **adjective** or an **adverb**.

1. Wait until choir practice is over to eat peanut butter. _____

2. Peanut butter on a spoon is a delicious and quick snack. _____

3. Have you ever enjoyed celery with peanut butter and raisins? _____

4. Try your peanut butter sandwich with cold milk. _____

5. I love peanut butter on toast. _____

6. I enjoy eating peanuts at a ball game. _____

Prepositional Phrases

A **prepositional phrase** is a group of words that begins with a preposition and ends with the object of the preposition.

Example: Water makes up about 65 percent
of the human body.

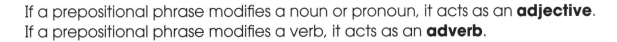

Circle the prepositional phrases in the sentences.

1. An adult skeleton consists
   of about 200 bones.

2. The body of a 160-pound man contains
   about 5 quarts of blood.

3. People who live in high altitudes may have more blood
   flowing in their veins.

4. Our skin helps protect our inner tissues from the outside world.

If a prepositional phrase modifies a noun or pronoun, it acts as an **adjective**.
If a prepositional phrase modifies a verb, it acts as an **adverb**.

Examples: Fluids **in the inner ear** help us maintain our balance. (adjective)
The doctors talked **in loud voices**. (adverb)

Circle the prepositional phrase in each sentence. Then, identify it as an **adjective**
or **adverb** on the line.

1. The muscles in the human body number 600. _____

2. All adults should brush their 32 teeth with great care. _____

3. Our skin might burn in the hot sun. _____

4. Every person on the Earth is warm-blooded. _____

5. The man went through the hospital doors. _____

6. The temperature inside the body is about 98.6°. _____

7. The dentist looked inside my mouth. _____

Prepositional Phrases as Adjectives

An adjective can be one word or an entire prepositional phrase.

Examples:
The **new** boy **with red hair**
The **tall** man **in the raincoat**
The **white** house **with green shutters**

Underline the prepositional phrases used as adjectives.

1. The boy in the blue cap is the captain.

2. The house across the street is 100 years old.

3. Jo and Ty love cookies with nuts.

4. I lost the book with the green cover.

5. Do you know the girl in the front row?

6. I like the pony with the long tail.

7. The dog in that yard is not friendly.

8. The picture in this magazine looks like you.

Complete these sentences with prepositional phrases used as adjectives.

9. I'd like a hamburger _____ .

10. Did you read the book _____?

11. The dog _____ is my favorite.

12. The woman _____ is calling you.

13. I bought a shirt _____ .

14. I'm wearing socks _____ .

15. I found a box _____ .

Prepositional Phrases as Adverbs

An adverb can be one word or an entire prepositional phrase.

Examples:
They'll be here **tomorrow**.
They always come **on time**.
Move it **down**.
Put it **under the picture**.
Drive **carefully**.
He drove **with care**.

Underline the adverb or prepositional phrase used as an adverb in each sentence. In the blank, write **how**, **when** or **where** to tell what the adverb or prepositional phrase explains.

1. Don't go swimming without a buddy. _____

2. Don't go swimming alone. _____

3. I wish you still lived here. _____

4. I wish you still lived on our street. _____

5. I will eat lunch soon. _____

6. I will eat lunch in a few minutes. _____

7. He will be here in a few hours. _____

8. He will be here later. _____

9. I'm going outside. _____

10. I'm going in the backyard. _____

11. She smiled happily. _____

12. She smiled with happiness. _____

Story Organizer

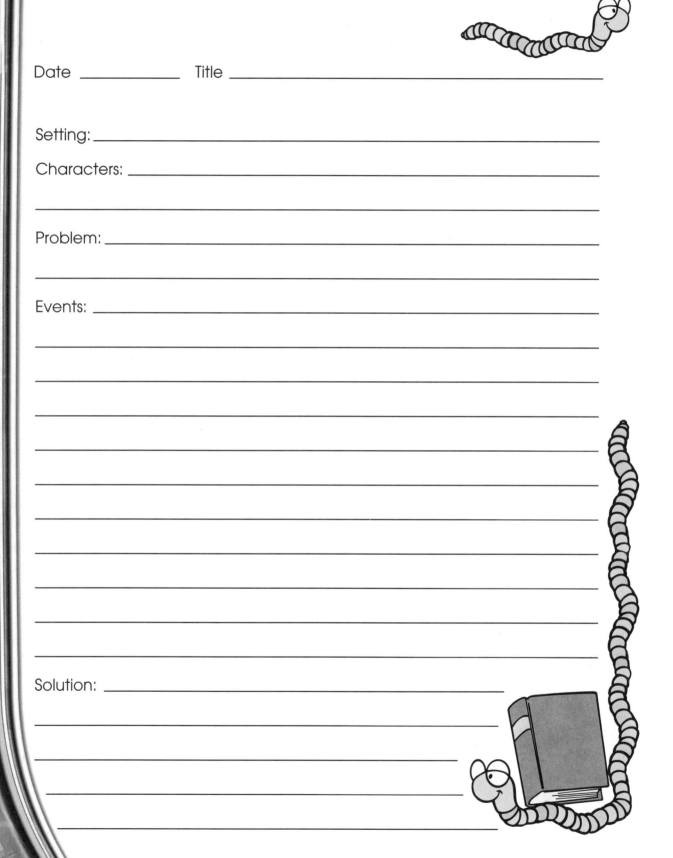

Date _____ Title _____

Setting: _____

Characters: _____

_____

Problem: _____

_____

Events: _____

_____

_____

_____

_____

_____

_____

_____

_____

_____

Solution: _____

_____

_____

_____

Multiplication and Division

Multiply or divide to find the answers.

Brianne's summer job is mowing lawns for three of her neighbors. Each lawn takes about 1 hour to mow and needs to be done once every week. At the end of the summer, she will have earned a total of $630. She collected the same amount of money from each job. How much did each neighbor pay for her summer lawn service?

_____

If the mowing season lasts for 14 weeks, how much will Brianne earn for each job each week? _____

If she had worked for two more weeks, how much would she have earned? _____

Brianne agreed to shovel snow from the driveways and sidewalks for the same three neighbors. They agreed to pay her the same rate. However, it only snowed seven times that winter.

How much did she earn shoveling snow? _____

What was her total income for both jobs? _____

Multiply or divide.

12 ⟌ 7,476   23 ⟌ 21,620   40 ⟌ 32,600

32 x 45 = _____   28 x 15 = _____   73 x 14 = _____   92 x 30 = _____

Multi-Step Problems

Some problems take more than one step to solve. First, plan each step needed to find the solution. Then solve each part to find the answer.

Example: Tickets for a bargain matinee cost $4 for adults and $3 for children. How much would tickets cost for a family of 2 adults and 3 children?

Step 1: Find the cost of the adults' tickets.

Step 2: Find the cost of the children's tickets.

Step 3: Add to find the sum of the tickets.

2 adults	x	$4 each ticket	=	$8 total
3 children	x	$3 each ticket	=	$9 total
$8 adults	+	$9 children	=	$17 total

The tickets cost $17 total.

Write the operations you will use to solve each problem. Then find the answer.

1. Arden and her father are riding their bikes 57 miles to Arden's grandma's house. They ride 13 miles, then take a water break. Then they ride 15 miles to a rest area for a picnic lunch. How many miles do Arden and her father have left to ride after lunch?

Operations: _____

Answer: _____

_____

2. A triathlete bikes 15 miles at 20 miles per hour, runs 5 miles at 6 miles per hour and swims 1 mile at 4 miles per hour. How long does the triathlon take her to complete?

Operations: _____

_____

Answer: _____

3. Ray bought strawberries for $1.99, blueberries for $1.40 and 2 pints of raspberries for $1.25 per pint. How much did Ray spend on berries?

Operations: _____

Answer: _____

_____

Multiply or Divide?

These key words will help you know when to multiply and when to divide.

multiplication key words: **in all, altogether, times** and **each**

division key words: **per, each**

Circle the key words and solve the story problems.

1. There are 9 classrooms at the vocational school. The average number of students per classroom is 27 students How many students altogether are there in the school? _____	2. Thirty-five students are studying auto mechanics. Three times that many are studying business. How many students are studying business? _____
3. The semester is 16 weeks long. Students attend class 5 days a week. How many days in all must a student attend class each semester? _____	4. In one class of 27 students, each student used $30.00 worth of materials. Altogether, how much did materials cost this class? _____
5. Lunch cost each student $11.50 for a 5-day week. How much does each lunch cost? _____	6. The average student drives a total of 8 miles per day to attend classes. How many miles in all does a student drive during the 80-day semester? _____

Shopping for Soccer Supplies

The soccer team members needed to buy their own shin guards, socks, shoes and shorts. A couple of the players volunteered to do some comparative shopping to find the store with the best deal. Use their chart to answer the questions below.

SPORTS CORNER	
Socks.................	3 pairs for $9.30
Shoes.................	2 pairs for $48.24
Shin Guards......	4 pairs for $32.48
Shorts.................	5 pairs for $60.30

JOE'S SOCCER	
Socks.................	2 pairs for $6.84
Shoes.................	3 pairs for $84.15
Shin Guards......	5 pairs for $35.70
Shorts.................	4 pairs for $36.36

1. Which store had the better price for socks? _____

   How much less were they per pair? _____

2. Which store had the better price for shin guards? _____

   How much would you save per pair? _____

3. How much would one pair of shoes and socks cost at Joe's Soccer? _____

   How much at Sports Corner? _____

4. Which store had the better price for shorts? _____

   How much less were they per pair? _____

5. Total the price per pair for each item at each store. If you could shop at only one store, which one would give you the best overall deal? _____

   How much would you save? _____

Week 11 Skills

Subject	Skill	Multi-Sensory Learning Activities
Reading and Language Arts	Use verbs, including helping verbs and linking verbs, correctly in writing.	• Complete Practice Pages 122–126. • Have your child choose a topic, make a plan for writing, then begin working on a rough draft. Have your child read through his or her rough draft and underline all the helping verbs and linking verbs.
Math	Understand and compare decimal numbers.	• Complete Practice Pages 127–129. • With your child, brainstorm situations in which decimal numbers are commonly used. Then, have your child look for numbers in a newspaper or magazine that are written as decimals.
	Add decimal numbers.	• Complete Practice Page 130. • Walk around the grocery store with your child. Ask him or her to make a list of all the decimals he or she sees and where they were found. Then, at home, choose two decimals from similar products and add them together. For example, if one box of cereal is 11.5 ounces and another box of cereal is 16.9 ounces, how many ounces are there total?

Verbs

A **verb** is the action word in a sentence. It tells what the subject does (**build**, **laugh**, **express**, **fasten**) or that it exists (**is**, **are**, **was**, **were**).

Examples: Randy **raked** the leaves into a pile.
I **was** late to school today.

In the following sentences, write verbs that make sense.

1. The quarterback _____ the ball to the receiver.

2. My mother _____ some cookies yesterday.

3. John _____ newspapers to make extra money.

4. The teacher _____ the instructions on the board.

5. Last summer, our family_____ a trip to Florida to visit relatives.

Sometimes, a verb can be two or more words. Verbs used to "support" other verbs are called **helping verbs**.

Examples: We **were** listening to music in my room.
Chris **has been** studying for over 2 hours.

In the following sentences, write helping verbs along with the correct form of the given verbs. The first one has been done for you.

1. Michelle (write) _is writing_ a letter to her grandmother right now.

2. My brother (have) _____ trouble with his math homework.

3. When we arrived, the movie (start) _____ already.

4. My aunt (live) _____ in the same house for 30 years.

5. Our football team (go) _____ to win the national championship this year.

6. My sister (talk)_____on the phone all afternoon!

7. I couldn't sleep last night because the wind (blow) _____ so hard.

8. Last week, Pat was sick, but now he (feel) _____ much better.

9. Tomorrow, our class (have) _____ a bake sale.

10. Mr. Smith (collect) _____ stamps for 20 years.

Linking or Helping Verbs?

The verb **be** (and its various forms) can be used as either a linking verb or a helping verb.

Examples: Sarah **is** a fine skater. (linking verb)
Gregory **is** helping Dad clean. (helping verb)

Read the sentences below. Underline the form of the verb **be** and decide how it is used. Write linking verb or helping verb on the line.

1. In ancient times, no one was using money. _____

2. Later on, they were trading goods and services. _____

3. The trading of goods and services is called bartering. _____

4. Finally, people were accepting certain objects as payment. _____

5. These objects were valuable to everyone. _____

6. The objects were anything from animal skins to shells. _____

7. Some of the objects were metal. _____

8. Gold and silver were demanded by many people. _____

9. Governments were given the power to mint coins. _____

10. One of the first coin-makers was an ancient Roman. _____

11. The first paper money was Chinese. _____

Write sentences using each verb as indicated.

is (linking verb)

_____

is (helping verb)

_____

are (helping verb)

_____

are (linking verb)

_____

was (linking verb)

_____

was (helping verb

_____

"Be" as a Helping Verb

A **helping verb** tells when the action of a sentence takes place. The helping verb **be** has several forms: **am**, **is**, **are**, **was**, **were** and **will**. These helping verbs can be used in all three tenses.

Examples:
    Past tense: Ken **was** talking. We **were** eating.
    Present tense: I **am** coming. Simon **is** walking. They **are** singing.
    Future tense: I **will** work. The puppies **will** eat.

In the present and past tense, many verbs can be written with or without the helping verb **be**. When the verb is written with a form of **be**, add **ing**. **Was** and **is** are used with singular subjects. **Were** and **are** are used with plural subjects.

Examples:
    Present tense: Angela **sings**. Angela **is singing**.
    The children **sing**. They **are singing**.
    Past tense: I **studied**. I **was studying**. They **studied**. They **were studying**.

The helping verb **will** is always needed for the future tense, but the **ing** ending is not used with **will**. **Will** is both singular and plural.

Examples:
    Future tense: I **will eat**. We **will watch**.

Underline the helping verbs.

1. Brian is helping me with this project.
2. We are working together on it.
3. Susan was painting the background yesterday.
4. Matt and Mike were cleaning up.
5. Tomorrow, we will present our project to the class.

Rewrite the verbs using a helping verb. The first one has been done for you.

6. Our neighborhood plans a garage sale.   <u>is planning</u>

7. The sale starts tomorrow.   _____

8. My brother Doug and I think about things we sell. _____

9. My grandfather cleans out the garage. _____

10. Doug and I help him. _____

"Be" as a Linking Verb

A **linking verb** links a noun or adjective in the predicate to the subject. Forms of the verb **be** are the most common linking verbs. Linking verbs can be used in all three tenses.

Examples:
Present: My father **is** a salesman.
Past: The store **was** very busy last night.
Future: Tomorrow **will be** my birthday.

In the first sentence, **is** links the subject (father) with a noun (salesman). In the second sentence, **was** links the subject (store) with an adjective (busy). In the third sentence, **will be** links the subject (tomorrow) with a noun (birthday).

Circle the linking verbs. Underline the two words that are linked by the verb.

The first one has been done for you.

1. <u>Columbus</u> (is) the <u>capital</u> of Ohio.

2. By bedtime, Nicole was bored.

3. Andy will be the captain of our team.

4. Tuesday is the first day of the month.

5. I hate to say this, but we are lost.

6. Ask him if the water is cold.

7. By the time I finished my paper, it was late.

8. Spaghetti is my favorite dinner.

9. The children were afraid of the big truck.

10. Karen will be a good president of our class.

11. These lessons are helpful.

12. Was that report due today?

Forms of "Be," "Do," and "Have"

Some forms of the verb **be** can be used as linking or helping verbs. Three forms of **be** cannot be used alone as verbs: **be, being** and **been**. These must always be used with helping verbs.

Examples:
Polar bears **are** carnivores. (**be** as linking verb)
The polar bear is hunting the seal. (**be** as helping verb)
A polar bear **has been** seen near here. (**be** with helping verb)
Forms of **be**: **am, is, are, was, were, be, being, been**

Complete each sentence below with the correct form of the verb **be** found in parentheses. Add helping verbs where needed.

1. Polar bears _____ excellent swimmers. (is, are)

2. The polar bear_____ seen running at a speed of 35 miles per hour.

(was, being)

3. I_____ sure I saw a polar bear swimming in the water. (am, are)

4. Polar bears _____ seen swimming many miles from shore.

(been, have been)

The verbs **do** and **have** can be used as main verbs or as helping verbs.

Examples:
I **have** traveled to Canada to see polar bears. (helping verb)
I **did** my report on polar bears yesterday. (main verb)
Forms of **do**: **do, did, done**
Forms of have: **have, has, had**

Complete the story below using the correct forms of the verbs **do** and **have**.

I_____ believe polar bears are very beautiful. I _____ seen them

along the coast of Alaska. I _____ see one come up to our tour bus. By

the age of 10 years, a male polar bear_____ grown to its full size.

Countries around the Arctic have _____a very good job of trying to

save the polar bear from extinction. Polar bears _____ beautiful coats

which_____ attracted hunters. Now the bears_____ protection

from hunters by law.

Decimals

A **decimal** is a number that includes a period called a **decimal point**. The digits to the right of the decimal point are a value less than one.

one whole

one tenth

one hundredth

The place value chart below helps explain decimals.

hundreds	tens	ones	tenths	hundredths	thousandths
6	3	2 .	4		
	4	7 .	0	5	
		8 .	0	0	9

A decimal point is read as "and." The first number, 632.4, is read as "six hundred thirty-two and four tenths." The second number, 47.05, is read as "forty-seven and five hundredths." The third number, 8.009, is read as "eight and nine thousandths."

Write the decimals shown below. Two have been done for you.

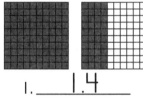

1. ___1.4___

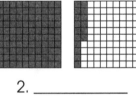

2. _____

3. _____

4. six and five tenths   ___6.5___

5. twenty-two and nine tenths   _____

6. thirty-six and fourteen hundredths   _____

7. forty-seven hundredths   _____

8. one hundred six and four tenths   _____

9. seven and three hundredths   _____

10. one tenth less than 0.6   _____

11. one hundredth less than 0.34   _____

12. one tenth more than 0.2   _____

Missing Train

Circle the...

1.	smallest number	0.31 (A)	0.05 (F)	0.20 (R)
2.	greatest number	0.001 (R)	0.137 (O)	0.100 (A)
3.	greatest number	9.910 (L)	9.010 (C)	9.909 (T)
4.	smallest number	0.110 (A)	0.09 (L)	0.3 (R)
5.	greatest number	0.090 (S)	0.10 (P)	0.12 (O)
6.	smallest number	0.131 (H)	0.2 (T)	0.08 (W)
7.	greatest number	1.310 (E)	1.03 (H)	1.33 (T)
8.	smallest number	2.001 (H)	2.9 (F)	2.010 (A)
9.	greatest number	0.3 (E)	0.03 (A)	0.003 (R)
10.	greatest number	1.01 (U)	1.001 (R)	1.1 (T)
11.	greatest number	3.04 (R)	3.009 (U)	3.039 (N)
12.	smallest number	6.01 (A)	6.11 (C)	6.030 (O)
13.	greatest number	0.001 (T)	0.100 (C)	0.090 (N)
14.	smallest number	1.027 (K)	1.270 (R)	1.207 (P)
15.	smallest number	9.909 (N)	9.09 (G)	9.009 (S)

Fill in the circled letters to solve the riddle below.
How do you search for a missing train?

___ ___ ___ ___ ___ ___ ___ ___ ___ ___ ___ ___ ___ ___ ___
 1   2   3   4   5   6   7   8   9   10 11 12 13 14 15

More Puzzling Problems

Across

3. 7.333 = seven and three hundred thirty-three _____

5. 67.02 = sixty-seven and _____ hundredths

6. 490.1 = four hundred _____ and one tenth

7. 0.512 = five _____ twelve thousandths

9. 8.06 = eight and _____ hundredths

10. 0.007 = _____ thousandths

12. 11.3 = _____ and three tenths

13. 300.12 = _____ hundred and twelve hundredths

15. 62.08 = sixty-two and _____ hundredths

18. 70.009 = _____ and nine thousandths

19. 9.3 = _____ and three tenths

20. 10.51 = _____ and fifty-one hundredths

21. 1,000.02 = one thousand and two ____

Down

1. 6.5 = six and five _____

2. 0.428 = four hundred _____ thousandths

3. 8,100.1 = eight _____ one hundred and one tenth

4. 3.02 = three and two _____

8. 0.685 = six hundred _____ thousandths

11. 50.19 = fifty and _____ hundredths

14. 0.015 = _____ thousandths

16. 430.7 = four hundred thirty and seven _____

17. 73.4 = seventy-three and four _____

Swiss Sentences

Complete these cheesy number sentences.

1.862	+	0.98534	=	
+		+		
0.53	+	6.72	=	
=		=		
	+		=	
				+
0.9076	+	0.995	=	
+		+		=
6.53	+	5.47	=	
=		=		
	+		=	

Week 12 Skills

Subject	Skill	Multi-Sensory Learning Activities
Reading and Language Arts	Understand verbs that are frequently confused.	• Complete Practice Page 132. • Give your child a list of word pairs that are often misused, such as **affect**, **effect**; **can**, **may**; **ascent**, **assent**; **your**, **you're**; **principal**, **principle**; **who**, **whom**; and **very**, **vary**. Have your child make an alphabetical glossary of these words. Then, choose three word pairs and have your child use each word correctly in a sentence.
	Understand present, past, and future verb tenses.	• Complete Practice Pages 133–135. • Give your child a list of five present-tense verbs to conjugate into the past and future tenses.
Math	Add and subtract decimal numbers, including money amounts.	• Complete Practice Pages 136–140. • Teach your child how to maintain a check register. Find an old register or get an extra from your bank. Show your child how to keep track of deposits and withdrawals using addition and subtraction.
Bonus: Social Studies		• Study a map of Washington, D.C., with your child. Ask him or her to locate major buildings and landmarks, such as the White House, the Capitol Building, the Supreme Court Building, the National Mall, the Pentagon, and the Lincoln Memorial.

Troublesome Verb Pairs

Don't confuse verbs that have similar meanings.

Lay means put or place.
Lie means rest or recline.

Teach means show how.
Learn means find out.

Set means put something somewhere.
Sit means sit down.

Lend means give to someone.
Borrow means get from someone.

Let means allow.
Leave means allow to remain.

Write the correct verb on each blank below.

"Mark, did you_____ (set, sit) the saddle on the fence?" David asked.

"Yes, David. I was going to _____(let, leave) it in the barn, but it was heavy."

Did you_____ (teach, learn) how to throw the saddle onto your horse's back yet?" Mark asked.

"Yes, and then I needed to _____ (lay, lie) down and rest," David answered.

"I was going to _____ (lend, borrow) you a hand, but I was too busy trying to _____ (teach, learn) how to rope," David remarked.

"Will you_____(let, leave) me _____ (lend, borrow) your horse tomorrow morning?" Mark inquired.

"Sure, Mark. I'm going to just_____ (set, sit) under a tree and read a book tomorrow morning," David responded.

Write the correct verb from the parentheses for each sentence.

1. Tell your dog to_____ (lay, lie) down in front of the barn.

2. Please,_____(lay, lie) that saddle down in front of the stall and _____ (set, sit) the bridle on the table.

3. _____ (Set, Sit) on that bale of hay and rest your tired legs.

4. Will you_____(let, leave) me wear your boots tomorrow?

5. Don't _____ (let, leave) those oats there.

6. I want to_____ (teach, learn) how to trim my horse's hooves.

7. We will certainly be happy to_____ (teach, learn) you.

Verb Tenses

Verbs have different forms to show whether something already happened, is happening right now or will happen.

Examples:

Present tense: **I walk.**
Past tense: **I walked.**
Future tense: **I will walk.**

Write **PAST** if the verb is past tense, **PRES** for present tense or **FUT** for future tense. The first one has been done for you.

PRES   1. My sister Sara works at the grocery store.

_____ 2. Last year, she worked in an office.

_____ 3. Sara is going to college, too.

_____ 4. She will be a dentist some day.

_____ 5. She says studying is difficult.

_____ 6. Sara hardly studied at all in high school.

_____ 7. I will be ready for college in a few years.

_____ 8. Last night, I read my history book for 2 hours.

Complete these sentences using verbs in the tenses listed. The first one has been done for you.

9. take: future tense   My friends and I __will take__ a trip.

10. talk: past tense   We _____ for a long time about where to go.

11. want: present tense   Pam _____ to go to the lake.

12. want: past tense   Jake _____ to go with us.

13. say: past tense   His parents _____ no.

14. ride: future tense   We _____ our bikes.

15. pack: past tense   Susan and Jared already _____ lunches for us.

Verb Tense

The **present tense** tells what is happening now.
  Example: Jamie runs today in the big race.
The **past tense** tells about an action which happened in the past.
  Example: Jamie ran in the preliminary race yesterday.
The **future tense** tells about an action which will occur in the future. It is formed by using the helping verb **will** with the present tense of the verb.
  Example: Jamie will run in the Olympics someday.

Underline the verb in each sentence. Tell whether the verb is in the present tense, past tense or future tense.

1. Thousands of years ago, the Chinese used more than one name. _____

2. Today, the Chinese still give their children three names. _____

3. Family names, or last names, came about in various ways. _____

4. These names will remain for centuries into the future. _____

5. Some writers use "pseudonyms," or fictitious names. _____

6. Eric Blair wrote under the assumed name George Orwell. _____

7. Immigrants will introduce new names to the United States. _____

8. Some people use nicknames instead of their legal names. _____

Fill in the chart below.

Verb	Present Tense	Past Tense	Future Tense
see	see, sees	saw	will see
hide			
swim			
catch			
leave			
run			
throw			

Verb Tenses

The past tense of many verbs is formed by adding **ed**.

Examples:
    remember + **ed** = remembered
    climb + **ed** = climbed

If a verb ends in **e**, drop the **e** before adding **ed**.

Examples:

Present	Past
phone	phoned
arrive	arrived

If a verb ends in **y**, change the **y** to **i** before adding **ed**.

Examples:

Present	Past
carry	carried
try	tried

If a verb ends in a short vowel followed by a single consonant, double the final consonant.

Examples:

Present	Past
trip	tripped
pop	popped

Circle the misspelled verb in each sentence and write it correctly in the blank.

1. They stopped at our house and then hurryed home. _____

2. I scrubed and mopped the floor. _____

3. The coach nameed the five starting players. _____

4. He popped the potatoes into the oil and fryed them. _____

5. I accidentally droped my papers on the floor. _____

6. I had hopeed you could go climbing with me. _____

7. He triped on the rug. _____

8. The baby cryed and screamed all night. _____

9. I moped the mess up after the glass dropped on the floor. _____

10. First, she frowned, and then she smileed. _____

Historical Harry

What were the large cannons that were used by Germany in World War I?
Solve the following subtraction problems and find the answers in the cannon.
Write the corresponding letter above the problem's number at the bottom of
the page to spell out the answer to this historical trivia question.

A = 8.01
E = 0.28
B = 8.57
I = 11.92
B = 19.46
R = 33.75
S = 1.98
G = 11.38
H = 0.33
T = 5.998

1. 9 – 0.43

2. 12 – 0.08

3. 15 – 3.62

4. 20 – 0.54

5. 1 – 0.72

6. 46 – 12.25

7. 6 – 0.002

8. 21 – 20.67

9. 9 – 0.99

10. 4 – 2.02

___ ___ ___   ___ ___ ___ ___ ___ ___ ___
 1   2   3   4   5   6   7   8   9   10

Blast Off

Hint: Decimal points take up their own square. Do not use a zero before the decimal.

Across

3.
$$\begin{array}{r} 8.237 \\ -2.083 \\ \hline \end{array}$$
4.
$$\begin{array}{r} 2.23 \\ -1.256 \\ \hline \end{array}$$
5.
$$\begin{array}{r} 1,376.33 \\ -542.13 \\ \hline \end{array}$$

6. 8.538 – 0.228   8. 3.099 – 2.406

12. 124.107 – 45.642   14. 465.52 – 104.1

15. 0.732 – 0.633   16. 67.549 – 55.412

Down

1.
$$\begin{array}{r} 33.333 \\ +0.896 \\ \hline \end{array}$$
2.
$$\begin{array}{r} 2.587 \\ +3.191 \\ \hline \end{array}$$
3.
$$\begin{array}{r} 5.78 \\ +1.09 \\ \hline \end{array}$$

7. 22.05 + 15.91   9. 2.057 + 0.008

10. 0.531 + .1911   7.852 + 1.489

13. 3.012 + 1.025

Big Bucks for You!

Solve the problems on another sheet of paper.   **Answer space**

1. You receive your first royalty check for $1,000.00 and deposit it in your checking account. You go directly to the music store and spend $234.56 on new CDs. What is your balance?

2. You naturally treat all your friends to pizza, which costs you $47.76. You pay with a check. What is your balance now?

3. You decide to restock your wardrobe and buy $389.99 worth of new clothes. What is your balance?

4. Your next royalty check arrives, and you deposit $1,712.34. You also treat yourself to a new 15-speed bicycle, which costs $667.09. What is your balance?

5. You buy your mother some perfume for a present. You write a check for $37.89. What is your balance?

6. You need a tennis racket and some other sports equipment. The bill comes to $203.45 What is your new balance?

7. You treat your family to dinner at **Snails in a Pail**, where the check comes to $56.17. What is your new balance?

8. You join a health club, and the first payment is $150.90. What is your new balance?

9. You deposit your latest royalty check, which amounts to $4,451.01. What is your new balance?

10. To celebrate this good fortune, you take your entire peewee football team to a professional football game. The bill comes to $4,339.98. What is your new balance?

Adding and Subtracting Decimals

Add and subtract with decimals the same way you do with whole numbers. Keep the decimal points lined up so that you work with hundredths, then tenths, then ones, and so on.

Add or subtract. Remember to keep the decimal point in the proper place.

```
   0.5          0.35         47.5          85.7
 + 0.8        + 0.25       - 32.7        - 9.8
```

```
  13.90         9.53         72.8          6.43
 + 4.23       - 8.16       - 63.9        + 4.58
```

```
 638.07       811.060      521.09
- 19.34      + 78.430     - 148.75
```

```
 916.635      287.768      467.05
+ 172.136    - 63.951     - 398.19
```

Sean ran a 1-mile race in 5.58 minutes. Carlos ran it in 6.38 minutes. How much less time did Sean need?

_____

Robin Hood's Loot

As you know, Robin Hood stole from the rich and gave to the poor. Follow his stealing and giving path to figure out how much he has left for himself at the end.

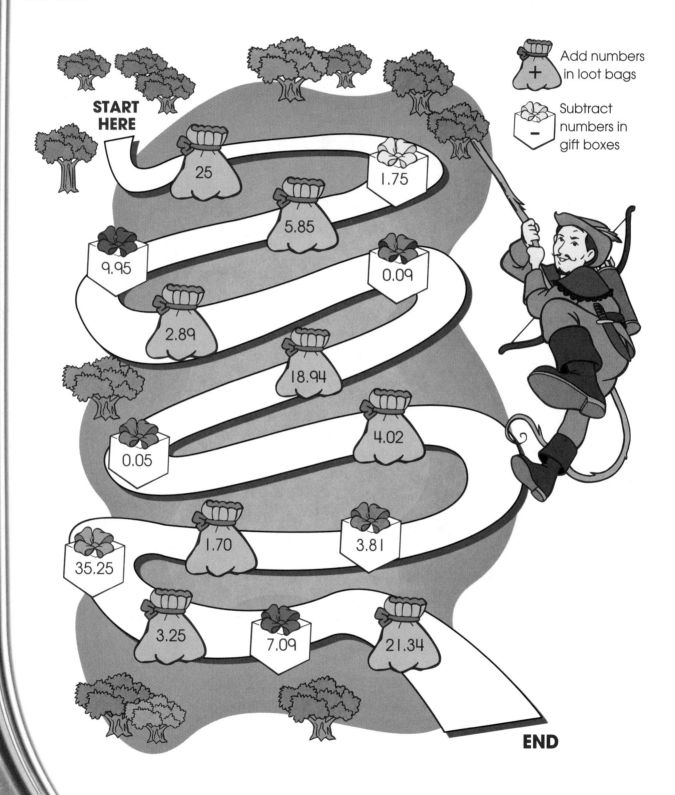

Add numbers in loot bags

Subtract numbers in gift boxes

START HERE

25

5.85

1.75

9.95

0.09

2.89

18.94

0.05

4.02

35.25

1.70

3.81

3.25

7.09

21.34

END

COMPLETE YEAR GRADE 5

Week 13 Skills

Subject	Skill	Multi-Sensory Learning Activities
Reading and Language Arts	Understand that many multisyllabic words are formed from Greek and Latin roots, prefixes, and suffixes.	• Complete Practice Pages 142–146. • Read the first two chapters of *Tuck Everlasting* by Natalie Babbitt. Have your child list words that contain prefixes and suffixes, and point out their root words. Then, finish the rest of the book.
Math	Add, subtract, and multiply decimal numbers.	• Complete Practice Pages 147–150. • After completing your weekly grocery list, ask your child to help you cut coupons for items on the list. Then, ask your child to sort the coupons by category (food, toiletries, cleaning supplies, etc.). Ask him or her to calculate the savings for each category and then add the savings in each category to get a total. Finally, ask your child to calculate how much you will save in a year if you use the same amount of coupons each week.
Bonus: Science		• Help your child make homemade ice cream. Mix a half cup of milk with a tablespoon of sugar and your favorite fruit in a small, resealable plastic bag. Place the bag inside a larger resealable bag. Add crushed ice and $\frac{1}{4}$ cup of salt to the large bag. Seal the large bag. Have your child put on mittens and shake and roll the bags until the ice-cream ingredients freeze (about 20 minutes).

Root Words

A **root word** is the common stem that gives related words their basic meanings.

Example: Separate is the root word for **separately**, **separation**, **inseparable** and **separator.**

Identify the root word in each group of words.
Look up the meaning of the root word in the dictionary and write its definition. The first one has been done for you.

1. colorless, colorful, discolor, coloration

   Root word: _____ color _____

   Definition: ___ any coloring matter, dye, ___
   ___ pigment or paint ___

2. creator, creation, creating, creative, recreate

   Root word: _____

   Definition: _____

3. remove, movement, movable, immovable, removable

   Root word: _____

   Definition: _____

4. contentment, malcontent, discontent, discontentment

   Root word: _____

   Definition: _____

5. pleasure, displeasure, pleasing, pleasant, unpleasant

   Root word: _____

   Definition: _____

6. successor, unsuccessful, successful

   Root word: _____

   Definition: _____

Greek and Latin Roots

Many word patterns in the English language are combinations of Greek or Latin words. When you know what part of a word means, you may be able to figure out the meaning of the rest of the word. For example, if **cycle** means "circle or wheel" and **bi** means "two," then you can figure out that **bicycle** means "two wheels." Root words are the words that longer words are based on. For example, **duct**, which means "to lead," is the root of **conduct** or **induct**. Look at the chart below. It has several root words and their meanings on it.

Root	Meaning	Example	Definition
act	to do	interact	to act with others
aqua	water	aquatint	dyed water
auto	self	automobile	to move oneself
centi	a hundred	centennial	one hundred years

Look at each word equation below. The meaning of one part is shown in parentheses. Consult the chart of root words to find the meaning of the other part. Write the meaning in the blank. Combine the two meanings. Write the dictionary definition in the space provided.

1. react   re (again) + act _____to do_____ = _____again to do_____

   Dictionary definition: _____To act or do again_____

2. automatic   auto _____ + matic (having a mind) = _____

   Dictionary definition: _____

3. transact   trans (across) + act _____ = _____

   Dictionary definition: _____

4. centimeter   centi _____ + meter (meter) = _____

   Dictionary definition: _____

5. aquanaut   aqua _____ + naut (sailor) = _____

   Dictionary definition: _____

Root Words

Root	Meaning	Example	Definition
cede	to go	supercede	to go beyond
cept	seize	intercept	to seize during
duce	lead	deduce	to find the lead
fer	carry	interfere	to carry into
port	carry	transport	to carry across
spect	to look	inspect	to look in
tain	to hold	obtain	to gain action
vene	to come	convene	to come to start

Complete the exercises below.

1. precede   pre (before) + cede _____to go_____ = __before to go__

Dictionary definition: _____to be, go or come before_____

2. report re (again) + port_____ = _____

Dictionary definition: _____

3. intervene inter (between) + vene_____ = _____

Dictionary definition: _____

4. induce in (in) + duce_____ = _____

Dictionary definition: _____

5. retrospect retro (backward) + spect _____ = _____

Dictionary definition: _____

6. refer re (again) + fer _____ = _____

Dictionary definition: _____

7. retain re (again) + tain _____ = _____

Dictionary definition: _____

8. concept con (with) + cept _____ = _____

Dictionary definition: _____

Adding Prefixes

A **prefix** is a syllable at the beginning of a word that changes its meaning. The prefixes **il**, **im**, **in** and **ir** all mean not.

Examples:

Illogical means not logical or practical.
Impossible means not possible.
Invisible means not visible.
Irrelevant means not relevant or practical.

Divide each word into its prefix and root word. The first one has been done for you.

	Prefix	**Root Word**
illogical	il	logical
impatient	_____	_____
immature	_____	_____
incomplete	_____	_____
insincere	_____	_____
irresponsible	_____	_____
irregular	_____	_____

Use the meanings in parentheses to complete the sentences with one of the above words.

1. I had to turn in my assignment _____ because I was sick last night. (not finished)

2. It was _____ for Jimmy to give me his keys because he can't get into his house without them. (not practical)

3. Sue and Joel were _____ to leave their bikes out in the rain. (not doing the right thing)

4. I sometimes get _____ waiting for my ride to school. (restless)

5. The boys sounded _____ when they said they were sorry. (not honest)

6. These towels didn't cost much because they are _____. (not straight or even)

Prefixes

The prefixes **un** and **non** also mean not.

Examples:
Unhappy means not happy.
Nonproductive means not productive.

Divide each word into its prefix and root word.
The first one has been done for you.

	Prefix	**Root Word**
1. unappreciated	un	appreciate
2. unlikely		
3. unkempt		
4. untimely		
5. nonstop		
6. nonsense		
7. nonprofit		
8. nonresident		

Use the clues in the first sentence to complete the second sentence with one of the words from the box. The first one has been done for you.

9. She didn't reside at school. She was a _____ nonresident. _____

10. He couldn't stop talking. He talked _____

11. The company did not make a profit. It was a _____ company.

12. She was not talking sense. She was talking _____

13. He visited at a bad time. His visit was _____

14. No one appreciated his efforts. He felt _____

15. He did not "keep up" his hair. His hair was _____

16. She was not likely to come. Her coming was _____

Adding and Subtracting Decimals

When adding or subtracting decimals, place the decimal points under each other. That way, you add tenths to tenths, for example, not tenths to hundredths. Add or subtract beginning on the right, as usual. Carry or borrow numbers in the same way. Adding 0 to the end of decimals does not change their value, but sometimes makes them easier to add and subtract.

Examples:	39.40	0.064	3.56	6.83
	+ 6.81	+ 0.470	- .09	-2.14
	46.21	0.534	3.47	4.69

Solve the following problems.

1. Write each set of numbers in a column and add them.

   a. 2.56 + 0.6 + 76 = _____

   b. 93.5 + 23.06 + 1.45 = _____

   c. 3.23 + 91.34 + 0.85 = _____

2. Write each pair of numbers in a column and subtract them.

   A. 7.89 – 0.56 = _____   B. 34.56 – 6.04 = _____   C. 7.6 – 3.24 = _____

3. In a relay race, Alice ran her part in 23.6 seconds, Cindy did hers in 24.7 seconds and Erin took 20.09 seconds. How many seconds did they take altogether? _____

4. Although Erin ran her part in 20.09 seconds today, yesterday it took her 21.55 seconds. How much faster was she today? _____

5. Add this grocery bill:
   potatoes—$3.49; milk—$2.09; bread—$0.99; apples—$2.30 _____

6. A yellow coat cost $47.59, and a blue coat cost $36.79. How much more did the yellow coat cost? _____

7. A box of Oat Boats cereal has 14.6 ounces. A box of Sugar Circles has 17.85 ounces. How much more is in the Sugar Circles box? _____

8. The Oat Boats cereal has 4.03 ounces of sugar in it. Sugar Circles cereal has only 3.76 ounces. How much more sugar is in a box of Oat Boats? _____

Multiplying Decimals by Two-Digit Numbers

To multiply by a 2-digit number, just repeat the same steps. In the example below, first multiply 4 times 9, 4 times 5 and 4 times 3. Then multiply 2 times 9, 2 times 5 and 2 times 3. You may want to place a 0 in the ones place to make sure this answer, 718, is one digit to the left. Now add 1,436 + 7,180 to get the final answer.

Example:

359	359	359	359	359	359
x 24	x 24	x 24	x 24	x 24	x 24
6	36	1,436	1,436	1,436	1,436
			80	180	7,180
					8,616

When one or both numbers in a multiplication problem have decimals, check to see how many digits are right of the decimal. Then place the decimal point the same number of places to the left in the answer. Here's how the example above would change if it included decimals:

35.9	3.59
x 0.24	x 24
8.616	86.16

The first example has one digit to the right of the decimal in 35.9 and two more in 0.24, so the decimal point is placed three digits to the left in the answer: 8.616. The second example has two digits to the right of the decimal in 3.59 and none in 24, so the decimal point is placed two digits to the left in the answer: 86.16. (Notice that you do not have to line up the decimals in a multiplication problem.)

Solve the following problems.

1. Jennie wants to buy 3 T-shirts that cost $15.99 each. How much will they cost altogether? _____

2. Steve is making $3.75 an hour packing groceries. How much will he make in 8 hours? _____

3. Justin made 36 cookies and sold them all at the school carnival for $0.75 each. How much money did he make? _____

4. Last year, the carnival made $467. This year it made 2.3 times as much. How much money did the carnival make this year? _____

5. Troy's car will go 21.8 miles on a gallon of gasoline. His motorcycle will go 1.7 times as far. How far will his motorcycle travel on one gallon of gas? _____

Multiplying Decimals

Multiply with decimals the same way you do with whole numbers. The decimal point moves in multiplication. Count the number of decimal places in the problem and use the same number of decimal places in your answer.

Example:

```
   3.5
x  1.4
  140
  35
 4.90
```

Multiply.

```
   2.5          67.4          83.7          13.35
x   .9        x 2.3         x 9.8         x 3.06
```

```
   9.06         28.97         33.41         28.7
x  2.38       x 5.16        x  .93        x 11.9
```

The jet flies 1.5 times faster than the plane with a propeller. The propeller plane flies 165.7 miles per hour. How fast does the jet fly?

_____

A Multiple Design

Solve the problems on a separate sheet of paper. Find the answers in the design and color correctly.

green
0.463
x   82

blue
28.5
x 7.4

red
6.51
x   6.9

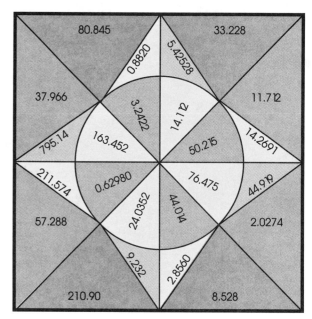

yellow
39.2
x 0.36

purple
7.54
x 0.43

purple
0.670
x   0.94

yellow
64.9
x 3.26

yellow
0.592
x 40.6

purple
7.46
x   5.9

green
92.4
x   0.62

blue
42.6
x   .78

blue
85.1
x 0.95

green
7.32
x   1.6

purple
6.05
x   8.3

green
3.27
x   0.62

blue
32.8
x 0.26

yellow
80.5
x 0.95

red
5.77
x   1.6

red
95.8
x   8.3

red
0.784
x 6.92

yellow
2.57
x 63.6

yellow
29.3
x 0.487

yellow
6.80
x   0.42

yellow
0.245
x   3.6

Week 14 Skills

Subject	Skill	Multi-Sensory Learning Activities
Reading and Language Arts	Understand the meanings of common prefixes.	• Complete Practice Pages 152–154. • Generate a list of root words, such as **school**, **kind**, **proper**, **aware**, and **happy**. Have your child add prefixes to the root words to create new words. Then, encourage your child to come up with his or her own list of root words and add prefixes to create new words.
	Use quotation marks correctly in writing.	• Complete Practice Page 155. • Seek out a passage in a fairy tale in which someone is speaking. Ask your child to read the passage aloud with lots of expression. Have your child write a new quotation following the format of a quotation from the fairy tale.
	Use italics for titles of books, newspapers, and other publications.	• Complete Practice Page 156. • Help your child find examples of book, magazine, and newspaper titles in book reviews and magazine articles. Have him or her note that the titles are italicized.
Math	Multiply and divide decimal numbers.	• Complete Practice Pages 157–160. • Give your child a problem to solve, such as **0.7 x 8** or **0.168 ÷ 0.8**. Use a penny or another small round object to represent a decimal point. Your child should move the decimal point around while solving the problem.

Prefixes

The prefixes **epi**, **hyper**, **over** and **super** mean "above" or "over." The prefixes **under** and **sub** mean "under."

Write each word's prefix and root word in the space provided.

Word	Prefix	Root Word
hyperactive	hyper	active
overanxious	_____	_____
superimpose	_____	_____
epilogue	_____	_____
underestimate	_____	_____
subordinate	_____	_____

Use the words above to complete the following sentences.

1. A photographer could _____ one image on top of another.

2. The _____ of the book may tell additional information about the story.

3. All the other children settled down for the night except the boy who was _____.

4. He could not sleep because he was _____ about the upcoming trip.

5. The company's president told his _____ to take over some of the responsibilities.

6. Just because you think you are weak, don't_____ how strong you could be.

Numerical Prefixes

Some prefixes are related to numbers. For example, in Latin **uni** means "one." The prefix **mono** means "one" in Greek. The chart below lists prefixes for numbers one through ten from both the Latin and Greek languages.

Number	Latin	Example	Greek	Example
1	uni	university	mon, mono	monopoly
2	du	duplex	di	digress
3	tri	tricycle	tri	trio
4	quad	quadrant	tetro	tetrameter
5	quin	quintuplets	penta	pentagon
6	sex	sexennial	hex	hexagon
7	sept	septuagenarian	hept	heptagon
8	oct	octopus	oct	octagon
9	nov	novena	enne	ennead (group of nine)
10	dec	decade	dec	decimal

Complete the exercises below.

1. unicycle   uni_____ + cycle (wheel) =

Dictionary definition: _____

2. monogram   mono_____ + gram (writing) = _____

Dictionary definition: _____

3. sextet   sex_____ + tet (group) = _____

Dictionary definition: _____

4. quadrant   quad _____ + rant (part) = _____

Dictionary definition: _____

5. decigram   dec_____ + gram (gram) = _____

Dictionary definition: _____

Practice With Prefixes

administer
advantage
adventure
defog
dehumidify
depart
derail
disagree
disappeared
dishonest
disinterested
explode
export
external
extricate
unequal
unprepared
untrue

prefixes

ex—out of, from   **dis, un**—not, opposite of
de—down, away from   **ad**—to, at, toward

Note the prefixes in the box above and how they change the meaning of a root word. **Write** each word under the appropriate category.

words with the
prefix **un**

1. _____

2. _____

3. _____

words with the
prefix **dis**

1. _____

2. _____

3. _____

4. _____

words with the
prefix **ad**

1. _____

2. _____

3. _____

words with the
prefix **ex**

1. _____

2. _____

3. _____

4. _____

Add the prefix **de** to each of these root words. Say each word to yourself as you write it on the line.

humidify   **part**   **fog**   **rail**

_____   _____   _____   _____

Quotation Marks

When a person's exact words are used in a sentence, **quotation marks** (" ") are used to identify those words. Commas are used to set off the quotation from the rest of the sentence. End punctuation is placed inside the final quotation mark.

Examples:
    "When are we leaving?" Joe asked.
    Marci shouted, "Go, team!"

When a sentence is interrupted by words that are not part of the quotation (he said, she answered, etc.), they are not included in the quotation marks. Note how commas are used in the next example.

Example: "I am sorry," the man announced, "for my rude behavior."

Place quotation marks, commas and other punctuation where needed in the sentences below.

1. Watch out yelled Dad.

2. Angela said I don't know how you can eat Brussels sprouts, Ted

3. Put on your coats said Mom. We'll be leaving in 10 minutes

4. Did you hear the assignment asked Joan.

5. Jim shouted This game is driving me up the wall

6. After examining our dog, the veterinarian said He looks healthy and strong

7. The toddlers both wailed We want ice cream

8. The judge announced to the swimmers Take your places

9. Upon receiving the award, the actor said I'd like to thank my friends and family

10. These are my favorite chips said Becky.

11. This test is too hard moaned the class.

12. When their relay team came in first place, the runners shouted, Hooray

13. Where shall we go on vacation this year Dad asked.

14. As we walked past the machinery, the noise was deafening. Cover your ears said Mom.

15. Fire yelled the chef as his pan ignited.

16. I love basketball my little brother stated.

Italics

Use **italics** or **underlining** for titles of books, newspapers, plays, magazines and movies.

Examples:
Book: Have you read *Gone with the Wind?*
Movie: Did you see *The Muppet Movie?*
Newspaper: I like to read *The New York Times.*
Magazine: Some children read *Sports Illustrated.*
Play: *A Doll's House* is a play by Henrik Ibsen.

Since we cannot write in italics, we underline words that should be in italics.

Underline the words that should be in italics.
The first one has been done for you.

1. I read about a play titled <u>Cats</u> in <u>The Cleveland Plain Dealer.</u>

2. You can find The New York Times in most libraries.

3. Audrey Wood wrote Elbert's Bad Word.

4. Parents and Newsweek are both popular magazines.

5. The original Miracle on 34th Street was filmed long ago.

6. Cricket and Ranger Rick are magazines for children.

7. Bon Appetit means "good appetite" and is a cooking magazine.

8. Harper's, The New Yorker and Vanity Fair are magazines.

9. David Copperfield was written by Charles Dickens.

10. Harriet Beecher Stowe wrote Uncle Tom's Cabin.

11. Paul Newman was in a movie called The Sting.

12. Have you read Ramona the Pest by Beverly Cleary?

13. The Louisville Courier Journal is a Kentucky newspaper.

14. Teen and Boy's Life are magazines for young readers.

15. Have you seen Jimmy Stewart in It's a Wonderful Life?

Multiplying Decimals

In some problems, you may need to add zeros in order to place the decimal point correctly.

$$
\begin{array}{r} 0.34 \\ \times\ 0.08 \\ \hline 0.0272 \end{array}
\qquad
\begin{array}{r} 0.0067 \\ \times\qquad 4 \\ \hline 0.0268 \end{array}
\qquad
\begin{array}{r} 0.046 \\ \times\ 0.07 \\ \hline 0.00322 \end{array}
$$

Solve the following problems.

1. $\begin{array}{r} 0.15 \\ \times\ 0.02 \\ \hline \end{array}$
2. $\begin{array}{r} 0.67 \\ \times\ 0.08 \\ \hline \end{array}$
3. $\begin{array}{r} 7.3 \\ \times\ 0.06 \\ \hline \end{array}$
4. $\begin{array}{r} 3.59 \\ \times\ 0.08 \\ \hline \end{array}$
5. $\begin{array}{r} 0.061 \\ \times\ 0.014 \\ \hline \end{array}$

6. $\begin{array}{r} 7.10 \\ \times\ 0.042 \\ \hline \end{array}$
7. $\begin{array}{r} 5.05 \\ \times\ 0.08 \\ \hline \end{array}$
8. $\begin{array}{r} 8.75 \\ \times\ 0.067 \\ \hline \end{array}$
9. $\begin{array}{r} 0.0647 \\ \times\ 0.3 \\ \hline \end{array}$
10. $\begin{array}{r} 3.62 \\ \times\ 0.003 \\ \hline \end{array}$

11. $\begin{array}{r} 1.07 \\ \times\ 0.05 \\ \hline \end{array}$
12. $\begin{array}{r} 3.03 \\ \times\ 0.07 \\ \hline \end{array}$
13. $\begin{array}{r} 0.02 \\ \times\ 0.02 \\ \hline \end{array}$
14. $\begin{array}{r} 0.501 \\ \times\ 0.03 \\ \hline \end{array}$
15. $\begin{array}{r} 0.321 \\ \times\ 0.09 \\ \hline \end{array}$

16. The players and coaches gathered around for refreshments after the soccer game. Of the 30 people there, 0.50 of them had fruit drinks, 0.20 of them had fruit juice and 0.30 of them had soft drinks. How many people had each type of drink?

fruit drink _____

fruit juice _____

soft drink _____

Comparison

Mr. Bigfoot's class was comparing numbers by multiplying decimals. Round your answer to the nearest hundredth.

$10.4 \times 1.2 =$

1. Andy's shoe is 10.4 inches long. Tony's is 1.2 times as long. How long is Tony's shoe?

   _____

2. Alicia can jump 24.8 inches. Jill can jump 1.05 times as high. How high can Jill jump?

   _____

3. The paper basket holds 288 sheets of paper. It is 0.25 full. How many sheets of paper are in it?

   _____

4. Misha's dog weighs 98.5 pounds. Tom's dog weighs 1.25 times as much. How much does Tom's dog weigh?

   _____

5. The area of Mr. Bigfoot's classroom is 981.75 square feet. The gym is 4.50 times as large. What is the area of the gym?

   _____

6. The box holds 48 pencils. It was 0.75 full. How many more pencils would fit in the box?

   _____

7. Amy is 5.250 feet tall. The ceiling is 2.075 times Amy's height. How tall is the ceiling?

   _____

Extension: Place the decimal point in the underlined number.

1. $213.05 \times 2.3 = \underline{490015}$ 2. $4.87 \times \underline{046} = 2.2402$ 3. $\underline{601} \times 0.08 = 4.808$

Dividing With Decimals

When the dividend has a decimal, place the decimal point for the answer directly above the decimal point in the dividend. The first one has been done for you.

$$
\begin{array}{r}
12.5 \\
3\overline{)37.5} \\
-3 \\
\hline
07 \\
-6 \\
\hline
15 \\
-15 \\
\hline
0
\end{array}
$$

$4\overline{)34.4}$ $2\overline{)31.6}$ $3\overline{)131.4}$

$5\overline{)187.5}$ $7\overline{)181.3}$ $6\overline{)340.8}$ $9\overline{)294.3}$

$3\overline{)135.6}$ $5\overline{)264.5}$ $2\overline{)134.6}$ $8\overline{)754.4}$

$5\overline{)35.25}$ $7\overline{)79.45}$ $9\overline{)28.71}$ $36\overline{)199.44}$

Decimal Dividends

Bring the decimal to the quotient. Solve.

1. $8\overline{)13.84}$

2. $12\overline{)27.96}$

3. $\dfrac{36.63}{11}$

4. $71.4 \div 51 =$

5. $93.09 \div 87$

6. $\dfrac{99.52}{32}$

7. Mandy wants to buy one bottle of soda pop. The advertised price is 3 bottles for $2.58. How much is one bottle? _____

8. Youngen and her 5 friends went to a movie together. Youngen paid $31.50 for all of the tickets. How much did each ticket cost? _____

9. Sang and Jon ate lunch for $12.58. They each had a turkey sandwich, fries and milk. How much did each boy pay? _____

Week 15 Skills

Subject	Skill	Multi-Sensory Learning Activities
Reading and Language Arts	Distinguish between facts and opinions.	• Complete Practice Pages 162–164. • Read *Bridge to Terabithia* by Katherine Paterson. Have your child list phrases from the book that express opinions and phrases that express facts.
	Find the main idea of a text.	• Complete Practice Page 165. • Have your child reread a favorite paragraph from *Bridge to Terabithia*. Ask him or her to state the main idea of the paragraph. What words does the author use to help the reader picture the main idea?
Math	Divide decimals by one- and two-digit whole numbers.	• Complete Practice Pages 166 and 167. • Give your child a catalog or sit with your child as he or she visits a shopping Web site. Give him or her an imaginary dollar amount to spend. Have your child choose one item he or she would like to buy, and ask how many identical items he or she could buy with the dollar amount you assigned.
	Divide decimals by decimals.	• Complete Practice Pages 168–170. • Make up real-life situations in which your child may need to divide a decimal by a decimal. For example, present a situation in which your child needs to purchase holiday presents for his or her friends. Say, "You have $30.50. Each toy costs $4.75. For how many friends can you buy these toys?"

Fact and Opinions

A **fact** is information that can be proved.

Example: Hawaii is a state.

An **opinion** is a belief. It tells what someone thinks. It cannot be proved.

Example: Hawaii is the prettiest state.

Write **f** (fact) or **o** (opinion) on the line by each sentence. The first one has been done for you.

___f___   1. Hawaii is the only island state.

_____   2. The best fishing is in Michigan.

_____   3. It is easy to find a job in Wyoming.

_____   4. Trenton is the capital of New Jersey.

_____   5. Kentucky is nicknamed the Bluegrass State.

_____   6. The friendliest people in the United States live in Georgia.

_____   7. The cleanest beaches are in California.

_____   8. Summers are most beautiful in Arizona.

_____   9. Only one percent of North Dakota is forest or woodland.

_____   10. New Mexico produces almost half of the nation's uranium.

_____   11. The first shots of the Civil War were fired in South Carolina on April 12, 1861.

_____   12. The varied geographical features of Washington include mountains, deserts, a rainforest and a volcano.

_____   13. In 1959, Alaska and Hawaii became the 49th and 50th states admitted to the Union.

_____   14. Wyandotte Cave, one of the largest caves in the United States, is in Indiana.

Write one fact and one opinion about your own state.

Fact: _____

Opinion: _____

_____

You Be The Judge

The lawyer is asking the witnesses many questions. Some of the answers are facts, some are opinions. The judge will only accept facts. Read each question and answer. Check fact or opinion next to each answer. If you checked fact, write a second answer that is an opinion. If you checked opinion, write a second answer that is a fact.

☐ **fact**
☐ **opinion**

1. **question:** Mr. Wallace, what was the stranger wearing?
   answer: He was wearing a blue coat, red scarf, black slacks and black shoes.

☐ **fact**
☐ **opinion**

2. **question:** Mr. Henry, what did you hear from your window?
   answer: I heard a sound that must have been the intruder breaking in.

☐ **fact**
☐ **opinion**

3. **question:** Ms. Harris, what time did you notice the broken lock?
   answer: It was 10:15 p.m., just as I arrived home.

☐ **fact**
☐ **opinion**

4. **question:** Mrs. Patterson, do you know the owner of the stolen painting?
   answer: He is the nicest boss I have ever worked for.

☐ **fact**
☐ **opinion**

5. **question:** Mr. Samuels, was the painting insured?
   answer: Yes, the painting was insured for ten thousand dollars.

☐ **fact**
☐ **opinion**

6. **question:** Miss Ryan, did you see the defendant take the painting?
   answer: Of course he took it! It had to be him.

Facts and Opinions

Read the articles about cats. List the facts and opinions.

Cats make the best pets. Domestic or house cats were originally produced by crossbreeding several varieties of wild cats. They were used in ancient Egypt to catch rats and mice, which were overrunning bins of stored grain. Today they are still the most useful domestic animal.

Facts:

_____

_____

_____

Opinions:

_____

_____

It is bad luck for a black cat to cross your path. This is one of the many legends about cats. In ancient Egypt, for example, cats were considered sacred, and often were buried with their masters. During the Middle Ages, cats often were killed for taking part in what people thought were evil deeds. Certainly, cats sometimes do bring misfortune.

Facts:

_____

_____

_____

Opinions:

_____

_____

Main Idea: New Corn

I will clothe myself in spring clothing

And visit the slopes of the eastern hill.

By the mountain stream, a mist hovers,

Hovers a moment and then scatters.

Then comes a wind blowing from the south

That brushes the fields of new corn.

Answer these questions about this ancient poem, which is translated from Chinese.

1. Circle the main idea:

The poet will dress comfortably and go to where the corn grows so he or she can enjoy the beauty of nature.

The poet will dress comfortably and visit the slopes of the eastern hill, where he or she will plant corn.

2. From which direction does the wind blow? _____

3. Where does the mist hover? _____

4. What do you think the poet means by "spring clothing"? _____

_____

The Perfect Sweet-Treat Solution

Solve each division problem on a separate sheet of paper. Draw a line from the popcorn (problem) to the correct drink (answer).

$3 \overline{\smash{)}7.95}$

6.84

$11 \overline{\smash{)}3.322}$

2.65

$5 \overline{\smash{)}0.31}$

0.905

$9 \overline{\smash{)}2.196}$

0.395

0.302

$2 \overline{\smash{)}0.016}$

$7 \overline{\smash{)}47.88}$

0.063

$5 \overline{\smash{)}11.4}$

0.244

$4 \overline{\smash{)}15.48}$

1.135

$8 \overline{\smash{)}7.24}$

0.008

3.87

2.28

$2 \overline{\smash{)}0.79}$

$8 \overline{\smash{)}0.504}$

0.062

$6 \overline{\smash{)}6.81}$

Dividing Decimals by Two-Digit Numbers

Dividing by a 2-digit divisor (34 in the example below) is very similar to dividing by a 1-digit divisor. In this example, 34 will divide into 78 twice. Then multiply 34 x 2 to get 68. Subtract 68 from 78. The answer is 10, which is smaller than the divisor, so 2 was the right number. Now bring down the next 8. 34 goes into 108 three times. Continue dividing as with a 1-digit divisor.

Example:

$$
\begin{array}{r}
2 \\
34\,\overline{)7{,}888} \\
68 \\
\hline
10
\end{array}
\qquad
\begin{array}{r}
23 \\
34\,\overline{)7{,}888} \\
68 \\
\hline
108 \\
102 \\
\hline
6
\end{array}
\qquad
\begin{array}{r}
232 \\
34\,\overline{)7{,}888} \\
68 \\
\hline
108 \\
102 \\
\hline
68 \\
68 \\
\hline
0
\end{array}
$$

To check your division, multiply: 34 x 232 = 7,888

When the dividend has a decimal, place the decimal point for the answer directly above the decimal point in the dividend.

Examples:

$$
\begin{array}{r}
3.6 \\
14\,\overline{)50.4}
\end{array}
\qquad
\begin{array}{r}
8.92 \\
34\,\overline{)303.28}
\end{array}
$$

Solve the following problems.

1. $56\,\overline{)7.28}$ 2. $23\,\overline{)18.63}$ 3. $62\,\overline{)255.44}$ 4. $71\,\overline{)82.36}$ 5. $4\,\overline{)8.580}$

6. If socks cost $8.97 for 3 pairs, how much does one pair cost? _____

7. If candy bars are 6 for $2.58, how much is one candy bar? _____

8. You buy a bike for $152.25 and agree to make 21 equal payments. How much will each payment be? _____

9. You and two friends agree to spend several hours loading a truck. The truck driver gives you $36.75 to share. How much will each person get? _____

10. You buy 14 hamburgers and the bill comes to $32.06. How much did each hamburger cost? _____

Dividing Decimals by Decimals

When a divisor has a decimal, eliminate it before dividing. If there is one digit right of the decimal in the divisor, multiply the divisor and dividend by 10. If there are two digits right of the decimal in the divisor, multiply the divisor and dividend by 100.

Multiply the divisor and dividend by the same number whether or not the dividend has a decimal. The goal is to have a divisor with no decimal.

Examples: $2.3\overline{)89} \times 10 = 23\overline{)890}$ $4.11\overline{)67.7} \times 100 = 411\overline{)6,770}$

  $4.9\overline{)35.67} \times 10 = 49\overline{)356.7}$ $0.34\overline{)789} \times 100 = 34\overline{)78,900}$

After removing the decimal from the divisor, work the problem in the usual way.

Solve the following problems.

1. $3.5\overline{)10.15}$ 2. $6.7\overline{)415.4}$ 3. $0.21\overline{)924}$ 4. $73\overline{)50.37}$

5. The body can burn only 0.00015 of an ounce of alcohol an hour. If an average-sized person has 1 drink, his/her blood alcohol concentration (BAC) is 0.0003. How many hours will it take his or her body to remove that much alcohol from the blood? _____

6. If the same person has 2 drinks in 1 hour, his or her blood alcohol concentration increases to 0.0006. Burning 0.00015 ounce of alcohol an hour, how many hours will it take that person's body to burn off 2 drinks? _____

7. If someone has 3 drinks in 1 hour, the blood alcohol concentration rises to 0.0009. At 0.00015 an hour, how many hours will it take to burn off 3 drinks? _____

8. After a drunk driving conviction, the driver's car insurance can increase by as much as $2,000. Still, this is only 0.57 of the total cost of the conviction. What is the total cost, in round numbers? _____

9. In Ohio in 1986, about 335 fatal car crashes were alcohol related. That was 0.47 of the total number of fatal car crashes. About how many crashes were there altogether, in round numbers? _____

Dividing Decimals by Decimals

When the divisor has a decimal point you must eliminate it before dividing. You can do this by moving the decimal point to the right to create a whole number. You must also move the decimal point the same number of spaces to the right in the dividend.

Sometimes you need to add zeros to do this.

Example

$$0.25 \overline{)85.50}$$ changes to

$$
\begin{array}{r}
342 \\
25\overline{)8550} \\
-75 \\
\hline
105 \\
-100 \\
\hline
50 \\
50 \\
\hline
0
\end{array}
$$

Divide.

$$0.3\overline{)27.9} \qquad 0.6\overline{)42.6} \qquad 0.9\overline{)81.9} \qquad 0.7\overline{)83.3}$$

$$0.4\overline{)23.2} \qquad 0.7\overline{)56.7} \qquad 1.2\overline{)10.8} \qquad 2.2\overline{)138.6}$$

$$12.6\overline{)5,670} \qquad 4.7\overline{)564} \qquad 8.6\overline{)842.8} \qquad 3.7\overline{)2,009.1}$$

$$5.9\overline{)1,917.5} \qquad 4.3\overline{)1,376} \qquad 2.9\overline{)922.2} \qquad 2.7\overline{)5613.3}$$

Dividing by Decimals

What kind of problems will these decimal glasses help you solve? Solve the problems. Then, write them in descending order (from greatest to least) beneath the blanks at the bottom of the page. Write each matching letter above the number to solve the riddle.

S $2.1\overline{)8.4}$ = $21.\overline{)84.}$ V $0.36\overline{)1.872}$ O $1.24\overline{)0.4712}$

N $8\overline{)1.12}$ D $0.3\overline{)17.7}$ I $6\overline{)126}$

I $.082\overline{)0.3772}$ — $7.4\overline{)103.6}$ I $5.5\overline{)3.025}$

___ ___ ___ ___ ___ ___ ___ ___ ___

Week 16 Skills

Subject	Skill	Multi-Sensory Learning Activities
Reading and Language Arts	Write a book report.	• Complete Practice Pages 172–174. • Ask your child to think of his or her favorite book. Have your child reread the book, if necessary, so it is fresh in his or her mind. Then, encourage your child to complete a project about the book, such as writing a sequel, writing a critique of the book, or illustrating a favorite scene.
Math	Review decimals.	• Complete Practice Pages 175–177. • Make up real-life situations for your child and ask him or her to give the answer as a decimal. For example, say, "A large pizza had eight slices. After dinner, there were six slices left. How much of the pizza was eaten?"
	Compare and convert decimals and fractions.	• Complete Practice Pages 178–180. • Draw a 10x10 grid (or a "base-ten square"). Give your child a series of fractions, ask him or her to convert the fractions to decimals, and shade in the correct number of squares. For example, if you give your child the fraction **60/100**, he or she will convert it to **0.60** and shade in six columns of the base-ten square.

How to Write a Book Report

Writing a book report should not be a chore. Instead, consider it an opportunity to share the good news about a book you have enjoyed. Simply writing, "I really liked this book. You will, too!" is not enough. You need to explain what makes the book worth reading.

Like other essays, book reports have three parts. An essay is a short report that presents the personal views of the writer. The three parts of an essay (and a book report) are introduction, body and conclusion.

The **introduction** to a book report should be a full paragraph that will capture the interest of your readers. The **body** paragraphs contain the main substance of your report. Include a brief overview of the plot of your book, along with supporting details that make it interesting. In the **conclusion**, summarize the central ideas of your report. Sum up why you would or would not recommend it to others.

Answer these questions about writing book reports.

1. Which of these introductory sentences is more interesting?

    ☐ Richie, a 12-year-old runaway, cries himself to sleep every night in the bowling alley where he lives.

    ☐ Many children run away from home, and this book is about one of them, a boy named Richie.

2. In a report on a fiction book about runaways, where would these sentences go?

    "Richie's mother is dead. He and his father don't get along."

    ☐ introduction

    ☐ conclusion

3. In the same report, where would these sentences go?

    "Author Clark Howard has written a sad and exciting book about runaways that shows how terrible the life of a runaway can be. I strongly recommend the book to people of all ages."

    ☐ body

    ☐ conclusion

Book Report: A Book I Devoured

Follow the writing prompts to write a short book report on a book you truly enjoyed.

Recently, I read a book I could not put down.

Its title is _____

One reason I "devoured" this book was _____

_____

_____

If I could be one of the characters, I'd be _____ because _____

_____

_____

_____

_____

My favorite part of the story was when _____

_____

_____

_____

_____

_____

_____

Book Report: Comparing Two Books

Follow the writing prompts to write a short book report comparing two books on the same subject.

Two books I recently read on the same subject

are _____

by _____

and _____

by _____

I liked _____ better because _____

_____

_____

_____

The best part of this book was when _____

_____

_____

_____

_____

_____

_____

Even though I did not like it as well, one good thing I can say about the other book

is _____

_____

_____

_____

Working With Decimals

1. Write 207.426 in words.

_____

2. Write forty-seven and thirteen thousandths in numerals. _____

3. Use > or < to indicate which decimal fraction is greater.

17.35 _____ 17.295

Fill in the blanks.

4. Round 12.836 to the nearest whole number. _____

5. Round 12.836 to the nearest tenth. _____

6. Round 12.836 to the nearest hundredth. _____

7. Write 0.36 as a fraction in lowest terms. _____

8. Write 0.25 as a fraction in lowest terms. _____

9. Write $\frac{3}{4}$ as a decimal number. _____

Solve.

10. $36.2 + 27.325 =$ _____

11. $87.36 - 84.95 =$ _____

12. $4.6 \times 1.2 =$ _____

13. $3.46 \times 10 =$ _____

14. $11.55 \div 7 =$ _____

15. $39 \div 12 =$ _____

16. $367.52 \div 10 =$ _____

Decimal Test

1. 0.45 + 0.96 + 0.52 = _____

2. 26.3 - 4.8 = _____

3. Use > or < to compare each pair of numbers.

   5.01_____ 5.003   6.15_____ 6.015   3.05_____ 5.03

4. Write sixty-one hundredths in numeral form. _____

5. 35.1 + 475.11 + 0.54 + 0.3 + 15 = _____

6. 81 - 0.04 = _____

7. Round 27.553 to the nearest tenth. _____

8. Round 62.814 to the nearest hundredth. _____

9. Round 5.06921 to the nearest hundredth. _____

10. Write 0.07 in words. _____

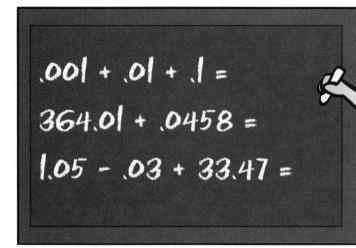

.001 + .01 + .1 =

364.01 + .0458 =

1.05 - .03 + 33.47 =

11. 16 x 0.18 = _____   15. 25.6 x 0.11 = _____

12. 0.504 ÷ 12 = _____   16. 22.1 + 0.008 = _____

13. 63 x 0.5 = _____   17. 3.65 ÷ 20 = _____

14. 90 - 10.50 = _____   18. 2.64 ÷ 5 = _____

Snails in a Pail

Sly Me Slugg, world-famous French chef, has made his
fast-food business, **Snails in a Pail**, the most popular
restaurant in the whole area. This is his menu:

Slime Soup $.49
Slugburger $1.69
Chicken-Fried Snails $2.99
Slimy Slush $.89
Snailcream Shake $1.49
Snailbits Salad $1.09

Solve the problems on another sheet of paper.

Answer space

1. Sly Me Slugg sold 60 Slimy Slushes and 40 Snailcream Shakes
   on Friday. How much did he make on drinks that day?

2. A coach treated 15 of his team players to Slugburgers. How
   much change did he receive from $40.00?

3. Your brother was so hungry that he ordered one of everything
   on the menu. How much change did he get from a $10.00 bill?

4. Sly Me Slugg sold $43.61 in Slime Soup orders on Wednesday
   and $38.22 in soup orders on Thursday. How many orders of
   slime Soup did he sell in those 2 days?

5. You had a party at **Snails in a Pail** and bought 9 Slugburgers,
   3 orders of Chicken-Fried Snails, 2 Snailbits Salads, 5 Snailcream
   Shakes and 10 Slimy Slushes. What was the total cost for
   the party?

6. In one week, Sly Me Slugg sold 200 Slugburgers and 79 orders
   of Chicken-Fried Snails. How much money did he earn from
   these 2 items?

7. You ordered 10 Slugburgers, 10 Snailcream Shakes and
   10 Slimy Slushes. What was your total cost?

8. On Friday, Sly Me earned $1,252. On Saturday, he earned
   $1,765. On Sunday, he earned $2,998. What was his average
   daily earnings for those 3 days?

Decimals

A **decimal** is a number with one or more places to the right of a decimal point.

Examples: 6.5 and 2.25

Fractions with denominators of 10 or 100 can be written as decimals.

Examples:

$\frac{7}{10}$ = 0.7

$\underset{\text{ones}}{0}$.	$\underset{\text{tenths}}{7}$	$\underset{\text{hundredths}}{0}$

$1\frac{52}{100}$ = 1.52

$\underset{\text{ones}}{1}$.	$\underset{\text{tenths}}{5}$	$\underset{\text{hundredths}}{2}$

Write the fractions as decimals.

$\frac{1}{2} = \overline{}10} = 0.\underline{}$

$\frac{2}{5} = \overline{}10} = 0.\underline{}$

$\frac{1}{5} = \overline{}10} = 0.\underline{}$

$\frac{3}{5} = \overline{}10} = 0.\underline{}$

			1/10
	$\frac{1}{4}$	$\frac{1}{5}$	1/10
$\frac{1}{2}$		$\frac{1}{5}$	1/10
	$\frac{1}{4}$		1/10
		$\frac{1}{5}$	1/10
	$\frac{1}{4}$		1/10
$\frac{1}{2}$		$\frac{1}{5}$	1/10
	$\frac{1}{4}$		1/10
		$\frac{1}{5}$	1/10

$\frac{63}{100}$ =	$2\frac{8}{10}$ =	$38\frac{4}{100}$ =	$6\frac{13}{100}$ =
$\frac{1}{4}$ =	$\frac{2}{5}$ =	$\frac{1}{50}$ =	$\frac{100}{200}$ =
$5\frac{2}{100}$ =	$\frac{4}{25}$ =	$15\frac{3}{5}$ =	$\frac{3}{100}$ =

COMPLETE YEAR GRADE 5

Comparing Decimals and Fractions

The symbol **>** means greater than. The number on its left is greater than that on its right. The symbol **<** means less than. The number on its left is less than that on its right. An equal sign, **=**, shows the same value on each side.

Use the sign >, = or < to make each statement true.

1. 0.4 $\bigcirc$ $\frac{2}{3}$ 2. 1.25 $\bigcirc$ $\frac{3}{2}$

3. 0.7 $\bigcirc$ $\frac{4}{5}$ 4. 0.68 $\bigcirc$ $\frac{5}{7}$

5. 0.1 $\bigcirc$ $\frac{1}{12}$ 6. 0.45 $\bigcirc$ $\frac{1}{2}$

7. 0.75 $\bigcirc$ $\frac{3}{8}$ 8. 0.6 $\bigcirc$ $\frac{5}{8}$

9. 0.54 $\bigcirc$ $\frac{2}{5}$ 10. 0.8 $\bigcirc$ $\frac{4}{6}$

11. 0.25 $\bigcirc$ $\frac{1}{7}$ 12. 1.8 $\bigcirc$ $\frac{12}{7}$

13. 0.625 $\bigcirc$ $\frac{4}{8}$ 14. 0.33 $\bigcirc$ $\frac{1}{3}$

15. Jenna looked carefully at the labels on two different types of cookies. The chocolate ones had $\frac{3}{4}$ pound in the package. The package of vanilla cookies claimed it had 0.67 pound of cookies inside. Were the chocolate cookies <, > or = to the vanilla cookies? _____

Decimals

1. Write out 36.124 in words. _____

2. Write two hundred thirty-seven and twenty-six hundredths in numerals.

   _____

3. Use > or < to indicate which decimal fraction is greater.

   3.147 _____ 3.205   3.06 _____ 3.059

4. Round 87.658 to the nearest whole number. _____

5. Round 87.658 to the nearest tenth. _____

6. Round 87.658 to the nearest hundredth. _____

7. Write 0.5 as a fraction in lowest terms. _____

8. Write 0.69 as a fraction in lowest terms. _____

9. Write 7.85 as a fraction in lowest terms. _____

10. Draw a model of 0.3.

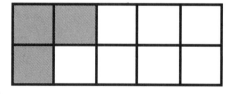

Week 17 Skills

Subject	Skill	Multi-Sensory Learning Activities
Reading and Language Arts	Understand the meaning of common suffixes.	• Complete Practice Pages 182–186. • Generate a list of root words, such as **kind**, **proper**, **talk**, **year**, and **walk**. Have your child add suffixes to the root words to create new words. Then, encourage your child to come up with his or her own list of root words and add suffixes to create new words.
Math	Understand equivalent fractions.	• Complete Practice Page 187. • Give your child 10 fractions. Have him or her name three equivalent fractions for each.
	Reduce fractions to their lowest terms.	• Complete Practice Pages 188 and 189. • Have your child list the common factors of pairs of numbers, such as **2** and **16** or **18** and **42**. Then, have your child circle the greatest common factor of each pair.
	Change mixed numbers to improper fractions.	• Complete Practice Page 190. • Write mixed numbers and corresponding improper fractions in two columns on a piece of paper. Have your child draw lines to match the equivalent numbers.

Adding Suffixes

A **suffix** is a syllable at the end of a word that changes its meaning.
The suffixes **ant** and **ent** mean a person or thing that does something.

Examples:

A person who occupies a place is an **occupant**.
A person who obeys is **obedient**.

A **root word** is the common stem that gives related words their basic meanings.

When a word ends in silent **e**, keep the **e** before adding a suffix beginning with a consonant.
Drop the **e** before adding a suffix beginning with a vowel.

Examples:

announce + ment = **announcement**
announce + ing = **announcing**

Announce is the root word in this example.

Combine each root word and suffix to make a new word. The first one has been done for you.

Root word	Suffix	New word
observe	ant	observant
contest	ant	
please	ant	
preside	ent	
differ	ent	

Use the meanings in parentheses to complete the sentences with one of the above new words. The first one has been done for you.

1. To be a good scientist, you must be very __observant__ . (pay careful attention)

2. Her perfume had a strong but very _____ smell. (nice)

3. Because the bridge was out, we had to find a _____ route home. (not the same)

4. The game show _____ jumped up and down when she won the grand prize. (person who competes)

5. Next week we will elect a new student council_____ . (highest officer)

Searching for Suffixes

In this group of words, suffixes were added without any changes to the root words.

Examples: clean + **ed** = cleaned
clean + **er** = cleaner
clean + **ing** = cleaning

attached
attended
avoiding
builder
catcher
concerned
drawing
enjoying
escorted
established
poster
prisoner
repeated
scalding
scooter
seller
spelling
younger

Exception: When a word ends in a single consonant preceded by a short vowel, the consonant is usually doubled before adding a suffix that begins with a vowel.

Examples: sit + **t** + **ing** = sitting
pad + **d** + **ed** = padded

Write each word in the appropriate category.

Root + er

1. _____
2. _____
3. _____
4. _____
5. _____
6. _____
7. _____

Root + ing

1. _____
2. _____
3. _____
4. _____
5. _____

Root + ed

1. _____
2. _____
3. _____
4. _____
5. _____
6. _____

Searching Suffixe

Circle the root word in each word.

1. clapping
2. canned
3. equipping
4. trimmer
5. slapped
6. beginning
7. quitter
8. dragging

Suffixes

The suffix **less** means lacking or without. The suffix **some** means full or like.

Examples:

Hopeless means without hope.
Awesome means filled with awe.

Create new words by adding **some** or **less** to these root words. Use a dictionary to check that the new words are correct. The first one has been done for you.

Root word		Suffixes		New Word
1. heart	+	less	=	heartless
2. trouble	+	_____	=	_____
3. home	+	_____	=	_____
4. humor	+	_____	=	_____
5. awe	+	_____	=	_____
6. child	+	_____	=	_____
7. win	+	_____	=	_____

Use the clues in the first sentence to complete the second sentence with one of the words from the box. The first one has been done for you.

8. Her smile was winning and delightful. She had a ___winsome___ smile.

9. The mean man seemed to have no heart. He was _____ .

10. She never smiled or laughed. She appeared to be _____ .

11. The solar system fills me with awe. It is _____ .

12. The couple had no children. They were _____ .

13. He had no place to live. He was _____ .

14. The pet caused the family trouble. It was _____ .

Suffixes

The suffix **ment** means the act of or state of. The suffixes **ible** and **able** mean able to.

Create new words by adding **ment** or **able** to these root words. Use a dictionary to check that the new words are correct. The first one has been done for you.

Root word		Suffixes		New Word
1. rely	+	able	=	reliable
2. retire	+	_____	=	_____
3. sense	+	_____	=	_____
4. commit	+	_____	=	_____
5. repair	+	_____	=	_____
6. love	+	_____	=	_____
7. quote	+	_____	=	_____
8. honor	+	_____	=	_____

Use the clues in the first sentence to complete the second sentence with one of the words from the box. The first one has been done for you.

9. Everyone loved her. She was __loveable (also lovable).__

10 He had a lot of sense. He was_____ .

11. She committed time to the project. She made a _____ .

12. He always did the right thing. His behavior was_____ .

13. The tire could not be fixed. It was not_____ .

14. They would not buy the car. The car was not _____ .

15. He gave the reporter good comments. His comments were_____ .

16. She was ready to retire. She looked forward to_____ .

Suffixes: "ance" and "ence"

Write words from the box to complete the sentences. Use a dictionary if you are unsure of the meaning of a word.

ance

performance	experience
correspondence	reliance
evidence	sequence
maintenance	absence
dependence	insurance

ence

1. The daycare position required _____ working with children.

2. During her _____ , a friend phoned each night with homework assignments.

3. My grandmother is known for her self- _____ .

4. The alphabet is a _____ of 26 letters.

5. A letter to my penpal is called long distance _____ .

6. The circus advertised a 2:00 P.M. _____ .

7. Many people have a great _____ on calculators for math.

8. Fortunately, most homeowners in the flooded area carried _____ .

9. The police gathered _____ in hopes of solving the burglary.

10. _____ of football and baseball fields requires much time and effort.

Equivalent Fractions

Match the pairs of equivalent fractions to find which line is longest—**A**, **B** or **C**.

Line A

$\frac{3}{8}$ ● $\frac{2}{4}$ ● — — — — — — — — — ● $\frac{1}{2}$ ● $\frac{6}{10}$

Line B

$\frac{6}{16}$ ● $\frac{2}{3}$ ●   ● $\frac{3}{5}$
$\frac{5}{6}$ ●   ● $\frac{4}{6}$ ● $\frac{3}{7}$
                                                ● $\frac{6}{14}$

$\frac{10}{12}$ ● $\frac{2}{8}$ ● $\frac{1}{2}$ ●   Line C $\frac{1}{3}$ ● $\frac{2}{6}$ ●
$\frac{6}{8}$ ●   ● $\frac{3}{4}$
$\frac{5}{8}$ ●   ● $\frac{1}{5}$
$\frac{10}{16}$ ●   ● $\frac{2}{10}$

Circle the longest line. **A B C**?

$\frac{2}{3}$ ● $\frac{2}{16}$ ●   Line A   ● $\frac{1}{3}$ ● $\frac{1}{2}$
$\frac{2}{6}$ ●   ● $\frac{3}{4}$

Line B

● $\frac{5}{8}$ ● $\frac{3}{8}$
$\frac{10}{17}$ ● $\frac{6}{16}$ ●

$\frac{9}{12}$ ●   Line C $\frac{1}{8}$ ●
$\frac{3}{12}$ ●   ● $\frac{1}{4}$ ● $\frac{5}{10}$
$\frac{4}{6}$ ●

Reducing Fractions

A fraction is in lowest terms when the GCF of both the numerator and denominator is 1. These fractions are in lowest possible terms: $\frac{2}{3}$, $\frac{5}{8}$ and $\frac{99}{100}$.

Example: Write $\frac{4}{8}$ in lowest terms.

Step 1: Write the factors of 4 and 8.

Factors of 4 are **4**, 2, 1.

Factors of 8 are 1, 8, 2, **4**.

Step 2: Find the GCF: 4.

Step 3: Divide both the numerator and denominator by 4.

$$\frac{4}{8} \div \frac{4}{4} = \frac{1}{2}$$

Write each fraction in lowest terms.

$\frac{6}{8} = $ —————— lowest terms $\frac{9}{12} = $ lowest terms

factors of 6: 6, 1, 2, 3   factors of 9: ___ , _____ , _____   ___GCF

factors of 8: 8, 1, 2, 4   factors of 12:___ , ____ , ____ , ____ , ____ , ____   ___GCF

$\frac{2}{6} = $	$\frac{10}{15} = $	$\frac{8}{32} = $	$\frac{4}{10} = $
$\frac{12}{18} = $	$\frac{6}{8} = $	$\frac{4}{6} = $	$\frac{3}{9} = $

Color the pizzas to show that $\frac{4}{6}$ in lowest terms is $\frac{2}{3}$.

 =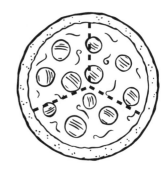

COMPLETE YEAR GRADE 5

Equivalent Fractions and the Lowest Term

Equivalent fractions name the same amount. For example, $\frac{1}{2}$, $\frac{5}{10}$, and $\frac{50}{100}$ are exactly the same amount. They all mean half of something. (And they are all written as the same decimal: 0.5.) To find an equivalent fraction, multiply the numerator and denominator of any fraction by the same number.

Examples: $\frac{3 \times 3}{4 \times 3} = \frac{9 \times 4}{12 \times 4} = \frac{36}{48}$ Thus, $\frac{3}{4}$, $\frac{9}{12}$ and $\frac{36}{48}$ are all equivalent fractions.

Most of the time, we want fractions in their lowest terms. It's easier to work with $\frac{3}{4}$ than $\frac{36}{48}$. To find a fraction's lowest term, instead of multiplying both parts of a fraction by the same number, divide.

Examples: $\frac{36 \div 12}{48 \div 12} = \frac{3}{4}$ The lowest term for $\frac{36}{48}$ is $\frac{3}{4}$.

If the numerator and denominator in a fraction can't be divided by any number, the fraction is in its lowest term. The fractions below are in their lowest terms.

Examples: $\frac{34}{61}$ $\frac{3}{5}$ $\frac{7}{9}$ $\frac{53}{90}$ $\frac{78}{83}$ $\frac{3}{8}$

Follow the instructions below.

1. Write two equivalent fractions for each fraction. Make sure you multiply the numerator and denominator by the same number. The first one is done for you.

a. $\frac{1 \times 3}{2 \times 3} = \frac{3}{6}$ $\frac{1 \times 4}{2 \times 4} = \frac{4}{8}$

b. $\frac{2 \times \underline{\ \ }}{3 \times \underline{\ \ }} = \frac{\underline{\ \ }}{\underline{\ \ }}$ $\frac{2 \times \underline{\ \ }}{3 \times \underline{\ \ }} = \frac{\underline{\ \ }}{\underline{\ \ }}$

c. $\frac{3 \times \underline{\ \ }}{5 \times \underline{\ \ }} = \frac{\underline{\ \ }}{\underline{\ \ }}$ $\frac{3 \times \underline{\ \ }}{5 \times \underline{\ \ }} = \frac{\underline{\ \ }}{\underline{\ \ }}$

d. $\frac{8 \times \underline{\ \ }}{9 \times \underline{\ \ }} = \frac{\underline{\ \ }}{\underline{\ \ }}$ $\frac{8 \times \underline{\ \ }}{9 \times \underline{\ \ }} = \frac{\underline{\ \ }}{\underline{\ \ }}$

2. Find the lowest terms for each fraction. Make sure your answers can't be divided by any other numbers. The first one has been done for you.

a. $\frac{2 \div 2}{36 \div 2} = \frac{1}{18}$

b. $\frac{12 \div \underline{\ \ }}{25 \div \underline{\ \ }} = \frac{\underline{\ \ }}{\underline{\ \ }}$

c. $\frac{12 \div \underline{\ \ }}{16 \div \underline{\ \ }} = \frac{\underline{\ \ }}{\underline{\ \ }}$

d. $\frac{3 \div \underline{\ \ }}{9 \div \underline{\ \ }} = \frac{\underline{\ \ }}{\underline{\ \ }}$

e. $\frac{25 \div \underline{\ \ }}{45 \div \underline{\ \ }} = \frac{\underline{\ \ }}{\underline{\ \ }}$

f. $\frac{11 \div \underline{\ \ }}{44 \div \underline{\ \ }} = \frac{\underline{\ \ }}{\underline{\ \ }}$

Mixed Numbers

A mixed number is a whole number and a fraction together. An example of a mixed number is $2\frac{3}{4}$. A mixed number can be changed to an improper fraction.

Example: $2\frac{3}{4}$

Step 1: Multiply the denominator by the whole number: $4 \times 2 = 8$

Step 2: Add the numerator: $8 + 3 = 11$

Step 3: Write the sum over the denominator: $\frac{11}{4}$

Follow the steps above to change the mixed numbers to improper fractions.

$3\frac{2}{3} =$	$6\frac{1}{5} =$	$4\frac{7}{8} =$	$2\frac{1}{2} =$
$1\frac{4}{5} =$	$5\frac{3}{4} =$	$7\frac{1}{8} =$	$9\frac{1}{9} =$
$8\frac{1}{2} =$	$7\frac{1}{6} =$	$5\frac{3}{5} =$	$9\frac{3}{8} =$
$12\frac{1}{5} =$	$25\frac{1}{2} =$	$10\frac{2}{3} =$	$14\frac{3}{8} =$

Week 18 Skills

Subject	Skill	Multi-Sensory Learning Activities
Reading and Language Arts	Use irregular verb forms correctly in writing.	• Complete Practice Pages 192–194. • With your child, brainstorm a list of at least 50 verbs. Then, help your child make a chart classifying verbs as regular or irregular.
	Write an opinion and support it with reasons.	• Complete Practice Pages 195 and 196. • Talk with your child about what it means to be a devil's advocate and intentionally argue against an opinion you support. Ask your child to play devil's advocate on an opinion he or she actually supports.
Math	Convert fractions to mixed numbers and vice-versa.	• Complete Practice Pages 197–200. • Give everyday examples of things that are divided or shared, such as eight candy bars for five kids, six toys for four puppies, or 12 sleds for 10 riders. Have your child give you the fraction and the mixed number that each situation represents.
Bonus: Social Studies		• Environmental awareness is important for everyone. Have your child read a newspaper article about pollution or conservation. Then, write a summary of the article and express an opinion.

Irregular Verbs

Verbs that do not add **ed** to show the past tense are called irregular verbs. **Irregular verbs** change in spelling in the past tense.

Examples:

Present	Past	Past with helpers
begin	began	(has, have) begun
see	saw	(has, have) seen
drive	drove	(has, have) driven

Fill in the blanks on the chart. You may refer to a dictionary.

Present	Past	Past with helpers
speak		
		taken
		ridden
choose		
	rang	
	went	
drink		
		driven
	drew	
know		
		eaten
do		

Underline the correct verb in each sentence below.

1. Martha has (began, begun) her research project.

2. First, she (chose, chosen) the topic.

3. She (drove, driven) many places to locate information.

4. Martha made a list of the interviews she had (did, done).

5. She (spoke, spoken) to people of many ages.

6. Many (knew, known) a great deal about the subject.

7. While interviewing people, Martha had (took, taken) notes.

8. Diagrams were (drew, drawn) for the project.

Irregular Verb Forms

The past tense of most verbs is formed by adding **ed**. Verbs that do not follow this format are called **irregular verbs**.

The irregular verb chart shows a few of the many verbs with irregular forms.

Irregular Verb Chart

Present Tense	Past Tense	Past Participle
go	went	has, have or had gone
do	did	has, have or had done
fly	flew	has, have or had flown
grow	grew	has, have or had grown
ride	rode	has, have or had ridden
see	saw	has, have or had seen
sing	sang	has, have or had sung
swim	swam	has, have or had swum
throw	threw	has, have or had thrown

The words **had**, **have** and **has** can be separated from the irregular verb by other words in the sentence.

Choose the correct verb form from the chart to complete the sentences. The first one has been done for you.

1. The pilot had never before ___flown___ that type of plane.

2. She put on her bathing suit and _____ 2 miles.

3. The tall boy had _____ 2 inches over the summer.

4. She insisted she had _____ her homework.

5. He _____ them walking down the street.

6. She _____ the horse around the track.

7. The pitcher has _____ the ball many times.

8. He can _____ safely in the deepest water.

Irregular Verb Forms

Use the irregular verb chart on the previous page. Write the correct verb form to complete each sentence.

1. Has she ever _____ carrots in her garden?

2. She was so angry she _____ a tantrum.

3. The bird had sometimes _____ from its cage.

4. The cowboy has never _____ that horse before.

5. Will you _____ to the store with me?

6. He said he had often _____ her walking on his street.

7. She insisted she has not _____ taller this year.

8. He _____ briskly across the pool.

9. Have the insects _____ away?

10. Has anyone _____ my sister lately?

11. He hasn't _____ the dishes once this week!

12. Has she been _____ out of the game for cheating?

13. I haven't _____ her yet today.

14. The airplane _____ slowly by the airport.

15. Have you _____ your bike yet this week?

COMPLETE YEAR GRADE 5

Reading Skills: It's Your Opinion

Your opinion is how you feel or think about something. Although other people may have the same opinion, their reasons could not be exactly the same because of their individuality.

When writing an opinion paragraph, it is important to first state your opinion. Then, in at least three sentences, support your opinion. Finally, end your paragraph by restating your opinion in different words.

Example:
I believe dogs are excellent pets. For thousands of years, dogs have guarded and protected their owners. Dogs are faithful and have been known to save the lives of those they love. Dogs offer unconditional love as well as company for the quiet times in our lives. For these reasons, I feel that dogs make wonderful pets.

Write an opinion paragraph on whether you would or would not like to have lived in Colonial America. Be sure to support your opinion with at least three reasons.

_____

_____

_____

_____

_____

_____

_____

_____

Writing Checklist

Reread your paragraph carefully.

- ☐ My paragraph makes sense.
- ☐ I have a good opening and ending.
- ☐ There are no jumps in ideas.
- ☐ I used correct spelling.
- ☐ I used correct punctuation.
- ☐ My paragraph is well-organized.
- ☐ My paragraph is interesting.

Writing: Supporting Your Opinion

Decide what your opinion is on each topic below. Then write a paragraph supporting your opinion. Begin with a topic sentence that tells the reader what you think. Add details in the next three or four sentences that show why you are right.

Example: Whether kids should listen to music while they do homework

Kids do a better job on their homework if they listen to music. The music makes the time more enjoyable. It also drowns out the sounds of the rest of the family. If things are too quiet while kids do homework, every little sound distracts them.

1. Whether young people should have a choice about going to school, no matter how old they are

   _____

   _____

   _____

2. Whether all parents should give their children the same amount of money for an allowance

   _____

   _____

   _____

3. Whether you should tell someone if you doubt he or she is telling the truth

   _____

   _____

   _____

Mixed Numbers and Improper Fractions

A **mixed number** is a whole number and a fraction, such as $1\frac{3}{4}$. An **improper fraction** has a numerator that is larger than its denominator, such as $\frac{16}{3}$. To write an improper fraction as a mixed number, divide the numerator by the denominator. The quotient becomes the whole number and the remainder becomes the fraction.

Example:

$$\frac{16}{3} = 3\overline{)16} \begin{array}{c} 5 \\ 15 \\ \hline 1 \end{array} = 5\frac{1}{3} \qquad \frac{28}{5} = 5\overline{)28} \begin{array}{c} 5 \\ 25 \\ \hline 3 \end{array} = 5\frac{3}{5}$$

To change a mixed number into an improper fraction, multiply the whole number by the denominator and add the numerator.

Example:
$$4\frac{1}{3} = 4 \times 3 = 12 + 1 = 13 \qquad \frac{13}{3}$$
$$8\frac{4}{7} = 8 \times 7 = 56 + 4 = 60 \qquad \frac{60}{7}$$

Follow the instructions below.

1. Change the improper fractions to mixed numbers and reduce to lowest terms. Use another sheet of paper if necessary. The first one has been done for you.

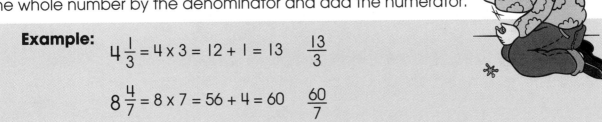

a. $\quad \frac{34}{6} = 6\overline{)34} \begin{array}{c} 5 \\ 30 \\ \hline 4 \end{array} = 5\frac{4}{6} = 5\frac{4}{6}$

b. $\frac{65}{4}$ 　　　　c. $\frac{23}{8}$ 　　　　d. $\frac{89}{3}$

e. $\frac{45}{9}$ 　　　　f. $\frac{32}{5}$ 　　　　g. $\frac{13}{7}$

h. $\frac{24}{9}$ 　　　　i. $\frac{31}{2}$ 　　　　j. $\frac{84}{23}$

2. Change these mixed numbers into improper fractions. The first one has been done for you.

a. $4\frac{6}{7} = 4 \times 7 = 28 + 6 = \frac{34}{7}$ 　　b. $2\frac{1}{9} =$ 　　c. $5\frac{4}{5} =$ 　　d. $6\frac{7}{8} =$

e. $3\frac{9}{11} =$ 　　f. $8\frac{3}{12} =$ 　　g. $1\frac{6}{14} =$ 　　h. $4\frac{2}{3} =$

Improper Fractions

An **improper fraction** has a numerator that is greater than its denominator. An example of an improper fraction is $\frac{7}{6}$. An improper fraction should be reduced to its lowest terms.

Example: $\frac{5}{4}$ is an improper fraction because its numerator is greater than its denominator.

Step 1: Divide the numerator by the denominator: $5 \div 4 = 1$, r1

Step 2: Write the remainder as a fraction: $\frac{1}{4}$

$\frac{5}{4} = 1\frac{1}{4}$ $1\frac{1}{4}$ is a mixed number—a whole number and a fraction.

Follow the steps above to change the improper fractions to mixed numbers.

$\frac{9}{8} =$	$\frac{11}{5} =$	$\frac{5}{3} =$	$\frac{7}{6} =$	$\frac{8}{7} =$	$\frac{4}{3} =$
$\frac{21}{5} =$	$\frac{9}{4} =$	$\frac{3}{2} =$	$\frac{9}{6} =$	$\frac{25}{4} =$	$\frac{8}{3} =$

Sara had 29 duplicate stamps in her stamp collection. She decided to give them to four of her friends. If she gave each of them the same number of stamps, how many duplicates will she have left? _____

Name the improper fraction in this problem. _____

What step must you do next to solve the problem? _____

_____

Write your answer as a mixed number. _____

How many stamps could she give each of her friends? _____

COMPLETE YEAR GRADE 5

Fractions: Mixed to Improper

Solve the problems. Connect the dots in the order of the numerator of the answers.

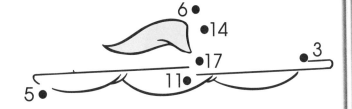

1. $1\frac{2}{5} = \frac{}{5}$
2. $1\frac{1}{3} = \frac{}{3}$

3. $1\frac{5}{7} = \frac{}{7}$
4. $2\frac{2}{3} = \frac{}{3}$

5. $2\frac{5}{8} = \frac{}{8}$
6. $2\frac{1}{2} = \frac{}{2}$

7. $1\frac{5}{6} = \frac{}{6}$
8. $1\frac{1}{5} = \frac{}{5}$

9. $2\frac{4}{5} = \frac{}{5}$
10. $1\frac{1}{16} = \frac{}{16}$

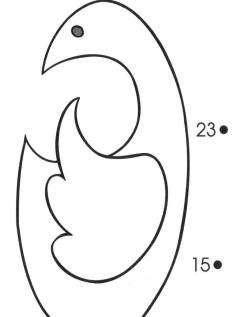

11. $1\frac{1}{2} = \frac{}{2}$
12. $3\frac{1}{5} = \frac{}{5}$

13. $1\frac{11}{12} = \frac{}{12}$
14. $1\frac{7}{8} = \frac{}{8}$

15. $1\frac{6}{7} = \frac{}{7}$
16. $2\frac{1}{4} = \frac{}{4}$

17. $1\frac{1}{12} = \frac{}{12}$
18. $1\frac{3}{7} = \frac{}{7}$

19. $6\frac{2}{3} = \frac{}{3}$
20. $3\frac{3}{5} = \frac{}{5}$

21. $1\frac{5}{21} = \frac{}{21}$
22. $1\frac{7}{36} = \frac{}{36}$

23. $1\frac{9}{20} = \frac{}{20}$
24. $1\frac{13}{24} = \frac{}{24}$

Fractions: Improper to Mixed

Change the fractions to mixed numbers. Shade in each answer to find the path to the pot of gold.

1. $\frac{11}{9} =$

2. $\frac{8}{3} =$

3. $\frac{8}{7} =$

4. $\frac{11}{6} =$

5. $\frac{7}{3} =$

6. $\frac{7}{6} =$

7. $\frac{9}{4} =$

8. $\frac{8}{5} =$

9. $\frac{4}{3} =$

10. $\frac{7}{2} =$

11. $\frac{3}{2} =$

12. $\frac{6}{5} =$

13. $\frac{7}{4} =$

14. $\frac{9}{2} =$

15. $\frac{11}{8} =$

16. $\frac{5}{2} =$

17. $\frac{9}{7} =$

18. $\frac{11}{4} =$

19. $\frac{17}{12} =$

20. $\frac{13}{12} =$

$1\frac{3}{5}$ $1\frac{1}{12}$ $2\frac{3}{4}$ $1\frac{4}{7}$ $2\frac{1}{6}$ $1\frac{5}{7}$ $1\frac{3}{8}$

$1\frac{11}{12}$ $4\frac{1}{3}$ $1\frac{1}{2}$ $1\frac{4}{5}$ $3\frac{3}{4}$ $4\frac{3}{4}$ $2\frac{1}{4}$ $2\frac{5}{6}$ $2\frac{6}{7}$

$4\frac{1}{2}$ $3\frac{1}{3}$ $2\frac{1}{2}$ $1\frac{7}{12}$ $1\frac{5}{8}$ $2\frac{1}{3}$ $3\frac{1}{2}$ $1\frac{1}{5}$ $1\frac{6}{7}$

$1\frac{2}{9}$ $2\frac{1}{5}$ $1\frac{5}{12}$ $1\frac{3}{4}$ $1\frac{1}{3}$ $1\frac{5}{6}$ $3\frac{1}{6}$ $4\frac{2}{3}$ $2\frac{4}{5}$

$1\frac{1}{7}$ $1\frac{4}{9}$ $1\frac{2}{3}$ $1\frac{3}{7}$ $1\frac{1}{6}$ $2\frac{2}{3}$ $1\frac{2}{7}$

Second Quarter Check-Up

Reading and Language Arts

❑ I can use prepositional phrases correctly in writing.
❑ I can plan an original story.
❑ I can use verbs, including helping verbs and linking verbs, correctly in writing.
❑ I understand verbs that are frequently confused.
❑ I understand present, past, and future verb tenses.
❑ I understand that many multisyllabic words are formed from Greek and Latin roots, prefixes, and suffixes.
❑ I understand the meanings of common prefixes and suffixes.
❑ I can use quotation marks correctly in writing.
❑ I can use italics for titles of books, newspapers, and other publications.
❑ I can distinguish between facts and opinions.
❑ I can find the main idea of a text.
❑ I can write a book report.
❑ I can use irregular verb forms correctly in writing.
❑ I can write an opinion and support it with reasons.

Math

❑ I can use multiplication and division to solve word problems.
❑ I understand and compare decimal numbers.
❑ I can add, subtract, multiply, and divide decimal numbers, including money amounts.
❑ I can divide decimals by one- and two-digit whole numbers.
❑ I can divide decimals by decimals.
❑ I can compare and convert decimals and fractions.
❑ I understand equivalent fractions.
❑ I can reduce fractions to their lowest terms.
❑ I can convert fractions to mixed numbers and vice-versa.

Final Project

Organize a fundraising project such as a book fair, garage sale, or bake sale to raise money for a charity of your child's choosing. Ask your child to generate publicity for the fundraiser by writing an opinion piece for your local newspaper about why he or she chooses to support the organization. After the fundraiser, ask your child to add all of the money he or she earned and donate it to the organization.

Third Quarter Introduction

In the weeks after the winter or mid-year break, students are often ready to tackle new learning challenges. In many classrooms, brand-new concepts and skills are introduced during third quarter that may be difficult for your child. You can help at home by encouraging your child and providing positive learning support using resources found in *Complete Year*.

Third Quarter Skills

Practice pages in this book for Weeks 19–27 will help your child improve the following skills.

Reading and Language Arts

- Understand verb tenses, including present, past, future, and past participle
- Use correct subject/verb agreement
- Use commas in a series and to separate a noun or pronoun in a direct address
- Understand and identify homographs, or words that have the same spelling but different meanings and pronunciations
- Answer questions about texts to determine reading comprehension
- Use editing marks to proofread and make corrections
- Understand the author's purpose to inform, persuade, or entertain
- Practice persuasive writing
- Use a dictionary to determine meaning and pronunciation of unfamiliar words
- Demonstrate correct punctuation
- Understand synonyms and antonyms
- Use context as a clue to the meaning of a word or phrase

Math

- Add and subtract fractions with like and unlike denominators
- Add, subtract, and multiply mixed numbers
- Multiply and divide fractions
- Divide fractions by whole numbers and whole numbers by fractions
- Measure length, weight, and capacity in customary and metric units

Multi-Sensory Learning Activities

Try these fun activities for enhancing your child's learning and development during the third quarter of the school year. Be sure to choose activities that include speaking, listening, touching, and active movement.

Reading and Language Arts

Write 10 sentences on a sheet of paper. Have your child underline the main verb in each and tell whether the verb form is past, present, or past participle.

Read *The Trumpet of the Swan* by E. B. White. Have your child monitor his or her own comprehension by asking questions and finding the answers him- or herself. Have your child look back through pages to find the answers and reread any confusing passages.

Have your child search a newspaper and a chapter book for examples of words in a series. Is a comma used after each word, including before **and** or **or**?

Take turns with your child reading several sentences that contain commas. Can you hear the pause indicated by the comma?

Discuss the editorial section of the newspaper. Have your child look at articles and letters on the editorial page as models of persuasive writing. Have your child choose a topic from the editorial section and write his or her own persuasive essay about it.

 **Math**

Show your child an addition problem in which the fractions have different denominators. Give your child several problems to solve using the LCM as a common denominator.

Have your child list multiples and find the LCM of several pairs of numbers, such as **2** and **3**, **4** and **5**, **3** and **6**, **3** and **5**, **4** and **8**, **4** and **7**, **9** and **6**.

Write numbers between **1** and **20** on at least 20 index cards, making sure that most of the numbers are not prime numbers. Split the cards evenly between two players. Then, both players simultaneously turn over the top card in their piles and place it between them. The first player to call out the correct lowest common multiple of the two numbers wins the round and adds both of the cards to the bottom of his or her pile. Continue playing until one player runs out of cards. The other player is the winner.

Third Quarter Introduction, cont.

 Science

Provide books and other resources on glaciers for your child's reference. Discuss well-known glaciers. Have your child choose a famous glacier and write about how it formed, where it is located, and other facts.

Have your child read about some of the major volcanoes on Earth. Discuss the Ring of Fire. Why do so many volcanoes appear around this ring? Watch a video on this phenomenon if possible, or look through a book with lots of photographs.

 **Social Studies**

Have your child read about famous Americans who were associated with events of the Revolutionary War, including Ethan Allen, Benedict Arnold, John Paul Jones, and George Washington. Then, have your child read about the government established immediately following the war. In 1781, Congress laid down basic laws for the new country. Why didn't these laws work?

Ask your child to interview several family members and neighbors about what it means to them to be Americans. Discuss each person's response, and have your child write a paragraph summary.

 Seasonal Fun

Create a mug cozy for your cup of hot cocoa. Have your child measure the height of a coffee mug, then cut a long strip of cardboard with the same height. Wrap the cardboard around the mug, leaving a gap for the handle. Have your child remove the cardboard ring and lay it on a sheet of construction paper. Trace it on the construction paper, and then cut it out and glue it to the top of the cardboard for a colorful cozy. Encourage your child to draw a sweater design or snowflakes onto felt or fabric for a winter-themed cozy. Carefully cut out and glue the felt shapes onto the cardboard and let them dry completely. Then, roll the cardboard into a ring, and glue the ends together.

Week 19 Skills

Subject	Skill	Multi-Sensory Learning Activities
Reading and Language Arts	Understand verb tenses, including present, past, future, and past participle.	• Complete Practice Pages 206–208. • There are three principal parts of every verb: present, past, and past participle. Have your child write sentences using these forms and explain why each verb tense was used in each situation.
	Use correct subject/verb agreement.	• Complete Practice Pages 209 and 210. • Choose a paragraph from a book your child has recently read. Have your child point out the subject and verb from each sentence and discuss the subject/verb agreement.
Math	Add fractions with like and unlike denominators.	• Complete Practice Pages 211–213. • Teach your child how to add fractions with the same denominator. Use models to show how it is done. For example, $\frac{1}{4} + \frac{2}{4} = \frac{3}{4}$. Have your child make models of addition problems using fractions with unlike denominators.
	Add mixed numbers.	• Complete Practice Page 214. • Ask your child to propose a procedure for solving the equation $\frac{4}{5} + 1\frac{3}{4}$. Try out your child's suggestion to see if it works. If it does, then continue to use it. If your child's suggestion does not work well, try another method.

Principal Parts of Verbs

Verbs have three principal parts. They are **present**, **past** and **past participle**.

Regular verbs form the past tense by adding **ed** to the present tense.

The past participle is formed by using the past tense verb with a helping verb: **has**, **have** or **had**.

Write the correct form of each verb. The first one has been done for you.

Present	Past	Past Participle
1. look	looked	has/have/had looked
2. _____	planned	_____
3. _____	_____	has/have/had closed
4. wash	_____	_____
5. _____	prepared	_____
6. _____	_____	has/have/had provided
7. invite	_____	_____
8. _____	discovered	_____
9. approve	_____	_____
10. _____	searched	_____
11. establish	_____	_____
12. _____	_____	has/have/had formed
13. _____	pushed	_____
14. travel	_____	_____

Writing: Future-Tense Verbs

Future-tense verbs tell about things that will happen in the future. To form future-tense verbs, use **will** before the verb.

Example: Tomorrow I **will walk** to school.

When you use **will**, you may also have to add a helping verb and the ending **ing**.

Example: Tomorrow I **will be walking** to school.

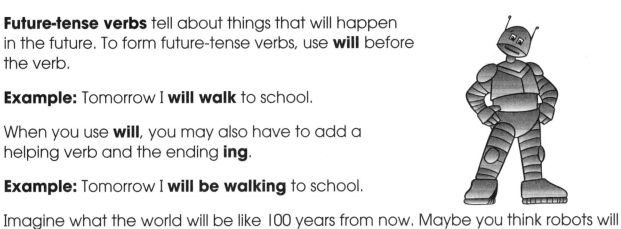

Imagine what the world will be like 100 years from now. Maybe you think robots will be doing our work for us, or that people will be living on the moon. What will our houses look like? What will school be like? Write a paragraph describing what you imagine. Be sure to use future-tense verbs.

_____

_____

_____

_____

_____

_____

_____

_____

_____

_____

_____

Verb Tense

Write a sentence using the present tense of each verb.

1. walk _____

_____

2. dream _____

_____

3. achieve _____

_____

Write a sentence using the past tense of each verb.

1. dance _____

_____

2. study _____

_____

3. hike _____

_____

Write a sentence using the future tense of each verb.

1. bake _____

_____

2. write _____

_____

3. talk _____

_____

Writing: Subjects and Verbs

Make each group of words below into a sentence by adding a subject, a verb, or a subject and a verb. Then write **S** over each subject and **V** over each verb.

Example: the dishes in the sink

      S   V

The dishes in the sink were dirty.

1. a leash for your pet

   _____

2. dented the table

   _____

3. a bowl of punch for the party

   _____

4. rinsed the soap out

   _____

5. a lack of chairs

   _____

6. bragging about his sister

   _____

7. the stock on the shelf

   _____

8. with a flip of the wrist

   _____

Subject/Verb Agreement

Singular subjects require singular verbs. **Plural subjects** require plural verbs. The subject and verb must agree in a sentence.

Example:

   Singular: My dog runs across the field.
   Plural: My dogs run across the field.

Circle the correct verb in each sentence.

1. Maria (talk/talks) to me each day at lunch.

2. Mom, Dad and I (is/are) going to the park to play catch.

3. Mr. and Mrs. Ramirez (dance/dances) well together.

4. Astronauts (hope/hopes) for a successful mission.

5. Trees (prevent/prevents) erosion.

6. The student (is/are) late.

7. She (ask/asks) for directions to the senior high gym.

8. The elephants (plod/plods) across the grassland to the watering hole.

9. My friend's name (is/are) Rebecca.

10. Many people (enjoy/enjoys) orchestra concerts.

11. The pencils (is/are) sharpened.

12. My backpack (hold/holds) a lot of things.

13. The wind (blow/blows) to the south.

14. Sam (collect/collects) butterflies.

15. They (love/loves) cotton candy.

Egyptian Math

Help build the pyramid by adding the fractions.

Reduce each to its lowest term.

Use the following rule:

$$a + b = c$$

$\dfrac{4}{15}$	$\dfrac{8}{15}$	$\dfrac{1}{15}$	$\dfrac{2}{15}$	$\dfrac{7}{15}$

Adding Unlike Fractions

Solve the problems. Shade in your answers on the pizzas below to show which pieces have been eaten.

$$\frac{1}{10} \atop + \frac{4}{5}$$ $$\frac{3}{12} \atop + \frac{1}{6}$$ $$\frac{1}{2} \atop + \frac{1}{3}$$ $$\frac{3}{4} \atop + \frac{1}{5}$$ $$\frac{1}{5} \atop + \frac{1}{3}$$

$$\frac{2}{3} \atop + \frac{1}{4}$$ $$\frac{5}{12} \atop + \frac{1}{6}$$ $$\frac{2}{5} \atop + \frac{9}{20}$$ $$\frac{1}{3} \atop + \frac{2}{9}$$ $$\frac{3}{5} \atop + \frac{1}{10}$$

$$\frac{1}{10} \atop + \frac{1}{5}$$ $$\frac{2}{3} \atop + \frac{1}{5}$$ $$\frac{1}{8} \atop + \frac{1}{3}$$ $$\frac{3}{8} \atop + \frac{1}{5}$$ $$\frac{1}{5} \atop + \frac{1}{9}$$

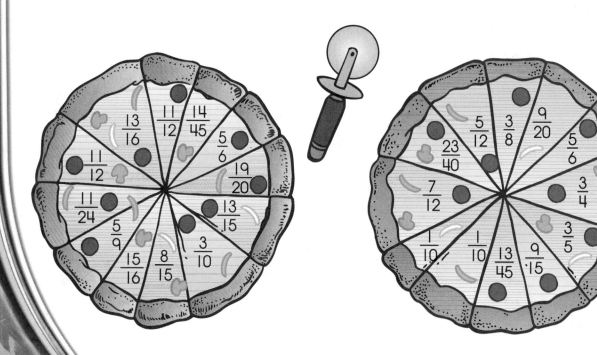

COMPLETE YEAR GRADE 5

Adding Unlike Fractions

Example: $\dfrac{4}{5} + \dfrac{1}{4}$

$$\dfrac{4}{5} + \dfrac{1}{4} = \dfrac{4(\times4)}{5(\times4)} + \dfrac{1(\times5)}{4(\times5)} = \dfrac{16}{20} \overset{\text{add}}{\longleftrightarrow} \dfrac{5}{20} = \dfrac{21}{20} = 1\dfrac{1}{20}$$

5, 10, 15, ⑳
4, 8, 12, 16, ⑳

Steps:
1. Find the LCM of both denominators (20).
2. Multiply the numerator and denominator of each fraction by a number to arrive at the LCM.
3. Add numerators.
4. Denominators stay the same.
5. Write improper fractions as mixed numbers.
6. Reduce to lowest terms.

Remember: Since you are multiplying both numerator and denominator by the same number, you are just multiplying the fraction by 1

$(\dfrac{4}{4} = 1, \dfrac{5}{5} = 1)$.

Add.

1. $\dfrac{2}{3} + \dfrac{1}{5}$

2. $\dfrac{3}{4} + \dfrac{1}{6}$

3. $\dfrac{7}{8} + \dfrac{5}{6}$

4. $\dfrac{1}{2} + \dfrac{8}{9}$

5. $\dfrac{11}{12} + \dfrac{1}{4}$

6. $\dfrac{3}{10} + \dfrac{1}{5}$

7. $\dfrac{3}{4} + \dfrac{2}{5}$

8. $\dfrac{5}{8} + \dfrac{9}{10}$

9. $\dfrac{1}{5} + \dfrac{7}{15}$

Adding Unlike Numbers

To add mixed numbers, first find the least common denominator.

Always reduce the answer to lowest terms.

Example:

$$5 \frac{1}{4}$$
$$+ 6 \frac{1}{3}$$

$$5 \frac{3}{12}$$
$$+ 6 \frac{4}{12}$$
$$11 \frac{7}{12}$$

Add. Reduce the answers to lowest terms.

$$8 \frac{1}{2}$$
$$+ 7 \frac{1}{4}$$

$$5 \frac{1}{4}$$
$$+ 2 \frac{3}{8}$$

$$9 \frac{3}{10}$$
$$+ 7 \frac{1}{5}$$

$$8 \frac{1}{5}$$
$$+ 6 \frac{7}{10}$$

$$4 \frac{4}{5}$$
$$+ 3 \frac{3}{10}$$

$$3 \frac{1}{2}$$
$$+ 7 \frac{1}{4}$$

$$4 \frac{1}{2}$$
$$+ 1 \frac{1}{3}$$

$$6 \frac{1}{12}$$
$$+ 3 \frac{3}{4}$$

$$5 \frac{1}{3}$$
$$+ 2 \frac{3}{9}$$

$$6 \frac{1}{3}$$
$$+ 2 \frac{2}{5}$$

$$2 \frac{2}{7}$$
$$+ 4 \frac{1}{14}$$

$$3 \frac{1}{2}$$
$$+ 3 \frac{1}{4}$$

The boys picked $3 \frac{1}{2}$ baskets of apples. The girls picked $5 \frac{1}{2}$ baskets. How many baskets of apples did the boys and girls pick in all? _____

COMPLETE YEAR GRADE 5

Week 20 Skills

Subject	Skill	Multi-Sensory Learning Activities
Reading and Language Arts	Review subject/verb agreement.	• Complete Practice Pages 216 and 217. • Have your child write a paragraph on a topic related to a nonfiction book of his or her choosing. Ask your child to include a variety of sentences and point out the subject/verb agreement of each.
	Use commas in a series and to separate a noun or pronoun in a direct address.	• Complete Practice Pages 218 and 219. • Write 10 sentences on a piece of paper, omitting the commas. For example, one sentence could be "The store window displayed a sled with a bear on it six wrapped boxes and a snow globe." Ask your child to add in the commas as needed.
Math	Add and subtract fractions with like and unlike denominators.	• Complete Practice Pages 220–224. • Show your child how to find the least common denominator before adding fractions. Give your child several problems with unlike denominators to practice this concept, such as $\frac{3}{8} + \frac{5}{12}$. What is the smallest multiple that 8 and 12 have in common?

Matching Subjects and Verbs

If the subject of a sentence is singular, the verb must be singular. If the subject is plural, the verb must be plural.

Example:

The **dog** with floppy ears **is eating**.
The **dogs** in the yard **are eating**.

Write the singular or plural form of the
subject in each sentence to match the verb.

1. The (yolk) _____ in this egg is bright yellow.

2. The (child) _____ are putting numbers in columns.

3. Both (coach) _____ are resigning at the end of the year.

4. Those three (class) _____ were assigned to the gym.

5. The (lunch) _____ for the children are ready.

6. (Spaghetti) _____ with meatballs is delicious.

7. Where are the (box) _____ of chalk?

8. The (man) _____ in the truck were collecting broken tree limbs.

9. The (rhythm) _____ of that music is exactly right for dancing.

10. Sliced (tomato) _____ on lettuce are good with salmon.

11. The (announcer) _____ on TV was condemning the dictator.

12. Two (woman) _____ are campaigning for mayor of our town.

13. The (group) _____ of travelers was on its way to three foreign countries.

14. The (choir) _____ of thirty children is singing hymns.

15. In spite of the parade, the (hero) _____ were solemn.

Agreement of Subject and Verb

A **singular subject** takes a singular verb.
Example: Bill washes the dishes.

A **plural subject** takes a plural verb.
Example: They watch television.

A **compound subject** connected by **and** takes a plural verb.
Example: Mary and Bill read books.

For a **compound subject** connected by **either/or** or **neither/nor**, the verb agrees with the subject closer to it.

Examples: Either my aunt or my uncle takes us.
Neither my grandfather nor my grandmothers are over 85.

A **singular indefinite pronoun** as the subject takes a singular verb (anybody, anyone, everybody, everyone, no one, somebody, someone, something).
Example: Everyone enjoys games.

Write the correct present-tense form of each verb on the line.

1. Everyone _____ wearing interesting hats. (enjoy)

2. Many people _____ hats for various activities. (wear)

3. One factory _____ only felt hats. (make)

4. Either bamboo grass or the leaves of a pine tree _____ wonderful straw hats. (make)

5. Factories _____ straw hats, too. (produce)

6. Somebody _____ the straw material. (braid)

7. Either machines or a worker _____ the braided material. (bleach)

8. Chemicals and gelatins _____ straw hats. (stiffen)

9. Ironing _____ the hat-making process. (finish)

Commas

Commas are used to separate items in a series.

Example:

The fruit bowl contains oranges, peaches, pears, and apples.

Commas are also used to separate geographical names and dates.

Example:

Today's date is January 13, 2000.
My grandfather lives in Tallahassee, Florida.
I would like to visit Paris, France.

Place commas where needed in these sentences.

1. I was born on September 21 1992.

2. John's favorite sports include basketball football hockey and soccer.

3. The ship will sail on November 16 2004.

4. My family and I vacationed in Salt Lake City Utah.

5. I like to plant beans beets corn and radishes in my garden.

6. Sandy's party will be held in Youngstown Ohio.

7. Periods commas colons and exclamation marks are types of punctuation.

8. Cardinals juncos blue jays finches and sparrows frequent our birdfeeder.

9. My grandfather graduated from high school on June 4 1962.

10. The race will take place in Burlington Vermont.

Write a sentence using commas to separate words in a series.

11. _____

Write a sentence using commas to separate geographical names.

12. _____

Write a sentence using commas to separate dates.

13. _____

Commas

Commas are used to separate a noun or pronoun in a direct address from the rest of the sentence. A noun or pronoun in a **direct address** is one that names or refers to the person addressed.

Examples:

John, this room is a mess!
This room**, John,** is a disgrace!
Your room needs to be more organized**, John**.

Commas are used to separate an appositive from the rest of the sentence. An **appositive** is a word or words that give the reader more information about a previous noun or pronoun.

Examples:

My teacher, **Ms. Wright,** gave us a test.
Thomas Edison, **the inventor of the lightbulb,** was an interesting man.

Place commas where needed in these sentences. Then write **appositive** or **direct address** on the line to explain why the commas were used.

1. Melissa do you know the answer? _____

2. John the local football hero led the parade through town. _____

3. Cancun a Mexican city is a favorite vacation destination. _____

4. Please help me move the chair Gail. _____

5. My great-grandfather an octogenarian has witnessed many events.

   _____

6. The president of the company Madison Fagan addressed his workers.

   _____

7. My favorite book *Anne of Green Gables* is a joy to read. _____

8. Your painting Andre shows great talent. _____

Adding and Subtracting Like Fractions

A **fraction** is a number that names part of a whole.

Examples of fractions are $\frac{1}{2}$ and $\frac{1}{3}$.

Like fractions have the same **denominator**, or bottom number. Examples of like fractions are $\frac{1}{4}$ and $\frac{3}{4}$.

To add or subtract fractions, the denominators must be the same. Add or subtract only the **numerators**, the numbers above the line in fractions.

Example:

numerators
denominators $\quad \frac{5}{8} - \frac{1}{8} = \frac{4}{8}$

$$\frac{5}{8} \qquad - \qquad \frac{1}{8} \qquad = \qquad \frac{4}{8}$$

Add or subtract these fractions.

$\frac{6}{12} - \frac{3}{12} =$	$\frac{4}{9} + \frac{1}{9} =$	$\frac{1}{3} + \frac{1}{3} =$	$\frac{5}{11} + \frac{4}{11} =$
$\frac{3}{5} - \frac{1}{5} =$	$\frac{5}{6} - \frac{2}{6} =$	$\frac{3}{4} - \frac{2}{4} =$	$\frac{5}{10} + \frac{3}{10} =$
$\frac{3}{8} + \frac{2}{8} =$	$\frac{1}{7} + \frac{4}{7} =$	$\frac{2}{20} + \frac{15}{20} =$	$\frac{11}{15} - \frac{9}{15} =$

Color the part of each pizza that equals the given fraction.

$$\frac{2}{4} \qquad + \qquad \frac{1}{4} \qquad = \qquad \frac{3}{4}$$

  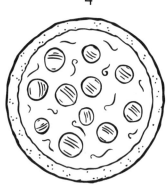

Adding and Subtracting Unlike Fractions

Unlike fractions have different denominators. Examples of unlike fractions are $\frac{1}{4}$ and $\frac{2}{5}$. To add or subtract fractions, the denominators must be the same.

Example:

Step 1: Make the denominators the same by finding the least common denominator. The LCD of a pair of fractions is the same as the least common multiple (LCM) of their denominators.

$$\frac{1}{3} + \frac{1}{4} =$$

Multiples of 3 are 3, 6, 9, **12**, 15.

Multiples of 4 are 4, 8, **12**, 16.

LCM (and LCD) = 12

Step 2: Multiply by a number that will give the LCD. The numerator and denominator must be multiplied by the same number.

A. $\frac{1}{3} \times \frac{4}{4} = \frac{4}{12}$ **B.** $\frac{1}{4} \times \frac{3}{3} = \frac{3}{12}$

Step 3: Add the fractions. $\frac{1}{3} + \frac{1}{4} = \frac{4}{12} + \frac{3}{12} = \frac{7}{12}$

Follow the above steps to add or subtract unlike fractions. Write the LCM.

$\frac{2}{4} + \frac{3}{8} =$ LCM - _____	$\frac{3}{6} + \frac{1}{3} =$ LCM - _____	$\frac{4}{5} - \frac{1}{4} =$ LCM - _____
$\frac{2}{3} + \frac{2}{9} =$ LCM - _____	$\frac{4}{7} - \frac{2}{14} =$ LCM - _____	$\frac{7}{12} - \frac{2}{4} =$ LCM - _____

The basketball team ordered two pizzas. They left $\frac{1}{3}$ of one and $\frac{1}{4}$ of the other. How much pizza was left?

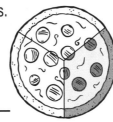 

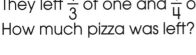

Fractions: Addition and Subtraction

Identify the shaded part.

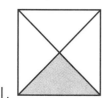 

1. _____ 2. _____ 3. _____

Complete. Reduce to lowest terms.

4. $\dfrac{2}{3} = \dfrac{}{15}$ 5. $\dfrac{9}{12} = \underline{\quad}$ 6. $\dfrac{18}{54} = \underline{\quad}$

Compare using > or <.

7. $\dfrac{13}{27} \qquad \dfrac{12}{27}$ 8. $\dfrac{5}{6} \qquad \dfrac{3}{4}$ 9. $2\dfrac{3}{4} \qquad \dfrac{13}{4}$

Add or subtract.

10. $\dfrac{1}{5} + \dfrac{2}{5} = $ _____   11. $\dfrac{3}{8} - \dfrac{2}{8} = $ _____   12. $\dfrac{3}{4} + \dfrac{1}{2} = $ _____

13. $\dfrac{7}{8} - \dfrac{3}{4} = $ _____   14. $5\dfrac{1}{2} + 2\dfrac{1}{2} = $ _____   15. $2\dfrac{1}{8} - 1\dfrac{5}{8} = $ _____

16. $\dfrac{21}{5} - \dfrac{21}{10} = $ _____   17. $5\dfrac{1}{6} + 3\dfrac{2}{4} = $ _____   18. $\dfrac{5}{3} + \dfrac{2}{5} = $ _____

Draw a model to show each fraction.

19. $3\dfrac{1}{4}$ 20. $\dfrac{10}{3}$

Tic-Tac-Toe Fractions

Solve each problem. Then, look in the boxes below for the answers to the problems. Draw an **X** over each correct answer. Circle the other numbers.

1. $\dfrac{7}{8} - \dfrac{5}{8} =$ _____

2. $\dfrac{8}{10} - \dfrac{3}{10} =$ _____

3. $2\dfrac{1}{2} - \dfrac{1}{2} =$ _____

4. $\dfrac{7}{9} - \dfrac{4}{9} =$ _____

5. $\dfrac{5}{3} - \dfrac{4}{3} =$ _____

6. $\dfrac{6}{7} - \dfrac{3}{7} =$ _____

7. $\dfrac{4}{5} - \dfrac{2}{5} =$ _____

8. $\dfrac{9}{11} - \dfrac{5}{11} =$ _____

9. $\dfrac{11}{12} - \dfrac{5}{12} =$ _____

10. $\dfrac{11}{6} - \dfrac{7}{6} =$ _____

11. $\dfrac{3}{4} - \dfrac{1}{4} =$ _____

12. $\dfrac{3}{3} - \dfrac{1}{3} =$ _____

$\dfrac{5}{8}$	$\dfrac{1}{7}$	$\dfrac{1}{3}$
$\dfrac{2}{4}$	$\dfrac{5}{10}$	$\dfrac{3}{4}$
2	$\dfrac{3}{5}$	$\dfrac{2}{9}$

$\dfrac{4}{5}$	$\dfrac{3}{7}$	$\dfrac{1}{9}$
$\dfrac{5}{6}$	$\dfrac{6}{12}$	$\dfrac{3}{11}$
$\dfrac{2}{5}$	$\dfrac{2}{3}$	$\dfrac{4}{6}$

$\dfrac{1}{5}$	$\dfrac{6}{7}$	$\dfrac{2}{8}$
$\dfrac{3}{8}$	$\dfrac{4}{11}$	$\dfrac{6}{12}$
$\dfrac{2}{7}$	$\dfrac{1}{10}$	$\dfrac{3}{9}$

Sandwich Solutions

Solve the following subtraction problems to find out who invented the sandwich. Write the letter next to each problem above its answer at the bottom.

A. $\frac{3}{5} - \frac{1}{4} =$ _____   A. $\frac{5}{6} - \frac{1}{3} =$ _____   E. $\frac{9}{16} - \frac{1}{4} =$ _____

I. $\frac{7}{10} - \frac{3}{5} =$ _____   D. $\frac{1}{2} - \frac{5}{12} =$ _____   C. $\frac{7}{8} - \frac{3}{4} =$ _____

W. $\frac{13}{18} - \frac{1}{6} =$ _____   N. $\frac{2}{3} - \frac{1}{12} =$ _____   H. $\frac{19}{20} - \frac{4}{5} =$ _____

F. $\frac{18}{25} - \frac{2}{5} =$ _____   L. $\frac{8}{9} - \frac{1}{6} =$ _____   R. $\frac{5}{8} - \frac{3}{16} =$ _____

O. $\frac{4}{5} - \frac{2}{3} =$ _____   S. $\frac{1}{7} - \frac{1}{14} =$ _____

$\frac{5}{16}$	$\frac{7}{20}$	$\frac{7}{16}$	$\frac{13}{18}$	$\frac{2}{15}$	$\frac{8}{25}$	$\frac{1}{14}$	$\frac{1}{2}$	$\frac{7}{12}$	$\frac{1}{12}$	$\frac{5}{9}$	$\frac{1}{10}$	$\frac{1}{8}$	$\frac{3}{20}$

Week 21 Skills

Subject	Skill	Multi-Sensory Learning Activities
Reading and Language Arts	Review commas.	• Complete Practice Pages 226 and 227. • Give your child 10–15 sentences that contain direct address and introductory words, omitting all commas. Have your child add commas as needed.
	Understand and identify homographs, or words that have the same spelling but different meanings and pronunciations.	• Complete Practice Pages 228–230. • Read *The War with Grandpa* by Robert Kimmel Smith. As you and your child are reading, make lists of any homographs you find. At the end of the book, compare lists to see whose is longer.
Math	Subtract fractions with like and unlike denominators.	• Complete Practice Pages 231 and 232. • Ask your child to explain why subtracting tenths and thirds is a little more difficult than subtracting thirds and thirds.
	Subtract mixed numbers.	• Complete Practice Pages 233 and 234. • Use models with the same fractional parts to demonstrate subtraction with mixed numbers (for example, all fourths or all thirds). First, ask your child to model the number $2\frac{3}{4}$. Then, have him or her remove the fraction $1\frac{2}{4}$ and determine the difference. Repeat several times, each time with different fractions.

Using Commas

Use commas to set off an **appositive**, a noun or phrase that explains or identifies the noun it follows.
Example: *Jack, the janitor, walked down the hall.*

Use commas to separate words or phrases in a **series**.
Example: *He ate the apple, the peach, and the plum.*

Use commas after **introductory** words or phrases.
Examples: *Yes, I'm going to the fair.*
By the way, did you bring a camera?

Use commas to set off a **noun of address,** the name of the person being addressed or spoken to.
Example: *Caroline, will you come with me?*

Use commas to set off **interrupting** words or phrases.
Example: *He was, as you know, an actor before he was elected.*

Add commas to the sentences where they are needed. On each line, explain why you added the comma by writing **appositive**, **series**, **introductory**, **noun of address** or **interrupting**.

1. Maryanne the new girl in school is a very good cook. _____

2. My favorite snacks are red apples pretzels and popcorn. _____

3. My skills however do not include cooking. _____

4. I know Sally that you love to cook. _____

5. That was in my opinion the best meal ever served. _____

6. After they finished the books Tom and Larry wrote the report. _____

7. Thomas Edison an inventor had failures before each success. _____

8. Pete our best soccer player won't be here for the big game. _____

9. No I won't be seeing the movie. _____

10. The coating on the pecans was sweet sugary and crisp. _____

11. That is if I'm not mistaken my yellow and green pencil. _____

12. Sam would you please pass me my pen? _____

Writing: Using Commas Correctly

A comma tells a reader where to pause when reading a sentence. Use commas when combining two or more complete sentences with a joining word.

Examples: We raked the leaves, and **we put them into bags.**
Brian dressed quickly, but **he still missed the school bus.**

Do not use commas if you are not combining complete sentences.

Examples: We raked the leaves and put them into bags.
Brian dressed quickly but still missed the school bus.

If either part of the sentence does not have both a subject and a verb, do not use a comma.

Read each sentence below and decide whether or not it needs a comma. If it does, rewrite the sentence, placing the comma correctly. If it doesn't, write **O.K.** on the line.

1. The cat stretched lazily and walked out of the room.

    _____

2. I could use the money to buy a new shirt or I could go to the movies.

    _____

3. My sister likes pizza but she doesn't like spaghetti.

    _____

4. Mom mixed the batter and poured it into the pan.

    _____

5. The teacher passed out the tests and she told us to write our names on them.

    _____

6. The car squealed its tires and took off out of the parking lot.

    _____

7. The snow fell heavily and we knew the schools would be closed the next day.

    _____

8. The batter hit the ball and it flew over the fence.

    _____

Homographs

Homographs are words that have the same spelling but different meanings and pronunciations.

pres´ent	n.	a gift
pre sent´	v.	to introduce or offer to view
rec´ord	n.	written or official evidence
re cord´	v.	to keep an account of
wind	n.	air in motion
wind	v.	to tighten the spring by turning a key
wound	n.	an injury in which the skin is broken
wound	v.	past tense of wind

Write the definition for the bold word in each sentence.

1. I would like to **present** our new student council president, Mindy Hall.

   _____

2. The store made a **record** of all my payments.

   _____

3. **Wind** the music box to hear the song.

   _____

4. His **wound** was healing quickly.

   _____

5. The **wind** knocked over my bicycle.

   _____

6. I bought her a birthday **present** with my allowance.

   _____

Present a Present

compact
conduct
conflict
content
contest
convict
impact
insult
object
permit
present
protest
rebel
record
refund
refuse
subject
suspect

Fill in the blank with the correct homograph. Place an accent mark on the accented syllable of each homograph.

1. They had to _____ the _____ for committing another terrible crime.

2. A young _____ will often _____ against parents or teachers.

3. I am _____ with the _____ of my research paper.

4. The nasty _____ used to _____ him made him feel bad.

5. I will _____ myself to this _____ .

6. Someday, my parents will _____ me to get my driver's _____ .

7. The singer hopes to _____ a hit _____ .

8. My mom will _____ if I throw this _____ .

9. We are expected to _____ ourselves with self-control and overall good _____ .

10. I will _____ her with a lovely _____ .

11. I _____ to touch that stinky _____ .

12. I _____ he is the guilty _____ .

Fill in the blanks with the remaining homographs. Place an accent mark on the appropriate syllable of each homograph.

Verbs: _____   Nouns: _____

_____   _____

_____   _____

_____   _____

_____   _____

Watch for Grandpa's Watch

Each "watch" in the title of this activity has a different meaning. One means "to look for," and the other means "timepiece." Write two meanings for each of the words below.

	Meaning 1	Meaning 2
1. spring		
2. run		
3. ruler		
4. duck		
5. suit		
6. cold		
7. fall		
8. tire		
9. rose		
10. face		
11. train		
12. play		
13. foot		
14. pen		
15. box		
16. dice		
17. fly		
18. seal		
19. bowl		
20. ride		

Choose some of the above words and illustrate both meanings on another sheet of paper.

COMPLETE YEAR GRADE 5

Subtracting Fractions

Subtracting fractions is very similar to adding them in that the denominators must be the same. If the denominators are different, use equivalent fractions.

Examples:

$$\frac{3}{4}$$
$$-\frac{1}{4}$$
$$\overline{\frac{2}{4}} = \frac{1}{2}$$

$$\begin{array}{r} 2 \times 8 = \frac{16}{40} \\ 5 \times 8 = \\ 1 \times 5 = \frac{5}{40} \\ -\ 8 \times 5 = \\ \hline \frac{11}{40} \end{array}$$

Adding and subtracting mixed numbers are also similar. Often, though, change the mixed numbers to improper fractions. If the denominators are different, use equivalent fractions.

Examples:

$$2\frac{3}{5} = \frac{13}{5}$$
$$-1\frac{4}{5} = \frac{9}{5}$$
$$\overline{\frac{4}{5}}$$

$$3\frac{3}{14} = \frac{45}{14} = \qquad = \frac{45}{14}$$
$$-2\frac{1}{7} = \frac{15 \times 2}{7 \times 2} = \frac{30}{14}$$
$$\overline{\frac{15}{14}} = 1\frac{1}{14}$$

Solve the following problems. Use equivalent fractions and improper fractions where necessary.

1. $\frac{6}{7}$
    $-\frac{5}{7}$

2. $1\frac{2}{9}$
    $-\ \frac{4}{9}$

3. $2\frac{3}{6}$
    $-\ \frac{4}{5}$

4. $\frac{3}{4}$
    $-\frac{1}{2}$

5. $2\frac{1}{3}$
    $-\ \frac{3}{4}$

6. Carol promised to weed the flower garden for $1\frac{1}{2}$ hours this morning. So far she has pulled weeds for $\frac{3}{4}$ of an hour. How much longer does she have to work?

7. Dil started out with $1\frac{1}{4}$ gallons of paint. He used $\frac{3}{8}$ gallon of the paint on his boat. How much paint is left?

8. A certain movie lasts $2\frac{1}{2}$ hours. Susan has already watched it for $1\frac{2}{3}$ hours. How much longer is the movie?

9. Bert didn't finish $\frac{1}{8}$ of the math problems on a test. He made mistakes on $\frac{1}{6}$ of the problems. The rest he answered correctly. What fraction of the problems did he answer correctly?

Fraction Frenzy

Subtract. Reduce your answers to lowest terms and write them here.

1. $\frac{3}{8}$
$-\frac{1}{4}$

2. $\frac{2}{5}$
$-\frac{2}{15}$

3. $\frac{3}{4}$
$-\frac{1}{12}$

4. $\frac{5}{6}$
$-\frac{1}{3}$

5. $\frac{3}{5}$
$-\frac{2}{10}$

6. $\frac{6}{7}$
$-\frac{3}{14}$

7. $\frac{5}{8}$
$-\frac{5}{16}$

8. $\frac{5}{10}$
$-\frac{2}{20}$

9. $\frac{2}{4}$
$-\frac{1}{12}$

10. $\frac{5}{15}$
$-\frac{1}{5}$

11. $\frac{7}{16}$
$-\frac{2}{8}$

12. $\frac{4}{9}$
$-\frac{1}{3}$

13. $\frac{5}{7}$
$-\frac{2}{14}$

14. $\frac{9}{10}$
$-\frac{2}{5}$

15. $\frac{2}{3}$
$-\frac{1}{9}$

16. $\frac{5}{8}$
$-\frac{1}{4}$

17. $\frac{2}{4}$
$-\frac{1}{2}$

18. $\frac{3}{6}$
$-\frac{1}{3}$

19. $\frac{1}{2}$
$-\frac{2}{8}$

20. $\frac{8}{9}$
$-\frac{3}{18}$

21. $\frac{6}{8}$
$-\frac{2}{16}$

22. $\frac{3}{4}$
$-\frac{5}{16}$

23. $\frac{7}{16}$
$-\frac{3}{8}$

24. $\frac{5}{6}$
$-\frac{2}{18}$

25. $\frac{7}{21}$
$-\frac{1}{7}$

26. $\frac{8}{24}$
$-\frac{2}{12}$

27. $\frac{5}{6}$
$-\frac{3}{16}$

28. $\frac{7}{10}$
$-\frac{1}{5}$

Subtracting Mixed Numbers

To subtract mixed numbers, first find the least common denominator. Reduce the answer to its lowest terms.

Subtract. Reduce to lowest terms.

Example:

$$6\frac{5}{8} \longrightarrow 6\frac{10}{16}$$
$$-\ 3\frac{4}{16} \longrightarrow -\ 3\frac{4}{16}$$
$$3\frac{6}{16} = 3\frac{6}{16}$$

$$2\frac{3}{7}$$
$$-\ 1\frac{1}{14}$$

$$7\frac{2}{3}$$
$$-\ 5\frac{1}{8}$$

$$6\frac{3}{4}$$
$$-\ 2\frac{3}{12}$$

$$9\frac{5}{12}$$
$$-\ 5\frac{9}{24}$$

$$5\frac{1}{2}$$
$$-\ 3\frac{1}{3}$$

$$7\frac{3}{8}$$
$$-\ 5\frac{1}{6}$$

$$8\frac{3}{8}$$
$$-\ 6\frac{5}{12}$$

$$11\frac{5}{6}$$
$$-\ 7\frac{1}{12}$$

$$9\frac{3}{5}$$
$$-\ 7\frac{1}{15}$$

$$4\frac{4}{5}$$
$$-\ 2\frac{1}{4}$$

$$9\frac{2}{3}$$
$$-\ 4\frac{1}{6}$$

$$14\frac{3}{8}$$
$$-\ 9\frac{3}{16}$$

The Rodriguez Farm has $9\frac{1}{2}$ acres of corn. The Johnson Farm has $7\frac{1}{3}$ acres of corn. How many more acres of corn does the Rodriguez Farm have? _____

COMPLETE YEAR GRADE 5

Subtracting Unlike Mixed Numbers

Example: $41\frac{2}{8} - 20\frac{2}{3}$

$41\frac{2}{8} - 20\frac{2}{3} = 41\frac{2(\times 3)}{8(\times 3)} - 20\frac{2(\times 8)}{3(\times 8)} = 41\frac{6}{24} - 20\frac{16}{24} = 40\frac{30}{24} - 20\frac{16}{24} =$

Subtract

Same

8, 16, ⑳
3, 6, 9, 12, 15, 18, 21, ㉔

$20\frac{14}{24} - 20\frac{7}{12}$

Steps:
1. Find the LCM of both denominators (24).
2. Multiply the numerator and denominator of each fraction by a number to arrive at the LCM.
3. When regrouping, borrow a whole number and write the fraction as an improper fraction.
4. Subtract whole numbers.
5. Subtract numerators.
6. Denominators stay the same.
7. Reduce your answer to lowest terms.

Subtract.

1. $24\frac{2}{9} - 11\frac{2}{3}$

2. $86\frac{1}{5} - 72\frac{7}{10}$

3. $44\frac{3}{8} - 26\frac{5}{6}$

4. $19\frac{1}{4} - 12\frac{2}{3}$

5. $17\frac{4}{5} - 8\frac{1}{4}$

6. $50\frac{2}{9} - 26\frac{1}{2}$

7. $10\frac{1}{2} - 3\frac{2}{3}$

8. $12\frac{1}{5} - 7\frac{2}{3}$

9. $28\frac{5}{12} - 11\frac{2}{3}$

Week 22 Skills

Subject	Skill	Multi-Sensory Learning Activities
Reading and Language Arts	Answer questions about texts to determine reading comprehension.	• Complete Practice Pages 236–240. • With your child, read *Baseball Saved Us*, a picture book by Ken Mochizuki. Ask questions to assess your child's comprehension. Have your child imagine what Shorty's life was like after camp and write a paragraph about it.
Math	Review subtracting fractions.	• Complete Practice Pages 241–244. • Have your child show you five wholes. Ask your child to take away one-half of one whole. Write the same problem on paper. Have your child "borrow" one whole from the five and make it a fraction with a like denominator ($\frac{2}{2}$). Then, your child can subtract the fractions.
Bonus: Science		• Canyons are deep valleys with steep sides cut through the land by the erosive forces of water and wind. A narrow canyon with steep sides is called a **gorge**. Have your child locate these canyons and gorges on a map: Bryce Canyon, Zion Canyon, Yellowstone, Grand Canyon, Kings Canyon, and Royal Gorge. Then, have your child look at photographs of these land formations and write about any differences he or she can see between canyons and gorges.

Comprehension: Old Gaelic Lullaby

A **Gaelic lullaby** is an ancient Irish or Scottish song some parents sing as they rock their babies to sleep.

Hush! The waves are rolling in,
White with foam, white with foam,
Father works amid the din,
But baby sleeps at home.

Hush! The winds roar hoarse and deep—
On they come, on they come!
Brother seeks the wandering sheep,
But baby sleeps at home.

Hush! The rain sweeps over the fields,
Where cattle roam, where cattle roam.
Sister goes to seek the cows,
But baby sleeps at home.

Answer these questions about the Gaelic lullaby.

1. What is Father doing while baby sleeps? _____

    _____

2. What is Brother doing? _____

    _____

3. What is Sister doing? _____

    _____

4. What do we assume Mother is doing? _____

    _____

5. Is it quiet or noisy while Father works?   ❑ quiet   ❑ noisy

6. Which is not mentioned in the poem?

    ❑ wind   ❑ sunshine   ❑ waves   ❑ rain

Comprehension: Pigs Are Particular

Have you ever wondered why pigs wallow in the mud? It's not because they are dirty animals. Pigs have no sweat glands. They can't sweat, so they roll in the mud to cool themselves. The next time you hear anyone who's hot say, "I'm sweating like a pig!" be sure to correct him or her. Humans can sweat, but pigs cannot.

Actually, pigs are particular about their pens. They are very clean animals. They prefer to sleep in clean, dry places. They move their bowels and empty their bladders in another area. They do not want to get their homes dirty.

Another misconception about pigs is that they are smooth. Only cartoon pigs are pink, smooth and shiny-looking. The skin of real pigs is covered with bristles—small, stiff hairs. Their bristles protect their tender skin. When pigs are slaughtered, their bristles are sometimes made into hair brushes or clothes brushes.

Female pigs are called sows. Sows have babies twice a year and give birth to 10 to 14 piglets at a time. The babies have a "gestation period" of 16 weeks before they are born. All the piglets together are called a "litter." Newborn piglets are on their tiny feet within a few minutes after birth. Can you guess why? They are hungrily looking for their mother's teats so they can get milk. As they nurse, piglets snuggle in close to their mother's belly to keep warm.

Answer these questions about pigs.

1. Why do pigs wallow in mud? _____

2. How long is the gestation period for pigs? _____

3. What are pig bristles used for? _____

4. Tell two reasons pigs are on their feet soon after they are born.

   1)_____ 2) _____

5. A female pig is called a

   ❑ bristle.   ❑ piglet.   ❑ sow.

6. Together, the newborn piglets are called a

   ❑ group.   ❑ family.   ❑ litter.

Main Idea

The **main idea** is the most important idea, or main point, in a sentence, paragraph or story.

Read the paragraphs below. For each paragraph, underline the sentence that tells the main idea.

Sometimes people think they have to choose between exercise and fun. For many people, it is more fun to watch television than to run 5 miles. Yet, if you don't exercise, your body gets soft and out of shape. You move more slowly. You may even think more slowly. But why do something that isn't fun? Well, there are many ways to exercise and have fun.

One family solved the exercise problem by using their TV. They hooked up the television to an electric generator. The generator was operated by an exercise bike. Anyone who wanted to watch TV had to ride the bike. The room with their television in it must have been quite a sight!

Think of the times when you are just "hanging out" with your friends. You go outside and jump rope, play ball, run races, and so on. Soon you are all laughing and having a good time. Many group activities can provide you with exercise and be fun, too.

Maybe there aren't enough kids around after school for group games. Perhaps you are by yourself. Then what? You can get plenty of exercise just by walking, biking or even dancing. In the morning, walk the long way to the bus. Ride your bike to and from school. Practice the newest dance by yourself. Before you know it, you will be the fittest dancer of all your friends!

Write other ideas you have for combining fun and exercise below.

_____

_____

_____

_____

_____

Recognizing Details: The Coldest Continent

Read the information about Antarctica. Then answer the questions.

Antarctica lies at the South Pole and is the coldest continent. It is without sunlight for months at a time. Even when the sun does shine, its angle is so slanted that the land receives little warmth. Temperatures often drop to 100 degrees below zero, and a fierce wind blows almost endlessly. Most of the land is covered by snow heaped thousands of feet deep. The snow is so heavy and tightly packed that it forms a great ice cap covering more than 95 percent of the continent.

Considering the conditions, it is no wonder there are no towns or cities in Antarctica. There is no permanent population at all, only small scientific research stations. Many teams of explorers and scientists have braved the freezing cold since Antarctica was sighted in 1820. Some have died in their effort, but a great deal of information has been learned about the continent.

From fossils, pieces of coal and bone samples, we know that Antarctica was not always an ice-covered land. Scientists believe that 200 million years ago it was connected to southern Africa, South America, Australia and India. Forests grew in warm swamps, and insects and reptiles thrived there. Today, there are animals that live in and around the waters that border the continent. In fact, the waters surrounding Antarctica contain more life than oceans in warmer areas of the world.

1. Where is Antarctica? _____

2. How much of the continent is covered by an ice cap? _____

3. When was Antarctica first sighted by explorers? _____

4. What clues indicate that Antarctica was not always an ice-covered land?

   _____

5. Is Antarctica another name for the North Pole?   Yes   No

Main Idea: Penguins

Read the information about penguins.

People are amused by the funny, duck-like waddle of penguins and by their appearance because they seem to be wearing little tuxedos. Penguins are among the best-liked animals on Earth, but are also a most misunderstood animal. People may have more wrong ideas about penguins than any other animal.

For example, many people are surprised to learn that penguins are really birds, not mammals. Penguins do not fly, but they do have feathers, and only birds have feathers. Also, like other birds, penguins build nests and their young hatch from eggs. Because of their unusual looks, though, you would never confuse them with any other bird!

Penguins are also thought of as symbols of the polar regions, but penguins do not live north of the equator, so you would not find a penguin on the North Pole. Penguins don't live at the South Pole, either. Only two of the seventeen **species** of penguins spend all of their lives on the frozen continent of Antarctica. You would be just as likely to see a penguin living on an island in a warm climate as in a cold area.

Draw an **X** on the blank for the correct answer.

1. The main idea is:

    _____ Penguins are among the best-liked animals on earth.

    _____ The penguin is a much misunderstood animal.

2. Penguins live

    _____ only at the North Pole.

    _____ only at the South Pole.

    _____ only south of the equator.

3. Based on the other words in the sentence, what is the correct definition of the word **species**?

    _____ number

    _____ bird

    _____ a distinct kind

4. List three ways penguins are like other birds.

    _____

Fun Facts

Some skyscrapers are so large that they have their own...

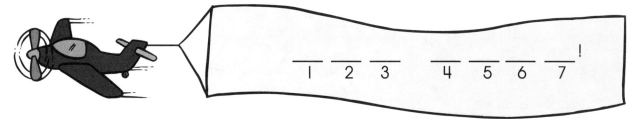

$$\overline{}_1 \ \overline{}_2 \ \overline{}_3 \quad \overline{}_4 \ \overline{}_5 \ \overline{}_6 \ \overline{}_7 !$$

To find the answer, follow the directions below.

Put an O above number 5 if the estimated difference between $13\frac{1}{3}$ and $5\frac{3}{7}$ is 8.

Put an A above number 6 if the estimated difference between $21\frac{5}{6}$ and $9\frac{4}{9}$ is 12.

Put an R above number 4 if the estimated difference between $16\frac{9}{20}$ and $13\frac{11}{15}$ is 3.

Put a B above number 1 if the estimated difference between $8\frac{3}{5}$ and $3\frac{7}{12}$ is 6.

Put a C above number 4 if the estimated difference between $25\frac{7}{20}$ and $13\frac{7}{12}$ is 11.

Put an E above number 7 if the estimated difference between $32\frac{7}{15}$ and $14\frac{9}{16}$ is 17.

Put a D above number 3 if the estimated difference between $18\frac{1}{3}$ and $11\frac{4}{13}$ is 2.

Put an I above number 2 if the estimated difference between $19\frac{7}{10}$ and $9\frac{6}{11}$ is 10.

Put a P above number 3 if the estimated difference between $58\frac{5}{12}$ and $42\frac{3}{10}$ is 16.

Put a D above number 6 if the estimated difference between $30\frac{13}{20}$ and $19\frac{7}{18}$ is 12.

Put an L above number 1 if the estimated difference between $11\frac{5}{7}$ and $5\frac{2}{5}$ is 6.

Put a Z above number 1 if the estimated difference between $16\frac{3}{8}$ and $9\frac{3}{7}$ is 7.

Fractions

Subtract. Reduce your answers to lowest terms and write them here. The first one has been done for you.

1. $5 \quad 4\frac{4}{4}$
   $-\frac{3}{4} \quad -\frac{3}{4}$
   $\quad\quad 4\frac{1}{4}$

2. 8
   $-\frac{7}{8}$

3. 4
   $-\frac{3}{6}$

4. 10
   $-\frac{3}{8}$

5. 14
   $-\frac{2}{5}$

6. 11
   $-\frac{7}{9}$

7. 4
   $-\frac{3}{5}$

8. 7
   $-\frac{5}{8}$

9. 6
   $-\frac{2}{4}$

10. 12
    $-\frac{3}{6}$

11. 9
    $-\frac{5}{8}$

12. 3
    $-\frac{6}{10}$

13. 7
    $-\frac{3}{4}$

14. 40
    $-\frac{3}{7}$

15. 5
    $-\frac{2}{3}$

16. 8
    $-\frac{5}{9}$

17. 11
    $-\frac{6}{12}$

18. 4
    $-\frac{3}{8}$

19. 6
    $-\frac{5}{7}$

20. 9
    $-\frac{3}{4}$

21. 12
    $-\frac{5}{9}$

22. 4
    $-\frac{6}{11}$

23. 7
    $-\frac{5}{10}$

24. 32
    $-\frac{5}{7}$

25. 25
    $-\frac{3}{4}$

26. 20
    $-\frac{5}{8}$

27. 5
    $-\frac{3}{6}$

28. 8
    $-\frac{2}{5}$

COMPLETE YEAR GRADE 5

A Trip to the Ocean

Maria's girls' club earned enough money from their cookie sale to go on a camping trip by the ocean. Read about their trip. Write your answers in complete sentences.

1. The bus started with $6\frac{1}{2}$ gallons of gasoline. When the driver added $9\frac{1}{2}$ more gallons of gasoline, how much gasoline did the bus have in it?

    _____

2. The girls and their leaders stopped for a picnic after driving $58\frac{1}{5}$ miles. After the picnic, they drove another $43\frac{4}{5}$ miles before reaching the ocean. How far were they from home?

    _____

3. Before leaving home, the girls made sandwiches for their lunch. They had $7\frac{1}{2}$ tuna sandwiches, $4\frac{1}{4}$ cheese sandwiches, $2\frac{3}{4}$ peanut butter sandwiches and $5\frac{1}{2}$ beef sandwiches. How many total sandwiches did they bring?

    _____

4. The leader cut a watermelon into 16 slices for lunch. The girls ate 8 of the slices. What fraction of the watermelon did they eat?

    _____

5. When they arrived, they took $1\frac{1}{3}$ hours to set up the tents. They spent another $\frac{2}{3}$ hour getting their bedrolls ready. How long did they work before they could play in the ocean?

    _____

6. The girls swam and played in the water for $1\frac{3}{4}$ hours. Then, they sat in the sun for $\frac{3}{4}$ hour. How many hours did they play and sunbathe?

    _____

7. After dinner, they had a campfire. First, they sang for $1\frac{1}{3}$ hours. Then, they told ghost stories for $\frac{2}{3}$ hour. If they put out the fire and went to sleep at 10:30 P.M., what time did they begin the campfire?

    _____

8. The next morning, $\frac{3}{8}$ of the girls went fishing. The rest of the girls hunted for shells. If there were 8 girls altogether,
    how many hunted for shells? _____

    How many went fishing? _____

Research Time

Mr. Write-A-Lot assigned research papers to his class. He divided the class into two groups. One person from each group was responsible for each part of the research process.

1. Marisha and John each found several books on their subjects. It took Marisha $2\frac{1}{2}$ hours to skim through her stack of books, and it took John $1\frac{3}{4}$ hours to look through his. How much longer did it take Marisha?

2. Neal and Geraldo were working on note cards. Neal was able to complete his in $48\frac{4}{6}$ minutes, and it took Geraldo $51\frac{3}{8}$ minutes to finish his. How much longer did Geraldo take?

3. Bobby and Gordon found it difficult to write outlines. It took Bobby $38\frac{2}{3}$ minutes and Gordon $36\frac{3}{4}$ minutes. How many more minutes did it take Bobby?

4. Anita finished the first draft of her report in 48 minutes, while it took Pablo $51\frac{3}{8}$ minutes to write his. How much longer did it take Pablo?

5. The final draft of their reports went smoothly for Katie and Laura. Katie zipped hers off in $18\frac{3}{4}$ minutes, and Laura's took $21\frac{1}{8}$ minutes. How much longer did Laura's final draft take?

Extension: Subtract $2\frac{7}{8}$ from . . .

a. 4

b. $5\frac{1}{8}$

c. $8\frac{7}{8}$

d. $6\frac{3}{8}$

e. $7\frac{5}{8}$

f. $9\frac{6}{8}$

COMPLETE YEAR GRADE 5

Week 23 Skills

Subject	Skill	Multi-Sensory Learning Activities
Reading and Language Arts	Use editing marks to proofread and make corrections.	• Complete Practice Pages 246–248. • Copy an interesting article or essay as one long paragraph. Have your child read the article carefully. Then, ask your child to divide the piece into paragraphs. Show your child how to use the paragraph sign to show where a new paragraph should begin.
Math	Multiply fractions.	• Complete Practice Pages 249–251. • Have your child draw a 3x4 grid of 12 boxes. Ask your child to shade different numbers of columns and rows to show these multiplication problems: $\frac{1}{4} \times \frac{1}{3}$, $\frac{1}{2} \times \frac{2}{3}$ and $\frac{1}{4} \times \frac{2}{3}$.
	Multiply mixed numbers.	• Complete Practice Pages 252 and 253. • Apply fractions to real-life situations. For example, say, "What is $\frac{3}{4}$ of $1\frac{1}{2}$ decks of cards?"
	Divide fractions by whole numbers.	• Complete Practice Page 254. • Write several problems for your child in which he or she must divide fractions by whole numbers. Then, write the numbers 1–9 and the symbols ÷ and x on small slips of paper. In the center of a large piece of paper, draw two horizontal lines. Ask your child to move the numbers and symbols above, below, and between the lines to act out solving the problems.

Editing

Editors and proofreaders use certain marks to note the changes that need to be made. In addition to circling spelling errors and fixing capitalization mistakes, editors and proofreaders also use the following marks to indicate other mistakes that need to be corrected.

~~the~~	Delete.	∧	Insert a comma.
a̲	Capitalize.	˅	Insert an apostrophe.
In#this	Insert a space.	˅	Insert quotation marks.
i̲s̲∧	Insert a word.	⊙	Insert a period.

Use editing marks to correct the errors in these sentences. Then write the sentences correctly on the lines.

1. Mr. Ramsey was a man who liked to do nothing

   _____

2. Lili a young hawaiian girl, liked to swim in the sea.

   _____

3. Youngsters who play baseballalways have a favorite player.

   _____

4. Too many people said, That movie was terrible."

   _____

5. I didn't wantto go to the movie with sally

   _____

6. Prince charles always wants to play polo

   _____

7. The little boy's name was albert leonard longfellow

   _____

Editing

⌒not⌒is⌒	Flip the words around; transpose.
wa⌒l⌒ut	Flip letters around; transpose.
¶That was when Peter began talking.	Indent the paragraph or start a new paragraph.
with you. The movie we went to see was good.	Move text down to line below.
There were no people there. Jason thought we should go.	Move text up to line above.

Use editing marks to edit this story.

The Fallen Log

There was once a log on the floor of a very damp and eerie forest two men

came upon the log and sat down for a rest. these two men, leroy and larry,

did not know that someone could hear every word they said. "I'm so

tired, moaned larry, as he began unlacing his heavy hikingboots. "and my feet

hurt, too."

"Quit complaining" friend his said. We've got miles to walk

before we'll find the cave with the hidden treasure. besides,

if you think you're tired at look feet my. with that he kicked

off his tennis shoe and discovered a very red big toe. "i think

i won't be able to go any farther.

"Sh-h-h, already!" the two men heard a voice. "enough

about feet, enough!" Larry and Leroy began loking around

them. theycouldn't see anyone, though. "I'm in hree the voice

said hoarsely.

Editing

Use editing marks to edit the continuing story of Larry and Leroy.

Larry and Leroy

larry and leroy jumped up from the log as soon as they realized that they were sitting on something that had a voice. "Hey, that was fast, said the voice. "How did you figure out where i was?"

By this time larry and leroy felt a little silly. Theycertainly didn't want to talk to a log. they looked at each other and then back at the log again. together they turned around and started walking down the path that had brought them to this point in the forest. "Hey were are you going?" the voice called.

"Well, i-i-i don't know," Larry replied, wondering if he sould be answering a log. "Who are you?"

"I'm a tiny elf who has been lostin this tree foryears," said the voice.

"Sure you are," replied larr. with that he and lroy began running for their lives.

Multiplying Fractions

To multiply fractions, follow these steps:

$\frac{1}{2}$ x $\frac{3}{4}$ = **Step 1:** Multiply the numerators.   1 x 3 = $\frac{3}{8}$

           = **Step 2:** Multiply the denominators.   2 x 4 =

When multiplying a fraction by a whole number, first change the whole number to a fraction.

Example:

$\frac{1}{2}$ x 8 = $\frac{1}{2}$ x $\frac{8}{1}$ = $\frac{8}{2}$ = 4   reduced to lowest terms

Multiply. Reduce your answers to lowest terms.

$\frac{3}{4}$ x $\frac{1}{6}$ =	$\frac{1}{2}$ x $\frac{5}{8}$ =	$\frac{2}{3}$ x $\frac{1}{6}$ =	$\frac{2}{3}$ x $\frac{1}{2}$ =
$\frac{5}{6}$ x 4 =	$\frac{3}{8}$ x $\frac{1}{16}$ =	$\frac{1}{5}$ x 5 =	$\frac{7}{8}$ x $\frac{3}{4}$ =
$\frac{7}{11}$ x $\frac{1}{3}$ =	$\frac{2}{9}$ x $\frac{9}{4}$ =	$\frac{1}{3}$ x $\frac{1}{3}$ x $\frac{1}{3}$ =	$\frac{1}{8}$ x $\frac{1}{4}$ x $\frac{1}{2}$ =

Jennifer has 10 pets. Two-fifths of the pets are cats, one-half are fish and one-tenth are dogs. How many of each pet does she have?

_____

_____

_____

Multiplying Fractions

To multiply two fractions, multiply the numerators and then multiply the denominators. If necessary, change the answer to its lowest term.

Examples: $\frac{3}{4} \times \frac{2}{3} = \frac{6}{12} = \frac{1}{2}$ $\frac{1}{8} \times \frac{4}{5} = \frac{4}{40} = \frac{1}{10}$

To multiply a whole number by a fraction, first write the whole number as a fraction (with 1 as the denominator). Then multiply as above. You may need to change an improper fraction to a mixed number.

Examples: $\frac{2}{3} \times \frac{4}{1} = \frac{8}{3} = 2\frac{2}{3}$ $\frac{3}{7} \times \frac{6}{1} = \frac{18}{7} = 2\frac{4}{7}$

Solve the following problems, writing answers in their lowest terms.

1. $\frac{1}{5} \times \frac{2}{3} =$ 2. $\frac{1}{3} \times \frac{4}{7} =$ 3. $\frac{2}{8} \times 3 =$ 4. $\frac{2}{6} \times \frac{1}{2} =$

5. Tim lost $\frac{1}{8}$ of his marbles. If he had 56 marbles, how many did he lose?

6. Jeff is making $\frac{2}{3}$ of a recipe for spaghetti sauce. How much will he need of each ingredient below?

   $1\frac{1}{4}$ cups water =   2 cups tomato paste =

   $\frac{3}{4}$ teaspoon oregano = $4\frac{1}{2}$ teaspoons salt =

7. Carrie bought 2 dozen donuts and asked for $\frac{3}{4}$ of them to be chocolate. How many were chocolate?

8. Christy let her hair grow 14 inches long and then had $\frac{1}{4}$ of it cut off. How much was cut off?

9. Kurt has finished $\frac{7}{8}$ of 40 math problems. How many has he done?

10. If Sherryl's cat eats $\frac{2}{3}$ can of cat food every day, how many cans should Sherryl buy for a week?

Puzzling Fractions

Multiply to solve the problems.

$7 \times \dfrac{1}{5} =$ _____ $9 \times \dfrac{1}{10} =$ _____ $8 \times \dfrac{1}{8} =$ _____ $8 \times \dfrac{1}{7} =$ _____

$7 \times \dfrac{1}{11} =$ _____ $9 \times \dfrac{1}{3} =$ _____ $3 \times \dfrac{1}{6} =$ _____ $12 \times \dfrac{1}{5} =$ _____

$\dfrac{1}{5} \times 4 =$ _____ $\dfrac{1}{3} \times 9 =$ _____ $\dfrac{1}{5} \times 20 =$ _____ $\dfrac{1}{6} \times 12 =$ _____

$\dfrac{1}{10} \times \dfrac{1}{100} =$ _____ $\dfrac{1}{6} \times \dfrac{1}{10} =$ _____ $\dfrac{1}{12} \times \dfrac{1}{3} =$ _____ $\dfrac{1}{6} \times \dfrac{1}{6} =$ _____

$\dfrac{1}{9} \times \dfrac{1}{8} =$ _____ $\dfrac{1}{9} \times \dfrac{1}{10} =$ _____ $\dfrac{1}{10} \times \dfrac{1}{10} =$ _____ $\dfrac{1}{20} \times \dfrac{1}{5} =$ _____

$8 \times \dfrac{1}{10} =$ _____ $\dfrac{1}{5} \times \dfrac{1}{8} =$ _____ $\dfrac{1}{6} \times \dfrac{1}{7} =$ _____ $\dfrac{1}{100} \times \dfrac{1}{100} =$ _____

$\dfrac{1}{9} \times 9 =$ _____ $\dfrac{1}{8} \times 7 =$ _____ $\dfrac{1}{7} \times 6 =$ _____ $12 \times \dfrac{1}{4} =$ _____

$\dfrac{1}{15} \times \dfrac{1}{13} =$ _____ $\dfrac{1}{3} \times \dfrac{1}{7} =$ _____ $\dfrac{1}{8} \times 3 =$ _____ $\dfrac{1}{7} \times 21 =$ _____

Multiplying Mixed Numbers

Multiply mixed numbers by first changing them to improper fractions. Always reduce your answers to lowest terms.

Example:

$$2\frac{1}{3} \times 1\frac{1}{8} = \frac{7}{3} \times \frac{9}{8} = \frac{63}{24} = 2\frac{15}{24} = 2\frac{5}{8}$$

Multiply. Reduce to lowest terms.

$4\frac{1}{4} \times 2\frac{1}{5} =$	$1\frac{1}{3} \times 3\frac{1}{4} =$	$1\frac{1}{9} \times 3\frac{3}{5} =$
$1\frac{6}{7} \times 4\frac{1}{2} =$	$2\frac{3}{4} \times 2\frac{3}{5} =$	$4\frac{2}{3} \times 3\frac{1}{7} =$
$6\frac{2}{5} \times 2\frac{1}{8} =$	$3\frac{1}{7} \times 4\frac{5}{8} =$	$7\frac{3}{8} \times 2\frac{1}{9} =$

Sunnyside Farm has two barns with 25 stalls in each barn. Cows use $\frac{3}{5}$ of the stalls, and horses use the rest.

How many stalls are for cows? _____

How many are for horses? _____

(Hint: First, find how many total stalls are in the

two barns.)

　　　　　　　　　　　　　　　　　　COMPLETE YEAR GRADE 5

Multiplication With Mixed Numbers

When multiplying by a mixed number, change the mixed number to an improper fraction. Cancel if possible. Multiply the numerators, then the denominators. Write the improper fractions as mixed numbers.

Multiply

Example A: $\frac{3}{4} \times 1\frac{1}{2} = \frac{3}{4} \times \frac{3}{2} = \frac{9}{8} = 1\frac{1}{8}$

Multiply

Multiply

Example B: $2\frac{4}{7} \times \frac{5}{9} = \frac{\overset{2}{\cancel{18}}}{7} \times \frac{5}{\cancel{9}} = \frac{10}{7} = 1\frac{3}{7}$

Multiply

Multiply.

1. $\frac{1}{2} \times 8\frac{3}{4} = \frac{1}{2} \times \frac{35}{4} =$

2. $5\frac{1}{3} \times \frac{6}{7} =$

3. $\frac{11}{12} \times 11\frac{1}{3} =$

4. $7\frac{1}{2} \times \frac{8}{9} =$

5. $\frac{2}{5} \times 2\frac{1}{12} =$

6. $8\frac{2}{3} \times \frac{1}{4} =$

Invert and Multiply

Solve the problems. Reduce
your answers to lowest terms.

1. $\dfrac{1}{5} \div 3$

2. $\dfrac{5}{7} \div 15$

3. $\dfrac{7}{8} \div 21$

4. $\dfrac{3}{5} \div 12$

5. $\dfrac{3}{7} \div 6$

6. $\dfrac{3}{8} \div 6$

7. $\dfrac{5}{6} \div 10$

8. $\dfrac{5}{6} \div 15$

9. $\dfrac{7}{10} \div 2$

10. $\dfrac{7}{8} \div 14$

11. $\dfrac{7}{9} \div 7$

12. $\dfrac{1}{4} \div 3$

Week 24 Skills

Subject	Skill	Multi-Sensory Learning Activities
Reading and Language Arts	Understand the author's purpose to inform, persuade, or entertain.	• Complete Practice Pages 256 and 257. • Look at each page of a magazine together with your child. Have your child identify whether the page was written to entertain, inform, or persuade.
	Practice persuasive writing.	• Complete Practice Pages 258 and 259. • Ask your child to write a persuasive paragraph about recycling. Encourage your child to form an opinion about recycling and write as many arguments as possible trying to persuade others to feel the same way.
Math	Divide fractions.	• Complete Practice Pages 260–263. • Ask your child to find a recipe to prepare for dinner. Challenge him or her to divide the ingredients to make the right number of servings for your family members. For each ingredient, which fraction of the package will be used?
	Divide whole numbers by fractions.	• Complete Practice Page 264. • Ask your child to think about what it means to divide a number by a fraction and think of a real-life example. For instance, dividing a one-hour chore into $\frac{1}{4}$-hour segments yields four segments.

Author's Purpose

Authors write to fulfill one of three purposes: to **inform**, to **entertain** or to **persuade**.

Authors who write to inform are providing facts for the reader in an informational context.

Examples: Encyclopedia entries and newspaper articles

Authors who write to entertain are hoping to provide enjoyment for the reader.

Examples: Funny stories and comics

Authors who write to persuade are trying to convince the reader to believe as they believe.

Examples: Editorials and opinion essays

Read each paragraph. Write **inform**, **entertain** or **persuade** on the line to show the author's purpose.

1. The whooping crane is a migratory bird. At one time, this endangered bird was almost extinct. These large white cranes are characterized by red faces and trumpeting calls. Through protection of both the birds and their habitats, the whooping crane is slowly increasing in number.

   _____

2. It is extremely important that all citizens place bird feeders in their yards and keep them full for the winter. Birds that spend the winter in this area are in danger of starving due to lack of food. It is every citizen's responsibility to ensure the survival of the birds.

   _____

3. Imagine being able to hibernate like a bear each winter! Wouldn't it be great to eat to your heart's content all fall? Then, sometime in late November, inform your teacher that you will not be attending school for the next few months because you'll be resting and living off your fat? Now, that would be the life!

   _____

4. Bears, woodchucks and chipmunks are not the only animals that hibernate. The queen bumblebee also hibernates in winter. All the other bees die before winter arrives. The queen hibernates under leaves in a small hole. She is cold-blooded and therefore is able to survive slightly frozen.

   _____

Author's Purpose

Write a paragraph of your own for each purpose. The paragraph can be about any topic.

1. to inform

   _____

   _____

   _____

   _____

2. to persuade

   _____

   _____

   _____

   _____

3. to entertain

   _____

   _____

   _____

   _____

Reread your paragraphs. Do they make sense? Check for grammar, spelling and punctuation errors and make corrections where needed.

Persuasive Writing

When trying to persuade someone, it helps to look at both sides of the issue. If you can understand both sides, you will have a better idea how to convince someone of your point of view.

Follow these steps to write two persuasive paragraphs about which form of transportation is better: airplanes or cars.

1. On another sheet of paper, list three or four reasons why planes are better and three or four reasons why cars are better.

2. Put each list of reasons in order. Often, persuasive writing is strongest when the best reason is placed last. Readers tend to remember the last reason best.

3. Write topic sentences for each paragraph.

4. Read each paragraph and make any necessary changes so one sentence leads smoothly to the next.

5. Write your paragraphs below.

    Airplanes Are Better Transportation Than Cars _____

    _____

    _____

    _____

    _____

    _____

    Cars Are Better Transportation Than Planes _____

    _____

    _____

    _____

    _____

    _____

6. Write two more paragraphs on another sheet of paper. Select any topic. Write from both points of view.

Persuasive Writing

Writing is usually more persuasive if written from the reader's point of view. If you made cookies to sell at a school fair, which of these sentences would you write on your sign?

>   I spent a lot of time making these cookies.

>   These cookies taste delicious!

If you were writing to ask your school board to start a gymnastics program, which sentence would be more persuasive?

>   I really am interested in gymnastics.

>   Gymnastics would be good for our school because both boys and girls can participate, and it's a year-round sport we can do in any weather.

In both situations, the second sentence is more persuasive because it is written from the reader's point of view. People care how the cookies taste, not how long it took you to make them. The school board wants to provide activities for all the students, not just you.

Write **R** if the statement is written from the reader's point of view or **W** if it's written from the writer's point of view.

_____ 1. If you come swimming with me, you'll be able to cool off.

_____ 2. Come swimming with me. I don't want to go alone.

_____ 3. Please write me a letter. I really like to get mail.

_____ 4. Please write me a letter. I want to hear from you.

Follow these steps to write an "invitation" on another sheet of paper to persuade people to move to your town or city.

1.   Think about reasons someone would want to live in your town. Make a list of all the good things there, like the schools, parks, annual parades, historic buildings, businesses where parents could work, scout groups, Little League, and so on. You might also describe your town's population, transportation, restaurants, celebrations or even holiday decorations.

2.   Now, select three or four items from your list. Write a sentence (or two) about each one from the reader's point of view. For example, instead of writing "Our Little League team won the championship again last year," you could tell the reader, "You could help our Little League team win the championship again this year."

3.   Write a topic sentence to begin your invitation, and put your support sentences in order after it.

4.   Read your invitation out loud to another person. Make any needed changes, and copy the invitation onto a clean sheet of paper.

Dividing Fractions

To divide fractions, follow these steps:

$$\frac{3}{4} \div \frac{1}{4} =$$

Step 1: "Invert" the divisor. That means to turn it upside down.

$$\frac{3}{4} \div \frac{4}{1} =$$

Step 2: Multiply the two fractions:

$$\frac{3}{4} \div \frac{4}{1} = \frac{12}{4}$$

Step 1: Reduce the fraction to lowest terms by dividing the denominator into the numerator.

$$12 \div 4 = 3$$

$$\frac{3}{4} \div \frac{1}{4} = 3$$

Follow the above steps to divide fractions.

$\frac{1}{4} \div \frac{1}{5} =$	$\frac{1}{3} \div \frac{1}{12} =$	$\frac{3}{4} \div \frac{1}{3} =$
$\frac{5}{12} \div \frac{1}{3} =$	$\frac{3}{4} \div \frac{1}{6} =$	$\frac{2}{9} \div \frac{2}{3} =$
$\frac{3}{7} \div \frac{1}{4} =$	$\frac{2}{3} \div \frac{4}{6} =$	$\frac{1}{8} \div \frac{2}{3} =$
$\frac{4}{5} \div \frac{1}{3} =$	$\frac{4}{8} \div \frac{1}{2} =$	$\frac{5}{12} \div \frac{6}{8} =$

Dividing Fractions

When dividing fractions, change the problem to multiplication. Invert the divisor. Cancel if possible. Multiply the numerators, then the denominators. Write improper fractions as mixed numbers.

Example A: $\frac{3}{10} \div \frac{4}{5} = \frac{3}{10} \times \frac{5}{4} = \frac{3}{10} \times \frac{5}{4} = \frac{3}{8}$

Example B: $\frac{5}{12} \div \frac{3}{8} = \frac{5}{12} \times \frac{8}{3} = \frac{5}{12} \times \frac{8}{3} = \frac{10}{9} = 1\frac{1}{9}$

Divide.

1. $\frac{1}{2} \div \frac{3}{4} = \frac{1}{2} \times \frac{4}{3} =$

2. $\frac{3}{8} \div \frac{1}{4} =$

3. $\frac{4}{9} \div \frac{2}{3} =$

4. $\frac{3}{8} \div \frac{5}{12} =$

5. $\frac{1}{10} \div \frac{2}{5} =$

6. $\frac{5}{6} \div \frac{11}{12} =$

7. $\frac{14}{15} \div \frac{2}{3} =$

8. $\frac{4}{5} \div \frac{3}{10} =$

Dividing Fractions

Reciprocals are two fractions that, when multiplied together, make 1. To divide a fraction by a fraction, turn one of the fractions upside down and multiply. The upside-down fraction is a reciprocal of its original fraction. If you multiply a fraction by its reciprocal, you always get 1.

Examples of reciprocals: $\frac{2}{3} \times \frac{3}{2} = \frac{6}{6} = 1$ $\frac{9}{11} \times \frac{11}{9} = \frac{99}{99} = 1$

Example of dividing by fractions: $\frac{2}{5} \div \frac{2}{7} = \frac{2}{5} \times \frac{7}{2} = \frac{14}{10} = 1\frac{4}{10} = 1\frac{2}{5}$

To divide a whole number by a fraction, first write the whole number as a fraction (with a denominator of 1). (Write a mixed number as an improper fraction.) Then finish the problem as explained above.

Examples: $4 \div \frac{2}{6} = \frac{4}{1} \times \frac{6}{2} = \frac{24}{2} = 12$ $3\frac{1}{2} \div \frac{2}{5} = \frac{7}{2} \times \frac{5}{2} = \frac{35}{4} = 8\frac{3}{4}$

Solve the following problems, writing answers in their lowest terms. Change any improper fractions to mixed numbers.

1. $\frac{1}{3} \div \frac{2}{5} =$ 2. $\frac{6}{7} \div \frac{1}{3} =$ 3. $3 \div \frac{3}{4} =$ 4. $\frac{1}{4} \div \frac{2}{3} =$

5. Judy has 8 candy bars. She wants to give $\frac{1}{3}$ of a candy bar to everyone in her class. Does she have enough for all 24 students?   _____

6. A big jar of glue holds $3\frac{1}{2}$ cups. How many little containers that hold $\frac{1}{4}$ cup each can you fill?   _____

7. A container holds 27 ounces of ice cream. How many $4\frac{1}{2}$-ounce servings is that?   _____

8. It takes $2\frac{1}{2}$ teaspoons of powdered mix to make 1 cup of hot chocolate. How many cups can you make with 45 teaspoons of mix?   _____

9. Each cup of hot chocolate also takes $\frac{2}{3}$ cup of milk. How many cups of hot chocolate can you make with 12 cups of milk?   _____

Dividing Fractions

$6 \div \frac{1}{4}$

Step 1: Write both numbers as fractions. $\frac{6}{1} \div \frac{1}{4}$

Step 2: Invert the second fraction and multiply. $\frac{6}{1} \times \frac{4}{1}$

Step 3: Reduce. $\frac{24}{1} = 24$

Solve each problem.

1. $7 \div \frac{1}{3}$

2. $8 \div \frac{1}{2}$

3. $16 \div \frac{1}{3}$

4. $6 \div \frac{1}{2}$

5. $5 \div \frac{1}{6}$

6. $18 \div \frac{1}{7}$

7. $8 \div \frac{1}{5}$

8. $7 \div \frac{1}{9}$

9. $15 \div \frac{1}{6}$

Dividing Whole Numbers by Fractions

Follow these steps to divide a whole number by a fraction:

$$8 \div \frac{1}{4} =$$

Step 1: Write the whole number as a fraction:

$$\frac{8}{1} \div \frac{1}{4} =$$

Step 2: Invert the divisor.

$$\frac{8}{1} \times \frac{4}{1} =$$

Step 3: Multiply the two fractions:

$$\frac{8}{1} \times \frac{4}{1} = \frac{32}{1}$$

Step 4: Reduce the fraction to lowest terms by dividing the denominator into the numerator: $32 \div 1 = 32$

Follow the above steps to divide a whole number by a fraction.

$6 \div \frac{1}{3} =$	$4 \div \frac{1}{2} =$	$21 \div \frac{1}{3} =$
$8 \div \frac{1}{2} =$	$3 \div \frac{1}{6} =$	$15 \div \frac{1}{7} =$
$9 \div \frac{1}{5} =$	$4 \div \frac{1}{9} =$	$12 \div \frac{1}{6} =$

Three-fourths of a bag of popcorn fits into one bowl.
How many bowls do you need if you have six bags of popcorn? _____

Week 25 Skills

Subject	Skill	Multi-Sensory Learning Activities
Reading and Language Arts	Use a dictionary to determine meaning and pronunciation of unfamiliar words.	• Complete Practice Pages 266–270. • Give your child a magazine on a topic that interests him or her. As your child is reading, ask him or her to make a list of unknown words and keep them in a journal. Then, have your child look up the definitions in a dictionary and use each word in a sentence. • Have your child make a glossary of animal kingdom words, such as *phylum*, *endangered*, and *vertebrates*. Have him or her arrange the entries in alphabetical order and write a definition for each word.
Math	Review addition, subtraction, multiplication, and division of fractions.	• Complete Practice Pages 271–274. • Help your child find a food package that provides nutrition facts including serving size, grams of protein, grams of sodium, etc. Can your child write and solve three problems that include fractions based on the information?
Bonus: Social Studies		• Teach your child about the different types of maps that are available, such as a political map, a physical map, a road map, and a precipitation map. Look at a variety of maps in textbooks and other resources. Discuss the purpose of each kind of map.

Multiple Meanings

Circle the correct definition of the bold word in each sentence. The first one has been done for you.

1. Try to **flag** down a car to get us some help!

   (to signal to stop)
   cloth used as symbol

2. We listened to the **band** play the National Anthem.

   group of musicians
   a binding or tie

3. He was the **sole** survivor of the plane crash.

   bottom of the foot
   one and only

4. I am going to **pound** the nail with this hammer.

   to hit hard
   a unit of weight

5. He lived on what little **game** he could find in the woods.

   animals for hunting
   form of entertainment

6. We are going to **book** the midnight flight from Miami.

   to reserve in advance
   a written work

7. The **pitcher** looked toward first base before throwing the ball.

   baseball team member
   container for pouring

8. My grandfather and I played a **game** of checkers last night.

   animals for hunting
   form of entertainment

9. They raise the **flag** over City Hall every morning.

   to signal to stop
   cloth used as symbol

COMPLETE YEAR GRADE 5

Learning New Words

Write a word from the box to complete each sentence. Use a dictionary to look up words you are unsure of.

bouquet	unconscious	inspire	disability
inherit	hovering	assault	enclosure
commotion	criticize		

1. He was knocked _____ by the blow to his head.

2. Megan never let her _____ stand in the way of accomplishing what she wanted.

3. The teacher burst into the noisy room and demanded to know what all the _____ was about.

4. He offered her a _____ of flowers as a truce after their argument.

5. The zoo was in the process of building a new _____ for the elephants.

6. The mother was _____ over her sick child.

7. The movie was meant to _____ people to do good deeds.

8. My friend will eventually _____ a fortune from his grandmother.

9. Not many people enjoy having someone _____ their work.

10. The female leopard led the _____ on the herd of zebras.

Using the Dictionary

Guide words are the words that appear at the top of dictionary pages. They show the first and last words on each page.

Read the guide words on each dictionary page below. Then look around for objects whose names come between the guide words. Write the names of the objects, and then number them in alphabetical order

babble	buzz

magic	myself

cabin	cycle

pea	puzzle

dairy	dwarf

scar	sword

feast	future

tack	truth

Using the Dictionary

Read about dictionaries. Then answer the questions.

> **Dictionaries** are books that give definitions of words. Dictionaries list words in alphabetical order. **Guide words** at the top of each page show the first and last words listed on the page. All other words on the page are listed in alphabetical order between the guide words. This helps you locate the word you want quickly and easily.
>
> In addition to definitions, dictionaries also show the following: how to pronounce, or say, each word; the individual syllables found in each word; the part of speech for each word; and the plural form or verb forms if the base word changes.
>
> Some dictionaries provide considerably more information. For example, The *Tormont Webster's Illustrated Encyclopedic Dictionary* includes many color illustrations of terms, a pronunciation key on every other page and two pages of introductory information on how to use the dictionary effectively.
>
> Other highlights of the Tormont Webster are **historic labels** that tell the history of words no longer in common use; **geographic labels** that tell in what part of the world uncommon words are used; **stylistic labels** that tell whether a word is formal, informal, humorous or a slang term; and **field labels** that tell what field of knowledge—such as medicine—the word is used in.

1. Where are guide words found? _____

_____

2. What is the purpose of guide words? _____

_____

3. Which label tells if a word is a slang term? _____

4. Which label tells the history of a word? _____

5. Which type of information is not provided for each word in the dictionary?

    ❏ definition

    ❏ part of speech

    ❏ picture

Using a Dictionary

Use the dictionary entry below to answer the questions.

ad·he·sive (ad-he'-siv) adj. 1. Tending to adhere; sticky. 2. Gummed so as to adhere. n. 3. An adhesive substance such as paste or glue. **ad·he·sive·ly** adv. **ad·he·sive·ness** n.

1. Based on the first definition of **adhesive**, what do you think **adhere** means?

   _____

   _____

2. Which definition of **adhesive** is used in this sentence?
   The tape was so **adhesive** that we couldn't peel it loose. _____

   _____

3. Which part of speech is **adhesive** used as in this sentence?
   We put a strong **adhesive** on the package to keep it sealed. _____

4. How many syllables does **adhesive** have? _____

5. Is **adhesive** used as a noun or an adjective in this sentence?
   The adhesive we chose to use was not very gummy. _____

6. **Adhesive** and variations of the word can be used as what parts of speech?

   _____

Write sentences using these words.

7. adhesiveness _____

   _____

8. adhesively _____

   _____

9. adhere _____

   _____

Fractions: Multiplication and Division

Solve.

1. $\frac{7}{9} \times \frac{1}{4} =$

2. $\frac{5}{6} \times \frac{1}{10} =$

3. $\frac{9}{10} \times \frac{2}{3} =$

4. $8 \times \frac{1}{4} =$

5. $\frac{1}{3} \times 15 =$

6. Jaime sat in his chair for $\frac{5}{6}$ of an hour. For $\frac{1}{3}$ of this time, he worked on this assignment. What fraction of an hour did he work on this assignment?

7. $\frac{1}{2} \div \frac{1}{5} =$

8. $\frac{1}{5} \div \frac{1}{2} =$

9. $\frac{3}{4} \div \frac{3}{8} =$

10. $\frac{7}{16} \div \frac{4}{7} =$

Art Shows

Ms. Creative had her students busy preparing for the year-end art show.

1. Kelly needed to finish seven paintings for the show. If she painted $\frac{1}{3}$ of a painting each session, how many sessions would it take her to finish all seven?

   _____

2. Fong's responsibility was to glaze six pieces of pottery. He was able to complete $\frac{1}{4}$ of a pot's glaze in one class. How many classes will it take him to glaze all six pieces?

   _____

3. Karen needed to have nine black-and-white sketches finished for the show. If she finished about $\frac{2}{4}$ of one in each class, how many classes would it take Karen to finish all nine?

   _____

4. Two sculptures were needed to highlight the entrance of the exhibit. One-sixteenth of each sculpture was completed in each art class. How many classes will it take to complete both sculptures?

   _____

5. The students took a sheet of art paper that was $\frac{8}{9}$ of a yard long to make a mural. Once the mural was complete it needed to be cut into sections, each $\frac{2}{18}$ of a yard long. How many pieces will there be?

   _____

6. A painted carousel horse was the hit of the show. Three-tenths was painted each day. How many days did it take to finish?

   _____

Extension:

Divide by $\frac{2}{4}$	
$\frac{3}{8}$	a.
5	b.
$\frac{10}{6}$	c.

Divide by $\frac{1}{3}$	
4	a.
$\frac{3}{8}$	b.
$\frac{8}{10}$	c.

COMPLETE YEAR GRADE 5

Stump the Teacher

The students in Ms. Davidson's class were playing "Stump the Teacher." See if you can solve their problems.

1. If baseball cards are worth $\frac{1}{10}$ of a dollar each, how much are Brad's 54 cards worth?

2. If $\frac{6}{8}$ of Sally's 8 puppies are female and $\frac{1}{2}$ of the female puppies have been sold, how many female puppies have been sold?

3. Felipe used $\frac{2}{3}$ cup of cheese for each pizza. If he made 4 pizzas, how much cheese did he need to buy?

4. Francis bought $\frac{15}{16}$ of a yard of fabric. She used $\frac{1}{2}$ of it to make a dress for her doll. What fraction of a yard did she use?

5. If a lot is $\frac{5}{8}$ of an acre, and the house covers $\frac{1}{2}$ of it, what fraction of an acre is covered by the house?

6. At the track meet, Rick entered 5 sprint contests. If each race was $\frac{1}{4}$ mile long, how many miles did Rick sprint in all?

7. The class had $\frac{1}{4}$ of an hour to take a math quiz. Nate used only $\frac{1}{3}$ of the time. What fraction of an hour did Nate use for the quiz?

8. Lisa and Kim live $\frac{3}{8}$ of a mile apart. If they each walked $\frac{1}{2}$ of the way and met in the middle, what part of a mile did each walk?

9. This year's summer vacation was $\frac{1}{6}$ of the year. How many months long was the summer vacation this year?

10. Paul's dog was asleep $\frac{2}{3}$ of the day. How many hours was it awake?

Fraction Test

1. $\frac{1}{6} + \frac{4}{6} =$

2. $4\frac{1}{12} + 3\frac{2}{12} =$

3. $18\frac{1}{3} + 12\frac{1}{3} =$

4. $19\frac{1}{5} + 4\frac{2}{3} =$

5. $37 - \frac{3}{11} =$

6. $\frac{4}{5} - \frac{1}{4} =$

7. $\frac{4}{5} \times \frac{3}{8} =$

8. $\frac{5}{6} \times 15 =$

9. $4\frac{1}{4} \times \frac{2}{5} =$

10. $3\frac{1}{2} \times 2\frac{1}{3} =$

11. $7 \times \frac{3}{5} =$

12. $\frac{3}{7} \div \frac{4}{5} =$

13. $\frac{2}{3} \div 9 =$

14. $2\frac{6}{7} \div \frac{5}{14} =$

15. $\frac{1}{2} \div \frac{1}{3} =$

16. $7\frac{1}{3} \div 2\frac{2}{6} =$

17. Write $\frac{3}{5}$ as a decimal.

18. Leroy got $\frac{7}{8}$ of his 24 homework problems correct. How many did he get correct?

19. Jean gave $\frac{3}{16}$ of her allowance to her sister and $\frac{1}{8}$ of her allowance to her brother. How much of her allowance did she give away?

20. Jack and Jill had a canteen full of 5 quarts of grape juice. They drank $3\frac{5}{9}$ quarts. How much was left?

Week 26 Skills

Subject	Skill	Multi-Sensory Learning Activities
Reading and Language Arts	Demonstrate correct punctuation.	• Complete Practice Pages 276 and 277. • Have your child write two declarative, interrogative, imperative, and exclamatory sentences, focusing on correct capitalization and punctuation. Have your child label each completed sentence and point out the ending punctuation.
	Understand synonyms, or words with similar meanings.	• Complete Practice Pages 278–280. • Catch your child using overused words, such as **like**, **nice**, **said**, **very**, **cool**, or **fun**. Challenge him or her to substitute a more interesting synonym. Let your child catch you using overused words, too.
Math	Measure length in customary and metric units.	• Complete Practice Pages 281 and 282. • Ask your child to use an online map to find the exact distance in miles between your home and his or her school. Then, ask your child to convert that distance into yards, feet, and inches.
	Measure weight in customary and metric units.	• Complete Practice Pages 283 and 284. • Give your child two objects of similar size. Ask him or her to predict which object weighs more. Then, weigh the objects on a kitchen scale. Was your child's prediction correct?

Tim Burr, Tall Tale Hero

Read the following tall tale about Tim Burr. Use proofreading marks to edit the paragraphs and correct the sentence fragments. Write the quotations correctly. Use proper capitalization and the appropriate homophones.

far up north, in the rugged, wooded regions of canada, their lived the famous lumberjack tim burr. his trusty sidekick, saw mills, lived there to. one day, saw and tim loaded up their axes and set off four the woods. To fell more trees. For the local mill, Log Lagoon. they took along they're pack mules, beauty and beast. they chopped so fast that the trees began falling onto each other. Creating quite a logjam. its knot my fault yelled saw. i can't see where you are cutting.

the problem grew worse. beauty, tim's beloved mule, almost got his tale sliced off. Buy a falling tree trunk. that does it yelled tim angrily when you cut down a tree. call for me. So i no where you are.

saw obeyed tim's wishes. From that day on as each tree was felled, saw cried "TIM BURR!"

Punctuation

Add commas where needed. Put the correct punctuation at the end of each sentence.

1. My friend Jamie loves to snowboard

2. Winter sports such as hockey skiing and skating are fun

3. Oh what a lovely view

4. The map shows the continents of Asia Africa Australia and Antarctica

5. My mother a ballet dancer will perform tonight

6. What will you do tomorrow

7. When will the plane arrive at the airport

8. Jason do you know what time it is

9. Friends of ours the Watsons are coming for dinner

10. Margo look out for that falling rock

11. The young child sat reading a book

12. Who wrote this letter

13. My sister Jill is very neat

14. The trampoline is in our backyard

15. We will have chicken peas rice and salad for dinner

16. That dog a Saint Bernard looks dangerous

Synonyms

A **synonym** is a word with the same or similar meaning as another word.

Examples: bucket — pail   happy — cheerful   dirty — messy

Match the words on the left with their synonyms on the right. The first one has been done for you.

tired	beverage
start	notice
get	boring
fire	busy
dull	sleepy
big	couch
noisy	receive
crowded	begin
sofa	loud
drink	halt
sign	large
stop	flames

Rewrite the sentences below using synonyms for the bold words.

1. Because the road was **rough**, we had a **hard** time riding our bikes on it.

_____

2. After the accident, the driver appeared to be **hurt**, so someone **ran** to call an ambulance.

_____

3. Yesterday everyone stayed after school to pick up litter, and now the school yard is **nice** and **clean**.

_____

Finding Synonyms

Circle a word, or group of words, in each sentence that is a synonym for a word in the box. Write the synonym on the line.

statue	imagination	jealous	future	arrangements
furniture	stranger	project	justice	capture

Example: She will ⟨lend⟩ me her book. loan　　　　　_____loan_____

1. He tried to catch the butterfly.　　　　　_____

2. No one knows what will happen in the time to come.　_____

3. They are loading the chairs and tables and beds into　_____

   the moving van.

4. We almost finished our team assignment.　　　_____

5. They made plans to have a class party.　　　_____

6. Penny made a model of a horse.　　　　　_____

7. The accused man asked the judge for fairness.　_____

Write your own sentences for these words: **stranger**, **imagination**, **jealous**.
Then choose one other word from the box and use it in a sentence. Make each sentence at least ten words long. The sentences should show that you know what the word means.

1. _____

   _____

2. _____

   _____

3. _____

   _____

4. _____

   _____

This Is So Fine

Rewrite each sentence below, replacing the word **fine** with one of the synonyms given. Since the synonyms have slight differences in meaning, be careful to choose the correct one.

Fine: clear, delicate, elegant, small, sharp, subtle

1. The queen wore a **fine** gown encrusted with jewels.

_____

_____

2. I wash this blouse by hand because of its **fine** lace collar.

_____

_____

3. The sand in an hourglass must be very **fine** to trickle as it does.

_____

_____

4. We need **fine** weather for sailing.

_____

_____

5. Dad used a whetstone to put a **fine** edge on the knife.

_____

_____

6. Sometimes there is a **fine** line between innocence and guilt.

_____

Length in Customary Units

The **customary system** of measurement is the most widely used in the United States. It measures length in inches, feet, yards and miles.

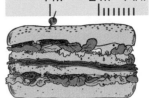

Examples:

12 inches (in.) = 1 foot (ft.)
3 ft. (36 in.) = 1 yard (yd.)
5,280 ft. (1,760 yds.) = 1 mile (mi.)

To change to a larger unit, divide. To change to a smaller unit, multiply.

Examples:

To change inches to feet, divide by 12.   24 in. = 2 ft.   27 in. = 2 ft. 3 in.
To change feet to inches, multiply by 12.   3 ft. = 36 in.   4 ft = 48 in.
To change inches to yards, divide by 36.   108 in. = 3 yd.   80 in. = 2 yd. 8 in.
To change feet to yards, divide by 3.   12 ft. = 4 yd.   11 ft. = 3 yd. 2 ft.

Sometimes in subtraction you have to borrow units.

Examples:

3 ft. 4 in.	=	2 ft. 16 in.		3 yd.	=	2 yd. 3 ft.
– 1 ft. 11 in.		– 1 ft. 11 in.		– 1 yd. 2 ft.		– 1 yd. 2 ft.
		1 ft. 5 in.				1 yd. 1 ft.

Solve the following problems.

1. 108 in. = _____ ft.

2. 68 in. = _____ ft. _____ in.

3. 8 ft. = _____ yd. _____ ft.

4. 3,520 yd. = _____ mi.

5. What form of measurement (inches, feet, yards or miles) would you use for each item below?

    a. pencil _____   b. vacation trip _____

    c. playground _____   d. wall _____

6. One side of a square box is 2 ft. 4 in.
    What is the perimeter of the box?   _____

7. Jason is 59 in. tall. Kent is 5 ft. 1 in. tall.
    Who is taller and by how much?   _____

8. Karen bought a doll 2 ft. 8 in. tall for her little sister.
    She found a box that is 29 in. long. Will the doll fit in that box? _____

9. Dan's dog likes to go out in the backyard, which is 85 ft. wide.
    The dog's chain is 17 ft. 6 in. long. If Dan attaches one end of
    the chain to a pole in the middle of the yard, will his dog be
    able to leave the yard?   _____

Length in Metric Units

The **metric system** measures length in meters, centimeters, millimeters, and kilometers.

Examples:

A **meter (m)** is about 40 inches or 3.3 feet.

A **centimeter (cm)** is $\frac{1}{100}$ of a meter or 0.4 inches.

A **millimeter (mm)** is $\frac{1}{1000}$ of a meter or 0.04 inches.

A **kilometer (km)** is 1,000 meters or 0.6 miles.

As before, divide to find a larger unit and multiply to find a smaller unit.

Examples:

To change cm to mm, multiply by 10.
To change cm to meters, divide by 100.
To change mm to meters, divide by 1,000.
To change km to meters, multiply by 1,000.

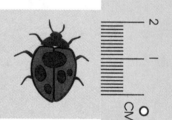

Solve the following problems.

1. 600 cm = _____ m 2. 12 cm = _____ mm 3. 47 m = _____ cm

4. In the sentences below, write the missing unit: m, cm, mm or km.

   a. A fingernail is about 1 _____ thick.

   b. An average car is about 5 _____ long.

   c. Someone could walk 1 _____ in 10 minutes.

   d. A finger is about 7 _____ long.

   e. A street could be 3 _____ long.

   f. The Earth is about 40,000 _____ around at the equator.

   g. A pencil is about 17 _____ long.

   h. A noodle is about 4 _____ wide.

   i. A teacher's desk is about 1 _____ wide.

5. A nickel is about 1 mm thick. How many nickels would be in a stack 1 cm high? _____

6. Is something 25 cm long closer to 10 inches or 10 feet? _____

7. Is something 18 mm wide closer to 0.7 inch or 7 inches? _____

8. Would you get more exercise running 4 km or 500 m? _____

Weight in Customary Units

Here are the main ways to measure weight in customary units:

16 ounces (oz.) = 1 pound (lb.)
2,000 lb. = 1 ton (tn.)
To change ounces to pounds, divide by 16.
To change pounds to ounces, multiply by 16.

As with measurements of length, you may have to borrow units in subtraction.

BRIDGE
UNSAFE
FOR TRUCKS
OVER
2 TONS

Examples:	4 lb. 5 oz. =	3 lb. 21 oz.
	– 2 lb. 10 oz.	– 2 lb. 10 oz.
		1 lb. 11 oz.

Solve the following problems.

1. 48 oz. = _____ lb.   2. 39 oz. = _____ lb.   3. 4 lb. = _____ oz.

4. What form of measurement would you use for each of these: ounces, pounds or tons?

a. pencil _____   b. elephant _____   c. person _____

5. Which is heavier, 0.25 ton or 750 pounds?   _____

6. Twenty-two people, each weighing an average of 150 lb., want to get on an elevator that can carry up to 1.5 tons. How many of them should wait for the next elevator?   _____

7. A one-ton truck is carrying 14 boxes that weigh 125 lb. each. It comes to a small bridge with a sign that says, "Bridge unsafe for trucks over 2 tons." Is it safe for the truck and the boxes to cross the bridge?   _____

8. A large box of Oat Boats contains 2 lb. 3 oz. of cereal, while a box of Honey Hunks contains 1 lb. 14 oz. How many more ounces are in the box of Oat Boats?   _____

9. A can of Peter's Powdered Drink Mix weighs 2 lb. 5 oz. A can of Petunia's Powdered Drink Mix weighs 40 oz. Which one is heavier?   _____

10. A can of Peter's Drink Mix is 12 cents an ounce. How much does it cost?   _____

Weight in Metric Units

A **gram** (**g**) is about 0.035 oz.

A **milligram** (**mg**) is $\frac{1}{1000}$ g or about 0.000035 oz.

A **kilogram** (**kg**) is 1,000 g or about 2.2 lb.

A **metric ton** (**t**) is 1,000 kg or about 1.1 tn.

To change g to mg, multiply by 1,000.
To change g to kg, divide by 1,000.
To change kg to g, multiply by 1,000.
To change t to kg, multiply by 1,000.

Solve the following problems.

1. 3 kg = _____ g

2. 2 g = _____ mg

3. 145 g = _____ kg

4. 3,000 kg = _____ t

5. _____ g = 450 mg

6. 3.5 t = _____ kg

7. Write the missing units below: g, mg, kg or t.

    a. A sunflower seed weighs less than 1 _____ .

    b. A serving of cereal contains 14 _____ of sugar.

    c. The same serving of cereal has 250 _____ of salt.

    d. A bowling ball weighs about 7 _____ .

    e. A whale weighs about 90 _____ .

    f. A math textbook weighs about 1 _____ .

    g. A safety pin weighs about 1 _____ .

    h. An average car weighs about 1 _____ .

8. Is 200 g closer to 7 oz. or 70 oz.? _____

9. Is 3 kg closer to 7 lb. or 70 lb.? _____

10. Does a metric ton weigh more or less than a ton measured by the customary system? _____

11. How is a kilogram different from a kilometer? _____

    _____

12. Which is heavier, 300 g or 1 kg? _____

Week 27 Skills

Subject	Skill	Multi-Sensory Learning Activities
Reading and Language Arts	Use context as a clue to the meaning of a word or phrase.	• Complete Practice Page 286. • Read *The Black Stallion* by Walter Farley. Have your child jot down any unfamiliar words, along with the sentence in which each word appears. Can your child guess each word's meaning from its context?
	Understand antonyms, or words with opposite meanings.	• Complete Practice Pages 287 and 288. • Read *Circle of Gold* by Candy Dawson Boyd. Discuss some unfamiliar words with your child. Challenge him or her to look the words up in a dictionary and then name an antonym for each.
	Review synonyms and antonyms.	• Complete Practice Page 289. • Write several sentences on a piece of paper, underlining a key word in each. Ask your child to copy the sentences and replace each underlined word with a synonym or an antonym. Then, have your child read the new sentences aloud.
Math	Measure capacity in customary and metric units.	• Complete Practice Pages 290–293. • Guide your child in making a favorite recipe. Which units of capacity are used?
	Review weight and capacity.	• Complete Practice Page 294. • Have your child use a metric measuring cup to determine the capacity of the following: a can of soda, a mug, a cereal bowl, and a drinking glass.

Multiple Meanings

Use context clues to determine the meaning of each bold word. The first one has been done for you.

1. My grandfather always has his **spectacles** perched on his nose.

   Meaning: _lenses worn in front of the eyes to aid vision_

2. The Fourth of July fireworks display was an amazing **spectacle**.

   Meaning: _____

3. We enjoy a rugged vacation, staying in a hunting **lodge** rather than a hotel.

   Meaning: _____

4. Don't let the baby have hard candy because it could **lodge** in his throat.

   Meaning: _____

5. Termites will **bore** through the rotten wood in our basement if we don't have it replaced.

   Meaning: _____

6. That television show could **bore** even a small child!

   Meaning: _____

7. Don't **resort** to lies just to get what you want!

   Meaning: _____

8. The **resort** is packed with tourists from May to September each year.

   Meaning: _____

Antonyms

An **antonym** is a word with the opposite meaning of another word.

Examples: hot — cold
up — down
start — stop

Match the words on the left with their antonyms on the right. The first one has been done for you.

asleep	sloppy
sit	shut
excited	full
north	awake
wild	tame
hairy	stand
open	bored
quick	bald
neat	south
hungry	slow

In the sentences below, replace each bold word with a synonym or an antonym so that the sentence makes sense. Write the word on the line. Then, write either **synonym** or **antonym** to show its relationship to the given word. The first one has been done for you.

1. If the weather stays warm, all the plants will **perish**. _____live-antonym_____

2. Last night, mom made my favorite meal, and it
   was **delicious**. _____

3. The test was **difficult**, and everyone in the class
   passed it. _____

4. The music from the concert was so **loud** we could
   hear it in the parking lot. _____

5. The bunks at camp were **comfortable**, and I didn't
   sleep very well. _____

Finding Antonyms

Write a word that is an antonym for each bold word in the sentences below.

1. Jared made his way **quickly** through the crowd. _____

2. My friends and I arrived **late** to the party. _____

3. My sister loves to watch airplanes **take off**. _____

4. The teacher seems especially **cheerful** this morning. _____

5. When are you going to **begin** your project? _____

Write antonyms for the following words on the lines. Then write a short paragraph using all the words you wrote.

dirty _____   whisper _____

old _____   carefully _____

down _____   night _____

sit _____   happy _____

_____

_____

_____

_____

_____

_____

_____

_____

COMPLETE YEAR GRADE 5

Synonym or Antonym?

Draw a green circle around each word
that is a synonym of the first word.
Draw an orange box around each word
that is its antonym. Use a dictionary to look
up any words you do not know.

forfeit	choose	generous	gain	lose
adjacent	sudden	nearby	clean	remote
pompous	modest	festive	noisy	proud
nosegay	unhappy	bouquet	puncture	weeds
exquisite	careful	beyond	hideous	delightful
impeccable	flawed	perfect	scarce	painful
wary	alert	brittle	unguarded	tired
harry	furry	attract	annoy	soothe
despondently	happily	elegantly	crazily	unhappily
interrogate	cross-examine	dislike	persecute	hush
cull	answer	charge	select	scatter
elude	confront	scold	avoid	frighten

Capacity in Customary Units

Here are the main ways to measure capacity (how much something will hold) in customary units:

8 fluid ounces (fl. oz.) = 1 cup (c.)
2 c. = 1 pint (pt.)
2 pt. = 1 quart (qt.)
4 qt. = 1 gallon (gal.)

To change ounces to cups, divide by 8.
To change cups to ounces, multiply by 8.
To change cups to pints or quarts, divide by 2.

As with measurements of length and weight, you may have to borrow units in subtraction.

Example: 3 gal. 2 qt. =   2 gal. 6 qt.
              - 1 gal. 3 qt   - 1 gal. 3 qt.
                                   1 gal. 3 qt.

Solve the following problems.

1. 32 fl. oz. = _____ pt.   2. 4 gal. = _____ pt.   3. _____ c. = 24 fl. oz.

4. 5 pt. = _____ qt.   5. 16 pt. = _____ gal.   6. 3 pt. = _____ fl. oz.

7. A large can of soup contains 19 fl. oz. A serving is about 8 oz.
    How many cans should you buy if you want to serve 7 people? _____

8. A container of strawberry ice cream holds 36 fl. oz. A container
    of chocolate ice cream holds 2 pt. Which one has more ice
    cream? How much more? _____

9. A day-care worker wants to give 15 children each 6 fl. oz. of milk.
    How many quarts of milk does she need? _____

10. This morning, the day-care supervisor bought 3 gal. of milk.
    The kids drank 2 gal. 3 c. How much milk is left for tomorrow? _____

11. Harriet bought 3 gal. 2 qt. of paint for her living room. She used
    2 gal. 3 qt. How much paint is left over? _____

12. Jason's favorite punch takes a pint of raspberry sherbet. If he
    wants to make $1\frac{1}{2}$ times the recipe, how many fl. oz. of sherbet
    does he need? _____

Capacity in Metric Units

A **liter (L)** is a little over 1 quart.
A **milliliter (mL)** is $\frac{1}{1000}$ of a liter or about 0.03 oz.
A **kiloliter (kL)** is 1,000 liters or about 250 gallons.

Solve the following problems.

1. 5,000 mL = _____ L

2. 2,000 L = _____ kL

3. 3 L = _____ mL

4. Write the missing unit: L, mL or kL.

   a. A swimming pool holds about 100 _____ of water.

   b. An eyedropper is marked for 1 and 2 _____ .

   c. A pitcher could hold 1 or 2 _____ of juice.

   d. A teaspoon holds about 5 _____ of medicine.

   e. A birdbath might hold 5 _____ of water.

   f. A tablespoon holds about 15 _____ of salt.

   g. A bowl holds about 250 _____ of soup.

   h. We drank about 4 _____ of punch at the party.

5. Which is more, 3 L or a gallon?   _____

6. Which is more, 400 mL or 40 oz.?   _____

7. Which is more, 1 kL or 500 L?   _____

8. Is 4 L closer to a quart or a gallon?   _____

9. Is 480 mL closer to 2 cups or 2 pints?   _____

10. Is a mL closer to 4 drops or 4 teaspoonsful?   _____

11. How many glasses of juice containing 250 mL
    each could you pour from a 1-L jug?   _____

12. How much water would you need to water an
    average-sized lawn, 1 kL or 1 L?   _____

Capacity

The **fluid ounce**, **cup**, **pint**, **quart** and **gallon** are used to measure capacity in the United States.

| I cup | I pint | I quart | I half gallon | I gallon |

8 fluid ounces (fl. oz.) = I cup (c.)

2 cups = I pint (pt.)

2 pints = I quart (qt.)

2 quarts = I half gallon (gal.)

4 quarts = I gallon (gal.)

Convert the units of capacity.

13 gal. = _____ qt.   10 pt. = _____ c.   12 c. = _____ pt.

4 gal. = _____ qt.   16 qt. = _____ gal.   5 c. = _____ pt.

36 pt. = _____ gal.   12 qt. = _____ pt.   6 gal. = _____ pt.

16 c. = _____ qt.   32 oz. = _____ c.   16 oz. = _____ pt.

Units of Capacity

Complete each equation so that it equals 1 gallon.

1. 3 qt. + _____ qt. = 1 gal.

| 1 pt. = 2 c.   1 qt. = 2 pt.   1 gal. = 4 qt. |

2. 4 c. + 2 pt. + _____ qt. = 1 gal.

3. 2 c. + 1 pt. + _____ qt. = 1 gal.

5. 2 pt. + _____ qt. + 1 qt. = 1 gal.

4. 3 qt. + 2 c. + _____ c. = 1 gal.

6. 6 c. + _____ c. + 2 qt. = 1 gal.

Match each equivalent capacity.

 = 1 c.   = 1 pt.   = 1 qt.   = 1/2 gal.   = 1 gal.

1. _____   a.

2. _____   b.

3. _____   c.

4. _____   d.

Which unit would best measure each example below?

1. Amount of water used to take a shower _____

2. Amount of flour to make bread _____

3. Amount of water to fill your pool _____

4. A single serving of yogurt _____

5. A container of motor oil _____

| gallons |
| cups |
| pints |
| quarts |

Weight and Capacity

Weight

1 pound (lb.) = 16 ounces (oz.)

1 ton (T.) = 2,000 pounds

Capacity

1 cup (c.) = 8 fluid ounces (fl. oz.)

1 pint (pt.) = 2 cups

1 quart (qt.) = 2 pints

1 gallon (gal.) = 4 quarts

Example 2

To change from a smaller unit to a larger unit, divide.

176 fl. oz. = _____ c.

8 fl. oz. = 1 c.

176 ÷ 8 = 22

176 fl. oz. = 22 c.

Example 1

To change from a larger unit to a smaller unit, multiply.

5 T. = _____ lb.

1 T. = 2,000 lb.

5 x 2,000 = 10,000

5 T. = 10,000 lb.

Example 3

Express remainders in terms of the original unit.

25 c. = 12 pt. 1 c.

25 c. = _____ pt.

2 c. = 1 pt.

25 ÷ 2 = 12 R1

Complete.

1. 16 pt. = _____ qt.

2. 12 gal. = _____ qt.

3. 5 lb. = _____ oz.

4. 150 oz. = _____ lb. ___ oz.

5. 5 gal. 3 qt. = _____ qt.

6. 2 lb. 3 oz. = _____ oz.

Compare using >, <, =.

7. 1 gal. [ ] 6 qt.

8. 560 oz. [ ] 35 lb.

9. 15 pt. [ ] 25 c.

Third Quarter Check-Up

Reading and Language Arts

☐ I understand verb tenses, including present, past, future, and past participle.

☐ I can use correct subject/verb agreement.

☐ I can use commas in a series and to separate a noun or pronoun in a direct address.

☐ I understand and identify homographs, or words that have the same spelling but different meanings and pronunciations.

☐ I can answer questions about texts to determine reading comprehension.

☐ I can use editing marks to proofread and make corrections.

☐ I understand the author's purpose to inform, persuade, or entertain.

☐ I can demonstrate persuasive writing.

☐ I can use a dictionary to determine meaning and pronunciation of unfamiliar words.

☐ I can demonstrate correct punctuation.

☐ I understand synonyms and antonyms.

☐ I can use context as a clue to the meaning of a word or phrase.

Math

☐ I can add and subtract fractions with like and unlike denominators.

☐ I can add, subtract, and multiply mixed numbers.

☐ I can multiply and divide fractions.

☐ I can divide fractions by whole numbers and whole numbers by fractions.

☐ I can measure length, weight, and capacity in customary and metric units.

Final Project

Have your child write a plot summary for an episode of his or her favorite television show. The summary should include the names of the characters, the setting, and the main idea of the episode. Once your child has mapped out the plot, have him or her begin work on a rough draft for the story. For a creative way to publish this script, have your child make a mini-television from a cardboard box. Let your child draw several scenes from the story and tape them together in a long horizontal strip, then pull the strip through the television set while narrating the episode.

Fourth Quarter Introduction

As the school year nears its end, many students are feeling confident about the new skills they have learned as fifth graders. This may be evident in their ability to edit and proofread their own writing, or their increasing understanding of fractions and decimals as they apply to real-life situations. As the days get warmer and children play outside in the evenings, don't forget to maintain school day routines and continue to support your child's academic growth at home.

Fourth Quarter Skills

Practice pages in this book for Weeks 28–36 will help your child improve the following skills.

Reading and Language Arts
- Recognize up to six-syllable words
- Practice spelling and pronunciation, and understand word meanings
- Identify simple and compound subjects and predicates
- Join sentences by using conjunctions **and**, **but**, **or**, **because**, and **so**
- Use context clues to interpret meaning
- Identify the topic sentence and supporting sentences of a paragraph
- Answer questions about texts to determine reading comprehension
- Understand and identify the main idea of a text
- Write an essay that compares and contrasts
- Identify **who**, **which**, and **that** clauses
- Use a thesaurus to find synonyms and antonyms
- Determine appropriate resource books for different situations

Math
- Measure temperature
- Compare and convert measurements
- Add and subtract inches and feet and pounds and ounces
- Add minutes and hours
- Understand volume, perimeter, and area
- Identify and classify quadrilaterals
- Build larger shapes from smaller shapes and use tangrams
- Identify polyhedrons
- Organize and interpret data from charts, bar graphs, picture graphs, circle graphs, and line graphs
- Locate points on a grid and plot ordered pairs

Multi-Sensory Learning Activities

Try these fun activities for enhancing your child's learning and development during the fourth quarter of the school year. Be sure to choose activities that include speaking, listening, touching, and active movement.

 Reading and Language Arts

Have your child divide the following words into syllables: **amusement**, **evasive**, **reverently**, **antagonistic**, **extricate**, **ruthless**, **antiquated**, **gingerly**, **blimey**, **horrendous**, and **suspect**. Then, have your child write a brief story using as many of these words as possible.

Read *Farmer Boy* by Laura Ingalls Wilder. Explain that some words and phrases, such as **butter-buyer**, are considered archaic or obsolete and are no longer used in common speech or writing. Discuss these words in their original context and find background information whenever possible.

Cut out an article from the front page of the newspaper. Leave off the headline. Have your child read the article, then write a headline that expresses the main idea of the article.

 **Math**

Ask your child to imagine designing a swimming pool for your yard or neighborhood. What could the dimensions of the pool be to fit the available space? What volume of water would the pool hold?

Ask your child to measure the dimensions of a shoe box, cereal box, or other box found around your home. Calculate volume in both cubic inches and cubic centimeters.

Gather examples of circle graphs for your child to examine. Choose two circle graphs to look at in greater depth. Give your child four or five questions pertaining to each graph that require him or her to analyze the information presented.

Talk about the different categories of spending, such as entertainment, food, clothes, charity, and savings. Help your child plan a budget. The budget should show how much money your child takes in (each week/each month/each year) and how he or she would like to spend or save

Fourth Quarter Introduction, cont.

that money. Then, have your child make a circle graph that shows how his or her total allowance will be spent.

Use self-sticking notes or masking tape to label the lines on one side of a checkerboard **A–H** and the lines on the other side **1–8**. Place a toy or other small item at the intersection of two squares. Can your child provide its coordinates?

Science

Discuss the differences between invertebrates and vertebrates. Gather a variety of pictures of different vertebrates (fish, amphibians, reptiles, birds, and mammals) and have your child sort the pictures into the five groups.

Ask your child to identify some of the fish and mammals that live in the sea. Have your child read about these unique animals. Ask your child to choose one fish and one sea mammal and compare them using a Venn diagram.

Social Studies

Have your child choose a quotation from Martin Luther King, Jr. to analyze. Have your child describe King's meaning and its significance in today's world.

Discuss the women's suffrage movement. The movement began in 1848 with Elizabeth Cady Stanton and Lucretia Mott. They held a convention that adopted a Declaration of Sentiments. This declaration called for women to have equal rights in education, ownership of property, voting, and other areas. Women were not granted the full right to vote in the United States until 1920. Have your child write a paragraph explaining why women were not allowed to vote in colonial times.

Seasonal Fun

Encourage your child to research your family by interviewing as many generations as possible. Find out about each person's life experiences and what makes him or her special. For each person your child interviews, cut out one large leaf from a sheet of construction paper. Then, help your child sum up each interview in a few sentences, and write them on a leaf. Use a hole punch to create a hole in and tie loops of string through the leaves so that they can easily be hung.

Week 28 Skills

Subject	Skill	Multi-Sensory Learning Activities
Reading and Language Arts	Recognize up to six-syllable words.	• Complete Practice Page 300. • Say words that have three or more syllables. Ask your child to listen carefully, clapping out the word, and tell which syllable is accented.
	Practice spelling and pronunciation, and understand word meanings.	• Complete Practice Pages 301–304. • Have your child use a dictionary to find all the accepted pronunciations of the following words: **tomato**, **practically**, **vase**, **bouquet**, **catsup**, **protocol**, **rodeo**, **horror**, and **pajamas**.
Math	Measure temperature.	• Complete Practice Page 305. • Look around your home for devices used to measure temperature (oral thermometer, candy or meat thermometer, outdoor thermometer, thermostat, etc.). Have your child choose one of these and take a temperature reading every hour.
	Compare and convert measurements.	• Complete Practice Pages 306 and 307. • Ask your child to measure his or her weight and convert it to ounces. Can your child convert the weight to kilograms?
	Add inches and feet.	• Complete Practice Page 308. • Measure the height of your child. Then, create math problems in which your child has to add inches to his or her height, such as, "If you grow 6 inches by next year, how tall will you be?"

Spelling: Syllables

A **syllable** is a part of a word with only one vowel sound. Some words have only one syllable, like **cat**, **leaf** and **ship**. Some words have two or more syllables. **Be-lief** and **trac-tor** have two syllables, **to-ge-ther** and **ex-cel-lent** have three syllables and **con-ver-sa-tion** has four syllables. Some words can have six or more syllables! The word **ex-tra-ter-res-tri-al**, for example, has six syllables.

Follow the instructions below.

1. Count the syllables in each word below, and write the number of syllables on the line.

   a. badger _____   f. grease _____

   b. location _____   g. relationship _____

   c. award _____   h. communication _____

   d. national _____   i. government _____

   e. necessary _____   j. Braille _____

2. Write four words with four syllables each in the blanks.

   a. _____   c. _____

   b. _____   d. _____

3. Write one word with five syllables and one with six syllables. If you need help, use a dictionary.

   Five syllables: _____

   Six syllables: _____

COMPLETE YEAR GRADE 5

Y Says "I"

Match each word from the list to its proper pronunciation. Refer to a dictionary, if necessary.

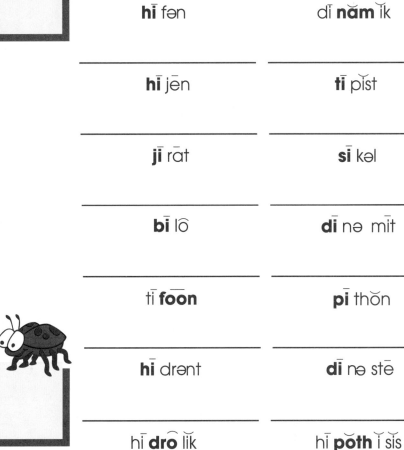

bylaw
cycle
cyclone
dynamic
dynamite
dynasty
gyrate
hydrant
hydraulic
hydrogen
hygiene
hyphen
hypothesis
lyre
python
typhoon
typist
tyrant

hī fən	dī **năm** ĭk
hī jĕn	**tī** pĭst
jī rāt	**sī** kəl
bī lô	**dī** nə mīt
tī **foon**	**pī** thŏn
hī drənt	**dī** nə stē
hī **drô** lĭk	hī **pŏth** ĭ sĭs

sī klōn	**tī** rənt
hī drə jən	līr

Write a metaphor using the words. A metaphor is a direct comparison that does not use **like** or **as** to compare one thing to another. **Example:** The typhoon was an enraged monster destroying the small oceanside town.

_____

_____

Spelling: Finding Mistakes

Circle the four spelling mistakes
in each paragraph. Then write the words
correctly on the lines below.

Last nite, our family went to a nice restaurant. As we were lookking at the menus, a waiter walked in from the kichen carrying a large tray of food. As he walked by us, he triped, and the tray went flying! The food flew all over our table and all over us, too!

_____   _____

_____   _____

Last week, while my dad was washing the car, our dog Jack dicided to help. He stuck his nose in the pale of soapy water, and it tiped over and soaked him! As he shook himself off, the water from his fur went all over the car. "Look!" Dad laffed. "Jack is doing his part!"

_____   _____

_____   _____

For our next feild trip, my class is going to the zoo. We have been studying about animals in sceince class. I'm very eksited to see the elephants, but my freind Karen really wants to see the monkeys. She has been to the zoo before, and she says the monkeys are the most fun to watch.

_____   _____

_____   _____

It seems the rain will never stop! It has been rainning for seven days now, and the sky is always dark and clowdy. Everyone at school is in a bad mood, because we have to stay inside during resess. Will we ever see the son again?

_____   _____

_____   _____

Spelling: Proofreading Practice

Circle the six spelling and pronoun mistakes in each paragraph. Write the words correctly on the lines below.

Jenna always braged about being ready to meet any chalenge or reach any gole. When it was time for our class to elekt it's new officers, Jenna said we should voat for her to be president.

_____   _____   _____

_____   _____   _____

Simon wanted to be ours president, too. He tried to coaks everyone to vote for his. He even lowned kids money to get their votes! Well, Jenna may have too much pryde in herself, but I like her in spit of that. At least she didn't try to buy our votes!

_____   _____   _____

_____   _____   _____

Its true that Jenna tried other ways to get us to vote for hers. She scrubed the chalkboards even though it was my dayly job for that week. One day, I saw her rinseing out the paintbrushes when it was Peter's turn to do it. Then she made sure we knew about her good deeds so we would praize her.

_____   _____   _____

_____   _____   _____

We held the election, but I was shalked when the teacher releesed the results. Simon won! I wondered if he cheeted somehow. I feel like our class was robed! Now Simon is the one who's braging about how great he is. I wish he knew the titel of president doesn't mean anything if no one wants to be around you!

_____   _____   _____

_____   _____   _____

Summer Daze

Write the number of the definition that applies to each **bold** word.

_____ 1. When Mr. Wong works, he never **putters** around.

_____ 2. Mabel would **cop** the prize as the best stickball player in the sixth grade.

_____ 3. The two small girls will **stalk** the tiger swallowtail very carefully.

_____ 4. The **cop** smiled as Shirley humbly scurried by.

_____ 5. I would wear gloves if I wished to climb that **spruce** in the forest.

_____ 6. Shirley imagined spiders **stalking** her in the furnace room.

_____ 7. She never considered that she might **cop** fruit from the market.

_____ 8. Will the students **spruce** up the playground before they leave for the summer?

_____ 9. The **putter** missed the ninth hole by a mile.

_____ 10. Shirley discovered that she liked celery **stalks** very much.

Glossary

stalk   1) a plant stem 2) to stealthily pursue one's prey

3) to walk with a slow, stiff stride

putter   1) a golf club used on the green 2) a golfer who putts 3) to work slowly

cop   1) to steal 2) to capture 3) a police officer

spruce   1) an evergreen tree 2) the wood from this tree 3) to make neat

COMPLETE YEAR GRADE 5

Temperature

The customary system measures temperature in Fahrenheit (F°) degrees.

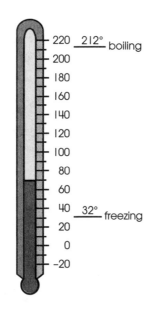

The metric system uses Celsius (C°) degrees.

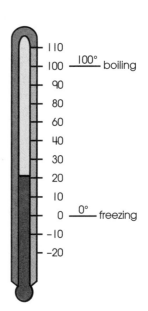

Study the thermometers and answer these questions.

1. Write in the temperature from both systems:

	Fahrenheit	**Celsius**
a. freezing	_____	_____
b. boiling	_____	_____
c. comfortable room temperature	_____	_____
d. normal body temperature	_____	_____

2. Underline the most appropriate temperature for both systems.

a. a reasonably hot day	34°	54°	84°	10°	20°	35°
b. a cup of hot chocolate	95°	120°	190°	60°	90°	120°
c. comfortable water to swim in	55°	75°	95°	10°	25°	40°

3. If the temperature is 35°C is it summer or winter? _____

4. Would ice cream stay frozen at 35°F? _____

5. Which is colder, –10°C or –10°F? _____

6. Which is warmer, 60°C or 60°F? _____

Comparing Measurements

Use the symbols greater than (>), less than (<) or equal to (=) to complete each statement.

10 inches   _____   10 centimeters

40 feet   _____   120 yards

25 grams   _____   25 kilograms

16 quarts   _____   4 gallons

2 liters   _____   2 milliliters

16 yards   _____   6 meters

3 miles   _____   3 kilometers

20 centimeters   _____   20 meters

85 kilograms   _____   8 grams

2 liters   _____   1 gallon

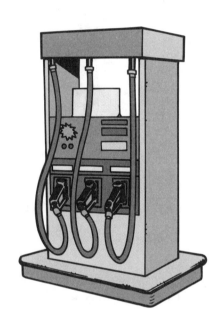

Conversion

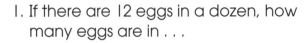

Find the number of units in each fraction described.

1. If there are 12 eggs in a dozen, how many eggs are in . . .

   $\frac{1}{2}$ dozen? _____

   $\frac{1}{4}$ dozen? _____

   $\frac{1}{3}$ dozen? _____

2. If there are 100 centimeters (cm) in a meter, how many cm are in . . .

   $\frac{1}{2}$ meter? _____

   $\frac{1}{4}$ meter? _____

   $\frac{1}{10}$ meter? _____

3. If there are 16 ounces in a pound, how many ounces are in . . .

   $\frac{1}{2}$ pound? _____

   $\frac{1}{4}$ pound? _____

   $\frac{3}{8}$ pound? _____

4. If there are 4 quarts in a gallon, how many quarts are in . . .

   $\frac{1}{2}$ gallon? _____

   $\frac{1}{4}$ gallon? _____

   $\frac{3}{4}$ gallon? _____

5. If there are 60 seconds in a minute, how many seconds are in . . .

   $\frac{1}{2}$ minute? _____

   $\frac{1}{4}$ minute? _____

   $\frac{3}{4}$ minute? _____

6. If there are 1,000 meters in a kilometer, how many meters are in . . .

   $\frac{1}{10}$ kilometer? _____

   $\frac{1}{2}$ kilometer? _____

   $\frac{1}{4}$ kilometer? _____

7. If there are 30 days in most months, how many days are in . . .

   $\frac{1}{3}$ month? _____

   $\frac{1}{6}$ month? _____

   $\frac{1}{10}$ month? _____

8. If there are 24 hours in a day, how many hours are in . . .

   $\frac{1}{3}$ day? _____

   $\frac{2}{3}$ day? _____

   $\frac{1}{4}$ day? _____

9. If there are 36 inches in a yard, how many inches are in . . .

   $\frac{2}{3}$ yard? _____

   $\frac{1}{4}$ yard? _____

   $\frac{1}{2}$ yard? _____

10. If there are 2,000 pounds in a ton, how many pounds are in . . .

   $\frac{1}{2}$ ton? _____

   $\frac{1}{4}$ ton? _____

   $\frac{1}{20}$ ton? _____

Adding Inches and Feet

When adding inches, regroup 1 foot for every 12 inches.

Examples:

a.   1 ft.   8 in.
   + 1 ft.   8 in.
          16 in.

     16 in. = 1 ft. 4 in.

b.   1
   1 ft.   8 in.
   + 1 ft.   8 in.
         4 in.

c.   1
   1 ft.   8 in.
   + 1 ft.   8 in.
   3 ft.   4 in.

1.   2 ft.   4 in.
   + 1 ft.   9 in.

2.   12 ft. 10 in.
   + 1 ft.   5 in.

3.   12 ft.   7 in.
   + 8 ft.   8 in.

4.   1 ft. 5 in.
   + 3 ft. 6 in.

5.   1 ft.   6 in.
   + 1 ft.   6 in.

6.   7 ft.   4 in.
   + 5 ft.   5 in.

7.   28 ft.   8 in.
   + 4 ft.   9 in.

8.   8 ft.   9 in.
   +   7 in.

9.   3 ft.   3 in.
   + 6 ft.   7 in.

Week 29 Skills

Subject	Skill	Multi-Sensory Learning Activities
Reading and Language Arts	Identify sentence subjects and predicates.	• Complete Practice Page 310. • Write sentence subjects and predicates on separate index cards. Have your child choose a card and say if it is a subject or a predicate.
	Identify compound subjects and predicates.	• Complete Practice Pages 311–313. • Have your child combine subjects and predicates to form original sentences, and use some of these sentences to make a story.
	Join sentences by using conjunctions **and**, **but**, **or**, **because**, and **so**.	• Complete Practice Page 314. • Write pairs of simple sentences, such as "The cows knew it was milking time. They walked slowly toward the barn." Ask your child to combine the sentences using a conjunction.
Math	Subtract feet and inches.	• Complete Practice Page 315. • Brainstorm a list of situations in which you measure things in inches and feet. Create subtraction problems from these scenarios.
	Add and subtract pounds and ounces.	• Complete Practice Pages 316 and 317. • Measure the weight of a package to be mailed. Then, give your child another object and ask how much the package will weigh if that object is added to the package.
	Add minutes and hours.	• Complete Practice Page 318. • Look at a clock and ask your child to tell you the current time. Ask what time it will be in 1 hour, 16 minutes.

Subjects and Predicates

The **subject** tells who or what a sentence is about. The **predicate** tells what the subject does, did or is doing. All complete sentences must have a subject and a predicate.

Examples:

Subject	Predicate
Hamsters	are common pets.
Pets	need special care.

Circle the subjects and underline the predicates.

1. Many children keep hamsters as pets.

2. Mice are good pets, too.

3. Hamsters collect food in their cheeks.

4. My sister sneezes around furry animals.

5. My brother wants a dog instead of a hamster.

Write subjects to complete these sentences.

6. _____ has two pet hamsters.

7. _____ got a new pet last week.

8. _____ keeps forgetting to feed his goldfish.

Write predicates to complete these sentences.

9. Baby hamsters_____ .

10. Pet mice _____ .

11. I _____ .

Write **S** if the group of words is a sentence or **NS** if the group of words is not a sentence.

12. _____ A new cage for our hamster.

13. _____ Picked the cutest one.

14. _____ We started out with two.

15. _____ Liking every one in the store.

Combining Subjects

Too many short sentences make writing sound choppy. Often, we can combine sentences with different subjects and the same predicate to make one sentence with a compound subject.

Example:

Lisa tried out for the play. Todd tried out for the play.
Compound subject: Lisa and Todd tried out for the play.

When sentences have different subjects and different predicates, we cannot combine them this way. Each subject and predicate must stay together. Two short sentences can be combined with a conjunction.

Examples:

Lisa got a part in the play. Todd will help make scenery.
Lisa got a part in the play, and Todd will help make scenery.

If a pair of sentences share the same predicate, combine them with compound subjects. If the sentences have different subjects and predicates, combine them using **and**.

1. Rachel read a book about explorers. Eric read the same book about explorers.

    _____

2. Rachel really liked the book. Eric agreed with her.

    _____

3. Vicki went to the basketball game last night. Dan went to the basketball game, too.

    _____

4. Vicki lost her coat. Dan missed his ride home.

    _____

5. My uncle planted corn in the garden. My mother planted corn in the garden.

    _____

6. Isaac helped with the food drive last week. Amy helped with the food drive, too.

    _____

Combining Predicates

If short sentences have the same subject and different predicates, we can combine them into one sentence with a compound predicate.

Example:

Andy got up late this morning.
He nearly missed the school bus.
Compound predicate: Andy got up late this  morning and nearly missed the school bus.

The pronoun **he** takes the place of Andy in the second sentence, so the subjects are the same and can be combined.

When two sentences have different subjects and different predicates, we cannot combine them this way. Two short sentences can be combined with a conjunction.

Examples:

Andy got up late this morning. Cindy woke up early.
Andy got up late this morning, but Cindy woke up early.

If the pair of sentences share the same subject, combine them with compound predicates. If the sentences have different subjects and predicates, combine them using **and** or **but**.

1. Kyle practiced pitching all winter. Kyle became the pitcher for his team.

    _____

2. Kisha studied two hours for her history test. Angela watched TV.

    _____

3. Jeff had an earache. He took medicine four times a day.

    _____

4. Nikki found a new hairstyle. Melissa didn't like that style.

    _____

5. Kirby buys his lunch every day. Sean brings his lunch from home.

    _____

Compound Subjects and Predicates

A compound subject has two or more nouns or pronouns joined by a conjunction. Compound subjects share the same predicate.

Examples:
   Suki and Spot walked to the park in the rain.
   Cars, buses and trucks splashed water on them.
   He and I were glad we had our umbrella.

A **compound predicate** has two or more verbs joined by a conjunction. Compound predicates share the same subject.

Examples:
   Suki **went** in the restroom **and wiped** off her shoes.
   Paula **followed** Suki **and waited** for her.

A sentence can have a compound subject and a compound predicate.

Example: Tina and Maria went to the mall **and shopped** for an hour.
Circle the compound subjects. Underline the compound predicates.

1.   Steve and Jerry went to the store and bought some gum.

2.   Police and firefighters worked together and put out the fire.

3.   Karen and Marsha did their homework and checked it twice.

4.   In preschool, the boys and girls drew pictures and colored them.

Write compound subjects to go with these predicates.

5.   _____ ate peanut butter sandwiches.

6.   _____ left early.

7.   _____ don't make good pets.

8.   _____ found their way home.

9.   _____ are moving to Denver.

Write compound predicates to go with these subjects.

10.   A scary book_____

11.   My friend's sister_____

12.   The shadow_____

13.   The wind_____

14.   The runaway car_____

Joining Sentences

Conjunctions are words that join sentences, words or ideas. When two sentences are joined with **and**, they are more or less equal.

Example: Julio is coming, **and** he is bringing cookies.

When two sentences are joined with **but**, the second sentence contradicts the first one.

Example: Julio is coming, **but** he will be late.

When two sentences are joined with **or**, they name a choice.

Example: Julio might bring cookies, **or** he might bring a cake.

When two sentences are joined with **because**, the second one names the reason for the first one.

Example: I'll bring cookies, too, **because** Julio might forget his.

When two sentences are joined with **so**, the second one names a result of the first one.

Example: Julio is bringing cookies, **so** we will have a snack.

Complete each sentence. The first one has been done for you.

1. We could watch TV, or _we could play a game._____

2. I wanted to seize the opportunity, but_____

3. You had better not deceive me, because _____

4. My neighbor was on vacation, so_____

5. Veins take blood back to your heart, and_____

6. You can't always yield to your impulses, because _____

7. I know that is your belief, but _____

8. It could be reindeer on the roof, or _____

9. Brent was determined to achieve his goal, so _____

10. Brittany was proud of her height, because _____

Subtracting Different Units

Subtract the units. Regroup the feet and inches.

Example:

3 ft. 5 in.	2 + 12 in. ~~3~~ ft. 5 in.	2 ~~3~~ ft. 17 in.
– 1 ft. 8 in.	– 1 ft. 8 in.	– 1 ft. 8 in.
		1 ft. 9 in.

Cannot take
8 from 5, so
regroup 1 foot.

1.   5 ft.   8 in.
     – 3 ft.   9 in.

2.   17 ft.   3 in.
     –   5 in.

3.   11 ft.   5 in.
     – 8 ft.   6 in.

4.   20 ft.   4 in.
     – 6 ft.   8 in.

5.   17 ft.   0 in.
     – 1 ft.   6 in.

6.   115 ft.
     – 7 ft.   8 in.

7. The carpenter's board was 8 ft. 8 in. long. She cut off 1 ft. 10 in. to use on a bench. How much of the board was left?

_____

Subtract the units. Regroup the days and weeks.

Example:

3 weeks 1 day	2 + 7 days ~~3~~ weeks 1 day	2 ~~3~~ weeks 8 days
– 1 week 5 days	– 1 week 5 days	– 1 week 5 days
		1 week 3 days

Cannot take 5 from 1,
so regroup 1 week.

8.   4 weeks   2 days
     – 2 weeks   5 days

9.   3 weeks   5 days
     – 1 week   2 days

10.   11 weeks   4 days
     – 7 weeks   4 days

Adding Ounces and Pounds

When adding ounces, regroup 1 pound for every 16 ounces.

Example:

a.   8 lb. 12 oz.
     + 1 lb. 8 oz.
          20 oz.
	b. 8 lb. 12 oz.
	     + 1 lb. 8 oz.
	          4 oz.
		c. 8 lb. 12 oz.
		     + 1 lb. 8 oz.
		    10 lb. 4 oz.

20 oz. = 1 lb. 4 oz.

1.   2 lb. 7 oz.
     + 1 lb. 11 oz.

2.   3 lb. 11 oz.
     + 1 lb. 11 oz.

3.   27 lb. 12 oz.
    + 9 lb. 12 oz.

4.   114 lb. 8 oz.
   + 59 lb. 10 oz.

5.   1 lb. 8 oz.
     + 1 lb. 8 oz.

6.   1 lb. 2 oz.
     + 1 lb. 14 oz.

7.   7 lb. 12 oz.
     +   13 oz.

8.   15 oz.
     + 3 lb. 5 oz.

9.   15 lb. 6 oz.
    + 17 lb. 9 oz.

10. Twins were born at St. Vincent Hospital today.
One weighs 5 lb. 8 oz.
The other weighs 5 lb. 12 oz.
How much do the babies weigh together?

Subtracting Different Units

Subtract the units. Regroup the pounds and ounces.

Example:

			16	+ 16 oz.			16		
17 lb.	3 oz.		1̸7̸ lb.	3 oz.		1̸7̸ lb.	19 oz.	
− 12 lb.	5 oz.		− 12 lb.	5 oz.		− 12 lb.	5 oz.	
						4 lb.	14 oz.	

1.   5 lb.   8 oz.
    − 3 lb.   8 oz.

2.   17 lb.   3 oz.
    − 12 lb.   11 oz.

3.   9 lb.   11 oz.
    − 3 lb.   14 oz.

4.   2 lb.   5 oz.
    −   8 oz.

5.   1 lb.   8 oz.
    −   9 oz.

6.   7 lb.
    − 1 lb.   9 oz.

Subtract the units. Regroup the minutes and seconds.

Example:

			2	+ 60 sec.			2	
3 min.	25 sec.		3̸ min.	25 sec.		3̸ min.	85 sec.	
− 1 min.	45 sec.		− 1 min.	45 sec.		− 1 min.	45 sec.	
						1 min.	40 sec.	

7.   7 min.   46 sec.
    − 3 min.   29 sec.

8.   4 min.   47 sec.
    − 3 min.   28 sec.

9.   9 min.   23 sec.
    − 8 min.   51 sec.

10.   4 min.   21 sec.
     − 2 min.   53 sec.

11.   12 min.   19 sec.
    − 8 min.   42 sec.

12.   16 min.   42 sec.
    − 8 min.   25 sec.

Adding Minutes and Hours

When adding hours and minutes, regroup 1 hour for every 60 minutes. The first one has been done for you.

1.
```
      1
   2 hr. 34 min.
 + 3 hr. 31 min.
   6 hr.  5 min.
```

2.
```
   5 hr. 24 min.
 + 7 hr. 19 min.
```

3.
```
   2 hr. 39 min.
 + 5 hr. 41 min.
```

4.
```
   16 hr. 51 min.
 +  4 hr.  8 min.
```

5.
```
   3 hr. 43 min.
 + 2 hr. 51 min.
```

6.
```
   3 hr. 14 min.
 + 6 hr. 72 min.
```

7.

+ 50 minutes

Time: _____

8.

+ 1 hour 5 minutes

Time: _____

9.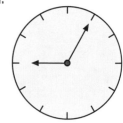

+ 30 minutes

Time: _____

10.

+ 4 hours 35 minutes

Time: _____

11. Geneva worked on her sculpture this week.

Monday:	2 hr.	14 min.
Tuesday:		30 min.
Wednesday:	1 hr.	16 min.
Thursday:	3 hr.	25 min.
Friday:	1 hr.	45 min.

Sum total: _____ _____

Week 30 Skills

Subject	Skill	Multi-Sensory Learning Activities
Reading and Language Arts	Use context clues to interpret meaning.	• Complete Practice Page 320. • Write sentences containing nonsense words. Ask your child to describe the meaning of each nonsense word based on the context.
	Identify the topic sentence of a paragraph.	• Complete Practice Page 321. • Have your child write a topic sentence about having cats as pets. Then, ask your child to fill out a paragraph by writing sentences that contain details to support the topic sentence.
	Answer questions about texts to determine reading comprehension.	• Complete Practice Pages 322 and 323. • Read *The Secret Garden* by Frances Hodgson Burnett with your child. Discuss the ways in which the characters changed over the course of the story.
Math	Understand volume as the number of cubic units that fit inside a figure.	• Complete Practice Pages 324–328. • Provide a die and encourage your child to think of it as a "unit cube." Use the die to measure the approximate volume of various small objects, like a bowl or a drinking glass.
	Understand perimeter as the distance around a figure and area as the number of square units needed to cover a region.	• Complete Practice Page 328. • Discuss some practical applications of perimeter and area, such as measuring for a fence or laying carpet. Teach your child to estimate the perimeter of your yard by pacing the measurement.

Comprehension: "The Ant and the Cricket"

A silly young cricket, who decided to sing
Through the warm sunny months of summer and spring,
Began to complain when he found that at home
His cupboards were empty and winter had come.

At last by starvation the cricket made bold
To hop through the wintertime snow and the cold.
Away he set off to a miserly ant
To see if to keep him alive he would grant
Shelter from rain, a mouthful of grain.
"I wish only to borrow—I'll repay it tomorrow—
If not, I must die of starvation and sorrow!"

Said the ant to the cricket, "It's true I'm your friend,
But we ants never borrow, we ants never lend;
We ants store up crumbs so when winter arrives
We have just enough food to keep ants alive."

Use context clues to answer these questions about the poem.

1. What is the correct definition of **cupboards**?

   ❑ where books are stored   ❑ where food is stored   ❑ where shoes are stored

2. What is the correct definition of **miserly**?

   ❑ selfish/stingy   ❑ generous/kind   ❑ mean/ugly

3. What is the correct definition of **grant**?

   ❑ to take away   ❑ to belch   ❑ to give

4. In two sentences, describe what the poet is trying to say with this poem.

   _____

   _____

   _____

   _____

Dolphins

Underline the topic sentence of each paragraph. Add the missing punctuation.

Dolphins are among the most intelligent animals on Earth. They are playful as well as smart and are easily trained for zoo and aquarium shows. They jump through hoops and fetch and grab objects from the trainer's hands Dolphins communicate with each other in a variety of ways using clicking whistling and slapping sounds.

Dolphins can locate objects easily under the water through a system called echolocation This is like a built-in sonar system. The dolphin makes a series of clicking sounds then listens for the sounds as echoes bounce back from the underwater object.

Many dolphins are caught and killed. These friendly mammals are killed by hunters of several nations for their meat and oils and are often caught in fishing nets intended to catch tuna cod and other fish. Steps have been taken to try to limit the number of dolphins killed

Rembrandt

Rembrandt was one of the greatest artists of all time. He was born on July 15, 1606, in Leiden, Holland. Rembrandt began painting at an early age. At the age of fifteen, he traveled to Amsterdam to study art but soon returned home to paint on his own.

Rembrandt's first paintings were of subjects from the Bible and from history. He used bright colors and glossy paints. These paintings were very popular, and soon, Rembrandt became well-known in his community.

In 1628, Rembrandt began to teach art. He was a respected teacher with many students.

In 1632, Rembrandt moved back to Amsterdam, where he began to paint portraits of many well-known people. He soon became famous in Holland for his beautiful portraits.

In 1634, he married a wealthy and educated girl named Saskia. They moved into a large home where Rembrandt hung many of the paintings he had collected.

Rembrandt continued to succeed as an artist, but tragedy struck. Three of Rembrandt's four children died very young. And, in 1642, his wife Saskia died.

Rembrandt became very sad. He began to paint with darker colors. But somehow, his painting grew even more beautiful. He used dark colors around the figures in his paintings.

The figures themselves were painted as if a soft light were shining on them. Rembrandt began to paint more for himself and less for other people. Although his work was brilliant, he was not able to make enough money to keep his house. In 1657, his house and his possessions were auctioned off. Rembrandt was bankrupt.

Rembrandt continued to paint until he died on October 4, 1669. His most famous painting was titled *The Night Watch.*

Rembrandt created over 600 paintings, 300 etchings and 1,400 drawings. Some of his most fascinating paintings were the one hundred portraits he painted of himself. These self-portraits are a remarkable record of his life.

Understanding Rembrandt

Answer the questions below from your reading of page 322.

True or False

Rembrandt . . .

_____ was one of the greatest artists of all time.

_____ was born on July 15, 1606, in Florence, Italy.

_____ began painting at an early age.

_____ traveled to Amsterdam at the age of fifteen to study architecture.

Check and write:

Rembrandt used ☐ soft ☐ bright colors and _____ paints.

Underline:

In 1634, Rembrandt married . . .
a wealthy and educated girl named Saskia.
a poor girl from Amsterdam named Saskia.

Check and write:

Although Rembrandt was successful as an artist,

☐ tragedy ☐ good fortune began to strike his family.

Three of his _____ children died at a very early age.

In 1642, ☐ Rembrandt's father died. ☐ Rembrandt's wife died.

Rembrandt's sadness caused him to use ☐ darker ☐ lighter colors.

Check, circle and write:

Rembrandt died on October 4, ☐ 1669. ☐ 1700.

Rembrandt's most famous painting was called _____.

Rembrandt's works included:

☐ paintings ☐ drawings ☐ etchings ☐ self-portraits

Volume

Volume is the measure of the inside of a figure. Find the volume. Count the boxes.

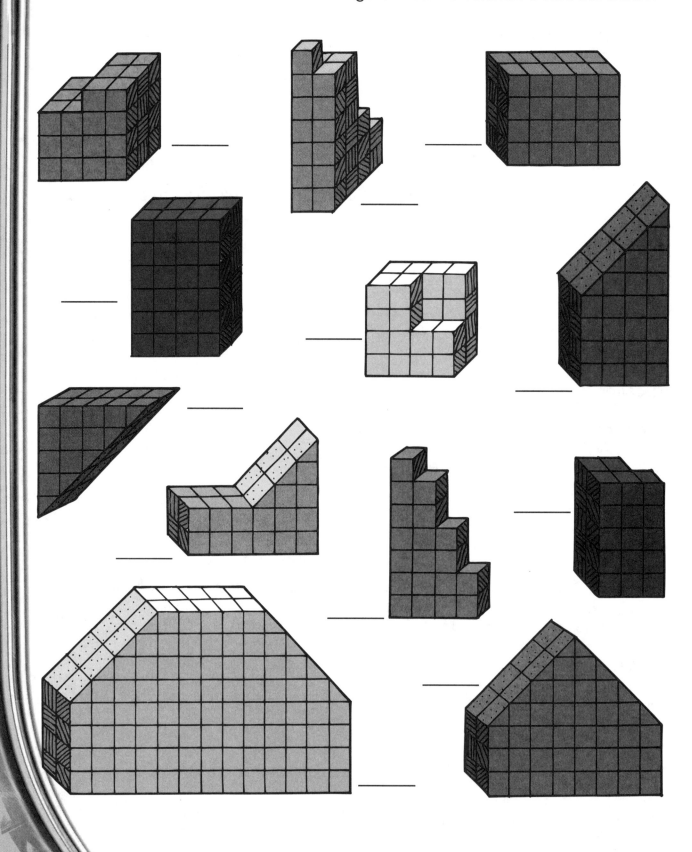

Volume

The formula for finding the volume of a box is length times width times height (**L** x **W** x **H**). The answer is given in cubic units.

Solve the problems.

Example:
Height   8 ft.
Length   8 ft.
Width   8 ft. **L** x **W** x **H** = **volume**
         8' x 8' x 8' = 512 cubic ft. or 512 ft.³

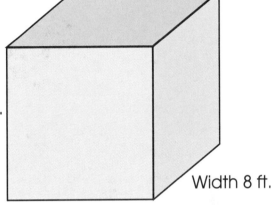

Height 8 ft.

Width 8 ft.

Length 8 ft.

4 ft.

6 ft.

12 ft.

V =_____

6 ft.

2 ft.

1.5 ft.

V =_____

7 ft.

9 ft.

V =_____

3 ft.

2 ft.

2 ft.

2 ft.

V =_____

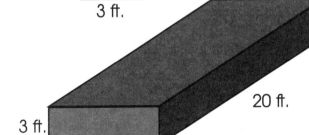

20 ft.

3 ft.

6 ft.

V =_____

5 in.

15 in.

22 in.

V =_____ in.³   V =_____ ft.³

Volume of Prisms

Volume is measured in cubic units.

Volume of a **nonrectangular prism**
= base area • height

$V = b \cdot h$

$V = (\frac{1}{2} \cdot 4 \cdot 6) \cdot 12$

$V = 144 \text{ in}^3$

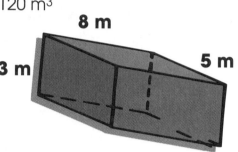

4 in.

6 in.

12 in

Volume of a **rectangular prism**
= l • w • h

$V = 8 \cdot 5 \cdot 3$

$V = 120 \text{ m}^3$

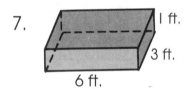

8 m

3 m

5 m

Find the volume of each prism.

1.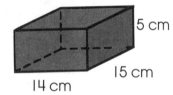

5 cm

15 cm

14 cm

4.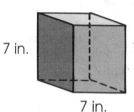

7 in.

7 in.

7 in.

7.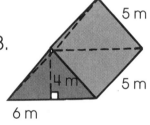

1 ft.

3 ft.

6 ft.

2.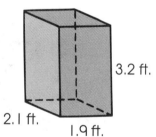

3.2 ft.

2.1 ft.

1.9 ft.

5.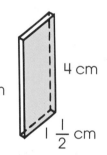

4 cm

$\frac{1}{5}$ cm

$1\frac{1}{2}$ cm

8.

5 m

4 m

5 m

6 m

3.

2 m

5 m

5 m

6.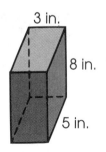

3 in.

8 in.

5 in.

Volume

Volume is the number of cubic units that fills a space. A **cubic unit** has 6 equal sides, like a child's block. To find the volume (**V**) of something, multiply the length (**l**) by the width (**w**) by the height (**h**), or **V = l x w x h**. The answer will be in cubic units (³). Sometimes it's easier to understand volume if you imagine a figure is made of small cubes.

Example: V = l x w x h

V = 4 x 6 x 5

V = 120 in.³

Solve the following problems.

1. What is the volume of a cube that is 7 inches on each side? _____

2. How many cubic inches of cereal are in a box that is
    10 inches long, 6 inches wide and 4.5 inches high? _____

3. Jeremy made a tower of five blocks that are each 2.5 inches
    square. How many cubic inches are in his tower? _____

4. How many cubic feet of gravel are in the back of a full dump
    truck that measures 7 feet wide by 4 feet tall by 16 feet long? _____

5. Will 1,000 cubic inches of dirt fill a flower box that is 32 inches
    long, 7 inches wide and 7 inches tall? _____

6. A mouse needs 100 cubic inches of air to live for an hour.
    Will your pet mouse be okay for an hour in an airtight box
    that's 4.5 inches wide by 8.25 inches long by 2.5 inches high? _____

7. Find the volume of the figures below. 1 cube = 1 inch³

A.  V = _____

B. 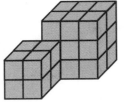 V = _____

C. 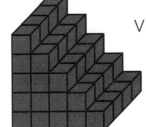 V = _____

D.  V = _____

Perimeter, Area, and Volume

Find the perimeter and area.

1. Length = 8 ft.

   Width = 11 ft.

   P = _____   A = _____

2. Length = 12 ft.

   Width = 10 ft.

   P = _____   A = _____

3. Length = 121 ft.

   Width = 16 ft.

   P = _____   A = _____

4. Length = 72 in.

   Width = 5 ft.

   P = _____   A = _____

Find the perimeter, area and volume.

5. Length = 7 ft.

   Width = 12 ft.

   Height = 10 ft.

   P = _____

   A = _____

   V = _____

7. Length = 12 in.

   Width = 15 in.

   Height = 20 in.

   P = _____

   A = _____

   V = _____

6. Length = 48 in.

   Width = 7 ft.

   Height = 12 in.

   P = _____

   A = _____

   V = _____

8. Length = 22 ft.

   Width = 40 ft.

   Height = 10 ft.

   P = _____

   A = _____

   V = _____

Week 31 Skills

Subject	Skill	Multi-Sensory Learning Activities
Reading and Language Arts	Review reading comprehension.	• Complete Practice Pages 330 and 331. • Share with your child memories about an eventful time in history that you lived through. Then, ask your child to read a book about that time. Ask your child to compare and contrast information from the reading with the story you told.
	Review editing and proofreading.	• Complete Practice Pages 332 and 333. • Read *Carry On, Mr. Bowditch* by Jean Lee Latham. Have your child write a review of the book as if for a newspaper. The review should include a summary of the story as well as your child's own opinions. Then, edit the article and have your child proofread it carefully.
Math	Identify and classify quadrilaterals.	• Complete Practice Pages 334–337. • Have your child find quadrilaterals around your home. Ask him or her to identify each shape.
	Build larger shapes from smaller shapes.	• Complete Practice Page 338. • Polygons are found everywhere—in art, design, architecture, nature, and mathematics. Help your child create a mosaic with polygon shapes.

Comprehension: Proserpine and Pluto

Proserpine was terrified in Pluto's palace in the underworld. She missed her mother, Ceres, and would not stop crying.

When Ceres discovered her daughter was missing, she searched the whole Earth looking for her. Of course, she did not find her. Ceres was so unhappy about Proserpine's disappearance that she refused to do her job, which was to make things grow. When Ceres did not work, rain could not fall and crops could not grow. Finally, Ceres went to Jupiter for help.

Jupiter was powerful, but so was Pluto. Jupiter told Ceres he could get Proserpine back from Pluto if she had not eaten any of Pluto's food. As it turned out, Proserpine had eaten something. She had swallowed six seeds from a piece of fruit. Because he felt sorry for the people on Earth who were suffering, Pluto told Jupiter that Proserpine could return temporarily to Ceres so she would cheer up and make crops grow again. But Pluto later came back for Proserpine and forced her to spend six months each year with him in the underworld— one month for each seed she had eaten. Every time she returned to the underworld, Ceres mourned and refused to do her job. This is how the Romans explained the seasons—when Proserpine is on Earth with Ceres, it is spring and summer; when Proserpine goes to the underworld, it is fall and winter.

Answer these questions about Proserpine and Pluto.

1. What happened to Ceres when Pluto took her daughter?

   _____

2. Whom did Ceres ask for help to get her daughter back?

   _____

3. Why did Proserpine have to return to Pluto's underworld?

   _____

4. How long did Proserpine have to stay in the underworld each time she returned?

   _____

Comprehension: Apollo and Phaethon

Apollo, the sun god, had a son named Phaethon (Fay-athun). Like most boys, Phaethon was proud of his father. He liked to brag to his friends about Apollo's important job, but no one believed that the great Apollo was his father.

Phaethon thought of a way to prove to his friends that he was telling the truth. He went to Apollo and asked if he could drive the chariot of the sun. If his friends saw him making the sun rise and set, they would be awestruck!

Apollo did not want to let Phaethon drive the chariot. He was afraid Phaethon was not strong enough to control the horses. But Phaethon begged until Apollo gave in. "Stay on the path," Apollo said. "If you dip too low, the sun will catch the Earth on fire. If you go too high, people will freeze."

Unfortunately, Apollo's worst fears came true. Phaethon could not control the horses. He let them pull the chariot of the sun too close to the Earth. To keep the Earth from burning, Jupiter, father of the gods, sent a thunderbolt that hit Phaethon and knocked him from the driver's seat. When Phaethon let go of the reins, the horses pulled the chariot back up onto the proper path. Phaethon was killed as he fell to earth. His body caught fire and became a shooting star.

Answer these questions about the Roman legend of Apollo and his son.

1. Who did not believe Apollo was Phaethon's father? _____

2. What did Phaethon do to prove Apollo was his father?

   _____

3. Why did Jupiter send a lightning bolt? _____

   _____

4. Which was not a warning from Apollo to Phaethon?

   ❏ Don't go too close to the Earth. It will burn up.

   ❏ Don't pet the horses. They will run wild.

   ❏ Don't go too far from the Earth. It will freeze.

Proofreading

Proofreading or "proofing" means to carefully look over what has been written, checking for spelling, grammar, punctuation and other errors. At a newspaper, this is the job of a copyeditor. All good writers carefully proofread and correct their own work before turning it in to a copyeditor—or a teacher.

Here are three common proofreading marks:

Correct spelling   dog ~~doi~~

Replace with lowercase letter   A̸

Replace with uppercase letter   a̲̲

Carefully read the following paragraphs. Use proofreading marks to mark errors in the second paragraph. Correct all errors. The first sentence has been done for you.

alarm
A six- ~~alurm~~ fire at 2121 w̲i̲ndsor Terrace on the northeast

side awoke apartment R̸esidents at 3 A.M. yesterday

morning. Elven people were in the biulding. No one was

hurt in the blase, which caused $200,000 of property

damage.

Proporty manager Jim smith credits a perfectly Functioning smoke alurm system

for waking residents so they could get out safely. A springkler system were also

in plase. "There was No panick," Smith said proudly. "Everone was calm and

Orderly."

Editing

Use editing marks to show the changes that need to be made in the following sentences.

1. billy bob branstool was the biggest bully at our school

2. mr. Smith told my mother that i was not a good student

3. I heard your mom say, "give your mother a kiss.

4. david and justin liked reading about dinosaurs especially tyrannosaurus rex.

5. milton said to to mabel "maybe we can play tomorrow."

6. lisa and Phil knew the answers to the questions but they would not raise hands.

7. too many people were going to see the movie so we decided to go get pizza instead

8. tillie's aunt teresa was coming to visit for the month of may

9. we lived in a small town called sophia, north carolina, for 20 days before we decided to move away.

10. little elves do not always live under bridges but sometimes little fish do.

11. i was reading the book called, *haunting at midnight.*

12. kevin and i decided that we would be detective bob and detective joe.

13. there were thirteen questions on the test. kevin missed all but the first one

14. thirty of us were going on a fieldtrip when suddenly the teachertold the bus driver to turn around.

Types of Quadrilaterals

A **quadrilateral** is a shape with four sides and four angles. The sum of angles in all quadrilaterals is 360°. Like triangles, quadrilaterals come in different shapes and are categorized by their sides and their angles.

A **square** has four parallel sides of equal length and four 90° angles.

A **rectangle** has four parallel sides, but only its opposite sides are equal length; it has four 90° angles.

A **parallelogram** has four parallel sides, with the opposite sides of equal length.

A **trapezoid** has two opposite sides that are parallel; its sides may or may not be equal length; its angles may include none, one or two that are 90°.

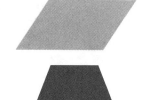

Study the examples. Then complete the exercises below.

1. Color in the correct quadrilaterals.

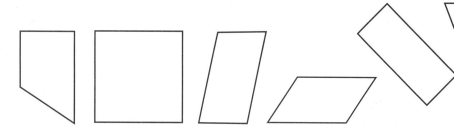

Color two squares blue.   Color two rectangles red.

Color two parallelograms yellow.   Color two trapezoids green.

2. Circle the number that shows the missing angle for each quadrilateral. Then name the possible quadrilaterals that could have those angles.

A. 90°, 90°, 90°   45°   90°   180°   _____

B. 65°, 115°, 65°   65°   90°   115°   _____

C. 90°, 110°, 90°   45°   70°   125°   _____

D. 100°, 80°, 80°   40°   80°   100°   _____

E. 90°, 120°, 50°   50°   75°   100°   _____

Identify the Quadrilateral

Cut out and sort the shapes. Make your own categories and name them.

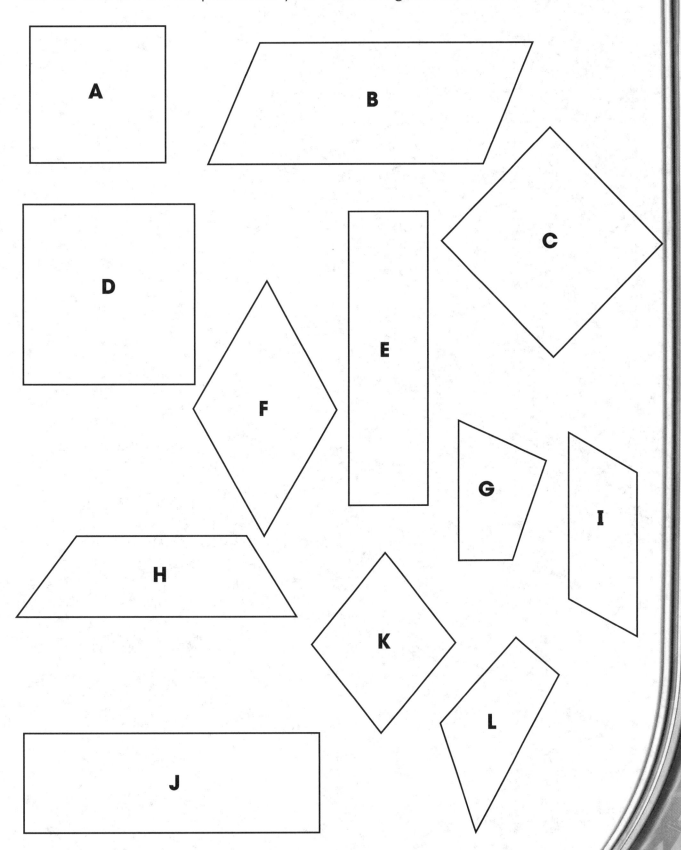

Classifying Quadrilaterals

The sum of the angles in any quadrilateral is 360°.

Name	Description	Example
trapezoid	I pair of opposite sides parallel	
parallelogram	opposite sides parallel, opposite sides and opposite angles congruent	
rhombus	parallelogram with all sides congruent	
rectangle	parallelogram with four right angles	
square	rectangle with four congruent sides	

Find x.

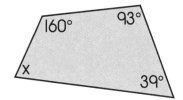

Example 1

93° + 39° + 160° = 292°

360° – 292° = 68°

x = 68°

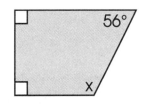

Example 2

90° + 90° + 56° = 236°

360° – 236° = 124°

x = 124°

Give all names for each quadrilateral. Then, find each missing angle measure.

1.
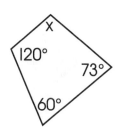

2.
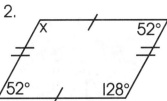

3.
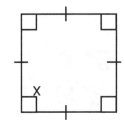

4.
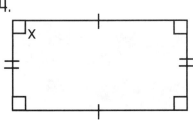

5.
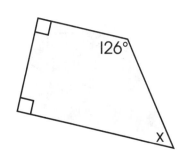

6.
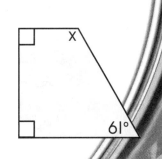

Shapes in Hiding

Shade triangles to make each shape.

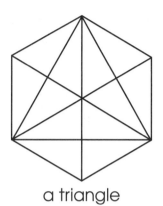

a triangle

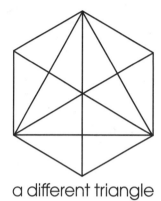

a different triangle

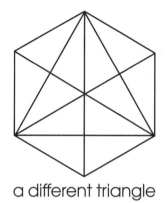

a different triangle

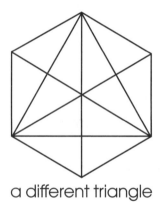

a different triangle

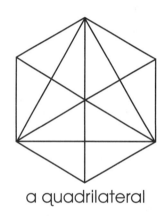

a quadrilateral

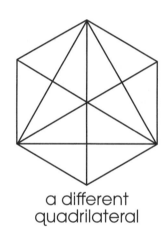

a different
quadrilateral

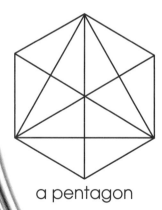

a pentagon

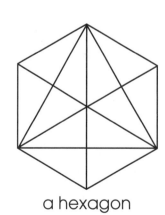

a hexagon

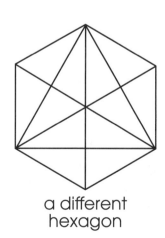

a different
hexagon

Week 32 Skills

Subject	Skill	Multi-Sensory Learning Activities
Reading and Language Arts	Review topic sentences.	• Complete Practice Page 340. • Copy paragraphs from a book, magazine, or newspaper. Eliminate the topic sentence, but leave a space where it was written. Have your child read each paragraph and write a topic sentence.
	Identify the supporting sentences of a paragraph.	• Complete Practice Page 341. • Have your child write an article about a famous scientist. Have him or her form a topic sentence and several supporting sentences for each paragraph.
	Understand and identify the main idea of a text.	• Complete Practice Pages 342 and 343. • Show your child a picture from a magazine or book. Ask your child to study the picture and tell the main idea.
Math	Build shapes and use tangrams.	• Complete Practice Pages 344–347. • Ask your child to look around your home for geometric shapes. Ask him or her to recreate those shapes using the tangram pieces on page 345.
	Identify polyhedrons.	• Complete Practice Page 348. • A pyramid has four faces that are triangles. Ask your child to research the dimensions of a famous pyramid in Egypt and determine whether or not it is a polyhedron.

Writing: Topic Sentences

The topic sentence in a paragraph usually comes first. Sometimes, however, the topic sentence can come at the end or even in the middle of a paragraph. When looking for the topic sentence, try to find the one that tells the main idea of a paragraph.

Read the following paragraphs and underline the topic sentence in each.

The maple tree sheds its leaves every year. The oak and elm trees shed their leaves, too. Every autumn, the leaves on these trees begin changing color. Then, as the leaves gradually begin to die, they fall from the trees. Trees that shed their leaves annually are called deciduous trees.

When our family goes skiing, my brother enjoys the thrill of going down the steepest hill as fast as he can. Mom and Dad like to ski because it gets them out of the house and into the fresh air. I enjoy looking at the trees and birds and the sun shining on the snow. There is something about skiing that appeals to everyone in my family. Even the dog came along on our last skiing trip!

If you are outdoors at night and there is traffic around, you should always wear bright clothing so that cars can see you. White is a good color to wear at night. If you are riding a bicycle, be sure it has plenty of reflectors, and if possible, headlamps as well. Be especially careful when crossing the street, because sometimes drivers cannot see you in the glare of their headlights. Being outdoors at night can be dangerous, and it is best to be prepared!

Writing: Supporting Sentences

A **paragraph** is a group of sentences that tell about one topic. The **topic sentence** in a paragraph usually comes first and tells the main idea of the paragraph. **Supporting sentences** follow the topic sentence and provide details about the topic.

Write at least three supporting sentences for each topic sentence below.

Example: Topic Sentence: Carly had an accident on her bike. **Supporting Sentences:** She was on her way to the store to buy some bread. A car came weaving down the road and scared her. She rode her bike off the road so the car wouldn't hit her. Now, her knee is scraped, but she's all right.

1. I've been thinking of ways I could make some more money after school.

   _____

   _____

   _____

2. In my opinion, cats (dogs, fish, etc.) make the best pets.

   _____

   _____

   _____

3. My life would be better if I had a(n) (younger sister, younger brother, older sister, older brother).

   _____

   _____

   _____

4. I'd like to live next door to a (swimming pool, video store, movie theater, etc.).

   _____

   _____

   _____

Beth Is Sick

Poor Beth is sick, and she doesn't know why. She felt great yesterday, but this morning she woke up with a headache, a fever and a horrible sore throat. Beth is disappointed because today is the day her class is going to the new science museum. Why did she have to be sick on a field trip day? How did she get ill so quickly?

Beth and Kim talk on the phone about Beth's situation for twenty minutes. Because they planned to be field trip partners, Kim is really sad Beth isn't going to school today. Kim tells Beth she probably got sick because she didn't wear a jacket to school yesterday, and it was a cold day. She tells Beth that if your body gets cold, you catch germs more easily. Beth tells Kim that is silly. She believes Kim has a virus.

Beth remembers learning about viruses in science class. Mr. Fridley told them that viruses are noncellular structures that can only be seen through an electron microscope, which magnifies them thousands of times. On its own, a virus is a lifeless particle that can't reproduce, but when a virus enters a living cell, it starts reproducing and can sometimes harm the host cell. Viruses that harm host cells cause disease like chicken pox, the flu and colds. Mr. Fridley told them that shaking hands with or being sneezed or coughed on by an infected person may infect you with the virus. Beth believes that she became infected from someone since lots of people are sick at this time of year. Kim promises Beth a full report on the science museum.

Underline the main idea of the story.

Beth has a headache, fever and a sore throat.

Beth and Kim try to discover why Beth is sick.

Viruses cause diseases.

Mr. Fridley taught them about viruses.

Check the correct answers.

Viruses... ❑ can't be seen through an ordinary light microscope.

❑ pass easily from one person to another.

❑ are thousands of times bigger than regular cells.

❑ enter living cells and start reproducing.

What are some ways to avoid viruses? _____

_____

Main Idea: Creating Art

No one knows exactly when the first human created the first painting. Crude drawings and paintings on the walls of caves show that humans have probably always expressed themselves through art. These early cave pictures show animals being hunted, people dancing and other events of daily life. The simplicity of the paintings reflect the simple lifestyles of these primitive people.

The subjects of early paintings also help to make another important point. Art is not created out of nothing. The subjects an artist chooses to paint reflect the history, politics and culture of the time and place in which he/she lives. An artist born and raised in New York City, for example, is not likely to paint scenes of the Rocky Mountains. An artist living in the Rockies is not likely to paint pictures of city life.

Of course, not all paintings are realistic. Many artists choose to paint pictures that show their own "inner vision" as opposed to what they see with their eyes. Many religious paintings of earlier centuries look realistic but contain figures of angels. These paintings combine the artist's inner vision of angels with other things, such as church buildings, that can be seen.

Answer these questions about creating art.

1. Circle the main idea:

    Art was important to primitive people because it showed hunting and dancing scenes, and is still important today.

    Through the ages, artists have created paintings that reflect the culture, history and politics of the times, as well as their own inner visions.

2. Why is an artist living in the Rocky Mountains less likely to paint city scenes?

    _____

    _____

3. In addition to what they see with their eyes, what do some artists' paintings also show?

    _____

    _____

Lines Across a Triangle

Draw the given number of straight lines to divide each triangle into the shapes listed. The first one has been done for you.

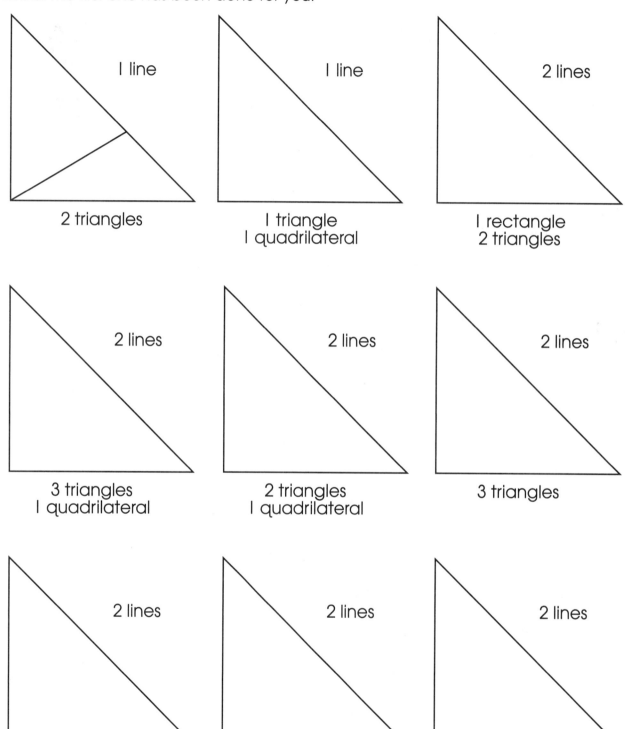

| 1 line | 1 line | 2 lines |
| 2 triangles | 1 triangle
1 quadrilateral | 1 rectangle
2 triangles |

| 2 lines | 2 lines | 2 lines |
| 3 triangles
1 quadrilateral | 2 triangles
1 quadrilateral | 3 triangles |

| 2 lines | 2 lines | 2 lines |
| 2 triangles
2 quadrilaterals | 2 triangles
1 pentagon | 2 triangles
1 square |

Making a Tangram Set

You will need: a piece of tagboard, a ruler, a pencil and scissors

Using the ruler to measure precisely, cut the tagboard into a 5" square. Cut the square according to the pattern below. Laminate the finished pieces (or cover with clear shelf paper).

Use the shapes to form triangles, quadrilaterals, and pictures. For a challenge, identify each shape and each type of angle.

Totally Tangram!

Use the Tangram pieces from page 345 to create the shapes below.

Now, use the tangram pieces to create your own pictures, shapes and designs. Trace around each image you make. Save the outlines and try to recreate the images another day.

Polyhedrons

A **polyhedron** is a solid figure with many flat faces shaped like polygons.

Parts of a Polyhedron

Faces: flat surfaces (sides) **F = 4**

Vertices: corners or points (where 3 edges meet) **V = 4**

Edges: parts of a line (where 2 faces meet) **E = 6**

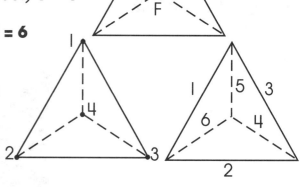

Use this formula to tell if a solid figure is a polyhedron.

$$E = F + V - 2$$

Example: 6 = 4 + 4 − 2
8 − 2
6 = 6

Find the parts of the figures and tell if they are polyhedrons.

1. F = ___
    V = ___
    E = ___
    E = F + V − 2
    Yes ___ No ___

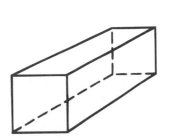

2. F = ___
    V = ___
    E = ___
    E = F + V − 2
    Yes ___ No ___

3. F = ___
    V = ___
    E = ___
    E = F + V − 2
    Yes ___ No ___

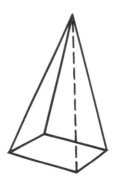

4. F = ___
    V = ___
    E = ___
    E = F + V − 2
    Yes ___ No ___

Week 33 Skills

Subject	Skill	Multi-Sensory Learning Activities
Reading and Language Arts	Review reading comprehension.	• Complete Practice Pages 350–352. • Ask your child to write a poem or short story in which at least one type of animal is personified.
	Write an essay that compares and contrasts.	• Complete Practice Page 353. • Read *The 500 Hats of Bartholomew Cubbins* by Dr. Seuss. Then, read another Dr. Seuss book of your child's choosing. Have your child write an essay comparing and contrasting the two books.
Math	Organize and interpret data from charts.	• Complete Practice Pages 354 and 355. • Show your child examples of charts from a newspaper or magazine. Ask your child questions about the information presented in the charts. Then, ask why charts are sometimes better at presenting data than a paragraph.
	Organize and interpret data from bar graphs.	• Complete Practice Pages 356–358. • Ask your child what mountain peaks he or she has heard of or seen. Help your child locate major mountains on a map or in a world atlas and have your child make a bar graph comparing their heights.

Comprehension: "The Eagle"

Personification is a figure of speech in which human characteristics are given to an animal or object.

Example: The trees danced in the wind.

Trees do not dance; therefore, the trees are being personified.

He clasps the crag with crooked hands:
Close to the sun in lonely lands,
Ringed with the azure world, he stands.

The wrinkled sea beneath him crawls;
He watches from his mountain walls,
And like a thunderbolt he falls.

       —*Alfred, Lord Tennyson*

Answer these questions about the poem.

1. What is the correct definition of **crag**? _____

   _____

2. What is the correct definition of **azure**? _____

3. Which phrases in the poem show personification? _____

   _____

4. Explain what one of these phrases actually means. _____

   _____

   _____

   _____

5. What is the author trying to say in the last line of the poem?

   _____

   _____

Comprehension: Epitaphs

Epitaphs are verses written on tombstones and were very popular in the past. The following epitaphs were written by unknown authors.

On a Man Named Merideth

Here lies one blown out of breath
Who lived a merry life and died a Merideth.

On a Dentist

Stranger, approach this spot with gravity:
John Brown is filling his last cavity.

On Leslie Moore

Here lies what's left
Of Leslie Moore
No Les
No more

Answer these questions about the epitaphs.

1. What does the phrase "blown out of breath" mean?

    _____

2. What does the author mean when he says "and died a Merideth"?

    _____

3. What cavity is John Brown filling? _____

4. Write an epitaph of your own.

    _____

    _____

    _____

    _____

    _____

Get the Facts, Max

Read the paragraphs to answer the questions below.

The islands of Aruba, Bonaire and Curaçao, sometimes known as the ABC islands, are part of the Netherlands Antilles. They lie 50 miles north off the coast of Venezuela. Three more islands, St. Eustatius, Saba and St. Martin (the northern half of which belongs to France), are approximately 500 miles northeast of the ABC islands.

Until 1949, the islands were known as the Dutch West Indies or Curaçao Territory. In 1986, Aruba separated to become a self-governing part of the Netherlands Realm.

On the island of Curaçao, most food is imported. Because it is so rocky, little farming is possible. The island is the largest and most heavily populated of the Netherlands Antilles. Its oil refineries, among the largest in the world, give its people a relatively high standard of living. Today, most people of Curaçao work in the shipping, refining or tourist industry.

Netherlands Antilles—other Facts

Area:

Aruba	75 square miles
Bonaire	111 square miles
Curaçao	171 square miles
Saba	5 square miles
St. Eustatius	11 square miles
St. Martin	13 square miles

Capital: Willemstad

Major languages: Dutch, Papiamento (a mixture of Spanish, Dutch, Portuguese, Carib and English), English, Spanish

1. Name the capital of the Netherlands Antilles. _____

2. What industry gives the people a high standard of living? _____

3. Name the ABC islands. _____

4. What is Papiamento? _____

5. Why must food be imported to Curaçao? _____

6. Which island is smallest? _____

7. Which two islands are the largest? _____

8. Which island belongs in part to France? _____

9. In what year did Aruba become self-governing? _____

Advantages and Disadvantages

As in the comparison/contrast essay, it is easiest to put all of the advantages in one paragraph and the disadvantages in another paragraph.

Write an essay in response to the prompt.

Writing Prompt: Think about what a society would be like if all people had the same skin tone, hair color, eye color, height and weight. What would the benefits of living in such a society be? Would there be any disadvantages? What would they be?

_____

_____

_____

_____

_____

_____

_____

_____

_____

_____

When you finish writing, reread your essay. Use this checklist to help make corrections.

❑ My essay makes sense.

❑ I used correct spelling, grammar and punctuation.

❑ I answered the writing prompt.

❑ I have varied sentence length.

Tables

Organizing data into tables makes it easier to compare numbers. As evident in the example, putting many numbers in a paragraph is confusing. When the same numbers are organized in a table, you can compare numbers at a glance. Tables can be arranged several ways and still be easy to read and understand.

Example: Money spent on groceries:
Family A: week 1 — $68.50; week 2 — $72.25; week 3 — $67.00; week 4 — $74.50.
Family B: week 1 — $42.25; week 2 — $47.50; week 3 — $50.25; week 4 — $53.50.

	Week 1	Week 2	Week 3	Week 4
Family A	$68.50	$72.25	$67.00	$74.50
Family B	$42.25	$47.50	$50.25	$53.50

Complete the following exercises.

1. Finish the table below. Then answer the questions. Data: Steve weighs 230 lb. and is 6 ft. 2 in. tall. George weighs 218 lb. and is 6 ft. 3 in. tall. Chuck weighs 225 lb. and is 6 ft. 1 in. tall. Henry weighs 205 lb. and is 6 ft. tall.

	Henry	George	Chuck	Steve
Weight				
Height				

   a. Who is tallest? _____   b. Who weighs the least? _____

2. On another sheet of paper, prepare 2 tables comparing the amount of money made by 3 booths at the school carnival this year and last year. In the first table, write the names of the games in the left-hand column (like **Family A** and **Family B** in the example). In the second table (using the same data), write the years in the left-hand column. Here is the data: fish pond—this year $15.60, last year $13.50; bean-bag toss—this year $13.45, last year $10.25; ring toss— this year $23.80, last year $18.80. After you complete both tables, answer the following questions.
   a. Which booth made the most money this year?

   _____

   b. Which booth made the biggest improvement from last year to this year?

   _____

Charting the Weather

For four months, the students in Ms. Forecaster's class charted the sunny, partly sunny and cloudy days. The following chart shows their findings to the nearest tenth.

MONTH	SUNNY	PARTLY SUNNY	CLOUDY
October	13.4	12.8	4.8
November	7	13.1	9.9
December	6.3	11	13.7
January	8.4	16.7	5.9

1. How many more sunny days did January have than December? _____

2. In November, how many more cloudy days were there than sunny days? _____

3. How many more partly sunny days were there than sunny days in January? _____

4. What is the difference in days between the month with the most cloudy days and the month that had the fewest cloudy days? _____

5. Which month had the most sunny days? How many more sunny days did it have than the month with the second most? Which month came in second? _____

6. Which month had the most cloudy days? Which month had the fewest cloudy days? How many total cloudy days were there in these four months? _____

Extension: Find the total number of sunny, partly sunny and cloudy days in these four months. Then, find the average number of days for each type of weather.

Bar Graphs

Another way to organize information is a **bar graph**. The bar graph in the example compares the number of students in 4 elementary schools. Each bar stands for 1 school. You can easily see that School A has the most students and School C has the least. The numbers along the left show how many students attend each school.

Example:

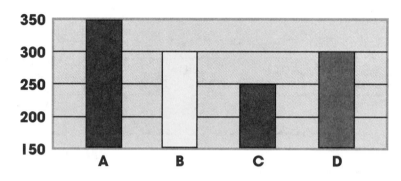

Complete the following exercises.

1. This bar graph will show how many calories are in 1 serving of 4 kinds of cereal. Draw the bars the correct height and label each with the name of the cereal. After completing the bar graph, answer the questions. Data: Korn Kernals—150 calories; Oat Floats—160 calories; Rite Rice—110 calories; Sugar Shapes—200 calories.

   A. Which cereal is the best to eat if you're trying to lose weight? _____

   B. Which cereal has nearly the same number of calories as Oat Floats?

   _____

2. On another sheet of paper, draw your own graph, showing the number of TV commercials in 1 week for each of the 4 cereals in the graph above. After completing the graph, answer the questions. Data: Oat Boats—27 commercials; Rite Rice—15; Sugar Shapes—35; Korn Kernals—28.

   A. Which cereal is most heavily advertised? _____

   B. What similarities do you notice between the graph of calories and the graph of TV commercials? _____

Dog and Jog Graphs

Answer the questions using the graphs indicated.

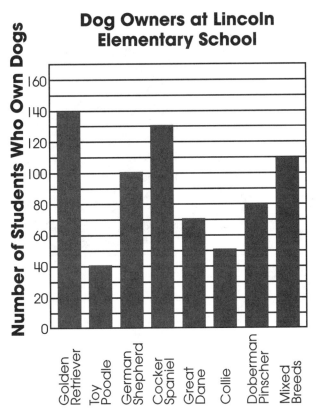

Dog Owners at Lincoln Elementary School

1. How many students own Great Danes at Lincoln Elementary School?

2. Which breed of dog is owned by the fewest students?

3. Which breed is owned by the most students?

4. How many students own Doberman pinschers?

5. How many more students own German shepherds than collies?

1. What class jogged the most during a one-week period?

2. Which class jogged the most miles during this four-week period? What was the difference between classes?

3. Which week had the greatest range between the two classes?

4. Which week had the smallest range?

5. What was the range for Mr. Halverson's class during these four weeks?

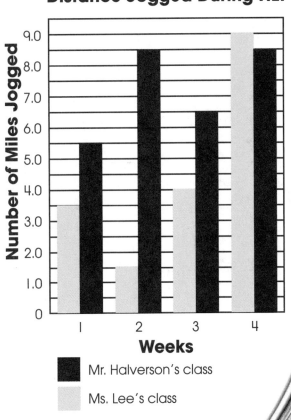

Distance Jogged During P.E.

Mr. Halverson's class

Ms. Lee's class

Graphs

Complete the graph using the information in the table.

Student	Books read in February
Sue	20
Joe	8
Peter	12
Cindy	16
Dean	15
Carol	8

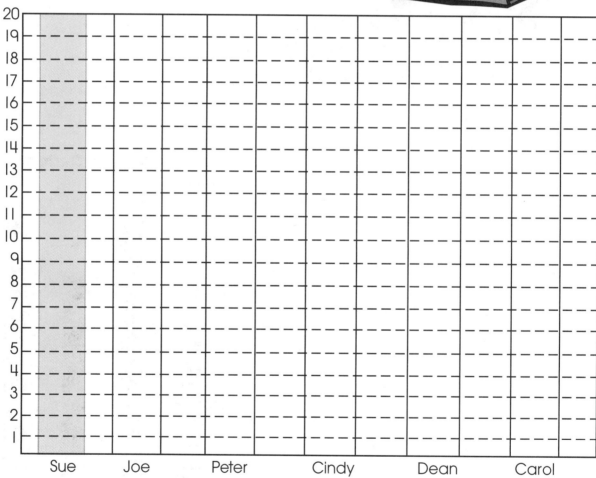

Week 34 Skills

Subject	Skill	Multi-Sensory Learning Activities
Reading and Language Arts	Identify **who**, **which**, and **that** clauses.	• Complete Practice Pages 360–363. • Write at least 10 dependent clauses and 10 independent clauses on index cards (one clause per card). Scramble the cards. Have your child match dependent clauses with independent clauses to make sentences that make sense.
	Identify simple sentences, compound sentences, complex sentences, and sentences with parallel structure.	• Complete Practice Pages 364 and 365. • Choose a nonfiction book from the library and ask your child to write a paragraph on what he or she learned by reading it. Ask your child to include a variety of sentences (simple, compound, and complex) and identify each kind.
Math	Organize and interpret data from picture graphs.	• Complete Practice Page 366. • Have your child bounce a ball for 30 seconds. Record the number of bounces. Then, have your child time you for 30 seconds and record the number of bounces you make. Make a pictograph to show the results. Have your child draw a ball for each of the bounces. Discuss the data on the graph. Who had the most bounces?
	Organize and interpret data from circle graphs.	• Complete Practice Pages 367 and 368. • Help your child interview friends and family members about their favorite ice cream flavors. Ask your child to present the results in a circle graph.

"Who" Clauses

A **clause** is a group of words with a subject and a verb. When the subject of two sentences is the same person or people, the sentences can sometimes be combined with a "who" clause.

Examples:

Mindy likes animals. Mindy feeds the squirrels.
Mindy, **who likes animals**, feeds the squirrels.

A "who" clause is set off from the rest of the sentence with commas.

Combine the pairs of sentences, using "who" clauses.

1. Teddy was late to school. Teddy was sorry later.

   _____

2. Our principal is retiring. Our principal will be 65 this year.

   _____

3. Michael won the contest. Michael will receive an award.

   _____

4. Charlene lives next door. Charlene has three cats.

   _____

5. Burt drew that picture. Burt takes art lessons.

   _____

6. Marta was elected class president. Marta gave a speech.

   _____

7. Amy broke her arm. Amy has to wear a cast for 6 weeks.

   _____

8. Dr. Bank fixed my tooth. He said it would feel better soon.

   _____

"Which" Clauses

When the subject of two sentences is the same thing or things, the sentences can sometimes be combined with a "which" clause.

Examples:

The guppy was first called "the millions fish." The guppy was later named after Reverend Robert Guppy in 1866. The guppy, which was first called "the millions fish," was later named after Reverend Robert Guppy in 1866.

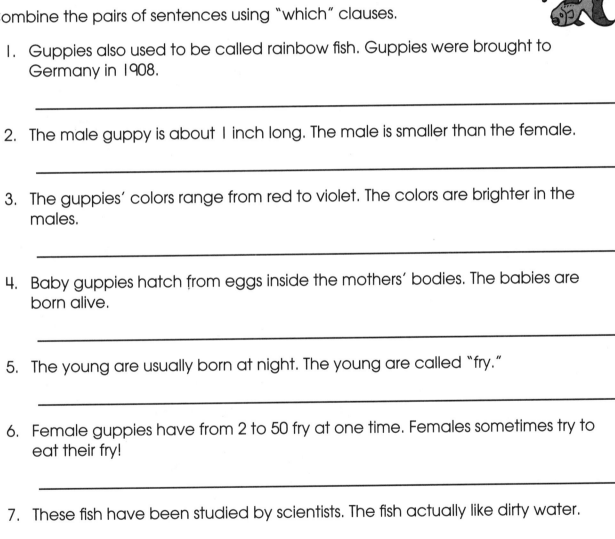

A "which" clause is set off from the rest of the sentence with commas.

Combine the pairs of sentences using "which" clauses.

1. Guppies also used to be called rainbow fish. Guppies were brought to Germany in 1908.

   _____

2. The male guppy is about 1 inch long. The male is smaller than the female.

   _____

3. The guppies' colors range from red to violet. The colors are brighter in the males.

   _____

4. Baby guppies hatch from eggs inside the mothers' bodies. The babies are born alive.

   _____

5. The young are usually born at night. The young are called "fry."

   _____

6. Female guppies have from 2 to 50 fry at one time. Females sometimes try to eat their fry!

   _____

7. These fish have been studied by scientists. The fish actually like dirty water.

   _____

8. Wild guppies eat mosquito eggs. Wild guppies help control the mosquito population.

   _____

"That" Clauses

When the subject of two sentences is the same thing or things, the sentences can sometimes be combined with a "that" clause. We use **that** instead of **which** when the clause is very important in the sentence.

Examples:

The store is near our house. The store was closed.
The store **that is near our house** was closed.

The words "**that is near our house**" are very important in the combined sentence. They tell the reader which store was closed. A "that" clause is not set off from the rest of the sentence with commas.

Examples:

Pete's store is near our house. Pete's store was closed.
Pete's store, which is near our house, was closed.

The words "**which is near our house**" are not important to the meaning of the combined sentence. The words **Pete's store** already told us which store was closed.

Combine the pairs of sentences using "that" clauses.

1. The dog lives next door. The dog chased me.

   _____

2. The bus was taking us to the game. The bus had a flat tire.

   _____

3. The fence is around the school. The fence is painted yellow.

   _____

4. The notebook had my homework in it. The notebook is lost.

   _____

5. A letter came today. The letter was from Mary.

   _____

6. The lamp was fixed yesterday. The lamp doesn't work today.

   _____

7. The lake is by our cabin. The lake is filled with fish.

   _____

Combining Sentences

Not every pair of sentences can be combined with "who," "which" or "that" clauses. These sentences can be combined in other ways, either with a conjunction or by renaming the subject.

Examples:

Tim couldn't go to sleep. Todd was sleeping soundly.
Tim couldn't go to sleep, **but** Todd was sleeping soundly.

The zoo keeper fed the baby ape. A crowd gathered to watch.
When the zoo keeper fed the baby ape, a crowd gathered to watch.

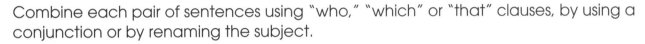

Combine each pair of sentences using "who," "which" or "that" clauses, by using a conjunction or by renaming the subject.

1. The box slipped off the truck. The box was filled with bottles.

    _____

    _____

2. Carolyn is our scout leader. Carolyn taught us a new game.

    _____

    _____

3. The girl is 8 years old. The girl called the emergency number when her grandmother fell.

    _____

    _____

4. The meatloaf is ready to eat. The salad isn't made yet.

    _____

    _____

5. The rain poured down. The rain canceled our picnic.

    _____

6. The sixth grade class went on a field trip. The school was much quieter.

    _____

    _____

Parallel Structure

Parts of a sentence are parallel when they "match" grammatically and structurally.

Faulty parallelism occurs when the parts of a sentence do not match grammatically and structurally.

For sentences to be parallel, all parts of a sentence—including the verbs, nouns and phrases—must match. This means that, in most cases, verbs should be in the same tense.

Examples:

Correct: She liked running, jumping and swinging outdoors.

Incorrect: She liked running, jumping and to swing outdoors.

In the correct sentence, all three of the actions the girl liked to do end in **ing**. In the incorrect sentence, they do not.

Rewrite the sentences so all elements are parallel.
The first one has been done for you.

1. Politicians like making speeches and also to shake hands.

    Politicians like making speeches and shaking hands.

2. He liked singing, acting and to perform in general.

    _____

3. The cake had icing, sprinkles and also has small candy hearts.

    _____

    _____

4. The drink was cold, frosty and also is a thirst-quencher.

    _____

5. She was asking when we would arrive, and I told her.

    _____

6. Liz felt like shouting, singing and to jump.

    _____

Sentences

A simple sentence has a complete subject and predicate.
Example: The little brown rabbit hopped all around the yard.

A compound sentence has two or more simple sentences joined together.
Example: Patrick tried to pick the rabbit up, but it quickly hopped away.

A complex sentence contains one independent clause and one or more dependent clauses.
Example: After several tries, Patrick finally caught the frightened rabbit.

Label the sentences below as simple, compound or complex.

1. Jack and Sam were planning their summer vacation. _____
2. Jack, who loved to hike and climb, wanted to go to the mountains. _____
3. Sam called the travel agency, but no one answered the phone. _____
4. They needed some advice about their travel plans. _____
5. Since they had been to the mountains last year, Sam thought going to a lake would be better this time. _____
6. They finally decided to fish the first week of their vacation and head for the mountains the second week. _____

Write the sentences below according to the directions.

1. Write a simple sentence with a compound subject.

   _____

2. Write a simple sentence with a compound verb.

   _____

3. Write a compound sentence using and as the conjunction.

   _____

4. Write a complex sentence using the subordinating conjunction after.

   _____

Picture Graphs

Newspapers and textbooks often use pictures in graphs instead of bars. Each picture stands for a certain number of objects. Half a picture means half the number. The picture graph in the example indicates the number of games each team won. The Astros won 7 games, so they have $3\frac{1}{2}$ balls.

Example:

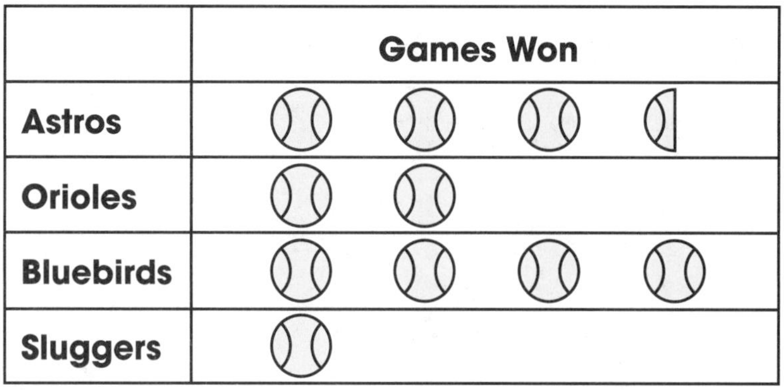

	Games Won
Astros	⚾ ⚾ ⚾ ◖
Orioles	⚾ ⚾
Bluebirds	⚾ ⚾ ⚾ ⚾
Sluggers	⚾

(1 ball = 2 games)

Complete the following exercises.

Finish this picture graph, showing the number of students who have dogs in 4 sixth-grade classes. Draw simple dogs in the graph, letting each drawing stand for 2 dogs. Data: Class 1—12 dogs; Class 2—16 dogs; Class 3—22 dogs; Class 4—12 dogs. After completing the graph, answer the questions.

	Dogs Owned by Students
Class 1	
Class 2	
Class 3	
Class 4	

(One dog drawing = 2 students' dogs)

1. Why do you think newspapers use picture graphs? _____

_____

2. Would picture graphs be appropriate to show exact number of dogs living in America? Why or why not?

_____

Circle Graphs

Circle graphs are useful in showing how something is divided into parts. The circle graph in the example shows how Carly spent her $10 allowance. Each section is a fraction of her whole allowance. For example, the movie tickets section is $\frac{1}{2}$ of the circle, showing that she spent $\frac{1}{2}$ of her allowance, $5, on movie tickets.

Complete the following exercises.

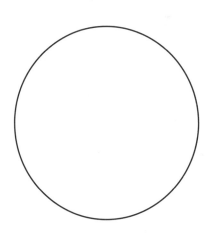

1. When the middle school opened last fall, $\frac{1}{2}$ of the students came from East Elementary, $\frac{1}{4}$ came from West Elementary, $\frac{1}{8}$ came from North Elementary and the remaining students moved into the town from other cities. Make a circle graph showing these proportions. Label each section. Then answer the questions.

    a. What fraction of students at the new school moved into the area from other cities?

    _____

b. If the new middle school has 450 students enrolled, how many used to go to East Elementary?

    _____

2. This circle graph will show the hair color of 24 students in one class. Divide the circle into 4 sections to show this data: black hair—8 students; brown hair—10 students; blonde hair—4 students; red hair—2 students. (Hint: 8 students are $\frac{8}{24}$ or $\frac{1}{3}$ of the class.) Be sure to label each section by hair color. Then answer the questions.

    a. Looking at your graph, what fraction of the class is the combined group of blonde- and red-haired students?

    _____

    b. Which two fractions of hair color combine to total half the class?

    _____

Circle Graph

Ned earns an allowance of $10.00 each week. He created this circle graph on his computer to show his parents how he spends the money. Refer to the graph to answer each question below.

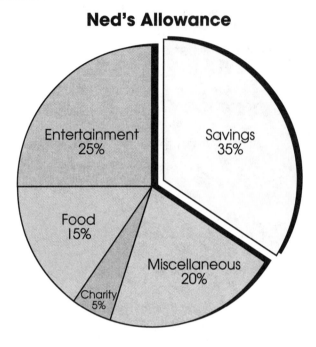

Ned's Allowance

1. Ned highlighted the savings segment of the circle graph because his family believes that having a savings account is very important. If Ned saves $3.50 each week, how much will he have left for other things?

   _____

2. Ned spends all of his entertainment allowance on movies. How much does he spend each week on movies?

   _____

3 How much does Ned spend each week on miscellaneous expenses? Name some things he might buy which would fall into this category.

   _____

4. You have an allowance, create your own circle graph detailing your spending habits. If you don't have an allowance, write two sentences describing how you would spend $10.00 differently than Ned.

   _____

   _____

Week 35 Skills

Subject	Skill	Multi-Sensory Learning Activities
Reading and Language Arts	Use a thesaurus to find synonyms and antonyms.	• Complete Practice Pages 370–372. • Have your child look up the same words in both a dictionary and a thesaurus. Discuss the differences in the entries.
	Determine appropriate resource books for different situations.	• Complete Practice Pages 373 and 374. • Have your child look at and compare geographical resources, such as maps, atlases, and globes. How are these resources different? How are they alike? What might you use each reference to find?
Math	Choose the correct meaning of a word.	• Complete Practice Page 375. • Read *The Dove Dove: Funny Homograph Riddles* by Marvin Terban. Then, brainstorm homographs with your child and ask him or her to write a story using as many as possible.
	Organize and interpret data from line graphs.	• Complete Practice Pages 376 and 377. • Have your child take his or her body temperature every hour throughout the day, then plot the temperatures on a graph. Discuss his or her observations.
	Review graphs.	• Complete Practice Page 378. • Ask your child to research local precipitation amounts for the past month. Have your child present the data in a graph of his or her choosing.

Using a Thesaurus

A **thesaurus** is a type of reference book that lists words in alphabetical order followed by their synonyms and antonyms. **Synonyms** are words that mean the same. **Antonyms** are words that mean the opposite.

A thesaurus is an excellent tool for finding "just the right word." It is also a valuable resource for finding a variety of synonyms and/or antonyms to make your writing livelier.

Each main entry in a thesaurus consists of a word followed by the word's part of speech, its definition, an example, a list of related words and other information.

Here is a typical entry in a thesaurus, with an explanation of terms below:

SLOW

ADJ **SYN** deliberate, dilatory, laggard, leisurely, unhasty, unhurried **REL** lateness, limited, measured, slowish, steady, unhurrying, slowfooted, plodding, pokey, straggling, snail-like **IDIOM** as slow as molasses in January; as slow as a turtle **CON** blitz, quick, rapid, swift **ANT** fast

ADJ means adjective

CON means contrasted words

SYN means synonym

ANT means antonym

REL means related words

idiom means a common phrase that is not literal

Use the thesaurus entry to answer the questions.

1. What is the antonym listed for **slow**? _____

2. How many contrasting words are listed for **slow**? _____

3. How many synonyms are listed for **slow**? _____

4. What is **slow** compared to in the two idioms listed? _____

5. What is the last related word listed for **slow**? _____

Using a Thesaurus to Find Synonyms

A thesaurus can help you find synonyms.

Example:
FIND:
VERB **SYN** locate, discover, detect, uncover, see, etc.
Use a thesaurus. Replace each word in bold with a synonym.

1. My father does not like our **artificial** Christmas tree.

   _____

2. The **fabulous** home sat on a large hill overlooking a wooded ravine.

   _____

3. My dog is allowed to be **loose** if someone is home.

   _____

4. A **peaceful** rally was held to bring attention to the needs of the homeless.

   _____

5. The artist completed his **sketch** of the girl.

   _____

6. The **timid** boy could not bring himself to speak to the man at the counter.

   _____

7. My family is cutting down the **timber** at the back of our property.

   _____

8. Her necklace was very **attractive**.

   _____

9. The girl looked hopelessly at her **clothes** and moaned that she had nothing to wear.

   _____

10. The team's **feat** of winning 20 games in a row was amazing.

   _____

Using a Thesaurus to Find Antonyms

Antonyms are words that mean the opposite. Antonyms can also be found in a thesaurus. They are identified by the abbreviation **ANT**.

Examples:

FOUND:
VERB **ANT** misplaced, gone, lost, missing, mislaid, etc.

RIDDLE:
NOUN **ANT** key, solution, answer, etc.

ANCIENT:
ADJECTIVE **ANT** new, recent, current, etc.

Use a thesaurus to replace each word in bold with an antonym.

_____ 1. Today's weather will undoubtedly be very **humid**.

_____ 2. Can you **give** my sister a napkin?

_____ 3. The man **insulted** me by laughing at my artwork.

_____ 4. I thought the rules for the classroom were too **lax**.

_____ 5. The broken leg was quite **painful**.

_____ 6. We made great **progress** last night on the parade float.

_____ 7. The girl received a **reward** for returning the lost wallet.

_____ 8. The teacher asked us to **separate** the types of art brushes.

_____ 9. The home was decorated in a **simple** manner.

_____ 10. They became very **tense** during the earthquake.

_____ 11. Mr. Kurtzman gave us a math test **today**.

_____ 12. My father loves hiking in the **hills**.

_____ 13. Stephen ran over my **new** red bike.

COMPLETE YEAR GRADE 5

The Right Stuff

Circle the resource book you would use to find . . .

1. A recipe for baking homemade bread.

   encyclopedia   cookbook   *The Life of a Beaver*

2. A description of how beavers make dams.

   almanac   *The Life of a Beaver*   *The Guinness Book of World Records*

3. A map of the United Kingdom.

   thesaurus   world atlas   *The Guinness Book of World Records*

4. The ingredients for Turkish delight.

   The Life of a Beaver   world atlas   cookbook

5. Information about the author, C. S. Lewis.

   almanac   encyclopedia   *Guidebook for Art Instructors*

6. The name of the world's most massive dam.

   The Guinness Book of World Records   dictionary   thesaurus

7. The oldest words in the English language.

   almanac   atlas   *The Guinness Book of World Records*

8. Another word for "trouble."

   thesaurus   atlas   cookbook

9. Why a beaver slaps its tail.

   dictionary   *The Life of a Beaver*   atlas

10. The pronunciation of "courtier."

    The Hobbit   dictionary   almanac

11. What camphor is used for.

    dictionary   *The Life of a Beaver*   thesaurus

Making Inferences: Encyclopedias

Read each question. Then check the answer for where you would find the information in an encyclopedia.

1. If you wanted to grow avocado pits on a windowsill, under which topic should you look?

   ❏ window   ❏ avocado   ❏ food

2. To find information about the Cuban revolution of 1959, which topic should you look up?

   ❏ Cuba   ❏ revolution   ❏ 1959

3. Information about Rudolph Diesel, the inventor of the Diesel engine, would be found under which topic?

   ❏ engine   ❏ Diesel   ❏ inventor

4. If you wanted to find out if the giant panda of China was really a bear or a raccoon, what should you look up?

   ❏ bear   ❏ China   ❏ panda

5. Under which topic should you look for information on how to plant a vegetable garden?

   ❏ plant   ❏ vegetable   ❏ gardening

6. If you wanted to write a report on both wild and pet gerbils, under which topic should you look for information?

   ❏ animal   ❏ gerbil   ❏ pet

7. To find out if World War I was fought only on European soil, which topic should you look up?

   ❏ Europe   ❏ World War I   ❏ war

8. Under which topic should you look for information on how bats guide themselves in the dark?

   ❏ guide   ❏ flying   ❏ bat

9. The distance of all the planets from the sun might be found under which topic?

   ❏ planets   ❏ sky   ❏ distance

Double Trouble

Fill in the blanks with the correct definition number for each underlined word.

Example: _3_ I was covered with <u>pitch</u> after climbing the pine tree.

winding	1. having bends or curves 2. the act of turning something around a central core
wolf	1. to gulp down 2. a large carnivorous member of the dog family
pitch	1. to sell or persuade 2. to throw a ball from the mound to the batter 3. a resin that comes from the sap of pine trees

_____ 1. Do girls' clubs <u>pitch</u> cookies?

_____ 2. We are <u>winding</u> the top's string tightly.

_____ 3. The adult <u>wolf</u> returned to her lair.

_____ 4. Red didn't <u>pitch</u> after the fourth inning.

_____ 5. The Mather family had a <u>winding</u> driveway.

_____ 6. The young ball player <u>wolfed</u> down his lunch and left.

choke	1. to strangle 2. to bring the hands up on the bat
hitch	1. obstacle 2. to fasten or tie temporarily
windup	1. the swing of the pitcher's arm just before the pitch 2. a concluding part

_____ 1. We <u>hitched</u> the mule to the cart.

_____ 2. Tip would not <u>choke</u> up on his bat.

_____ 3. Paul wished to play, but there was just one <u>hitch</u>.

_____ 4. The program's <u>windup</u> was filled with more of Joe's record hits.

_____ 5. Mom was afraid the dog would <u>choke</u> itself on its leash.

_____ 6. He has a great <u>windup</u> and curve ball.

Line Graphs

Still another way to display information is a **line graph**. The same data can often be shown in both a bar graph and a line graph. Nevertheless, line graphs are especially useful in showing changes over a period of time.

The line graph in the example shows changes in the number of students enrolled in a school over a 5-year period. Enrollment was highest in 1988 and has decreased gradually each year since then. Notice how labeling the years and enrollment numbers makes the graph easy to understand.

Example: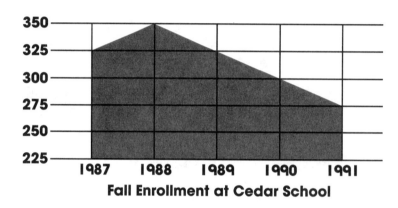

Fall Enrollment at Cedar School

Complete the following exercises.

1. On another sheet of paper, draw a line graph that displays the growth of a corn plant over a 6-week period. Mark the correct points, using the data below, and connect them with a line. After completing the graph, answer the questions. Data: week 1—3.5 in.; week 2—4.5 in.; week 3—5 in.; week 4—5.5 in.; week 5—5.75 in.; week 6—6 in.

   a. Between which weeks was the growth fastest? _____

   b. Between which weeks was the growth slowest? _____

2. On another sheet of paper draw a line graph to show how the high temperature varied during one week. Then answer the questions. Data: Sunday—high of 53 degrees; Monday—51; Tuesday—56; Wednesday—60; Thursday—58; Friday—67; Saturday—73. Don't forget to label the numbers.

   a. In general, did the days get warmer or cooler?

   _____

   b. Do you think this data would have been as clear in a bar graph? Explain your answer.

   _____

   _____

Graphs

Graphs have a vertical axis and a horizontal axis. The axes are labeled to show what is being compared.

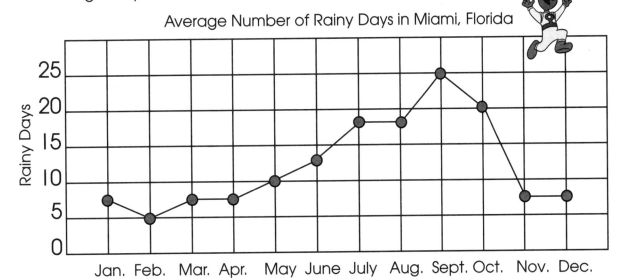

Average Number of Rainy Days in Miami, Florida

Use the data plotted on the graph to answer the following questions.

1. What is the title of the graph?

   _____

2. How is the vertical axis labeled?

   _____

3. What is contained in the horizontal axis?

   _____

4. Which month had the greatest number of rainy days?

   _____

5. Which two-month period shows the greatest change in the number of rainy days?

   _____

6. Which month was the driest?

   _____

Use the graph to fill in the blanks below.

7. range: _____   8. mean: _____   9. median: _____   10. mode: _____

Graphing Data

Complete the following exercises.

1. Use the following information to create a bar graph.

Cities	Population (in 1,000's)
Dover	20
Newton Falls	12
Springdale	25
Hampton	17
Riverside	5

2. Study the data and create a line graph showing the number of baskets Jonah scored during the season.

   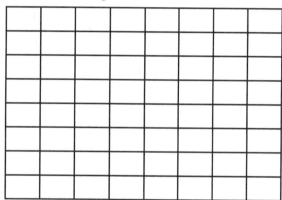

   Game 1–10
   Game 2–7
   Game 3–11
   Game 4–10
   Game 5–9
   Game 6–5
   Game 7–9

   Fill in the blanks.
   a. High game:

   _____

   b. Low game:

   _____

   c. Average baskets per game:

   _____

3. Study the graph, then answer the questions.

   a. Which flavor is the most popular?

   _____

   b. Which flavor sold the least?

   _____

   c. What decimal represents the two highest sellers?

   _____

   d. Which flavor had $\frac{1}{10}$ of the sales?

   _____

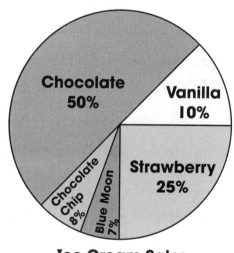

Ice-Cream Sales

Week 36 Skills

Subject	Skill	Multi-Sensory Learning Activities
Reading and Language Arts	Review context clues and reading comprehension.	• Complete Practice Pages 380–383. • Use a black marker to black out every 10th word in an article before you give it to your child to read. Have your child fill in the missing words using context clues.
Math	Locate points on a grid.	• Complete Practice Pages 384 and 385. • Encourage your child to research and learn about imaginary latitude and longitude lines that cover the globe. What are the coordinates of the place where you live?
	Understand and plot ordered pairs.	• Complete Practice Pages 386–388. • Have your child use graph paper to create a large grid. Pin it to a bulletin board. Then, name ordered pairs such as (2, 6), (3, 7), (5, 1), and (8, 6). Challenge your child to insert a thumbtack at each point you name.
Bonus: Science		• Sir Isaac Newton's first law of motion says "an object at rest tends to remain at rest, and an object in motion tends to remain in motion unless acted on by a force." Ask your child to recall a time riding in a car when the brakes were applied quickly and apply that experience to Newton's first law of motion.
Bonus: Social Studies		• Have your child make flash cards to help learn the state capitals. Have your child use the flash cards for several weeks until he or she has memorized the capitals.

Comprehension: "The Lark and the Wren"

"Goodnight, Sir Wren!" said the little lark.
"The daylight fades; it will soon be dark.
I've sung my hymn to the parting day.
So now I fly to my quiet glen
In yonder meadow—Goodnight, Wren!"

"Goodnight, poor Lark," said the haughty wren,
With a flick of his wing toward his happy friend.
"I also go to my rest profound
But not to sleep on the cold, damp ground.
The fittest place for a bird like me
Is the topmost bough of a tall pine tree."

Use context clues for these definitions.

1. What is the correct definition of **hymn**?

   ❑ whisper   ❑ song   ❑ opposite of her

2. What is the correct definition of **yonder**?

   ❑ distant   ❑ mountaintop   ❑ seaside

3. What is the correct definition of **haughty**?

   ❑ happy   ❑ friendly   ❑ pompous

4. What is the correct definition of **profound**?

   ❑ restless   ❑ deep   ❑ uncomfortable

5. What is the correct definition of **bough**?

   ❑ to bend over   ❑ tree roots   ❑ tree branch

6. Write another verse of the poem.

   _____

   _____

   _____

   _____

Comprehension: Proverbs

Proverbs are bits of advice for daily life. The following proverbs were written by Benjamin Franklin in 1732. They were published in *Poor Richard's Almanack.*

1. Keep conscience clear,
   Then never fear.

2. Little strokes
   Fell great oaks.

3. From a slip of foot you may soon recover,
   But a slip of the tongue you may never get over.

4. Doing an injury puts you below your enemy;
   Revenging one makes you but even with him;
   Forgiving it sets you above him.

Explain the meaning of each proverb.

1. _____
   _____

2. _____
   _____

3. _____
   _____

4. _____
   _____
   _____

Write a proverb of your own.

_____
_____
_____
_____

The Sign of the Beaver

Read the following sentences. Based on context, write a definition for each bold word. Then, look up the definitions and circle yes if you were correct. If you were not correct, change your answer.

1. "... when his rage died down, that he felt a **prickle** of fear."

   Prickle means_____ yes

2. "... he saw the sunlight glinted through the **chinks** on the roof."

   Chinks means _____ yes

3. "... but he thought he'd rather have the **pesky** insects himself."

   Pesky means _____ yes

4. "Matt sat **pondering** the strange idea."

   Pondering means _____ yes

5. "He strutted and pranced in ridiculous **contortions** ..."

   Contortions means _____ yes

6. "Now **wampum** no good to pay for gun."

   Wampum means_____ yes

7. "**Warily**, he made his way through the brush."

   Warily means _____ yes

8. "The brown eyes looked up at the Indian boy with **admiration**."

   Admiration means_____ yes

9. "... they **wielded** their bats with no heed to each other's heads. .."

   Wielded means _____ yes

10. "Matt forced himself to eat **sparingly** of these things."

    Sparingly means _____ yes

The Prairie Food Web

In complex grassland communities like the prairie, the flow of food and energy cannot be described by a simple food chain. Instead, it is represented by a series of interconnected food chains called a **food web.** The many kinds of producers and consumers in the prairie community provide a wide variety of food sources.

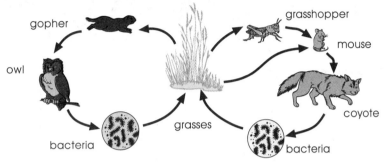

1. Name at least four relationships shown in the food web pictured above.

   1. _____   3. _____

   2. _____   4. _____

2. If there were no coyotes left in the prairie community, what would happen to the mouse population? Why? _____

   _____

   _____

3. If there was a decrease in the owl population, what would happen to the gopher population? Why? _____

   _____

   _____

4. If the prairie grasses were destroyed by fire, what would happen to the coyote population? Why? _____

   _____

   _____

5. What does it mean when we say, "The death of one species in a food web upsets the rest of the web"? _____

   _____

   _____

Locating Points on a Grid

To locate points on a grid, read the first coordinate and follow it to the second coordinate.

Example: C, 3

Maya is new in town. Help her learn the way around her new neighborhood. Place the following locations on the grid below.

Grocery	C, 10
Home	B, 2
School	A, 12
Playground	B, 13
Library	D, 6
Bank	G, 1
Post Office	E, 7
Ice-Cream Shop	D, 3

Is her home closer to the bank or the grocery? _____

Does she pass the playground on her way to school? _____

If she needs to stop at the library after school, will she be closer to home or farther away? _____

Plotting North American Cities

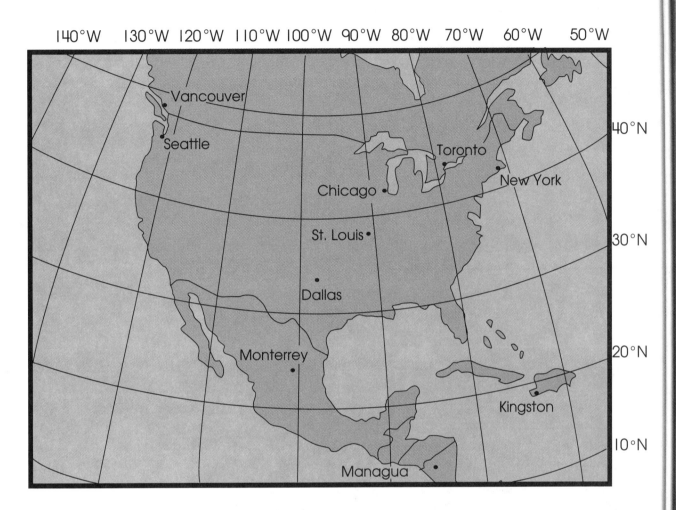

Determine the approximate coordinates of the North American cities on the map above. Write the coordinates for each city in the blanks below.

	Latitude	Longitude		Latitude	Longitude
1. Seattle	_____	_____	2. St. Louis	_____	_____
3. Kingston	_____	_____	4. Toronto	_____	_____
5. Dallas	_____	_____	6. New York	_____	_____
7. Vancouver	_____	_____	8. Monterrey	_____	_____
9. Managua	_____	_____	10. Chicago	_____	_____

Ordered Pairs

Ordered pairs is another term used to describe pairs of integers used to locate points on a graph.

Complete the following exercises.

1. Place the following points on the graph, using the ordered pairs as data.

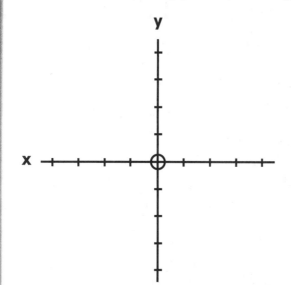

x	y
+3,	+3
–2,	+4
+1,	–2
+4,	–3
–4,	–4
+2,	+3
–1,	+4

2. Create your own set of ordered pairs. Use your home as the center of your coordinates—zero. Let the x axis serve as East and West. The y axis will be North and South. Now select things to plot on your graph—the school, playground, grocery store, a friend's house, and so on.

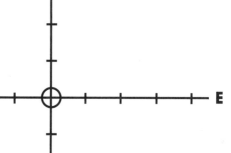

Place	Ordered pair of coordinates
School	_____
Grocery store	_____
Playground	_____
Friend's house	_____

Hidden Picture

Graph the ordered pairs in each group. Number each dot. Connect each point
with the next point using a straight line. Do not connect the last point in one group
with the first point in another group. The first one is done for you.

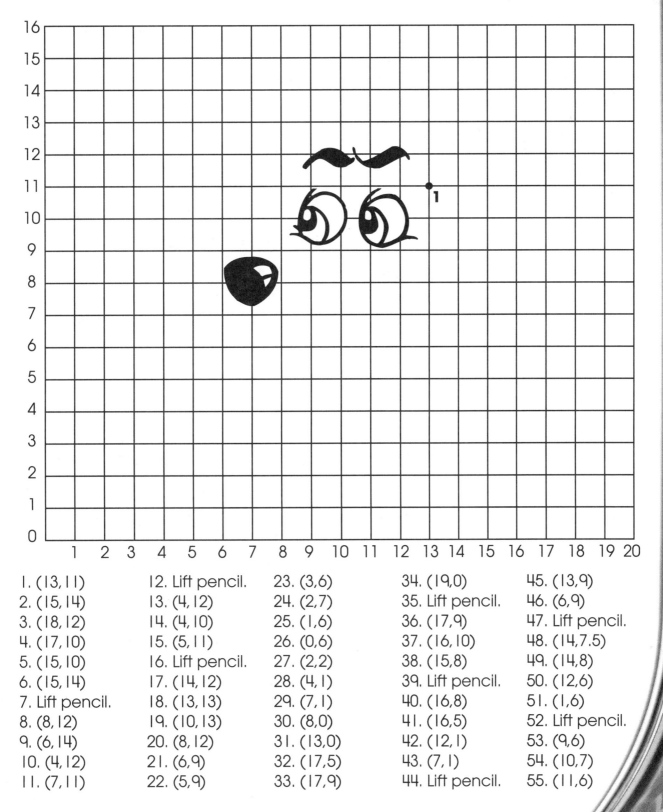

1. (13,11)	12. Lift pencil.	23. (3,6)	34. (19,0)	45. (13,9)
2. (15,14)	13. (4,12)	24. (2,7)	35. Lift pencil.	46. (6,9)
3. (18,12)	14. (4,10)	25. (1,6)	36. (17,9)	47. Lift pencil.
4. (17,10)	15. (5,11)	26. (0,6)	37. (16,10)	48. (14,7.5)
5. (15,10)	16. Lift pencil.	27. (2,2)	38. (15,8)	49. (14,8)
6. (15,14)	17. (14,12)	28. (4,1)	39. Lift pencil.	50. (12,6)
7. Lift pencil.	18. (13,13)	29. (7,1)	40. (16,8)	51. (1,6)
8. (8,12)	19. (10,13)	30. (8,0)	41. (16,5)	52. Lift pencil.
9. (6,14)	20. (8,12)	31. (13,0)	42. (12,1)	53. (9,6)
10. (4,12)	21. (6,9)	32. (17,5)	43. (7,1)	54. (10,7)
11. (7,11)	22. (5,9)	33. (17,9)	44. Lift pencil.	55. (11,6)

Plotting Graphs

A graph with horizontal and vertical number lines can show the location of certain points. The horizontal number line is called the **x axis**, and the vertical number line is called the **y axis**. Two numbers, called the **x coordinate** and the **y coordinate**, show where a point is on the graph.

The first coordinate, x, tells how many units to the right or left of 0 the point is located. On the example graph, point A is +2, two units to the right of 0.

The second coordinate, y, tells how many units above or below 0 the point is located. On the example, point A is –3, three units below 0.

Thus, the coordinates of A are +2, –3. The coordinates of B are –3, +2. (Notice the order of the coordinates.) The coordinates of C are +3, +1; and D, –2, –2.

Study the example. Then answer these questions about the graph below.

1. What towns are at these coordinates?

+1, +3 _____

+1, –3 _____

–4, +1 _____

–2, –3 _____

–3, –2 _____

–3, +3 _____

2. What are the coordinates of these towns?

Hampton _____

Wooster _____

Beachwood _____

Middletown _____

Kirby _____

Arbor _____

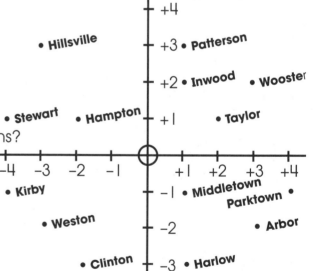

Fourth Quarter Check-Up

Reading and Language Arts

❏ I can recognize up to six-syllable words.

❏ I know spelling and pronunciation, and understand word meanings.

❏ I can identify simple and compound subjects and predicates.

❏ I can join sentences by using conjunctions **and**, **but**, **or**, **because**, and **so**.

❏ I can use context clues to interpret meaning.

❏ I can identify the topic sentence and supporting sentences of a paragraph.

❏ I can answer questions about texts to determine reading comprehension.

❏ I can understand and identify the main idea of a text.

❏ I can write an essay that compares and contrasts.

❏ I can identify **who**, **which**, and **that** clauses.

❏ I can use a thesaurus to find synonyms and antonyms.

❏ I can determine appropriate resource books for different situations.

Math

❏ I can measure temperature.

❏ I can compare and convert measurements.

❏ I can add and subtract inches and feet and pounds and ounces.

❏ I can add minutes and hours.

❏ I understand volume, perimeter, and area.

❏ I can identify and classify quadrilaterals.

❏ I can build larger shapes from smaller shapes and use tangrams.

❏ I can identify polyhedrons.

❏ I can organize and interpret data from charts and graphs.

❏ I can locate points on a grid and plot ordered pairs.

Final Project

Read *Mr. Popper's Penguins* by Richard and Florence Atwater. Summarize the main idea of each chapter with a single sentence. Then, make a chart of the cities that the performers visit. Estimate how much money they are making on tour.

Student Reference

Multiplication Chart

x	1	2	3	4	5	6	7	8	9	10
1	1	2	3	4	5	6	7	8	9	10
2	2	4	6	8	10	12	14	16	18	20
3	3	6	9	12	15	18	21	24	27	30
4	4	8	12	16	20	24	28	32	36	40
5	5	10	15	20	25	30	35	40	45	50
6	6	12	18	24	30	36	42	48	54	60
7	7	14	21	28	35	42	49	56	63	70
8	8	16	24	32	40	48	56	64	72	80
9	9	18	27	36	45	54	63	72	81	90
10	10	20	30	40	50	60	70	80	90	100

Customary and Metric Measurement

Length	Weight
12 inches = 1 foot	16 ounces = 1 pound
3 feet = 1 yard	2,000 pounds = 1 ton
5,280 feet = 1 mile	1 milligram = about 0.000035 ounces
1 millimeter = about 0.04 inch	1 gram = about 0.035 ounces
1 centimeter = about 0.4 inch	1 kilogram = about 2.2 pounds
1 meter = about 40 inches or 3.3 feet	1 metric ton = about 1.1 ton
1 kilometer = about 0.6 mile	

Capacity

8 fluid ounces (fl. oz.) = 1 cup (c.)   2 cups = 1 pint (pt.)   2 pints = 1 quart (qt.)

2 quarts = $\frac{1}{2}$ gallon (gal.)   4 quarts = 1 gallon (gal.)

Temperature

The customary system measures temperature in Fahrenheit (F°) degrees.

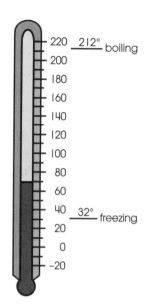

220
212° boiling
200
180
160
140
120
100
80
60
40
32° freezing
20
0
−20

The metric system uses Celsius (C°) degrees.

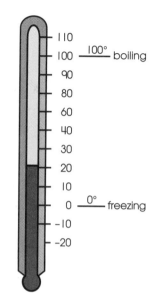

110
100
100° boiling
90
80
60
40
30
20
10
0
0° freezing
−10
−20

Perimeter, Area, and Volume

8 cm

12 cm

Perimeter = length + width + length + width
P = 8 + 12 + 8 + 12
P = 40 cm

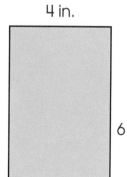

4 in.

6 in.

Area = length x width
A = 4 x 6
A = 24 square inches or 24 in.²

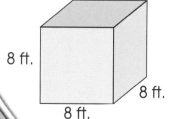

8 ft.

8 ft.

8 ft.

Volume = length x width x height
V = 8 x 8 x 8
V = 512 cubic feet or 512 ft.³

Quadrilaterals

Name	Description	Example
trapezoid	1 pair of opposite sides parallel	
parallelogram	opposite sides parallel, opposite sides and opposite angles congruent	
rhombus	parallelogram with all sides congruent	
rectangle	parallelogram with four right angles	
square	rectangle with four congruent sides	

Polyhedrons

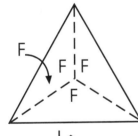

Faces: flat surfaces (sides) **F = 4**

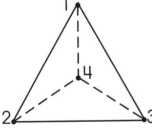

Vertices: corners or points (where 3 edges meet) **V = 4**

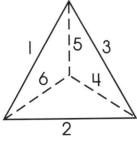

Edges: parts of a line (where 2 faces meet) **E = 6**

Prepositions

across	before	around	to	into
by	from	between	with	about
after	in	over	at	as
behind	for	off	on	like
through	near	beyond	of	during

Conjunctions

and	but	or	because	so

Recommended Read-Alouds for Grade 5

❑ *Kit's Wilderness* by David Almond

❑ *Chasing Vermeer* by Blue Balliett

❑ *The Shakespeare Stealer* by Gary Blackwood

❑ *The Secret Garden* by Frances Burnett

❑ *I Am the Ice Worm* by MaryAnn Easley

❑ *The Slave Dancer* by Paula Fox

❑ *The Pepins and Their Problems* by Polly Horvath

❑ *The Phantom Tollbooth* by Norton Juster

❑ *From the Mixed-Up Files of Mrs. Basil E. Frankweiler* by E.L. Konigsburg

❑ *Number the Stars* by Lois Lowry

❑ *The White Darkness* by Geraldine McCaughrean

❑ *Island of the Blue Dolphins* by Scott O'Dell

❑ *Airborn* by Kenneth Oppel

❑ *Bread and Roses, Too* by Katherine Paterson

❑ *Hatchet* by Gary Paulsen

❑ *On the Wings of Heroes* by Richard Peck

❑ *The Wall: Growing Up Behind the Iron Curtain* by Peter Sis

❑ *Peak* by Roland Smith

Answer Key

Page 18 — Similes and Metaphors in Poetry

Week 1 Practice

Similes and Metaphors in Poetry

Many poems use similes and metaphors to create a more interesting description of what the poem is about.

Read the following poems and underline any similes or metaphors you see.

Flint

An emerald is as green as grass,
A ruby red as blood;
A sapphire shines as blue as heaven;
A flint lies in the mud.

A diamond is a brilliant stone,
To catch the world's desire;
An opal holds a fiery spark;
But a flint holds fire.

—Christina Rossetti

The Night Is a Big Black Cat

The night is a big black cat
The moon is her topaz eye.
The stars are the mice she hunts at night.
In the field of the sultry sky.

—G. Orr Clark

Now, write your own poem, using at least one simile and one metaphor.

Poems will vary.

COMPLETE YEAR GRADE 5

18

Page 19 — Like...a Simile!

Week 1 Practice

Like...a Simile!

Underline the two being compared in each sentence. On the blank, write if the comparison is a **simile** or a **metaphor**. Remember, a simile uses **like** or **as**; a metaphor does not.

1. Angel was as mean as a wild bull. _simile_
2. Toni and Mattie were like toast and jam. _simile_
3. Mr. Ashby expected the students to be as busy as beavers. _simile_
4. The pin was a masterpiece in Mattie's mind. _metaphor_
5. The pork's peacefulness was a friend to Mattie. _metaphor_
6. The words came as slow as molasses into Mattie's mind. _simile_
7. Mrs. Stamps's apartment was like a museum. _simile_
8. Mrs. Benson was as happy as a lark when Mattie won the contest. _simile_
9. Mr. Phillip's smile was a glowing beam to Mattie and Mrs. Benson. _metaphor_
10. Mattie ran like the wind to get her money. _simile_
11. Angel's mean words cut through Charlene like glass. _simile_
12. Mr. Bacon was a fairy godmother to Mattie. _metaphor_
13. The gingko tree's leaves were like fans. _simile_

Complete the following similes. _Answers may include:_
1. Matt was as artistic as _Van Gogh._
2. Hannibal's teeth were like _a vampire's._
3. Toni's mind worked fast like _a well-oiled machine._
4. Mattie was as sad as _a clown._
5. Mrs. Stamps was like _sugar._

COMPLETE YEAR GRADE 5

19

Page 20 — Personification

Week 1 Practice

Personification

Sometimes, writers use descriptions like: The fire engine **screamed** as it rushed down the street. The sun **crawled** slowly across the sky. We know that fire engines do not really scream, and the sun does not really crawl. Writers use descriptions like these to make their writing more interesting and vivid. When a writer gives an object or animal human qualities, it is called **personification**.

For each object below, write a sentence using personification. The first one has been done for you.

1. the barn door
   The old, rusty barn door groaned loudly when I pushed it open.

2. the rain

3. the pickup truck

4. the radiator

5. the leaves

6. the television

7. the kite

8. the river

Sentences will vary.

COMPLETE YEAR GRADE 5

20

Page 21 — Analogies

Week 1 Practice

Analogies

An **analogy** is a way of comparing objects to show how they relate.

Example: Nose is to smell as tongue is to taste.

Write the correct word on the blank to fill in the missing part of each analogy. The first one has been done for you.

1. Scissors are to paper as saw is to wood. fold (scissors) thin
2. Man is to boy as woman is to _girl_. mother (girl) lady
3. _Attic_ is to cellar as sky is to ground. down (attic) up
4. Rag is to dust as _broom_ is to sweep. floor straw (broom)
5. Freezer is to cold as stove is to _hot_. cook (hot) recipe
6. Car is to _garage_ as book is to bookshelf. ride gas (garage)
7. Window is to _glass_ as car is to metal. (glass) clear house
8. Eyes are to seeing as feet are to _walking_. legs (walking) shoes
9. Gas is to car as _electricity_ is to lamp. (electricity) plug cord
10. Refrigerator is to food as _closet_ is to clothes. fold material (closet)
11. Floor is to down as ceiling is to _up_. high over (up)
12. Pillow is to soft as rock is to _hard_. dirt (hard) hurt
13. Carpenter is to house as poet is to _verse_. (verse) novel writing
14. Lamp is to light as clock is to _time_. (time) hands numbers
15. _Palm_ is to hand as sole is to foot. wrist finger (palm)

COMPLETE YEAR GRADE 5

21

Page 22 — Place Value

Week 1 Practice

Place Value

The place value of a digit or numeral is shown by where it is in the number. In the number **1,234**, 1 has the place value of thousands, 2 is hundreds, 3 is tens and 4 is ones.

Example: 1,250,000,000

Read: One billion, two hundred fifty million

Write: 1,250,000,000

Billions	Millions	Thousands	Ones
h t o	h t o	h t o	h t o
1,	2 5 0,	0 0 0,	0 0 0

Read the words. Then write the numbers.

twenty million, three hundred four thousand — 20,304,000

five thousand, four hundred twenty-three — 5,423

one hundred fifty billion, eight million, one thousand, five hundred — 150,008,001,500

sixty billion, seven hundred million, one hundred thousand, three hundred twelve — 60,700,100,312

four hundred million, fifteen thousand, seven hundred one — 400,015,701

six hundred ninety-nine million, four thousand, nine hundred forty-two — 699,004,942

Here's a game to play with a partner.

Write a ten-digit number using each digit, 0 to 9, only once. Do not show the number to your partner. Give clues like: "There is a five in the hundreds place." The clues can be given in any order. See if your partner can write the same number you have written.

COMPLETE YEAR GRADE 5

22

Page 23 — Place Value

Week 1 Practice

Place Value

Draw a line to connect each number to its correct written form.

1. 791,000 — Three hundred fifty thousand
2. 350,000 — Seventeen million, five hundred thousand
3. 17,500,000 — Seven hundred ninety-one thousand
4. 3,500,000 — Seventy thousand, nine hundred ten
5. 70,910 — Three million, five hundred thousand
6. 35,500,000 — Seventeen million, five hundred thousand
7. 17,000,500,000 — Thirty-five million, five hundred thousand

Look carefully at this number: **2,071,463,548.** Write the numeral for each of the following places.

8. _6_ ten thousands
9. _1_ millions
10. _5_ hundreds
11. _2_ billions
12. _4_ hundred thousands
13. _7_ ten millions
14. _3_ one thousands
15. _0_ hundred millions

2,342

COMPLETE YEAR GRADE 5

23

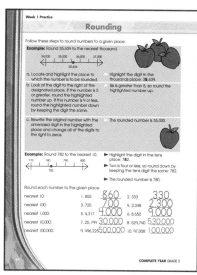

24

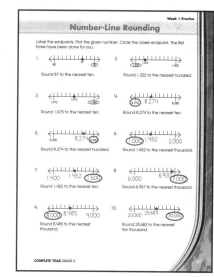

25

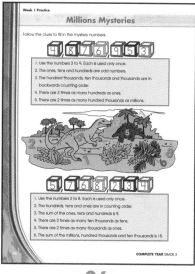

26

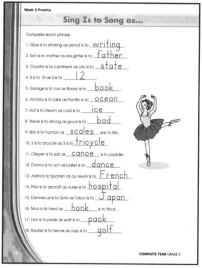

28

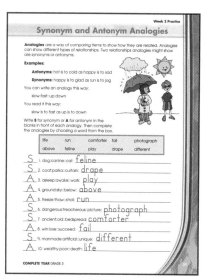

29

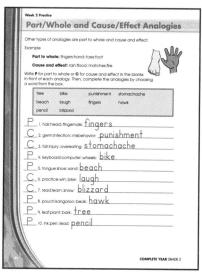

30

31

Up a Tree

Week 2 Practice

Match these expressions with their meanings.

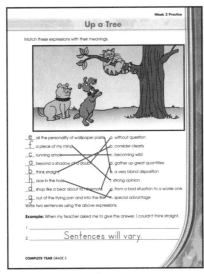

- e all the personality of wallpaper paste — a. without question
- f a piece of my mind — b. consider clearly
- c running amok — c. becoming wild
- a beyond a shadow of a doubt — d. gather up great quantities
- b think straight — e. a very bland disposition
- h ace in the hole — f. strong opinion
- d shop like a bear about to hibernate — g. from a bad situation to a worse one
- g out of the frying pan and into the fire — h. special advantage

Write two sentences using the above expressions.

Example: When my teacher asked me to give the answer, I couldn't think straight.

1. _____
2. _____ Sentences will vary. _____

COMPLETE YEAR GRADE 5

32

Week 2 Practice

Place Value

Place value is the position of a digit in a number. A digit's place in a number shows its value. Numbers left of the decimal point represent whole numbers. Numbers right of the decimal point represent a part, or fraction, of a whole number. These parts are broken down into tenths, hundredths, thousandths, and so on.

Example:
3,443,221.621

millions	hundred thousands	ten thousands	thousands	hundreds	tens	ones	tenths	hundredths	thousandths
3	4	4	3	2	2	1	6	2	1

◄——— Whole Numbers ——— ——— Fractions ———►

Write the following number words as numbers.

1. Three million, forty-four thousand, six hundred twenty-one **3,044,621**
2. One million, seventy-seven **1,000,077**
3. Nine million, six hundred thousand, one hundred two **9,600,102**
4. Twenty-nine million, one hundred three thousand and nine tenths **29,103,000.9**
5. One million, one hundred thousand, one hundred seventy-one and thirteen hundredths **1,100,171.13**

In each box, write the corresponding number for each place value.

1. 4,822,000.00 **0** hundreds
2. 55,907,003.00 **7** thousands
3. 190,641,225.07 **6** hundred thousands
4. 247,308,211.59 **5** tenths
5. 7,594,097.33 **7** millions
6. 201,480,110.01 **4** hundred thousands
7. 42,367,109,074.25 **5** hundredths

10.25

COMPLETE YEAR GRADE 5

33

Week 2 Practice

Place Value

The chart below shows the place value of each number.

trillions	billions	millions	thousands	ones
h t o	h t o	h t o	h t o	h t o
2	1 4 0	9 0 0	6 8 0	3 5 0

Word form: two trillion, one hundred forty billion, nine hundred million, six hundred eighty thousand, three hundred fifty

Draw a line to the correct value of each underlined digit. The first one is done for you.

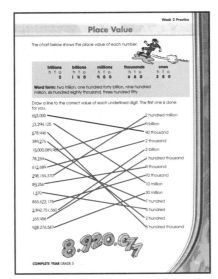

693,000 — 2 hundred million
13,294,125 — 4 billion
678,446 — 40 thousand
389,276 — 2 thousand
13,000,089,485 — 2 billion
78,264 — 1 hundred thousand
612,689 — 8 thousand
298,154,370 — 70 thousand
83,256 — 10 million
1,370 — 30 million
853,622,175 — 7 hundred
2,842,751,360 — 5 hundred
163,456 — 2 hundred
438,276,587 — 6 hundred thousand

8,920,077

COMPLETE YEAR GRADE 5

34

Week 2 Practice

Expanded Notation

Expanded notation is writing out the value of each digit in a number.

Example:
8,920,077 = 8,000,000 + 900,000 + 20,000 + 70 + 7
Word form: Eight million, nine hundred twenty thousand, seventy-seven

Write the following numbers using expanded notation.

1. 20,769,033 **20,000,000 + 700,000 + 60,000 + 9,000 + 30 + 3**
2. 1,183,541,029 **1,000,000,000 + 100,000,000 + 80,000,000 + 3,000,000 + 500,000 + 40,000 + 1,000 + 20 + 9**
3. 776,003,091 **700,000,000 + 70,000,000 + 6,000,000 + 3,000 + 90 + 1**
4. 6,920,100,808 **5,000,000,000 + 900,000,000 + 20,000,000 + 100,000 + 800 + 8**
5. 14,141,543,760 **10,000,000,000 + 4,000,000,000 + 100,000,000 + 40,000,000 + 1,000,000 + 500,000 + 40,000 + 3,000 + 700 + 60**

Write the following numbers.

1. 700,000 + 900 + 50 + 7 **700,967**
2. 35,000,000 + 600,000 + 400 + 40 + 2 **35,600,442**
3. 12,000,000 + 700,000 + 60,000 + 4,000 + 10 + 4 **12,764,014**
4. 80,000,000,000 + 8,000,000,000 + 400,000,000 + 80,000,000 + 10,000 + 400 + 30 **88,480,010,430**
5. 4,000,000,000 + 16,000,000 + 30 + 2 **4,016,000,032**

COMPLETE YEAR GRADE 5

35

Week 2 Practice

Place Value

Read and solve.

1. Write the number 2,058,763 in words. **two million, fifty-eight thousand, seven hundred sixty-three**
2. Write the following in numerals: eight billion, two hundred thirty-seven million, eighty-five thousand, three hundred four. **8,237,085,304**
3. In the number 9,876,543,210 . . .
   which digit is in the hundred thousands place? **5**
   which digit is in the ones place? **0**
   In what place is the 9? **billions**
4. Add.
   3,259 + 32,769 + 305 = **36,333**
   8,759,233 + 3,410 + 655,200 = **9,417,843**
5. Round . . .
   84,239 to the nearest ten. **84,240**
   7,857,355 to the nearest ten million. **7,860,000**
6. Estimate the sum.
   34,396 → 30,000
   + 6,875   6,000
            36,000

COMPLETE YEAR GRADE 5

36

Week 2 Practice

Place Value Games

1. Choose any 2-digit number. Multiply the tens digit by 5. Add 7. Now, double this number. Add the ones digit of the original number. Now subtract 14. The answer is the original number.

2. Choose any 3-digit number. Multiply the hundreds digit by 2. Add 3. Now, multiply by 5. Add 7. Add the tens digit. Add 3. Multiply by 5. Add the ones digit. Now, subtract 235. The answer is the original number.

3. One week (Sunday through Saturday) there is a birthday party every day. No two children are invited to the same party. Find out the day that each child attends a party.

   Hint: Use a chart with days of the week across and children's names down the side.

   a. Lisa and Pat don't go to a party on a Friday or a Saturday.
   b. Pat and Alice don't go on a Tuesday, but Sandy does.
   c. Jennifer goes to a party on Wednesday.
   d. Jim goes to a party the day after Jennifer.
   e. Lisa goes to a party the day before Pat.
   f. Paul goes to a party on a Saturday.

Sunday	—	Lisa
Monday	—	Pat
Tuesday	—	Sandy
Wednesday	—	Jennifer
Thursday	—	Jim
Friday	—	Lisa
Saturday	—	Paul

COMPLETE YEAR GRADE 5

Answer Key

Week 3 Practice

What's the Idea?

Circle the sentence that best expresses the main idea of each paragraph.

1. Edmund began to question whether or not the lion in the Queen's courtyard was alive. The large creature looked as if it were about to pounce on a dwarf. But it did not move. Then Edmund noticed the snow on the lion's head and back. Only a statue would be covered like that!
   - The statue is snow-covered.
   - Edmund wonders if the lion is alive.
   - **The lion is ready to jump.**

2. The resting party of children and beavers heard the sound of jingling bells. Mr. Beaver dashed out of his hiding place and soon called the others to join him. He could hardly contain himself with excitement. Father Christmas is here!
   - Mr. Beaver is a brave animal.
   - **Father Christmas has come to Narnia.**
   - The group hears a jingling sound.

3. **Poor Edmund Because he came to the Queen**, he expected her to reward him gratefully with Turkish delight. After all, he had traveled so far and had suffered miserably in the cold. When the Queen finally commanded that he receive food and drink, the cruel dwarf brought Edmund a bowl of water and a hunk of dry bread.
   - Edmund is not rewarded as he expects.
   - Edmund receives bread and water.
   - **The young boy suffered from the cold.**

4. Peter knew he must rescue Susan from the wolf. When the wolf charged, Susan climbed up a nearby tree. The wolf's snapping and snarling mouth was inches away. When Peter looked more closely, he realized that his sister was about to faint. Rushing in with his sword, Peter slashed at the beast.
   - **Peter kills the wolf.**
   - The wolf snarls at Susan.
   - **Peter realizes he must save his sister.**

Choose one of the following sentences as your main idea and write a paragraph.
1. The Queen demands that Edmund be returned to her.
2. Aslan's army loses the Queen and her dwarf.
3. Father Christmas gives gifts to the beavers and the three children.

Paragraphs will vary.

COMPLETE YEAR GRADE 5

38

Week 3 Practice

Taking Notes: Egyptian Mummies

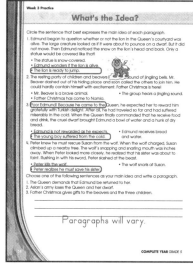

Taking notes is the process of writing important points to remember, such as taking notes from material prepared by your teacher or from what is discussed in class or from an article you read. Taking notes is useful when preparing for a test or when writing a report. When taking notes, follow these steps:

1. Read the article carefully.
2. Select one or two important points from each paragraph.
3. Write your notes in your own words.
4. Reread your notes to be sure you understand what you have written.
5. Abbreviate words to save time.

Read about Egyptian mummies. Select one or two important points from each paragraph. Write your notes in your own words.

After the Egyptians discovered that bodies buried in the hot, dry sand of the desert became mummified, they began searching for ways to improve the mummification process. The use of natron became a vital part of embalming.

Natron is a type of white powdery salt found in oases throughout Egypt. An oasis is a place in the desert where underground water rises to the surface. This water contains many types of salts, including table salt. It also contains natron. As the water evaporates in the hot sun of the desert, the salts are left behind. Natron was collected for use in the mummification process.

The body was dried in natron for up to 40 days. The natron caused the body to shrink and the skin to become leathery. For thousands of years, natron was a vital ingredient in preserving the bodies of kings, queens and other wealthy Egyptian citizens.

Sample notes:

Paragraph 1: Bodies buried in hot dry sand became mummified. Natron is vital for embalming.

Paragraph 2: Natron is a salt that is found when water from an oasis evaporates, leaving behind salts that were in it.

Paragraph 3: The body was soaked in natron for up to 40 days, causing it to shrink and the skin to become leathery. Natron was used for thousands of years.

COMPLETE YEAR GRADE 5

39

Week 3 Practice

Summarizing

A **summary** includes the main points from an article, book or speech.

Example:
Tomb robbing was an important business in ancient Egypt. Often entire families participated in the plunder of tombs. These robbers may have been laborers, officials, tomb architects or guards, but they all probably had one thing in common. They were involved in the building or designing of the tomb or they wouldn't have had the knowledge necessary to successfully rob the burial sites. Not only did tomb robbing ensure a rich life for the robbers but it also enabled them to be buried with many riches themselves.

Summary:
Tomb robbing occurred in ancient Egypt. The robbers stole riches to use in their present lives or in their burials. Tomb robbers usually had some part in the building or design of the tomb. This allowed them to find the burial rooms where the treasures were stored.

Read about life in ancient Egypt. Then write a three- to five-sentence summary.

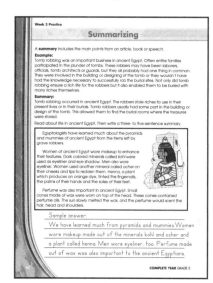

Egyptologists have learned much about the pyramids and mummies of ancient Egypt from the items left by grave robbers.

Women of ancient Egypt wore makeup to enhance their features. Dark colored minerals called *kohl* were used as eyeliner and eye shadow. Men also wore eyeliner. Women used another mineral called ocher on their cheeks and lips to redden them. Henna, a plant which produces an orange dye, tinted the fingernails, the palms of their hands and the soles of their feet.

Perfume was also important in ancient Egypt. Small cones made of wax were worn on top of the head. These cones contained perfume oils. The sun slowly melted the wax, and the perfume would scent the hair, head and shoulders.

Sample answer:
We have learned much from pyramids and mummies. Women wore makeup made out of the minerals kohl and ocher and a plant called henna. Men wore eyeliner, too. Perfume made out of wax was also important to the ancient Egyptians.

COMPLETE YEAR GRADE 5

40

Week 3 Practice

Outlining

Outlining is a way to organize information before you write an essay or informational paragraph. Outlining helps you understand the information you read.

This sample form will help you get started. When outlining, you can add more main points, more smaller points and/or more examples.

Title
I. First Main Idea
   A. A smaller idea
      1. An example
      2. Another example
   B. Another smaller idea
II. Second Main Idea
   A. A smaller idea
   B. Another smaller idea
      1. An example
      2. Another example
III. Third Main Idea
   A. A smaller idea
   B. A smaller idea

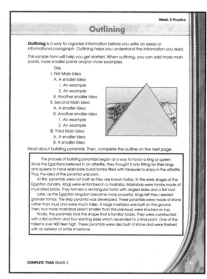

Read about building pyramids. Then, complete the outline on the next page.

The process of building pyramids began as a way to honor a king or queen. Since the Egyptians believed in an afterlife, they thought it only fitting for their kings and queens to have elaborate burial tombs filled with treasures to enjoy in the afterlife. One of the pyramid was born.

At first, pyramids were not built as they are known today. In the early stages of the Egyptian dynasty, kings were entombed in a mastaba. Mastabas were tombs made of mud-dried bricks. They formed a rectangular tomb with angled sides and a flat roof.

Later, as the Egyptian kingdom became more powerful, kings felt they needed grander tombs. The step pyramid was developed. These pyramids were made of stone rather than mud and were much taller. A large mastaba was built on the ground. Then, four smaller mastabas (each smaller than the previous) were stacked on top.

Finally, the pyramids took the shape that is familiar today. They were constructed with a flat bottom and four slanting sides which ascended to a final point. One of the tallest is over 400 feet high. These pyramids were also built of stone and were finished with an exterior of white limestone.

COMPLETE YEAR GRADE 5

41

Week 3 Practice

Outlining: Egyptian Pyramids

Complete the outline. Then answer the question.

Egyptian Pyramids
(Title)

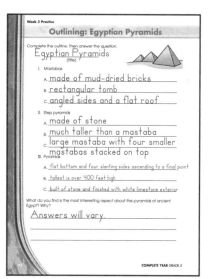

I. Mastabas
   A. made of mud-dried bricks
   B. rectangular tomb
   C. angled sides and a flat roof
II. Step pyramids
   A. made of stone
   B. much taller than a mastaba
   C. large mastaba with four smaller mastabas stacked on top
III. Pyramids
   A. flat bottom and four slanting sides ascending to a final point
   B. tallest is over 400 feet high
   C. built of stone and finished with white limestone exterior

What do you find is the most interesting aspect about the pyramids of ancient Egypt? Why?

Answers will vary.

COMPLETE YEAR GRADE 5

42

Week 3 Practice

Trial and Error

Use trial and error to complete each diagram so all the equations work.

Example:

$$6, 7 \begin{cases} + & 13 \\ \times & 42 \end{cases}$$

$$7, 4 \begin{cases} + & 11 \\ \times & 28 \end{cases} \qquad 4, 8 \begin{cases} + & 12 \\ \times & 32 \end{cases}$$

$$4, 4 \begin{cases} + & 8 \\ \times & 16 \end{cases} \qquad 7, 0 \begin{cases} + & 7 \\ \times & 0 \end{cases}$$

$$8, 7 \begin{cases} + & 15 \\ \times & 56 \end{cases} \qquad 8, 9 \begin{cases} + & 17 \\ \times & 72 \end{cases}$$

$$6, 9 \begin{cases} + & 15 \\ \times & 54 \end{cases} \qquad 15, 16 \begin{cases} + & 31 \\ \times & 240 \end{cases}$$

$$10, 1 \begin{cases} + & 11 \\ \times & 10 \end{cases} \qquad 100, 1 \begin{cases} + & 101 \\ \times & 100 \end{cases}$$

COMPLETE YEAR GRADE 5

43

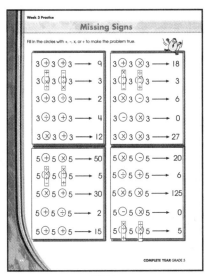

Page 44 — Missing Signs

Missing Signs

Fill in the circles with +, -, x, or + to make the problem true.

$3 \oplus 3 \oplus 3 \rightarrow 9$ $3 \oplus 3 \otimes 3 \rightarrow 18$

$3 \otimes 3 \oplus 3 \rightarrow 3$ $3 \oplus 3 \oplus 3 \rightarrow 3$

$3 \oplus 3 \ominus 3 \rightarrow 2$ $3 \otimes 3 \ominus 3 \rightarrow 6$

$3 \oslash 3 \oplus 3 \rightarrow 4$ $3 \ominus 3 \otimes 3 \rightarrow 0$

$3 \otimes 3 \oplus 3 \rightarrow 12$ $3 \otimes 3 \otimes 3 \rightarrow 27$

$5 \oplus 5 \otimes 5 \rightarrow 50$ $5 \otimes 5 \ominus 5 \rightarrow 20$

$5 \oslash 5 \oplus 5 \rightarrow 5$ $5 \oslash 5 \oplus 5 \rightarrow 6$

$5 \otimes 5 \oplus 5 \rightarrow 30$ $5 \otimes 5 \otimes 5 \rightarrow 125$

$5 \oplus 5 \oslash 5 \rightarrow 2$ $5 \ominus 5 \otimes 5 \rightarrow 0$

$5 \oplus 5 \oplus 5 \rightarrow 15$ $5 \oplus 5 \oplus 5 \rightarrow 5$

44

Page 45 — A Number Challenge

A Number Challenge

Fill in the blanks to make each problem true. To check your work, start at the left and do each operation in order to get the given answer.

1. __ + __ - __ = 2
2. __ - __ + __ = 3
3. __ + __ + __ = 4
4. __ x __ - __ =
5. __
6. __ __ = 3
7. __ + __ + __ = 4
8. __ + __ - __ = 5

9. __ + __ x __ = 6
10. __ x __ + __ : 7
11. __ = 12
12. __ = 15
13. __ + __ x __ = 20
14. __ x __ + __ = 8
15. __ + __ x __ = 24

Answers will vary

45

Page 46 — Equations

Equations

Write the correct operation signs in the blanks to make accurate equations.

1. $5 + 5 + 5 = 3 \times 5 + 0$
2. $(50 + 0) \times 2 = 25 \times 2 \times 2$
3. $2 \times 2 \times 2 \times 2 = 2 \times 2 \times 4$
4. $(4 \times 5) + 5 + 5 = 2 \times 3 \times 5$
5. $(25 + 5) \times 2 \times 3 = 3 \times 6 \times 2 \times 5$
6. $(125 \times 2 + 3 = 100 \times 2 \times 4 + 70 + 10$
7. $(100 \times 10) \times 5 + 10 = 10 \times 5 \times 100 + 10$
8. $35 + 35 + 5 \times 2 = 5 \times 3 \times 2 \times 5$
9. $(50 + 2) \times 3 = 3 \times 3 \times 3 \times 0 + 15 + (5 \times 15)$
10. $(120 \times 4) + 7 + 3 = (7 \times 7) \times (2 \times 5)$
11. $(9) + 3 + 6) \times 3 = 2 \times 5 \times 3 \times (2 \times 5)$
12. $(16 \times 4) - 8 = 5 \times 5 \times (2 + 3) + 6$
13. $0 \times 5 + 15 - 4 = 3 - 3 + 3 + 8$
14. $16 \times 3 + 12 - (2 \times 20) = (2 \times 2) \times 6 + 10 - (2 \times 7)$
15. $21 + (3 \times 3) - 3 - 1 = 3 + 1 \times 2 + 20$

46

Page 48 — What's the Difference?

What's the Difference?

One day, David and Donald were discussing alligators. David insisted that alligators and crocodiles were the same animal but that people called them by different names. Donald insisted, however, that the two animals were entirely different reptiles. Kim walked up just in time to save the boys from further squabbling. Kim, who had lived in Florida for ten years, could settle this one.

She told David that alligators and crocodiles are separate reptiles. She told them that although they are similar looking and are both called crocodilians, they are very different. Both have a long, low, cigar-shaped body, short legs and a long, powerful tail to help them swim. But most crocodiles have a pointed snout instead of a round one like the alligator's. She also pointed out that while both have tough hides, long snouts and sharp teeth to grasp their prey, the crocodile is only about two-thirds as heavy as an American alligator of the same length and can therefore move much more quickly. David and Donald were impressed with Kim's knowledge.

Kim also told the boys another way to tell the two reptiles apart. She said that both have an extra long lower fourth tooth. This tooth fits into a pit in the alligator's upper jaw, while in the crocodile, it fits into a groove in the side of the upper jaw and shows when the crocodile's mouth is closed. David and Donald thanked Kim for the information, looked at each other sheepishly and walked away laughing.

Match:
crocodile — fourth tooth shows when mouth is shut
— round snout
— called crocodilian
alligator — fourth tooth is in a pocket in upper jaw
— pointed snout

Write three ... they are different.

Answers may include:

Alike
tough hide
short legs
long powerful tail

Different
Alligators have round snout;
crocodiles have pointed
crocodiles are lighter
crocodiles are faster

Name two other animals that are sometimes thought to be the same.

toad   frog

Answers will vary.

48

Page 49 — Comprehension: The Lusitania

Comprehension: The *Lusitania*

The *Lusitania* was a British passenger steamship. It became famous when it was torpedoed and sunk by the Germans during World War I. On May 7, 1915, the *Lusitania* was traveling off the coast of Ireland when a German submarine fired on it without warning. The ship stood no chance of surviving the attack and sunk in an astonishing 20 minutes. 1,198 people perished, of whom 128 were American citizens. At the time the ship was torpedoed, the United States was not yet involved in the war. Public opinion over the attack put pressure on President Woodrow Wilson to declare war on Germany. The Germans proclaimed that the *Lusitania* was carrying weapons for the use of the allies.

This claim was later proven to be true. President Wilson demanded that the German government apologize for the sinking and make amends. Germany did not accept responsibility but did promise to avoid sinking any more passenger ships without first giving no warning.

Answer these questions about the *Lusitania*.

1. What does **proclaimed** mean? _____
2. What does **perished** mean? _____
3. What does **amends** mean? _____
4. What does **allies** mean? _____
5. If the *Lusitania* ... you think the Germans had a right to sink it? Why or why not?

Answers will vary.

49

Page 50 — Comprehension: The Titanic

Comprehension: The *Titanic*

The British passenger ship, *Titanic*, debuted in the spring of 1912. It was billed as an unsinkable ship due to its construction. It had 16 watertight compartments that would hold the ship afloat even in the event that four of the compartments were damaged.

But on the evening of April 14, 1912, during *Titanic*'s first voyage, its design proved unworthy. Just before midnight, *Titanic* struck an iceberg, which punctured 5 of the 16 compartments. The ship sunk in a little under 3 hours. Approximately 1,513 of the over 2,220 people onboard died. Most of these people died because there weren't enough lifeboats to accommodate everyone onboard. These people were left floating in the water. Many died from exposure, since the Atlantic Ocean was near freezing in temperature. It was one of the worst ocean disasters in history.

Because of the investigations that followed the *Titanic* disaster, the passenger ship industry instituted many reforms. It is now required that there is ample lifeboat space for all passengers and crew. An international ice patrol and full-time radio coverage were also instituted to prevent such disasters in the future.

Answer these questions about the *Titanic*.

1. How did most of the 1,513 people onboard the *Titanic* die? exposure to cold
2. Why did this "unsinkable" ship sink? An iceberg punctured five compartments.
3. What changes have been made in ship safety as a result of the *Titanic* tragedy? They must have enough lifeboats, international ice patrol, and full-time radio coverage.
4. There have been many attempts to rescue artifacts from the *Titanic*. But many families of the dead wish the site to be left alone, as it is the final resting place of their relatives. They feel burial sites should not be disrupted. Do you agree or disagree? Why?

Answers will vary.

50

Answer Key

Page 51

Venn Diagram: *Lusitania* and *Titanic*

A **Venn diagram** is used to chart information that shows similarities and differences between two things.

Example:

Dogs	Both	Cats
bark	good pets	one size
dependent	can live inside or outside	kill mice
large and small breeds	have fur	can use litterbox
protect the home	four legs	independent

Complete the Venn diagram for the *Lusitania* and the *Titanic*.

Sample answers

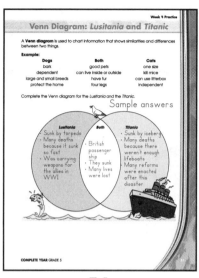

Lusitania
- Sunk by torpedo
- Many deaths because it sunk so fast
- Was carrying weapons for the allies in WWI

Both
- British passenger ship
- They sunk
- Many lives were lost

Titanic
- Sunk by iceberg
- Many deaths because there weren't enough lifeboats
- Many reforms were enacted after this disaster

COMPLETE YEAR GRADE 5

Page 52

Equations

In an **equation**, the value on the left of the equal sign must equal the value on the right. Remember the order of operations: solve from left to right, multiply or divide numbers before adding or subtracting and do the operation inside parentheses first. Write the correct operation signs in the blanks to make accurate equations.

Example: 6 + 4 − 2 = 4 x 2
10 − 2 = 8
8 = 8

Write the correct operation signs in the blanks to make accurate equations.

1. (25 __+__ 25) __÷__ 2 = 100 __−__ 75

2. (76 __+__ 24) __X__ 3 = 150 __X__ 2

3. 140 __÷__ 2 __X__ 10 = 500 __−__ 50 __+__ 150

4. 2,100 __−__ 2,000 __+__ 60 = 80 __X__ 2

5. 80 __X__ 8 __÷__ 4 = 160 __+__ 160 __−__ 160

6. (55 __X__ 100) __÷__ 11 = (1,000 __X__ 2) __÷__ 4

7. 137 __+__ 81 __÷__ 3 = 150 __X__ 90

8. 3,000 __÷__ 10 __÷__ 10 = (600 __+__ 300) __÷__ 30

9. (720 __+__ 20) __÷__ 4 = 37 __X__ 5

10. (457 __+__ 43) __−__ 500 = (21 __+__ 40) x 0

COMPLETE YEAR GRADE 5

Page 53

Equations

Solve the equations on another sheet of paper. Write your answers here.

1. 5 + 64 = **69**   2. (3 x 4) + 3 = **4**   3. (32 + 8) + 3 = **7**

4. (40 + 8) x 2 = **10**   5. 6 + (8 x 3) = **30**   6. 14 + 12 − 6 = **20**

7. (2 x 9) + 4 = **22**   8. (8 x 8) ÷ 6 = **70**   9. 6 + (6 + 6) = **7**

10. 45 + (5 x 3) = **3**   11. 9 + 7 − 10 = **6**   12. (15 x 2) + 3 = **10**

13. (3 x 7) − 1 = **20**   14. (18 ÷ 9) x 8 = **16**   15. (36 + 9) + 8 = **12**

16. (21 + 7) + 6 = **9**   17. 7 + 8 − 8 = **7**   18. 9 + 6 − 12 = **3**

19. 12 + 7 − 8 = **11**   20. (56 + 8) + 4 = **11**   21. (64 + 8) + 5 = **13**

22. 14 + (2 x 8) = **30**   23. (7 + 9) ÷ 2 = **8**   24. (15 x 3) x 2 = **10**

25. (5 + 3) x 3 = **24**   26. 15 − 7 + 3 = **11**   27. (3 + 7) x (10 − 2) = **80**

28. 6 + (8 + 2) = **10**   29. 3 x (5 + 6) = **33**   30. 15 + (3 x 2) = **21**

31. 14 − (8 − 2) − 1 = **7**   32. 16 − (10 − 4) = **10**   33. (14 + 6) + 5 = **4**

34. (3 + 2) x (4 + 6) = **50**   35. 12 x (3 + 2) = **60**   36. 6 x (4 + 5) = **54**

37. 3 + (6 x 2) + 5 = **20**   38. 4 + (4 x 5) = **28**   39. (6 x 8) + 2 = **50**

40. 30 + (16 x 2) = **62**   41. 3 x (9 + 2) = **33**   42. 52 − (5 + 3) = **44**

43. (64 + 8) x 3 = **24**   44. 25 − (3 + 8) = **14**   45. 21 + (3 + 4) = **3**

COMPLETE YEAR GRADE 5

Page 54

Timed Multiplication

1 × 1	9 × 3	4 × 10	8 × 3	2 × 10	5 × 7	7 × 4	12 × 3
1	27	40	24	20	35	28	36

10 × 3	12 × 9	10 × 5	4 × 9	7 × 5	11 × 2	6 × 6	3 × 2
30	108	50	36	35	22	36	6

5 × 8	10 × 4	9 × 4	3 × 3	5 × 9	9 × 6	8 × 5	6 × 7
40	40	36	9	45	54	40	42

4 × 8	11 × 3	12 × 5	1 × 4	7 × 7	10 × 6	7 × 2	4 × 7
32	33	60	4	49	60	14	28

3 × 4	6 × 8	9 × 5	5 × 10	11 × 9	3 × 5	7 × 10	1 × 5
12	48	45	50	99	15	70	5

2 × 6	8 × 7	9 × 2	4 × 6	9 × 8	8 × 8	7 × 9	4 × 5
12	56	18	24	72	64	63	20

10 × 8	3 × 6	11 × 6	9 × 6	2 × 3	12 × 10	7 × 10	
80	18	60	6	63	10	120	70

COMPLETE YEAR GRADE 5

Page 55

Multiplication (One-Digit Multiplier)

Example A (no regrouping)
234 × 2 = 468
- Step 1 Multiply ones. 2 x 4 = 8
- Step 2 Multiply tens. 2 x 3 = 6
- Step 3 Multiply hundreds. 2 x 2 = 4

Example B (regrouping)
563 × 4 = 2,252
- Step 1 Multiply ones. 4 x 3 = 12 ones = 1 ten 2 ones. Carry the 1.
- Step 2 Multiply tens. 4 x 6 + 1 = 25 tens = 2 hundreds 5 tens. Carry the 2.
- Step 3 Multiply hundreds. 4 x 5 + 2 = 22 hundreds = 2 thousands 2 hundreds.

Example C (regrouping and zeros)
7,086 × 9 = 63,774
- Step 1 Multiply ones. 9 x 6 = 54 ones = 5 tens 4 ones. Carry the 5.
- Step 2 Multiply tens. 9 x 8 + 5 = 77 tens = 7 hundreds 7 tens. Carry the 7.
- Step 3 Multiply hundreds. 9 x 0 + 7 = 7 hundreds.
- Step 4 Multiply thousands. 9 x 7 = 63 thousands = 6 ten-thousands 3 thousands.

Multiply.

1. 323 × 8 = **2,584**   2. 1,132 × 2 = **2,264**   3. 789 × 5 = **3,945**

4. 4,008 × 7 = **28,056**   5. 2,580 × 3 = **7,740**   6. 888 × 6 = **5,328**

7. 4,234 × 4 = **16,936**   8. 589 × 9 = **5,301**   9. 3,211 × 3 = **9,633**

COMPLETE YEAR GRADE 5

Page 56

Multiplication

Multiply the following numbers. Be sure to keep the numbers aligned and place a 0 in the ones place when multiplying by the tens digit.

Example:

	Correct	Incorrect
	55	55
	x 15	x 15
	275	275
	550	55
	825	330

1. 12 × 6 = **72**   2. 44 × 9 = **396**   3. 27 × 7 = **189**   4. 92 × 6 = **552**   5. 85 × 9 = **765**

6. 78 × 24 = **1,872**   7. 32 × 17 = **544**   8. 19 × 46 = **874**   9. 63 × 12 = **756**   10. 38 × 77 = **2,926**

11. 125 × 6 = **750**   12. 641 × 25 = **16,025**   13. 713 × 47 = **33,511**   14. 586 × 45 = **26,370**   15. 294 × 79 = **23,226**

16. 20 x 4 x 7 = **560**   17. 9 x 5 x 11 = **495**

18. 16 x 2 x 2 = **64**   19. 7 x 6 x 3 = **126**

20. 33 x 11 x 3 = **1,089**   21. 2 x 8 x 10 = **160**

COMPLETE YEAR GRADE 5

Answer Key

58

Conjunctions (page 58)

Week 5 Practice

The conjunctions **and, or, but** and **nor** can be used to make a compound subject, a compound predicate or a compound sentence.

Examples:
Compound subject: My friend **and** I will go to the mall.
Compound predicate: We ran **and** jumped in gym class.
Compound sentence: I am a talented violinist, **but** my father is better.

Write two sentences of your own in each section.

Compound subject:
1. _____
2. _____

Compound predicate:
1. _____
2. _____

Compound sentence:
1. _____
2. _____

Answers will vary.

COMPLETE YEAR GRADE 5

Conjunctions (page 59)

Week 5 Practice

A conjunction joins words, groups of words or entire sentences. The most common conjunctions are **and, or, but.**

Examples:
Christian Huygens **and** Jean Cassini made discoveries about Saturn. (joins subjects)

The Italian astronomer Galileo first saw Saturn's rings through a telescope, **but** the rings weren't very clear. (joins sentences)

He discovered the rings in the early 1600s **and** thought they were large satellites. (joins predicates)

Add a conjunction to each sentence below.

1. Did you know that Saturn takes about 29 ½ Earth-years to orbit the Sun, **or** are you still looking up that fact?
2. Saturn **and** Earth have very different day lengths.
3. Earth's day is about 24 hours, **but** Saturn's is only about 10 ½ hours.
4. Saturn has 23 satellites that have been discovered, **and** Earth has only one.
5. Saturn's natural satellites all have different names, **but** Earth's satellite is just called "the Moon."
6. Saturn has many rings that surround it, **but** Earth has none.

Add a conjunction to each phrase below that describes Saturn.

1. beautiful **and** majestic
2. far away, **but** gigantic
3. larger than Earth, **but** lighter in comparison
4. shorter days than Earth **and** faster rotation
5. atmosphere of mostly hydrogen **and** helium
6. beautiful rings **but** not the only planet with them

COMPLETE YEAR GRADE 5

59

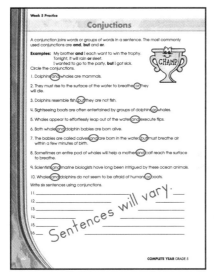

60

Conjunctions (page 60)

Week 5 Practice

A conjunction joins words or groups of words in a sentence. The most commonly used conjunctions are **and, but** and **or.**

Examples: My brother **and** I each want to win the trophy.
Tonight, it will rain **or** sleet.
I wanted to go to the party, **but** I got sick.

Circle the conjunctions.

1. Dolphins (and) whales are mammals.
2. They must rise to the surface of the water to breathe (or) they will die.
3. Dolphins resemble fish, (but) they are not fish.
4. Sightseeing boats are often entertained by groups of dolphins (or) whales.
5. Whales appear to effortlessly leap out of the water (and) execute flips.
6. Both whale (and) dolphin babies are born alive.
7. The babies are called calves (and) are born in the water, (but) must breathe air within a few minutes of birth.
8. Sometimes an entire pod of whales will help a mother (and) calf reach the surface to breathe.
9. Scientists (and) marine biologists have long been intrigued by these ocean animals.
10. Whales (and) dolphins do not seem to be afraid of humans (or) boats.

Write six sentences using conjunctions.

11. _____
12. _____
13. _____
14. _____
15. _____
16. _____

Sentences will vary.

COMPLETE YEAR GRADE 5

Writing: Conjunctions (page 61)

Week 5 Practice

Too many short sentences make writing seem choppy. Short sentences can be combined to make writing flow better. Words used to combine sentences are called **conjunctions.**

Examples: but, before, after, because, when, or, so, and

Use **or, but, before, after, because, when, and** or **so** to combine each pair of sentences. The first one has been done for you.

1. I was wearing my winter coat. I started to shiver.
I was wearing my winter coat, but I started to shiver.

2. Animals all need water. They may perish without it.
_____

3. The sun came out. The ice began to thaw.
_____

4. The sun came out. The day was still chilly.
_____

5. Will the flowers perish? Will they thrive?
_____

6. The bear came closer. We began t...
_____

7. Winning was ... ...n't have much experience.
_____

8. Winr... ...allenge. Our team was up to it.
_____

Sentences will vary.

Write three sentences of your own. Use a conjunction in each sentence.
_____

COMPLETE YEAR GRADE 5

61

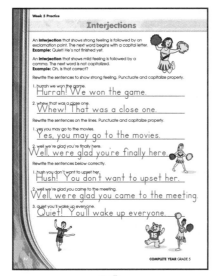

62

Interjections (page 62)

Week 5 Practice

An **interjection** that shows strong feeling is followed by an exclamation point. The next word begins with a capital letter.
Example: Quiet! He's not finished yet.

An **interjection** that shows mild feeling is followed by a comma. The next word is not capitalized.
Example: Oh, is that correct?

Rewrite the sentences to show strong feeling. Punctuate and capitalize properly.

1. hurrah we won the game.
Hurrah! We won the game.

2. whew that was a close one.
Whew! That was a close one.

Rewrite the sentences on the lines. Punctuate and capitalize properly.

1. yes you may go to the movies.
Yes, you may go to the movies.

2. well we're glad you're finally here.
Well, we're glad you're finally here.

Rewrite the sentences below correctly.

1. hush you don't want to upset her.
Hush! You don't want to upset her.

2. well we're glad you came to the meeting.
Well, we're glad you came to the meeting.

3. quiet you'll wake up everyone.
Quiet! You'll wake up everyone.

COMPLETE YEAR GRADE 5

Interjections and Direct Address (page 63)

Week 5 Practice

Strong interjections, which show great feeling, are followed by exclamation points.
Mild interjections, such as **now, well** and **yes,** are set apart by commas.
A comma or commas are used to set apart the name of a person being directly spoken to, or addressed, in a sentence. This is called **direct address.**

Examples:
Ugh! That soup is horrible. (strong interjection)
No, I haven't finished my homework yet. (mild interjection)
Sue, please hand me the pencil. (direct address)
Thank you, **Jean,** for your contribution. (direct address)

Add commas and exclamation points where they are needed in the following sentences.

1. Yes, we will finish the science project soon.
2. Wow! I forgot that it must be completed by Friday.
3. Oh! I forgot that the materials for the experiment are at home.
4. Jim, bring the microscope to the science lab.
5. Now, Leonard, it's your turn to work on the experiment.
6. Will the research for the project be completed soon, Amy?
7. No, Mrs. Clarke, it will take at least another week.
8. Yikes! That was a scary experiment you did, Mark.

Add commas and exclamation points where they are needed in the following sentences. In the blank, write the letter of the reason each punctuation mark is used. Some have two answers.

A. Interjection **B.** Direct Address

1. B Lewis, will you attempt this experiment on air pressure?
2. A No, I need to work on my electricity project, Sam.
3. B I need some help, Mr. Johnson, with my electrical circuit.
4. B The science lab is too crowded to set up the project, Ms. Chang.
5. A Cool! I would love to use the other lab.
6. A/B Yes, I'll try to set up the project in that room, Sarah.
7. A Well, that solved my problem.

COMPLETE YEAR GRADE 5

63

Answer Key

Page 64

Week 5 Practice

Multiplication

Multiplication is a process of quick addition of a number a certain number of times.

Example: 3 × 15 = 45   is the same as adding   15 + 15 + 15 = 45
15 three times.

Multiply.

32 × 3 = **96**	48 × 7 = **336**	26 × 5 = **130**	19 × 6 = **114**	63 × 2 = **126**
251 × 4 = **1,004**	523 × 8 = **4,184**	915 × 3 = **2,745**	431 × 7 = **3,017**	275 × 3 = **825**
412 × 21 = **8,652**	643 × 17 = **10,931**	526 × 22 = **11,572**	742 × 35 = **25,970**	
256 × 74 = **18,944**	874 × 15 = **13,110**	372 × 45 = **16,740**	951 × 34 = **32,334**	

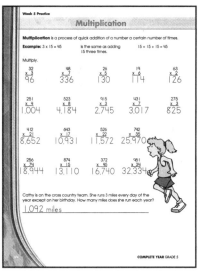

Cathy is on the cross country team. She runs 3 miles every day of the year except on her birthday. How many miles does she run each year?
1,092 miles

COMPLETE YEAR GRADE 5

Page 65

Week 5 Practice

Multiplication

Multiply.

1. 649 × 8 = **5,192**	2. 858 × 7 = **6,006**	3. 7,642 × 5 = **38,210**	4. 8,219 × 3 = **24,657**	5. 5,238 × 6 = **31,428**
6. 8,249 × 4 = **32,996**	7. 6,518 × 7 = **45,626**	8. 8,943 × 9 = **80,487**	9. 3,268 × 5 = **16,340**	10. 4,637 × 8 = **37,096**
11. 5,387 × 4 = **21,548**	12. 8,264 × 9 = **74,376**	13. 4,875 × 7 = **34,125**	14. 5,689 × 8 = **45,512**	15. 9,243 × 4 = **36,972**
16. 8,540 × 6 = **51,240**	17. 3,726 × 5 = **18,630**	18. 83,243 × 6 = **499,458**	19. 74,254 × 7 = **519,778**	20. 62,435 × 9 = **561,915**
21. 73,643 × 8 = **589,144**	22. 51,476 × 4 = **205,904**	23. 73,629 × 5 = **368,145**	24. 87,642 × 7 = **613,494**	25. 25,624 × 4 = **102,496**
26. 98,215 × 6 = **589,290**	27. 41,826 × 9 = **376,434**	28. 53,214 × 8 = **425,712**	29. 83,265 × 4 = **333,060**	30. 65,429 × 5 = **327,145**
31. 46,254 × 7 = **323,778**	32. 91,242 × 8 = **729,936**	33. 73,263 × 6 = **439,578**	34. 35,584 × 2 = **71,168**	35. 79,267 × 2 = **158,534**

COMPLETE YEAR GRADE 5

Page 66

Week 5 Practice

Multiplying With Zeros

Multiply the following numbers. If a number ends with zero, you can eliminate it while calculating the rest of the answer. Then count how many zeros you took off and add them to your answer.

Example: 55̶0̶ Take off 2 zeros
× 5̶0̶
27,500 Add on 2 zeros

5̶0̶0̶ Take off 2 zeros
× 5̶
2,500 Add on 2 zeros

1. 300 × 6 = **1,800**	2. 400 × 7 = **2,800**	3. 620 × 5 = **3,100**	4. 290 × 7 = **2,030**
5. 142 × 20 = **2,840**	6. 505 × 50 = **25,250**	7. 340 × 70 = **23,800**	8. 600 × 60 = **36,000**
9. 550 × 380 = **209,000**	10. 290 × 150 = **43,500**	11. 2,040 × 360 = **734,400**	12. 8,800 × 200 = **1,760,000**

13. Bruce traveled 600 miles each day of a 10-day trip.
How far did he go during the entire trip? **6,000 miles**

14. 30 children each sold items for the school fund-raiser.
Each child earned $100 for the school.
How much money did the school collect? **$3,000**

15. 10 × 40 × 2 = **800**   16. 30 × 30 × 10 = **9,000**

17. 100 × 60 × 10 = **60,000**   18. 500 × 11 × 2 = **11,000**

19. 9 × 10 × 10 = **900**   20. 7,000 × 20 × 10 = **1,400,000**

COMPLETE YEAR GRADE 5

Page 68

Week 6 Practice

Homophones

Homophones are words that sound alike but have different spellings and meanings.

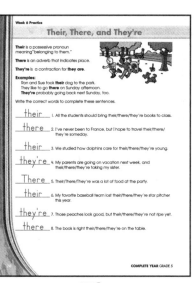

Write the correct homophone in the blank.

Their house is around the corner from us. (their, there)

1. We couldn't decide **whether** to visit Boston or St. Louis. (weather, whether)

2. We chose to visit Boston, the **capital** of Massachusetts. (capital, capitol)

3. We drove **to** the city in **two** days. (to, too, two)

4. Our **route** was over interstate highways. (route, root)

5. We **read** many signs along the way. (read, red)

6. My brothers couldn't hide **their** excitement. (their, there)

7. We found that **it's** an exciting city. (its, it's)

8. It was interesting to **hear** the accent of the people. (hear, here)

9. Many people related interesting **tales** about the city's history. (tales, tails)

10. We appreciated the **peace** and quiet of the parks. (peace, piece)

11. We walked up and down **rows** of houses in the historic district. (rows, rose)

12. I wore a **hole** in one of my shoes from **so** much walking. (whole, hole) (so, sew)

13. Luckily, this caused me **no** **pain**. (know, no) (pain, pane)

14. I had to have the **sole** of the shoe repaired. (soul, sole)

COMPLETE YEAR GRADE 5

Page 69

Week 6 Practice

Who's and Whose

Who's is a contraction for **who is**.

Whose is a possessive pronoun.

Examples:
Who's going to come?
Whose shirt is this?

To know which word to use, substitute the words "who is." If the sentence makes sense, use **who's**.

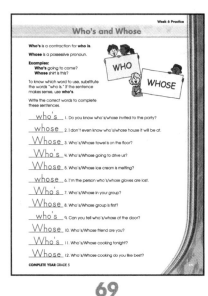

Write the correct words to complete these sentences.

who's 1. Do you know who's/whose invited to the party?

whose 2. I don't even know who's/whose house it will be at.

Whose 3. Who's/Whose towel is on the floor?

Who's 4. Who's/Whose going to drive us?

Whose 5. Who's/Whose ice cream is melting?

whose 6. I'm the person who's/whose gloves are lost.

Who's 7. Who's/Whose in your group?

Whose 8. Who's/Whose group is first?

who's 9. Can you tell who's/whose at the door?

Whose 10. Who's/Whose friend are you?

Who's 11. Who's/Whose cooking tonight?

Whose 12. Who's/Whose cooking do you like best?

COMPLETE YEAR GRADE 5

Page 70

Week 6 Practice

Their, There, and They're

Their is a possessive pronoun meaning "belonging to them."

There is an adverb that indicates place.

They're is a contraction for **they are**.

Examples:
Ron and Sue took **their** dog to the park.
They like to go **there** on Sunday afternoon.
They're probably going back next Sunday, too.

Write the correct words to complete these sentences.

their 1. All the students should bring their/there/they're books to class.

there 2. I've never been to France, but I hope to travel their/there/they're someday.

their 3. We studied how dolphins care for their/there/they're young.

they're 4. My parents are going on vacation next week, and their/there/they're taking my sister.

There 5. Their/There/They're was a lot of food at the party.

their 6. My favorite baseball team lost their/there/they're star pitcher this year.

they're 7. Those peaches look good, but their/there/they're not ripe yet.

there 8. The book is right their/there/they're on the table.

COMPLETE YEAR GRADE 5

64   **65**   **66**   **68**   **69**   **70**

Answer Key

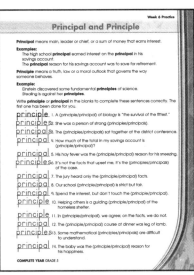

Principal and Principle

Principal means main, leader or chief, or a sum of money that earns interest.

Examples:
The high school **principal** earned interest on the **principal** in his savings account.
The **principal** reason for his savings account was to save for retirement.

Principle means a truth, law or a moral outlook that governs the way someone behaves.

Example:
Einstein discovered some fundamental **principles** of science.
Stealing is against her **principles**.

Write **principle** or **principal** in the blanks to complete these sentences correctly. The first one has been done for you.

principle 1. A (principle/principal) of biology is "the survival of the fittest."
principle 2. She was a person of strong (principles/principals).
principals 3. The (principles/principals) sat together at the district conference.
principal 4. How much of the total in my savings account is (principle/principal)?
principal 5. His hay fever was the (principle/principal) reason for his sneezing.
principle 6. It's not the facts that upset me, it's the (principles/principals) of the case.
principal 7. The jury heard only the (principle/principal) facts.
principal 8. Our school (principle/principal) is strict but fair.
principal 9. Spend the interest, but don't touch the (principle/principal).
principle 10. Helping others is a guiding (principle/principal) of the homeless shelter.
principle 11. In (principle/principal), we agree; on the facts, we do not.
principal 12. The (principle/principal) course at dinner was leg of lamb.
principles 13. Some mathematical (principles/principals) are difficult to understand.
principal 14. The baby was the (principle/principal) reason for his happiness.

COMPLETE YEAR GRADE 5

71

Multiplication (Two-Digit Multiplier)

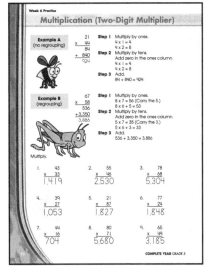

Example A (no regrouping)

	21
x	44
	84
+	840
	924

Step 1 Multiply by ones.
4 x 1 = 4
4 x 2 = 8
Step 2 Multiply by tens.
Add zero in the ones column.
4 x 1 = 4
4 x 2 = 8
Step 3 Add.
84 + 840 = 924

Example B (regrouping)

	67
x	58
	536
+	3,350
	3,886

Step 1 Multiply by ones.
8 x 7 = 56 (Carry the 5.)
8 x 6 + 5 = 53
Step 2 Multiply by tens.
Add zero in the ones column.
5 x 7 = 35 (Carry the 3.)
5 x 6 + 3 = 33
Step 3 Add.
536 + 3,350 = 3,886

Multiply.

1. 43 x 33 = 1,419
2. 55 x 46 = 2,530
3. 78 x 68 = 5,304
4. 39 x 27 = 1,053
5. 21 x 87 = 1,827
6. 77 x 24 = 1,848
7. 44 x 16 = 704
8. 80 x 71 = 5,680
9. 65 x 49 = 3,185

COMPLETE YEAR GRADE 5

72

Multiplication Maze

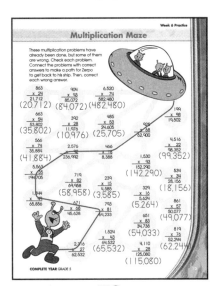

These multiplication problems have already been done, but some of them are wrong. Check each problem. Connect the problems with correct answers to make a path to get back to his ship for Zerpo. Then, correct each wrong answer.

863 x 24 = 21,712 (20,712)
904 x 93 = 85,072 (84,072)
6,520 x 74 = 582,480 (482,480)
663 x 54 = 53,802 (35,802)
392 x 28 = 11,976 (10,976)
485 x 53 = 24,605 (25,705)
199 x 98 = 19,502
566 x 74 = 35,884 (41,884)
2,576 x 92 = 236,992
466 x 18 = 8,388
925 x 68 = 62,900
4,516 x 22 = 98,352 (99,352)
5,563 x 35 = 194,705
719 x 82 = 69,958 (58,958)
239 x 15 = 3,585
1,530 x 93 = 152,290 (142,290)
534 x 34 = 28,156 (18,156)
1,944 x 49 = 65,856
671 x 68 = 45,628
793 x 81 = 64,233
329 x 16 = 5,624 (5,264)
861 x 57 = 50,077 (49,077)
651 x 83 = 34,738 (54,033)
819 x 76 = 52,244 (62,244)
2,316 x 27 = 62,532 (65,532)
1,624 x 43 = 64,532
4,110 x 28 = 125,080 (115,080)

COMPLETE YEAR GRADE 5

73

Multiplication

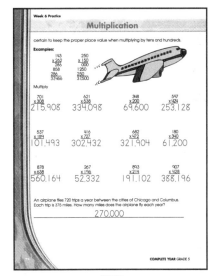

certain to keep the proper place value when multiplying by tens and hundreds.

Examples:

143	250
x 262	x 150
286	000
858	1250
286	250
37,466	37,500

Multiply.

701 x 308 = 215,908
621 x 538 = 334,098
348 x 200 = 69,600
597 x 424 = 253,128

537 x 189 = 101,493
416 x 727 = 302,432
682 x 472 = 321,904
180 x 340 = 61,200

878 x 638 = 560,164
267 x 196 = 52,332
893 x 214 = 191,102
907 x 428 = 388,196

An airplane flies 720 trips a year between the cities of Chicago and Columbus. Each trip is 375 miles. How many miles does the airplane fly each year?

_270,000_

COMPLETE YEAR GRADE 5

74

Multiplication

Solve.

1. 467 x 35 = 16,345
2. 538 x 47 = 25,286
3. 393 x 82 = 32,226
4. 304 x 529 = 160,816
5. 246 x 824 = 202,704

6. 146 x 532 = 77,672
7. 308 x 236 = 72,688
8. 326 x 92 = 29,992
9. 735 x 45 = 33,075
10. 268 x 39 = 10,452

11. 486 x 513 = 249,318
12. 314 x 249 = 78,186

COMPLETE YEAR GRADE 5

75

Puzzling Cross Number

Solve the multiplication problems below. Write the answers in the puzzle.

Across

1. 462 x 212 = 97,944
5. 234 x 101 = 23,634
7. 926 x 815 = 754,690

8. 624 x 783 = 488,592
11. 832 x 458 = 381,056

13. 336 x 817 = 274,512
14. 801 x 101 = 80,901

Down

2. 634 x 756 = 478,670
3. 208 x 422 = 87,776
4. 672 x 833 = 559,776

6. 547 x 900 = 492,300
9. 926 x 950 = 879,700

10. 698 x 741 = 517,218
12. 111 x 111 = 12,321

COMPLETE YEAR GRADE 5

76

403

Answer Key

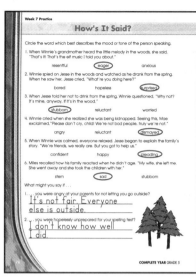

Week 7 Practice

How's It Said?

Circle the word which best describes the mood or tone of the person speaking.

1. When Winnie's grandmother heard the little melody in the woods, she said, "That's it! That's the elf music I told you about."
   resentful   (eager)   anxious

2. Winnie spied on Jesse in the woods and watched as he drank from the spring. When he saw her, Jesse cried, "What're you doing here?"
   bored   hopeless   (surprised)

3. When Jesse told her not to drink from the spring, Winnie questioned, "Why not? It's mine, anyway. If it's in the wood."
   (stubborn)   reluctant   worried

4. Winnie cried when she realized she was being kidnapped. Seeing this, Mae exclaimed, "Please don't cry, child! We're not bad people, truly we're not."
   angry   reluctant   (dismayed)

5. When Winnie was calmed, everyone relaxed. Jesse began to explain the family's story. "We're friends, we really are. But you got to help us."
   confident   happy   (pleading)

6. Miles recalled how his family reacted when he didn't age. "My wife, she left me. She went away and she took the children with her."
   stern   (sad)   stubborn

What might you say if . . .

1. . . . you were angry at your parents for not letting you go outside?
   It's not fair. Everyone else is outside.

2. . . . you were hopelessly unprepared for your spelling test?
   I don't know how well I did.

COMPLETE YEAR GRADE 5

78

Week 7 Practice

Writing: Different Points of View

A **fact** is a statement that can be proved. An **opinion** is what someone thinks or believes.

Write **F** if the statement is a fact or **O** if it is an opinion.

1. F The amusement park near our town just opened last summer.
2. O It's the best one in our state.
3. F It has a roller coaster that's 300 feet high.
4. O You're a chicken if you don't go on it.

Think about the last movie or TV show you saw. Write one fact and one opinion about it.

Fact:
Opinion: *Answers will vary.*

In a story, a **point of view** is how one character feels about an event and reacts to it. Different points of view show how characters feel about the same situation.

What if you were at the mall with a friend and saw a CD you really wanted on sale? You didn't bring enough money, so you borrowed five dollars from your friend to buy the CD. Then you lost the money in the store!

Write a sentence describing what happened from the point of view of each person named below. Explain how each person felt.

Yourself
Your friend
The store clerk who watched *Answers will vary.*
The person money.

COMPLETE YEAR GRADE 5

79

Week 7 Practice

Writing: Point of View

People often have different opinions about the same thing. This is because each of us has a different "point of view." **Point of view** is the attitude someone has about a particular topic as a result of his or her personal experience or knowledge.

Read the topic sentence below about the outcome of a basketball game. Then write two short paragraphs, one from the point of view of a player for the Reds and one from the point of view of a player for the Cowboys. Be sure to give each person's opinion of the outcome of the game.

Topic Sentence: In the last second of the basketball game between the Reds and the Cowboys, the Reds scored and won the game.

Terry, a player for the Reds :
Chris, a player for the *Paragraphs will vary.*

Here's a different situation. Read the topic sentence, and then write three short paragraphs from the points of view of Katie, her dad and her brother.

Topic Sentence: Katie's dog had chewed up another one of her father's shoes.

Katie :
Katie's father : *Paragraphs will vary.*
Katie's brother : have a cat.

COMPLETE YEAR GRADE 5

80

Week 7 Practice

Division Facts

COMPLETE YEAR GRADE 5

81

Week 7 Practice

Division in Three Ways

The equation 12 ÷ 3 can also be written as 3⟌12 or 12/3

Write each equation in the three forms. The first one has been done for you.

1. 12 ÷ 3 = 3⟌12 = 12/3
2. 24 ÷ 8 = 8⟌24 = 24/8
3. 56 ÷ 8 = 8⟌56 = 56/8
4. 63 ÷ 9 = 9⟌63 = 63/9
5. 42 ÷ 6 = 6⟌42 = 42/6
6. 15 ÷ 5 = 5⟌15 = 15/5
7. 42 ÷ 7 = 7⟌42 = 42/7
8. 72 ÷ 9 = 9⟌72 = 72/9

Solve.

9. 20⟌440 = 22
10. 440 ÷ 20 = 22
11. 440/20 = 22
12. 12⟌780 = 65
13. 650 ÷ 13 = 50
14. 720/15 = 48

COMPLETE YEAR GRADE 5

82

Week 7 Practice

Multiplication's Opposite

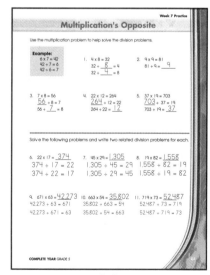

Use the multiplication problem to help solve the division problems.

Example:
6 × 7 = 42
42 ÷ 7 = 6
42 ÷ 6 = 7

1. 4 × 8 = 32
   32 ÷ 8 = 4
   32 ÷ 4 = 8

2. 9 × 9 = 81
   81 ÷ 9 = 9

3. 7 × 8 = 56
   56 ÷ 8 = 7
   56 ÷ 7 = 8

4. 22 × 12 = 264
   264 ÷ 12 = 22
   264 ÷ 22 = 12

5. 37 × 19 = 703
   703 ÷ 37 = 19
   703 ÷ 19 = 37

Solve the following problems and write two related division problems for each.

6. 22 × 17 = 374
   374 ÷ 17 = 22
   374 ÷ 22 = 17

7. 45 × 29 = 1,305
   1,305 ÷ 45 = 29
   1,305 ÷ 29 = 45

8. 19 × 82 = 1,558
   1,558 ÷ 82 = 19
   1,558 ÷ 19 = 82

9. 671 × 63 = 42,273
   42,273 ÷ 63 = 671
   42,273 ÷ 671 = 63

10. 663 × 54 = 35,802
    35,802 ÷ 663 = 54
    35,802 ÷ 54 = 663

11. 719 × 73 = 52,487
    52,487 ÷ 73 = 719
    52,487 ÷ 719 = 73

COMPLETE YEAR GRADE 5

83

Page 84

Week 7 Practice

Zeros in the Quotient

Zero holds a place in the quotient.

Example:

$$\begin{array}{r}1\\5\overline{)545}\\-5\\\hline 04\end{array}$$ Five goes into 4 zero times.

$$\begin{array}{r}10\\5\overline{)545}\\-5\\\hline 45\end{array}$$ Five goes into 45 nine times.

$$\begin{array}{r}109\\5\overline{)545}\\-5\\\hline 45\\-45\\\hline 0\end{array}$$

1. $4\overline{)420}$ = 105
2. $6\overline{)636}$ = 106
3. $9\overline{)963}$ = 107

4. $9\overline{)945}$ = 105
5. $9\overline{)963}$ = 107
6. $8\overline{)816}$ = 102

7. $3\overline{)312}$ = 104
8. $3\overline{)9,021}$ = 3,007
9. $7\overline{)1,386}$ = 198

COMPLETE YEAR GRADE 5

Page 85

Week 7 Practice

Division

Solve.

1. $9\overline{)3,654}$ = 406
2. $8\overline{)835}$ = 104 R3
3. $6\overline{)618}$ = 103

Estimate.

4. $36\overline{)660}$ = 18
5. $23\overline{)4,280}$ = 200
6. $158 \div 21$ = 10

Solve.

7. $24\overline{)228}$ = 9 R12
8. $1298 \div 37$ = 35 R3
9. $7\overline{)1,386}$ = 203 R6

10. What is the cost for 1 golf ball?

$3.36 \div 12 = $.28$

On Sale Today Only
One dozen golf balls
Only $3.36

COMPLETE YEAR GRADE 5

Page 86

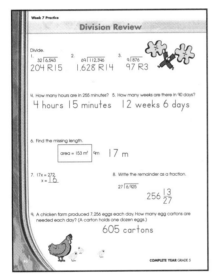

Week 7 Practice

Division Review

Divide.

1. $32\overline{)6,543}$ = 204 R15
2. $69\overline{)112,346}$ = 1,628 R14
3. $9\overline{)876}$ = 97 R3

4. How many hours are in 255 minutes? 4 hours 15 minutes

5. How many weeks are there in 90 days? 12 weeks 6 days

6. Find the missing length.

area = 153 m² 9m   17 m

7. $17x = 272$ $x = 16$

8. Write the remainder as a fraction. $27\overline{)6,925}$ $256\frac{13}{27}$

9. A chicken farm produced 7,256 eggs each day. How many egg cartons are needed each day? (A carton holds one dozen eggs.) 605 cartons

COMPLETE YEAR GRADE 5

Page 88

Week 8 Practice

Writing: Sequencing

When writing paragraphs, it is important to write events in the correct order. Think about what happens first, next, later and last.

The following sentences tell about Chandra's day, but they are all mixed up.

Read each sentence and number them in the order in which they happened.

3 She arrived at school and went to her locker to get her books.
8 After dinner, she did the dishes, then read a book for a while.
9 Chandra brushed her teeth and put on her pajamas.
5 She rode the bus home, then she fixed herself a snack.
2 She ate breakfast and went out to wait for the bus.
1 Chandra woke up and picked out her clothes for school.
4 She met her friend Sarah on the way to the cafeteria.
6 She worked on homework and watched TV until her mom called her for dinner.

Write a short paragraph about what you did today. Use words like **first, next, then, later** and **finally** to indicate the order in which you did things.

Paragraphs will vary.

COMPLETE YEAR GRADE 5

Page 89

Week 8 Practice

Personal Narratives

A **personal narrative** tells about a person's own experiences.

Read the example of a personal narrative. Write your answers in complete sentences.

My Worst Year

When I look back on that year, I can hardly believe that one person could have such terrible luck for a whole year. But then again, I should have realized that if things could begin to go wrong in January. It didn't bode well for the rest of the year.

It was the night of January 26. One of my best friends was celebrating her birthday at the local roller-skating rink, and I had been invited. The evening began well enough with pizza and laughs. I admit I have never been a cracker jack roller skater, but I could hold my own. After a few minutes of skating, I decided to exit the rink for a cold soda.

Unfortunately, I did not notice the trailing ribbons of carpet which wrapped around the wheel of my skate, yanking my left leg from under me. My leg was broken. It wasn't just broken in one place but in four places! At the hospital, the doctor set the bone and put a cast on my leg. Three months later, I felt like a new person.

Sadly, the happiness wasn't meant to last. Five short months after the final cast was removed, I fell and broke the same leg again. Not only did it rebreak but it broke in the same four places! We found out later that it hadn't healed correctly. Three months later, it was early December and the end of a year I did not wish to repeat.

1. List the sequence of events in the personal narrative.
   January 26: fell while skating and broke leg in four places
   Three months later: fell and broke leg again in same four places.

2. From reading the personal narrative, what do you think were the author's feelings toward the events that occurred?
   Answers will vary.

COMPLETE YEAR GRADE 5

Page 90

Week 8 Practice

Personal Narratives

A **narrative** is a spoken or written account of an actual event. A **personal narrative** tells about your own experience. It can be written about any event in your life and may be serious or comical.

When writing a personal narrative, remember to use correct sentence structure and punctuation. Include important dates, sights, sounds, smells, tastes and feelings to give your reader a clear picture of the event.

Write a personal narrative about an event in your life that was funny.

Narratives will vary.

COMPLETE YEAR GRADE 5

91

Week 8 Practice

Describing Characters

When you write a story, your characters must seem like real people. You need to let your reader know not only how they look but how they act and how they feel. You could just tell the reader that a character is friendly, scared or angry, but your story will be more interesting if you show these feelings by the characters' actions.

Example:
Character: A frightened child
Adjectives and adverbs: red-haired, freckled, scared, lost, worried
Simile: as frightened as a mouse cornered by a cat
Action: He peeked between his fingers, but his mother was nowhere in sight.

Write adjectives, adverbs, similes and/or metaphors that tell how each character feels. Then write a sentence that shows how the character feels.

1. an angry woman
Adjectives and adverbs: _____
Metaphor or simile: _____
Sentence: _____

2. a disappointed man
Adjectives and adverbs: _____
Metaphor or simile: _____
Sentence: _____

3. a hungry ch...
Adjec...
Metaph...
Sentence: _____

4. a tired boy
Adjectives and adverbs: _____
Metaphor or simile: _____
Sentence: _____

Answers will vary.

COMPLETE YEAR GRADE 5

92

Week 8 Practice

Writing Fiction

Use descriptive writing to complete each story. Write at least five sentences.

1. It was a cold, wintry morning in January. Snow had fallen steadily for 4 days. I was staring out my bedroom window when I saw the bedraggled dog staggering through the snow.

2. Mindy was home Saturday studying for a big science test. P... ts were due next Friday, and the test on Monday would be on the ... dy needed to do well on the test to get an A in Science ... her best friend, Jenny.

Answers will vary.

3. Mc... works every weekend delivering newspapers. He wakes up at 5:30 A.M. and begins his route at 6:00 A.M. He delivers 150 newspapers on his bike. He enjoys his weekend job because he is working toward a goal.

COMPLETE YEAR GRADE 5

93

Week 8 Practice

Division

The remainder in a division problem must always be less than the divisor.

Example:
```
     261 r 23
26| 6,367
    5.2
    116
    104
    127
    104
     23
```

Divide.

53| 1,220 = **23 r 1**   37| 1,528 = **41 r 11**   83| 6,270 = **75 r 45**   26| 3,618 = **139 r 4**

14| 389 = **27 r 11**   29| 2,645 = **91 r 6**   60| 8,010 = **133 r 30**   57| 5,406 = **94 r 48**

35| 2,546 = **72 r 26**   43| 492 = **11 r 19**   83| 4,608 = **55 r 43**   19| 185 = **9 r 14**

The Oregon Trail is 2,197 miles long. How long would it take a covered wagon traveling 20 miles a day to complete the trip?
110 days

COMPLETE YEAR GRADE 5

94

Week 8 Practice

Dividing with Zeros

Sometimes you have a remainder in division problems. You can add a decimal point and zeros to the dividend and keep dividing until you have the answer.

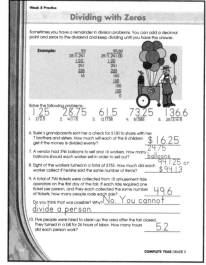

Example:
```
      49              49.64
25| 1,241         25| 1,241.00
    1.00               1.00
    241                241
    225                225
     16                160
                       150
                       100
                       100
                         0
```

Solve the following problems.

1. 2| 2.5 = **1.25**   2. 4| 115 = **28.75**   3. 12| 738 = **61.5**   4. 8| 586 = **73.25**   5. 25| 3,415 = **136.6**

6. Susie's grandparents sent her a check for $130 to share with her 7 brothers and sisters. How much will each of the 8 children get if the money is divided evenly? **$16.25**

7. A vendor had 396 balloons to sell and 16 workers. How many balloons should each worker sell in order to sell out? **24.75 balloons**

8. Eight of the workers turned in a total of $753. How much did each worker collect if he/she sold the same number of items? **94.125 or $94.13**

9. A total of 744 tickets were collected from 15 amusement ride operators on the first day of the fair. If each ride required one ticket per person, and they each collected the same number of tickets, how many people rode each ride? **49.6**
Do you think that was possible? Why? **No. You cannot divide a person.**

10. Five people were hired to clean up the area after the fair closed. They turned in a bill for 26 hours of labor. How many hours did each person work? **5.2**

COMPLETE YEAR GRADE 5

95

Week 8 Practice

Artifact Facts

Help the archaeologist find the artifact. First, solve the division problems. Then, connect the quotients in numerical order, starting at 788, to make his path.

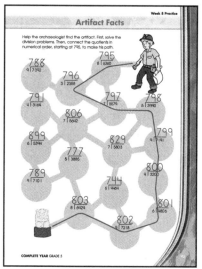

9| 7,092 = **788**   8| 6,360 = **795**
3| 2,388 = **796**
4| 3,164 = **791**   7| 5,579 = **797**   5| 3,990 = **798**
7| 5,642 = **806**
6| 5,394 = **899**   7| 5,803 = **829**   9| 7,191 = **799**
5| 3,885 = **777**
9| 7,101 = **789**   4| 3,200 = **800**
6| 4,464 = **744**
8| 6,424 = **803**   6| 4,806 = **801**
9| 7,218 = **802**

COMPLETE YEAR GRADE 5

96

Week 8 Practice

Wisconsin's Nickname

What is Wisconsin known as? To find out, solve the division problems below. Then, find the answers at the bottom of the page and write the corresponding letter on the line above the answer.

T. 14| 1218 = **87**   E. 23| 1633 = **71**   S. 53| 2756 = **52**

A. 38| 1596 = **42**   A. 61| 5185 = **85**   E. 18| 1764 = **98**

T. 22| 1628 = **74**   R. 40| 2520 = **63**   D. 55| 4400 = **80**

G. 31| 1364 = **44**   B. 12| 780 = **65**

B A D G E R   S T A T E
65 85 80 44 71 63   52 74 42 87 98

COMPLETE YEAR GRADE 5

Answer Key

Week 9 Practice

Because...

The sentences below are about the book *Tuck Everlasting* by Natalie Babbitt.

Remember:
The **cause** is the reason for the action or **why** something happened. The **effect** is the result of the action or **what** actually happened.

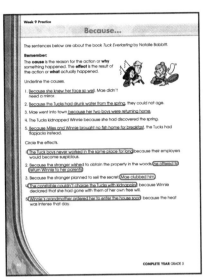

Underline the causes.

1. Because she knew her face so well, Mae didn't need a mirror.
2. Because the Tucks had drunk water from the spring, they could not age.
3. Mae went into town because her two boys were returning home.
4. The Tucks kidnapped Winnie because she had discovered the spring.
5. Because Miles and Winnie brought no fish home for breakfast, the Tucks had flapjacks instead.

Circle the effects.

1. The Tuck boys never worked in the same place for long because their employers would become suspicious.
2. Because the stranger wished to obtain the property in the woods, he offered to return Winnie to her parents.
3. Because the stranger planned to sell the secret, Mae clubbed him.
4. The constable couldn't charge the Tucks with kidnapping because Winnie declared that she had gone with them of her own free will.
5. Winnie's grandmother ordered her to enter the house soon because the heat was intense that day.

COMPLETE YEAR GRADE 5

98

Week 9 Practice

What Do You Think?

Read each sentence. Write two sentences explaining what could have caused each event to happen.

1. The bird ceased its singing in the forest.
   a. A predator was nearby.
   b. _____

2. Tim came home crying. His backpack was open.
   a. _____
   b. _____

3. Five hundred people laughed at Lana as she stood in the bright light.
   a. _____
   b. _____

4. The saddled horse galloped onto the track without a jockey.
   a. _____
   b. _____

5. Pam sat soaking wet on the bench with her towel.
   a. _____
   b. _____

6. Martin stared with his mouth agape at his teacher, Mr. Lancaster.
   a. _____ *Answers will vary.*
   b. _____

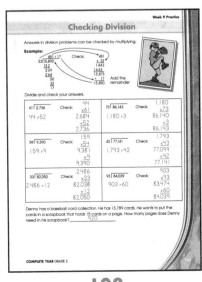

COMPLETE YEAR GRADE 5

99

Week 9 Practice

Cause and Effect

A **cause** is an event or reason which has an effect on something else.

Example:
The heavy rains produced flooding in Chicago.
Heavy rains were the **cause** of the flooding in Chicago.

An **effect** is an event that results from a cause.

Example:
Flooding in Chicago was due to the heavy rains.
Flooding was the **effect** caused by the heavy rains.

Read the paragraphs. Complete the charts by writing the missing cause (reason) or effect (result).

Club-footed toads are small toads that live in the rainforests of Central and South America. Because they give off a poisonous substance on their skins, other animals cannot eat them.

Cause:	Effect:
They give off a poisonous substance.	Other animals cannot eat them.

Civets (siv its) are weasel-like animals. The best known of the civets is the mongoose, which eats rats and snakes. For this reason, it is welcome around homes in its native India.

Cause:	Effect:
It eats rats and snakes.	It is welcome around homes in its native India.

Bluebirds can be found in most areas of the United States. Like other members of the thrush family of birds, young bluebirds have speckled breasts. This makes them difficult to see and helps them hide from their enemies. The Pilgrims called them "blue robins" because they are much like the English robin. They are the same size and have the same red breast and friendly song as the English robin.

Cause:	Effect:
Young bluebirds have speckled breasts.	It helps them hide from enemies.
They are much like English robins.	The Pilgrims called them "blue robins."

COMPLETE YEAR GRADE 5

100

Week 9 Practice

Prepositions

A **preposition** is a word that comes before a noun or pronoun and shows the relationship of that noun or pronoun to other words in the sentence.

The **object of a preposition** is a noun or pronoun that follows a preposition and completes its meaning. A **prepositional phrase** includes a preposition and the object(s) of the preposition.

Examples:
The girl **with red hair** spoke first.
With is the preposition.
Hair is the object of the preposition.
With red hair is a prepositional phrase.

In addition to being subjects, direct and indirect objects and nouns and pronouns can also be objects of prepositions.

Prepositions					
across	behind	from	near	over	to	on
by	through	in	around	off	with	of
after	before	for	between	beyond	at	into

Underline the prepositional phrases in these sentences. Circle the prepositions.
The first sentence has been done for you.

1. The name of our street is Redsail Court.
2. We have lived in our house for three years.
3. In our family, we eat a lot of hamburgers.
4. We like hamburgers on toasted buns with mustard.
5. Sometimes we eat in the living room in front of the TV.
6. In the summer, we have picnics in the backyard.
7. The ants crawl into our food and into our clothes.
8. Behind our house is a park with swings.
9. Kids from the neighborhood walk through our yard to the park.
10. Sometimes they cut across Mom's garden and stomp on her beans.
11. Mom says we need a tall fence without a gate.
12. With a fence around our yard, we could get a dog!

COMPLETE YEAR GRADE 5

101

Week 9 Practice

Preposition, Adverb, or Verb?

Don't confuse prepositions with adverbs or with phrases made of **to** plus a verb.

Examples: All the students went **to** the zoo. (preposition)
We really wanted **to** go. (verb part)
We started getting excited **before** the trip. (preposition)
Have you gone to the zoo **before**? (adverb)

Identify each **bold** word as a preposition, adverb or verb part.

1. It was incredible how they had trained the animals **to** move like that! ___verb part___
2. A monkey followed me **to** the concession stand. ___preposition___
3. A beautiful dove flew **around** the audience. ___preposition___
4. A seal tossed a ball **around** to show off. ___adverb___
5. We took pictures of the walrus **before** the show. ___preposition___
6. I had never seen a walrus up close **before**. ___adverb___
7. The walrus waddled beyond the stage over **to** the audience. ___preposition___
8. My friends were brave, and they decided **to** stay and pet him. ___verb part___
9. David asked us, "Who wants to see the Dolphin Show at 2:00?" ___verb part___
10. The whale catapulted **to** the top and grabbed the fish. ___preposition___
11. The monkeys would have liked **to** swing through the trees. ___verb part___
12. I looked **up** when I heard the parrot talk. ___adverb___
13. I noticed a pigeon flying **around**. ___adverb___
14. The elephants came **near**. ___adverb___
15. The pigeon carried the message **to** its destination. ___preposition___
16. The chimpanzees shouted **across** the water. ___preposition___

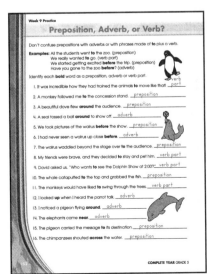

COMPLETE YEAR GRADE 5

102

Week 9 Practice

Checking Division

Answers in division problems can be checked by multiplying.

Example:

$$481 \text{ r } 17$$
$$33\overline{)15,890}$$
Check
$$\begin{array}{r} 481 \\ \times 33 \\ \hline 1443 \\ 1443 \\ \hline 15,873 \\ + 17 \\ \hline 15,890 \end{array}$$
Add the remainder

Divide and check your answers.

	Check			Check
$61\overline{)2,736}$ 44 r52	$\begin{array}{r}44\\\times 61\\\hline 44\\264\\\hline 2,684\\+52\\\hline 2,736\end{array}$		$73\overline{)86,143}$ 1,180 r3	$\begin{array}{r}1,180\\\times 73\\\hline 86,140\\+3\\\hline 86,143\end{array}$
$59\overline{)9,390}$ 159 r9	$\begin{array}{r}159\\\times 59\\\hline 9,381\\+9\\\hline 9,390\end{array}$		$43\overline{)77,141}$ 1,793 r42	$\begin{array}{r}1,793\\\times 43\\\hline 77,099\\+42\\\hline 77,141\end{array}$
$33\overline{)82,050}$ 2,486 r12	$\begin{array}{r}2,486\\\times 33\\\hline 82,038\\+12\\\hline 82,050\end{array}$		$93\overline{)84,039}$ 903 r60	$\begin{array}{r}903\\\times 93\\\hline 83,474\\+60\\\hline 84,039\end{array}$

Denny has a baseball card collection. He has 13,789 cards. He wants to put the cards in a scrapbook that holds 15 cards on a page. How many pages does Denny need in his scrapbook? ___920___

COMPLETE YEAR GRADE 5

103

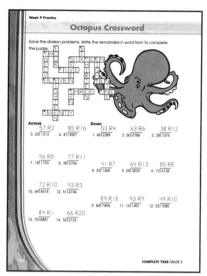

Week 9 Practice

Octopus Crossword

Solve the division problems. Write the remainders in word form to complete the puzzle.

Across

3. 23⟌1313 57 R2
4. 41⟌3501 85 R16
7. 18⟌1733 96 R5
8. 36⟌2706 77 R11
10. 64⟌4618 72 R10
12. 51⟌4746 93 R3
13. 70⟌5881 84 R1
14. 32⟌2132 66 R20

Down

1. 45⟌2389 53 R4
2. 60⟌3786 63 R6
3. 28⟌1076 38 R12
4. 33⟌1360 41 R7
5. 58⟌3533 64 R13
6. 72⟌6128 85 R8
9. 84⟌7494 89 R18
11. 16⟌1497 93 R9
12. 22⟌1088 49 R10

104

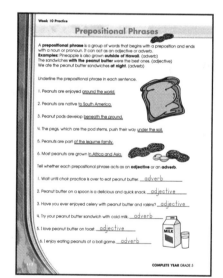

Week 9 Practice

Division Word Problems

In the example below, 368 is being divided by 4. 4 won't divide into 3, so move over one position and divide 4 into 36. 4 goes into 36 nine times. Then multiply 4 x 9 to get 36. Subtract 36 from 36. The answer is 0, less than the divisor, so 9 is the right number. Now bring down the 8, divide 4 into it and repeat the process.

Example:

$$4⟌368$$

To check your division, multiply 4 x 92 = 368.

Solve the following division problems. (For some problems, you will also need to add or subtract.)

1. Kristy helped the kindergarten teacher put a total of 192 crayons into 8 boxes. How many crayons did they put into each box? — **24 crayons**

2. The scout troop has to finish a 12-mile hike in 3 hours. How many miles an hour will they have to walk? — **4 miles per hour**

3. At her slumber party, Shelly had 4 friends and 25 pieces of candy. If she kept 5 pieces and divided the rest among her friends, how many pieces did each friend get? — **5 pieces**

4. Kenny's book has 147 pages. He wants to read the same number of pages each day and finish reading the book in 7 days. How many pages should he read each day? — **21 pages**

5. Brian and 2 friends are going to share 27 marbles. How many will each person get? — **9 marbles**

6. To help the school, 5 parents agreed to sell 485 tickets for a raffle. How many tickets will each person have to sell to do his or her part? — **97 tickets**

7. Tim is going to weed his neighbor's garden for $3 an hour. How many hours does he have to work to make $72? — **24 hours**

105

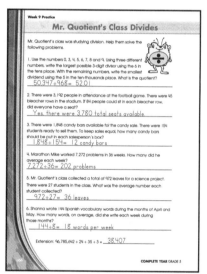

Week 9 Practice

Mr. Quotient's Class Divides

Mr. Quotient's class was studying division. Help them solve the following problems.

1. Use the numbers 0, 3, 4, 5, 6, 7, 8 and 9. Using three different numbers, write the largest possible 3-digit divisor using the 6 in the tens place. With the remaining numbers, write the smallest dividend using the 5 in the ten-thousands place. What is the quotient?
50,347÷968= **52 01**

2. There were 3,192 people in attendance at the football game. There were 45 bleacher rows in the stadium. If 84 people could sit in each bleacher row, did everyone have a seat?
Yes, there were 3,780 total seats available.

3. There were 1,848 candy bars available for the candy sale. There were 154 students ready to sell them. To keep sales equal, how many candy bars should be put in each salesperson's box?
1,848÷154= **12 candy bars**

4. Marathon Mike worked 7,272 problems in 36 weeks. How many did he average each week?
7,272÷36= **202 problems**

5. Mr. Quotient's class collected a total of 972 leaves for a science project. There were 27 students in the class. What was the average number each student collected?
972÷27= **36 leaves**

6. Shanna wrote 144 Spanish vocabulary words during the months of April and May. How many words, on average, did she write each week during those months?
144÷8= **18 words per week**

Extension: 96,785,642 ÷ 24 + 35 + 3 = **38,407**

106

Week 10 Practice

Prepositional Phrases

A **prepositional phrase** is a group of words that begins with a preposition and ends with a noun or pronoun. It can act as an adjective or adverb.
Examples: Pineapple is also grown **outside of Hawaii**. (adverb)
The sandwiches **with the peanut butter** were the best ones. (adjective)
We ate the peanut butter sandwiches **at night**. (adverb)

Underline the prepositional phrase in each sentence.

1. Peanuts are enjoyed around the world.

2. Peanuts are native to South America.

3. Peanut pods develop beneath the ground.

4. The pegs, which are the pod stems, push their way under the soil.

5. Peanuts are part of the legume family.

6. Most peanuts are grown in Africa and Asia.

Tell whether each prepositional phrase acts as an **adjective** or an **adverb**.

1. Wait until choir practice is over to eat peanut butter. **adverb**

2. Peanut butter on a spoon is a delicious and quick snack. **adjective**

3. Have you ever enjoyed celery with peanut butter and raisins? **adjective**

4. Try your peanut butter sandwich with cold milk. **adverb**

5. I love peanut butter on toast. **adjective**

6. I enjoy eating peanuts at a ball game. **adverb**

112

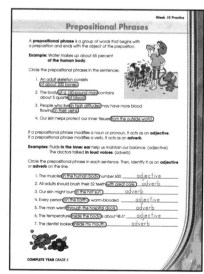

Week 10 Practice

Prepositional Phrases

A **prepositional phrase** is a group of words that begins with a preposition and ends with the object of the preposition.

Example: Water makes up about 65 percent **of the human body**.

Circle the prepositional phrases in the sentences.

1. An adult skeleton consists of about 200 bones.
2. The body of a 160-pound man contains about 5 quarts of blood.
3. People who live in high altitudes may have more blood flowing in their veins.
4. Our skin helps protect our inner tissues from the outside world.

If a prepositional phrase modifies a noun or pronoun, it acts as an **adjective**. If a prepositional phrase modifies a verb, it acts as an **adverb**.

Examples: Fluids in the inner ear help us maintain our balance. (adjective)
The doctors talked in loud voices. (adverb)

Circle the prepositional phrase in each sentence. Then, identify it as an **adjective** or **adverb** on the line.

1. The muscles in the human body number 600. **adjective**
2. All adults should brush their 32 teeth with great care. **adverb**
3. Our skin might burn in the hot sun. **adverb**
4. Every person on the earth is warm-blooded. **adjective**
5. The man went through the hospital doors. **adverb**
6. The temperature inside the body is about 98.6°. **adjective**
7. The dentist looked inside my mouth. **adverb**

113

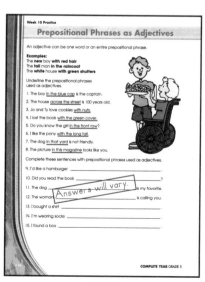

Week 10 Practice

Prepositional Phrases as Adjectives

An adjective can be one word or an entire prepositional phrase.

Examples:
The **new** boy **with red hair**
The **tall** man **in the raincoat**
The **white** house **with green shutters**

Underline the prepositional phrases used as adjectives.

1. The boy in the blue cap is the captain.
2. The house across the street is 100 years old.
3. Jo and Ty love cookies with nuts.
4. I lost the book with the green cover.
5. Do you know the girl in the front row?
6. I like the pony with the long tail.
7. The dog in that yard is not friendly.
8. The picture in this magazine looks like you.

Complete these sentences with prepositional phrases used as adjectives.

9. I'd like a hamburger _____.
10. Did you read the book _____?
11. The dog _____ is my favorite.
12. The woman _____ is calling you.
13. I bought a shirt _____.
14. I'm wearing socks _____.
15. I found a box _____.

Answers will vary.

114

Answer Key

115

Prepositional Phrases as Adverbs

An adverb can be one word or an entire prepositional phrase.

Examples:
They'll be here **tomorrow**.
They always come **on time**.
Move it **down**.
Put it **under the picture**.
Drive **carefully**.
He drove **with care**.

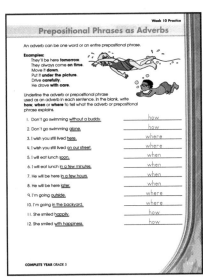

Underline the adverb or prepositional phrase used as an adverb in each sentence. In the blank, write **how**, **when** or **where** to tell what the adverb or prepositional phrase explains.

1. Don't go swimming without a buddy. — how
2. Don't go swimming alone. — how
3. I wish you still lived here. — where
4. I wish you still lived on our street. — where
5. I will eat lunch soon. — when
6. I will eat lunch in a few minutes. — when
7. He will be here in a few hours. — when
8. He will be here later. — when
9. I'm going outside. — where
10. I'm going in the backyard. — where
11. She smiled happily. — how
12. She smiled with happiness. — how

COMPLETE YEAR GRADE 5

116

Story Organizer

Date _____ Title _____

Setting: _____
Characters: _____

Problem: _____

Events: _____

Answers will vary.

Solution: _____

COMPLETE YEAR GRADE 5

117

Multiplication and Division

Multiply or divide to find the answers.

Brianne's summer job is mowing lawns for three of her neighbors. Each lawn takes about 1 hour to mow and needs to be done once every week. At the end of the summer, she will have earned a total of $630. She collected the same amount of money from each job. How much did each neighbor pay for her summer lawn service?
$210

If the mowing season lasts for 14 weeks, how much will Brianne earn for each job each week? $15

If she had worked for two more weeks, how much would she have earned? $720

Brianne agreed to shovel snow from the driveways and sidewalks for the same three neighbors. They agreed to pay her the same rate. However, it only snowed seven times that winter.
How much did she earn shoveling snow? $315

What was her total income for both jobs? $945

Multiply or divide.
623
12) 7,476

940
23) 21,620

815
40) 32,600

32 × 45 = 1,440   28 × 15 = 420   73 × 14 = 1,022   92 × 30 = 2,760

COMPLETE YEAR GRADE 5

118

Multi-Step Problems

Some problems take more than one step to solve. First, plan each step needed to find the solution. Then solve each part to find the answer.

Example: Tickets for a bargain matinee cost $4 for adults and $3 for children. How much would tickets cost for a family of 2 adults and 3 children?

Step 1: Find the cost of the adults' tickets.
2 × $4 = $8
adults / each ticket / total

Step 2: Find the cost of the children's tickets.
3 × $3 = $9
children / each ticket / total

Step 3: Add to find the sum of the tickets.
$8 + $9 = $17
adults / children / total

The tickets cost $17 total.

Write the operations you will use to solve each problem. Then find the answer.

1. Arden and her father are riding their bikes 57 miles to Arden's grandma's house. They ride 13 miles, then take a water break. Then they ride 15 miles to a rest area for a picnic lunch. How many miles do Arden and her father have left to ride after lunch?
Operations: 1. Add the miles they've gone. 2. Subtract from total miles.
Answer: 29 total miles.

2. A triathlete bikes 15 miles at 20 miles per hour, runs 5 miles at 6 miles per hour and swims 1 mile at 4 miles per hour. How long does the triathlon take her to complete?
Operations: 1. Devise a formula number of mi. ÷ mph = time;
2. Add the time totals. 3. Convert to hours.
Answer: 3 hrs. and 5 min.

3. Ray bought strawberries for $1.99, blueberries for $1.40 and 2 pints of raspberries for $1.25 per pint. How much did Ray spend on berries?
Operations: 1. Find total cost of raspberries. 2. Add to the
Answer: cost of blueberries and strawberries.
$5.89

COMPLETE YEAR GRADE 5

119

Multiply or Divide?

These key words will help you know when to multiply and when to divide.
multiplication key words: **in all, altogether, times** and **each**
division key words: **per, each**

Circle the key words and solve the story problems.

1. There are 9 classrooms at the vocational school. The average number of students per classroom is 27 students How many students (altogether) are there in the school?
27
× 9
243
243 students

2. Thirty-five students are studying auto mechanics. Three (times) that many are studying business. How many students are studying business?
35
× 3
105
105 students

3. The semester is 16 weeks long. Students attend class 5 days a week. How many days (in all) must a student attend class each semester?
16
× 5
80
80 days

4. In one class of 27 students, (each) student used $30.00 worth of materials. (Altogether) How much did materials cost this class?
27
× 30
810
$810.00

5. Lunch cost each student $11.50 for a 5-day week. How much does (each) lunch cost?
$11.50 ÷ 5 = $2.30
$2.30

6. The average student drives a total of 8 miles per day to attend classes. How many miles (in all) does a student drive during the 80-day semester?
80
× 8
640
640 miles

COMPLETE YEAR GRADE 5

120

Shopping for Soccer Supplies

The soccer team members needed to buy their own shin guards, socks, shoes and shorts. A couple of the players volunteered to do some comparative shopping to find the store with the best deal. Use their chart to answer the questions below.

SPORTS CORNER		JOE'S SOCCER	
Socks	3 pairs for $9.30	Socks	2 pairs for $6.84
Shoes	2 pairs for $48.24	Shoes	3 pairs for $84.15
Shin Guards	3 pairs for $32.48	Shin Guards	5 pairs for $35.70
Shorts	5 pairs for $60.30	Shorts	4 pairs for $36.36

1. Which store had the better price for socks? — Sports Corner
How much less were they per pair? — $0.32

2. Which store had the better price for shin guards? — Joe's Soccer
How much would you save per pair? — $0.98

3. How much would one pair of shoes and socks cost at Joe's Soccer? — $31.47
How much at Sports Corner? — $27.22

4. Which store had the better price for shorts? — Joe's Soccer
How much less were they per pair? — $2.97 less

5. Total the price per pair for each item at each store. If you could shop at only one store, which one would give you the best overall deal? — Sport's Corner
How much would you save? — $0.30

COMPLETE YEAR GRADE 5

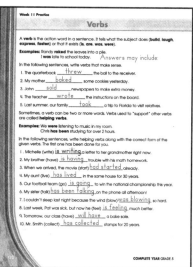

Page 122

Verbs

Week 11 Practice

A **verb** is the action word in a sentence. It tells what the subject does (**build, laugh, express, fasten**) or that it exists (**is, are, was, were**).

Examples: Randy **raked** the leaves into a pile.
I **was** late to school today.   Answers may include:

In the following sentences, write verbs that make sense.
1. The quarterback ___threw___ the ball to the receiver.
2. My mother ___baked___ some cookies yesterday.
3. John ___sold___ newspapers to make extra money.
4. The teacher ___wrote___ the instructions on the board.
5. Last summer, our family ___took___ a trip to Florida to visit relatives.

Sometimes, a verb can be two or more words. Verbs used to "support" other verbs are called **helping verbs**.

Examples: We **were** listening to music in my room.
Chris **has been** studying for over 2 hours.

In the following sentences, write helping verbs along with the correct form of the given verbs. The first one has been done for you.
1. Michelle (write) ___is writing___ a letter to her grandmother right now.
2. My brother (have) ___is having___ trouble with his math homework.
3. When we arrived, the movie (start) ___had started___ already.
4. My aunt (live) ___has lived___ in the same house for 30 years.
5. Our football team (go) ___is going___ to win the national championship this year.
6. My sister (talk) ___has been talking___ on the phone all afternoon!
7. I couldn't sleep last night because the wind (blow) ___was blowing___ so hard.
8. Last week, Pat was sick, but now he (feel) ___is feeling___ much better.
9. Tomorrow, our class (have) ___will have___ a bake sale.
10. Mr. Smith (collect) ___has collected___ stamps for 20 years.

COMPLETE YEAR GRADE 5

Page 123

Linking or Helping Verbs?

Week 11 Practice

The verb **be** (and its various forms) can be used as either a linking verb or a helping verb.
Examples: Sarah **is** a fine skater. (linking verb)
Gregory **is** helping Dad clean. (helping verb)

Read the sentences below. Underline the form of the verb **be** and decide how it is used. Write linking verb or helping verb on the line.
1. In ancient times, no one **was** using money. ___helping verb___
2. Later on, they **were** trading goods and services. ___helping verb___
3. The trading of goods and services **is** called bartering. ___helping verb___
4. Finally, people **were** accepting certain objects as payment ___helping verb___
5. These objects **were** valuable to everyone. ___linking verb___
6. The objects **were** anything from animal skins to shells. ___linking verb___
7. Some of the objects **were** metal. ___linking verb___
8. Gold and silver **were** demanded by many people. ___helping verb___
9. Governments **were** given the power to mint coins. ___helping verb___
10. One of the first coin-makers **was** an ancient Roman. ___linking verb___
11. The first paper money **was** Chinese. ___linking verb___

Write sentences using each verb as indicated.
is (linking verb)
is (helping verb)
are (linking verb)   Sentences will vary.
are (helping verb)
was (linking verb)
was (helping verb)

COMPLETE YEAR GRADE 5

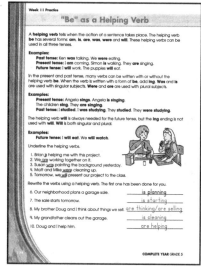

Page 124

"Be" as a Helping Verb

Week 11 Practice

A **helping verb** tells when the action of a sentence takes place. The helping verb **be** has several forms: **am, is, are, was, were** and **will**. These helping verbs can be used in all three tenses.

Examples:
Past tense: Ken **was** talking. We **were** eating.
Present tense: I **am** coming. Simon **is** walking. They **are** singing.
Future tense: I **will** work. The puppies **will** eat.

In the present and past tense, many verbs can be written with or without the helping verb **be**. When the verb is written with a form of **be**, add **ing**. **Was** and **is** are used with singular subjects. **Were** and **are** are used with plural subjects.

Examples:
Present tense: Angela **sings**. Angela **is singing**.
The children **sing**. They **are singing**.
Past tense: I **studied**. I **was studying**. They **studied**. They **were studying**.

The helping verb **will** is always needed for the future tense, but the **ing** ending is not used with **will**. **Will** is both singular and plural.

Examples:
Future tense: I **will** eat. We **will** watch.

Underline the helping verbs.
1. Brian **is** helping me with this project.
2. We **are** working together on it.
3. Susan **was** painting the background yesterday.
4. Matt and Mike **were** cleaning up.
5. Tomorrow, we **will** present our project to the class.

Rewrite the verbs using a helping verb. The first one has been done for you.
6. Our neighborhood plans a garage sale. ___is planning___
7. The sale starts tomorrow. ___is starting___
8. My brother Doug and I think about things we sell. ___are thinking/are selling___
9. My grandfather cleans out the garage. ___is cleaning___
10. Doug and I help him. ___are helping___

COMPLETE YEAR GRADE 5

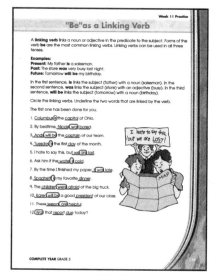

Page 125

"Be" as a Linking Verb

Week 11 Practice

A **linking verb** links a noun or adjective in the predicate to the subject. Forms of the verb **be** are the most common linking verbs. Linking verbs can be used in all three tenses.

Examples:
Present: My father **is** a salesman.
Past: The store **was** very busy last night.
Future: Tomorrow **will be** my birthday.

In the first sentence, **is** links the subject (father) with a noun (salesman). In the second sentence, **was** links the subject (store) with an adjective (busy). In the third sentence, **will be** links the subject (tomorrow) with a noun (birthday).

Circle the linking verbs. Underline the two words that are linked by the verb.
The first one has been done for you.
1. Columbus **is** the capital of Ohio.
2. By bedtime, Nicole **was** bored.
3. Andy **will be** the captain of our team.
4. Tuesday **is** the first day of the month.
5. I hate to say this, but we **are** lost.
6. Ask him if the water **is** cold.
7. By the time I finished my paper, I **was** late.
8. Spaghetti **is** my favorite dinner.
9. The children **were** afraid of the big truck.
10. Karen **will be** a good president of our class.
11. These lessons **are** helpful.
12. **Was** that report due today?

COMPLETE YEAR GRADE 5

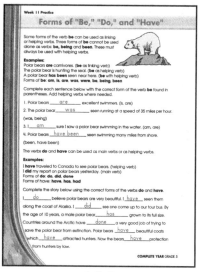

Page 126

Forms of "Be," "Do," and "Have"

Week 11 Practice

Some forms of the verb **be** can be used as linking or helping verbs. Three forms of **be** cannot be used alone as verbs: **be, being** and **been**. These must always be used with helping verbs.

Examples:
Polar bears **are** carnivores. (**be** as linking verb)
The polar bear **is** hunting the seal. (**be** as helping verb)
A polar bear has **been** seen near here. (**be** with helping verb)
Forms of be: **am, is, are, was, were, be, being, been**

Complete each sentence below with the correct form of the verb **be** found in parentheses. Add helping verbs where needed.
1. Polar bears ___are___ excellent swimmers. (is, are)
2. The polar bear ___was___ seen running at a speed of 35 miles per hour. (was, being)
3. I ___am___ sure I saw a polar bear swimming in the water. (am, are)
4. Polar bears ___have been___ seen swimming many miles from shore. (been, have been)

The verbs **do** and **have** can be used as main verbs or as helping verbs.

Examples:
I **have** traveled to Canada to see polar bears. (helping verb)
I **did** my report on polar bears yesterday. (main verb)
Forms of have: **have, has, had**
Forms of do: **do, does, did, done**

Complete the story below using the correct forms of the verbs **do** and **have**.
I ___do___ believe polar bears are very beautiful. I ___have___ seen them along the coast of Alaska. I ___did___ see one come up to our tour bus. By the age of 10 years, a male polar bear ___has___ grown to its full size. Countries around the Arctic have ___done___ a very good job of trying to save the polar bear from extinction. Polar bears ___have___ beautiful coats which ___have___ attracted hunters. Now the bears ___have___ protection from hunters by law.

COMPLETE YEAR GRADE 5

Page 127

Decimals

Week 11 Practice

A **decimal** is a number that includes a period called a **decimal point**. The digits to the right of the decimal point are a value less than one.

one whole   one tenth   one hundredth

The place value chart below helps explain decimals.

hundreds	tens	ones	tenths	hundredths	thousandths
6	3	2 .	4		
	4	7 .	0	5	
		8 .	0	0	9

A decimal point is read as "and." The first number, 632.4, is read as "six hundred thirty-two and four tenths." The second number, 47.05, is read as "forty-seven and five hundredths." The third number, 8.009, is read as "eight and nine thousandths."

Write the decimals shown below. Two have been done for you.
1. ___1.4___
2. ___1.6___
3. ___1.78___
4. six and five tenths ___6.5___
5. twenty-two and nine tenths ___22.9___
6. thirty-six and fourteen hundredths ___36.14___
7. forty-seven hundredths ___0.47___
8. one hundred six and four tenths ___106.4___
9. seven and three hundredths ___7.03___
10. one tenth less than 0.6 ___0.5___
11. one hundredth less than 0.34 ___0.33___
12. one tenth more than 0.2 ___0.3___

COMPLETE YEAR GRADE 5

Answer Key

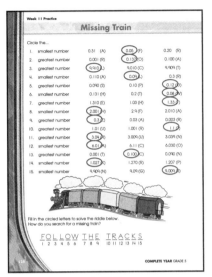

Week 11 Practice

Missing Train

Circle the...

1.	smallest number	0.31 (A)	(0.05)(F)	0.20 (R)
2.	greatest number	0.001 (R)	(0.137)(O)	0.100 (A)
3.	greatest number	(9.910)(L)	9.010 (C)	9.909 (T)
4.	smallest number	0.110 (A)	(0.09)(L)	0.3 (T)
5.	greatest number	0.090 (S)	0.10 (P)	(0.12)(O)
6.	greatest number	0.131 (H)	0.2 (T)	(0.06)(W)
7.	greatest number	1.310 (E)	1.03 (H)	(1.33)(T)
8.	greatest number	(2.001)(H)	2.9 (F)	2.010 (A)
9.	greatest number	(0.3)(E)	0.03 (A)	0.003 (R)
10.	greatest number	(1.01)(U)	1.001 (R)	(1.1)(E)
11.	greatest number	(3.04)(R)	3.009 (U)	3.039 (O)
12.	smallest number	(6.01)(A)	6.11 (C)	6.030 (O)
13.	smallest number	0.001 (T)	(7.100)(C)	0.090 (N)
14.	smallest number	(1.027)(K)	1.270 (R)	1.207 (P)
15.	smallest number	9.909 (N)	9.09 (G)	(9.009)(S)

Fill in the circled letters to solve the riddle below.
How do you search for a missing train?

F O L L O W   T H E   T R A C K S
1 2 3 4 5 6   7 8 9   10 11 12 13 14 15

COMPLETE YEAR GRADE 5

128

Week 11 Practice

More Puzzling Problems

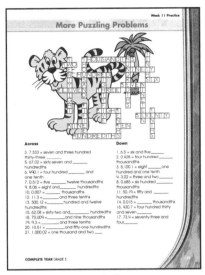

Across

3. 7.333 = seven and three hundred thirty-three
5. 67.02 = sixty-seven and _____ hundredths
6. 490.1 = four hundred _____ and one tenth
7. 0.512 = five _____ twelve thousandths
9. 8.06 = eight and _____ hundredths
10. 0.007 = _____ thousandths
12. 11.3 = _____ and three tenths
13. 300.12 = _____ hundred and twelve hundredths
15. 62.08 = sixty-two and _____ hundredths
18. 70.009 = _____ and nine thousandths
19. 9.3 = _____ and three tenths
20. 10.51 = _____ and fifty-one hundredths
21. 1,000.02 = one thousand and two

Down

1. 6.5 = six and five _____
2. 0.428 = four hundred twenty-eight thousandths
3. 8,100.1 = eight _____ one hundred and one tenth
4. 3.02 = three and two _____
8. 0.685 = six hundred _____ thousandths
11. 50.19 = fifty and _____ hundredths
14. 0.015 = _____ thousandths
16. 430.7 = four hundred thirty and seven _____
17. 73.4 = seventy-three and four _____

COMPLETE YEAR GRADE 5

129

Week 11 Practice

Swiss Sentences

Complete these cheesy number sentences.

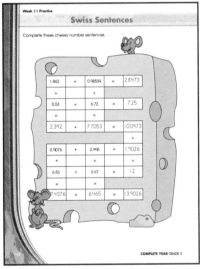

1.862	+	0.98534	=	2.8473
+		+		
0.53	+	6.72	=	7.25
=		=		
2.392	+	7.7053	=	10.0973

0.9076	+	0.995	=	1.9026
+		+		
6.53	+	5.47	=	12
=		=		
7.4376	+	6.465	=	13.9026

COMPLETE YEAR GRADE 5

130

Week 12 Practice

Troublesome Verb Pairs

Don't confuse verbs that have similar meanings.

Lay means put or place.
Lie means rest or recline.

Set means put something somewhere.
Sit means sit down.

Let means allow.
Leave means allow to remain.

Teach means show how.
Learn means find out.

Lend means give to someone.
Borrow means get from someone.

Write the correct verb on each blank below.

"Mark, did you __set__ (set, sit) the saddle on the fence?" David asked.
"Yes, David. I was going to __leave__ (let, leave) it in the barn, but it was heavy.
Did you __learn__ (teach, learn) how to throw the saddle onto your horse's back yet?" Mark asked.
"Yes, and then I needed to __lie__ (lay, lie) down and rest." David answered.
"I was going to __lend__ (lend, borrow) you a hand, but I was too busy trying to __learn__ (teach, learn) how to rope," David remarked.
"Will you __let__ (let, leave) me __borrow__ (lend, borrow) your horse tomorrow morning?" Mark inquired.
"Sure, Mark. I'm going to just __sit__ (set, sit) under a tree and read a book tomorrow morning," David responded.

Write the correct verb from the parentheses for each sentence.

1. Tell your dog to __lie__ (lay, lie) down in front of the barn.
2. Please __lay__ (lay, lie) that saddle down in front of the stall and __set__ (set, sit) the bridle on the table.
3. __Sit__ (Set, Sit) on that bale of hay and rest your tired legs.
4. Will you __let__ (let, leave) me wear your boots tomorrow?
5. Don't __leave__ (let, leave) those oats there.
6. I want to __learn__ (teach, learn) how to trim my horse's hooves.
7. We will certainly be happy to __teach__ (teach, learn) you.

COMPLETE YEAR GRADE 5

132

Week 12 Practice

Verb Tenses

Verbs have different forms to show whether something already happened, is happening right now or will happen.

Examples:
Present tense: **I walk.**
Past tense: **I walked.**
Future tense: **I will walk.**

Write **PAST** if the verb is past tense, **PRES** for present tense or **FUT** for future tense. The first one has been done for you.

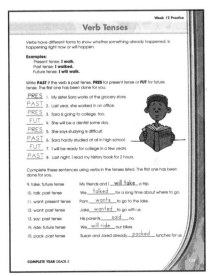

__PRES__ 1. My sister Sara works at the grocery store.
__PAST__ 2. Last year, she worked in an office.
__PRES__ 3. Sara is going to college, too.
__FUT__ 4. She will be a dentist some day.
__PRES__ 5. She says studying is difficult.
__PAST__ 6. Sara hardly studied at all in high school.
__FUT__ 7. I will be ready for college in a few years.
__PAST__ 8. Last night, I read my history book for 2 hours.

Complete these sentences using verbs in the tenses listed. The first one has been done for you.

9. take: future tense My friends and I __will take__ a trip.
10. talk: past tense We __talked__ for a long time about where to go.
11. want: present tense Pam __wants__ to go to the lake.
12. want: past tense Jake __wanted__ to go with us.
13. say: past tense His parents __said__ no.
14. ride: future tense We __will ride__ our bikes.
15. pack: past tense Susan and Jared already __packed__ lunches for us.

COMPLETE YEAR GRADE 5

133

Week 12 Practice

Verb Tense

The **present tense** tells what is happening now.
   Example: Jamie runs today in the big race.
The **past tense** tells about an action which happened in the past.
   Example: Jamie ran in the preliminary race yesterday.
The **future tense** tells about an action which will occur in the future. It is formed by using the helping verb: **will** with the present tense of the verb.
   Example: Jamie will run in the Olympics someday.

Underline the verb in each sentence. Tell whether the verb is in the present tense, past tense or future tense.

1. Thousands of years ago, the Chinese used more than one name. __past__
2. Today, the Chinese still give their children three names. __present__
3. Family names, or last names, came about in various ways. __past__
4. These names will remain for centuries into the future. __future__
5. Some writers use "pseudonyms," or fictitious names. __present__
6. Eric Blair wrote under the assumed name George Orwell. __past__
7. Immigrants will introduce new names to the United States. __future__
8. Some people use nicknames instead of their legal names. __present__

Fill in the chart below.

Verb	Present Tense	Past Tense	Future Tense
see	see, sees	saw	will see
hide	hide, hides	hid	will hide
swim	swim, swims	swam	will swim
catch	catch, catches	caught	will catch
leave	leave, leaves	left	will leave
run	run, runs	ran	will run
throw	throw, throws	threw	will throw

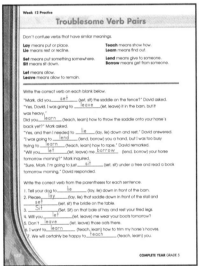

COMPLETE YEAR GRADE 5

134

Answer Key

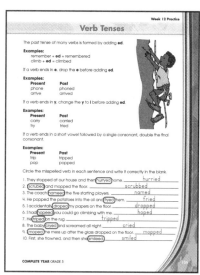

135

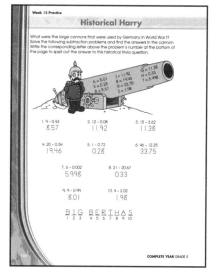

136

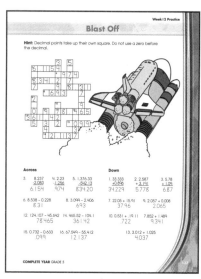

137

Big Bucks for You!

Solve the problems on another sheet of paper.

	Answer space
1. You receive your first royalty check for $1,000.00 and deposit it in your checking account. You go directly to the music store and spend $234.56 on new CDs. What is your balance?	$765.44
2. You naturally treat all your friends to pizza, which costs you $47.76. You pay with a check. What is your balance now?	$717.68
3. You decide to restock your wardrobe and buy $389.99 worth of new clothes. What is your balance?	$327.69
4. Your next royalty check arrives, and you deposit $1,712.34. You also treat yourself to a new 15-speed bicycle, which costs $667.09. What is your balance?	$1,372.94
5. You buy your mother some perfume for a present. You write a check for $37.89. What is your balance?	$1,335.05
6. You need a tennis racket and some other sports equipment. The bill comes to $203.45. What is your new balance?	$1,131.60
7. You treat your family to dinner at **Snails in a Pail**, where the check comes to $56.17. What is your balance?	$1,075.43
8. You join a health club, and the first payment is $150.90. What is your new balance?	$924.53
9. You deposit your latest royalty check, which amounts to $4,451.01. What is your new balance?	$5,375.54
10. To celebrate this good fortune, you take your entire peewee football team to a professional football game. The bill comes to $4,339.98. What is your new balance?	$1,035.56

138

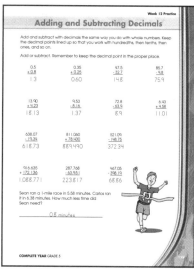

139

140

Page 142

Root Words

A **root word** is the common stem that gives related words their basic meanings.

Example: Separate is the root word for **separately, separation, inseparable** and **separator.**

Identify the root word in each group of words. Look up the meaning of the root word in the dictionary and write its definition. The first one has been done for you.

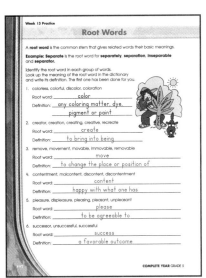

1. colorless, colorful, discolor, coloration
   Root word: **color**
   Definition: **any coloring matter, dye, pigment or paint**

2. creator, creation, creating, creative, recreate
   Root word: **create**
   Definition: **to bring into being**

3. remove, movement, movable, immovable, removable
   Root word: **move**
   Definition: **to change the place or position of**

4. contentment, malcontent, discontent, discontentment
   Root word: **content**
   Definition: **happy with what one has**

5. pleasure, displeasure, pleasing, pleasant, unpleasant
   Root word: **please**
   Definition: **to be agreeable to**

6. successor, unsuccessful, successful
   Root word: **success**
   Definition: **a favorable outcome**

COMPLETE YEAR GRADE 5

142

Page 143

Greek and Latin Roots

Many word patterns in the English language are combinations of Greek or Latin words. When you know what part of a word means, you may be able to figure out the meaning of the rest of the word. For example, it **cycle** means "circle or wheel" and **bi** means "two," then you can figure out that **bicycle** means "two wheels." Root words are the words that longer words are based on. For example, **duct**, which means "to lead," is the root of **conduct** or **induct**. Look at the chart below. It has several root words and their meanings on it.

Root	Meaning	Example	Definition
act	to do	interact	to act with others
aqua	water	aquatint	dyed water
auto	self	automobile	to move oneself
centi	a hundred	centennial	one hundred years

Look at each word equation below. The meaning of one part is shown in parentheses. Consult the chart of root words to find the meaning of the other part. Write the meaning in the blank. Combine the two meanings. Write the dictionary definition in the space provided.

1. react re (again) + act **to do** = **again to do**
   Dictionary definition: **To act or do again**

2. automatic auto **self** + matic (having a mind) = **self having a mind**
   Dictionary definition: **self-acting or self-moving**

3. transact trans (across) + act **to do** = **to do across**
   Dictionary definition: **to carry on or conduct to a settlement**

4. centimeter centi **a hundred** + meter (meter) = **a hundred meters**
   Dictionary definition: **one hundredth of a meter**

5. aquanaut aqua **water** + naut (sailor) = **water sailor**
   Dictionary definition: **an underwater explorer**

COMPLETE YEAR GRADE 5

143

Page 144

Root Words

Root	Meaning	Example	Definition
cede	to go	supercede	to go beyond
cept	seize	intercept	to seize during
duce	lead	deduce	to find the lead
fer	carry	interfere	to carry into
port	carry	transport	to carry across
spect	to look	inspect	to look in
tain	to hold	obtain	to gain action
vene	to come	convene	to come to start

Complete the exercises below.

1. precede pre (before) + cede **to go** = **before to go**
   Dictionary definition: **to be, go or come before**

2. report re (again) + port **carry** = **carry again**
   Dictionary definition: **to carry and repeat, as in a message**

3. intervene inter (between) + vene **to come** = **to come between**
   Dictionary definition: **to come between**

4. induce (in) + duce **lead** = **lead in**
   Dictionary definition: **to lead by persuasion**

5. retrospect retro (backward) + spect **to look** = **to look backward**
   Dictionary definition: **to look back at past events**

6. refer re (again) + fer **carry** = **carry again**
   Dictionary definition: **to hand over for consideration**

7. retain re (again) + tain **to hold** = **to hold again**
   Dictionary definition: **to keep possession of**

8. concept con (with) + cept **seize** = **seize with**
   Dictionary definition: **a general notion or idea**

COMPLETE YEAR GRADE 5

144

Page 145

Adding Prefixes

A **prefix** is a syllable at the beginning of a word that changes its meaning. The prefixes **il, im, in** and **ir** all mean not.

Examples:
Illogical means not logical or practical.
Impossible means not possible.
Invisible means not visible.
Irrelevant means not relevant or practical.

Divide each word into its prefix and root word. The first one has been done for you.

	Prefix	Root Word
illogical	il	logical
impatient	im	patient
immature	im	mature
incomplete	in	complete
insincere	in	sincere
irresponsible	ir	responsible
irregular	ir	regular

Use the meanings in parentheses to complete the sentences with one of the above words.

1. I had to turn in my assignment **incomplete** because I was sick last night. (not finished)

2. It was **illogical** for Jimmy to give me his keys because he can't get into his house without them. (not practical)

3. Sue and Joel were **irresponsible** to leave their bikes out in the rain. (not doing the right thing)

4. I sometimes get **impatient** waiting for my ride to school. (restless)

5. The boys sounded **insincere** when they said they were sorry. (not honest)

6. These towels didn't cost much because they are **irregular**. (not straight or even)

COMPLETE YEAR GRADE 5

145

Page 146

Prefixes

The prefixes **un** and **non** also mean not.

Examples:
Unhappy means not happy.
Nonproductive means not productive.

Divide each word into its prefix and root word. The first one has been done for you.

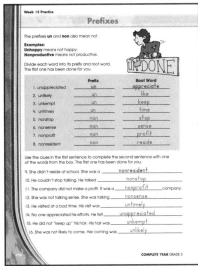

	Prefix	Root Word
1. unappreciated	un	appreciate
2. unlikely	un	like
3. unkempt	un	keep
4. untimely	un	time
5. nonstop	non	stop
6. nonsense	non	sense
7. nonprofit	non	profit
8. nonresident	non	reside

Use the clues in the first sentence to complete the second sentence with one of the words from the box. The first one has been done for you.

9. She didn't reside at school. She was a **nonresident.**
10. He couldn't stop talking. He talked **nonstop.**
11. The company did not make a profit. It was a **nonprofit** company.
12. She was not talking sense. She was talking **nonsense.**
13. He visited at a bad time. His visit was **untimely.**
14. No one appreciated his efforts. He felt **unappreciated.**
15. He did not "keep up" his hair. His hair was **unkempt.**
16. She was not likely to come. Her coming was **unlikely.**

COMPLETE YEAR GRADE 5

146

Page 147

Adding and Subtracting Decimals

When adding or subtracting decimals, place the decimal points under each other. That way, you add tenths to tenths, not tenths to hundredths. Add or subtract beginning on the right, as usual. Carry or borrow numbers in the same way. Adding 0 to the end of decimals does not change their value, but sometimes makes them easier to add and subtract.

Examples:
39.40	0.064	3.56	6.83
+ 8.81	+ 0.470	− .09	− 2.74
48.21	0.534	3.47	4.09

Solve the following problems.

1. Write each set of numbers in a column and add them.
   a. 2.56 + 0.6 + 76 = **79.16**
   b. 93.5 + 23.06 + 1.45 = **118.01**
   c. 3.23 + 91.34 + 0.85 = **95.42**

2. Write each pair of numbers in a column and subtract them.
   A. 7.89 − 0.56 = **7.33** B. 34.56 − 6.04 = **28.52** C. 7.6 − 3.24 = **4.36**

3. In a relay race, Alice ran her part in 23.6 seconds, Cindy did hers in 24.7 seconds and Erin took 20.09 seconds. How many seconds did they take altogether? **68.39 seconds**

4. Although Erin ran her part in 20.09 seconds today, yesterday it took her 21.55 seconds. How much faster was she today? **1.46 seconds**

5. Add this grocery bill: potatoes—$3.49; milk—$2.09; bread—$0.99; apples—$2.30 **$8.87**

6. A yellow coat cost $47.59, and a blue coat cost $36.79. How much more did the yellow coat cost? **$10.80**

7. A box of Oat Boats cereal has 14.6 ounces. A box of Sugar Circles has 17.85 ounces. How much more is in the Sugar Circles box? **3.25 ounces**

8. The Oat Boats cereal has 4.03 ounces of sugar in it. Sugar Circles cereal has only 3.76 ounces. How much more sugar is in a box of Oat Boats? **0.27 ounces**

COMPLETE YEAR GRADE 5

147

Answer Key

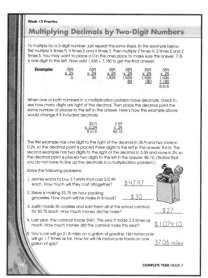

Week 13 Practice

Multiplying Decimals by Two-Digit Numbers

To multiply by a 2-digit number, just repeat the same steps. In the example below, first multiply 4 times 9, 4 times 5 and 4 times 3. Then multiply 2 times 9, 2 times 5 and 2 times 3. You may want to place a 0 in the ones place to make sure this answer, 718, is one digit to the left. Now add 1,436 + 7,180 to get the final answer.

Example:

359	359	359	359	359	359
x 24	x 24	x 24	x 24	x 24	x 24
6	36	1,436	1,436	1,436	1,436
			80	180	7,180
					8,616

When one or both numbers in a multiplication problem have decimals, check to see how many digits are right of the decimal. Then place the decimal point the same number of places to the left in the answer. Here's how the example above would change if it included decimals:

35.9	3.59
x 0.24	x 24
8.616	86.16

The first example has one digit to the right of the decimal in 35.9 and two more in 0.24, so the decimal point is placed three digits to the left in the answer: 8.616. The second example has two digits to the right of the decimal in 3.59 and none in 24, so the decimal point is placed two digits to the left in the answer: 86.16. (Notice that you do not have to line up the decimals in a multiplication problem.)

Solve the following problems.

1. Jennie wants to buy 3 T-shirts that cost $15.99 each. How much will they cost altogether? **$47.97**

2. Steve is making $3.75 an hour packing groceries. How much will he make in 8 hours? **$30**

3. Justin made 36 cookies and sold them all at the school carnival for $0.75 each. How much money did he make? **$27**

4. Last year, the carnival made $467. This year it made 2.3 times as much. How much money did the carnival make this year? **$1074.10**

5. Troy's car will go 21.8 miles on a gallon of gasoline. His motorcycle will go 1.7 times as far. How far will his motorcycle travel on one gallon of gas? **37.06 miles**

COMPLETE YEAR GRADE 5

148

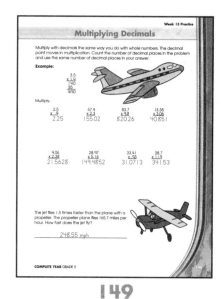

Week 13 Practice

Multiplying Decimals

Multiply with decimals the same way you do with whole numbers. The decimal point moves in multiplication. Count the number of decimal places in the problem and use the same number of decimal places in your answer.

Example:

3.5
x 1.4
140
35
4.90

Multiply.

2.5	67.4	83.7	13.35
x .9	x 2.3	x 9.8	x 3.06
2.25	155.02	820.26	40.851

9.06	28.97	33.41	28.7
x 2.38	x 5.16	x .93	x 11.9
21.5628	149.4852	31.0713	341.53

The jet flies 1.5 times faster than the plane with a propeller. The propeller plane flies 165.7 miles per hour. How fast does the jet fly?

248.55 mph

COMPLETE YEAR GRADE 5

149

Week 13 Practice

A Multiple Design

Solve the problems on a separate sheet of paper. Find the answers in the design and color correctly.

green
0.463
x .82
37.966

blue
28.5
x 7.4
210.9

red
6.51
x .69
44.919

yellow
39.2
x 0.36
14.112

purple
7.54
x .043
3.2422

purple
0.670
x .94
0.62980

yellow
64.9
x 3.26
211.574

yellow
0.592
x 40.6
240.352

purple
7.46
x 5.9
44.014

green	blue	blue	green	purple
92.4	42.6	85.1	7.32	6.05
x 0.62	x .78	x .096	x 1.6	x 8.3
57.288	33.228	8.0845	11.712	50.215

green	blue	yellow	red	red
3.27	32.8	80.5	5.77	95.8
x 0.62	x .26	x .95	x 1.6	x 8.3
2.0274	8.528	76.475	9.232	795.14

red	yellow	yellow	yellow	yellow
0.784	2.57	29.3	6.80	0.245
x 6.92	x 63.6	x 0.487	x 0.42	x 3.6
5.42528	163.452	14.2691	2.856	0.8820

COMPLETE YEAR GRADE 5

150

Week 14 Practice

Prefixes

The prefixes **epi**, **hyper**, **over** and **super** mean "above" or "over." The prefixes **under** and **sub** mean "under."

Write each word's prefix and root word in the space provided.

Word	Prefix	Root Word
hyperactive	hyper	active
overanxious	over	anxious
superimpose	super	impose
epilogue	epi	logue
underestimate	under	estimate
subordinate	sub	ordinate

Use the words above to complete the following sentences.

1. A photographer could **superimpose** one image on top of another.
2. The **epilogue** of the book may tell additional information about the story.
3. All the other children settled down for the night except the boy who was **hyperactive**.
4. He could not sleep because he was **overanxious** about the upcoming trip.
5. The company's president told his **subordinate** to take over some of the responsibilities.
6. Just because you think you are weak, don't **underestimate** how strong you could be.

COMPLETE YEAR GRADE 5

152

Week 14 Practice

Numerical Prefixes

Some prefixes are related to numbers. For example, in Latin **uni** means "one." The prefix **mono** means "one" in Greek. The chart below lists prefixes for numbers one through ten from both the Latin and Greek languages.

Number	Latin	Example	Greek	Example
1	uni	university	mon, mono	monopoly
2	du	duplex	di	digress
3	tri	tricycle	tri	trio
4	quad	quadrant	tetra	tetrameter
5	quin	quintuplets	penta	pentagon
6	sex	sexennial	hex	hexagon
7	sept	septuagenarian	hept	heptagon
8	oct	octopus	oct	octagon
9	nov	novena	enne	ennead (group of nine)
10	dec	decade	dec	decimal

Answers may vary.

Complete the exercises below.

1. unicycle uni **one** + cycle (wheel) = **one wheel**

Dictionary definition: **one-wheeled vehicle**

2. monogram mono **one** + gram (writing) = **one writing**

Dictionary definition: **interlaced initials of a name**

3. sextet sex **six** + tet (group) = **six group**

Dictionary definition: **a group of six**

4. quadrant quad **four** + rant (part) = **four part**

Dictionary definition: **one of four parts**

5. decigram dec **ten** + gram (gram) = **ten grams**

Dictionary definition: **one tenth of a gram**

COMPLETE YEAR GRADE 5

153

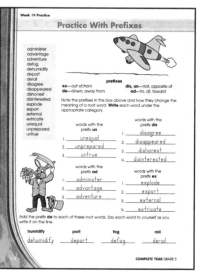

Week 14 Practice

Practice With Prefixes

administer
advantage
adventure
defog
dehumidify
depart
derail
disagree
disappeared
dishonest
disinterested
explode
export
external
extricate
unequal
unprepared
untrue

prefixes

ex—out of, from
de—down, away from
dis, un—not, opposite of
ad—to, at, toward

Note the prefixes in the box above and how they change the meaning of a root word. **Write** each word under the appropriate category.

words with the prefix **un**
1. unequal
2. unprepared
3. untrue

words with the prefix **dis**
1. disagree
2. disappeared
3. dishonest
4. disinterested

words with the prefix **ad**
1. administer
2. advantage
3. adventure

words with the prefix **ex**
1. explode
2. export
3. external
4. extricate

Add the prefix **de** to each of these root words. Say each word to yourself as you write it on the line.

humidify	part	fog	rail
dehumidify	depart	defog	derail

COMPLETE YEAR GRADE 5

154

Answer Key

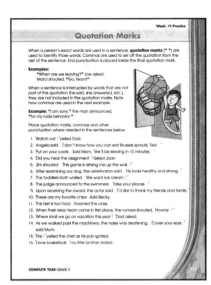

155

156

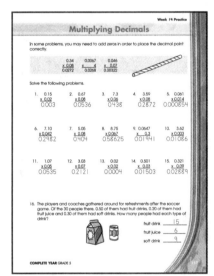

157

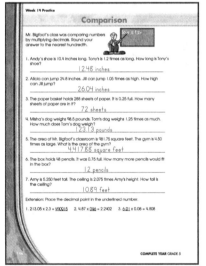

158

159

160

Answer Key

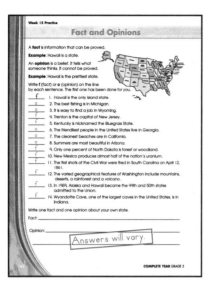

Week 15 Practice

Fact and Opinions

A **fact** is information that can be proved.

Example: Hawaii is a state.

An **opinion** is a belief. It tells what someone thinks. It cannot be proved.

Example: Hawaii is the prettiest state.

Write **f** (fact) or **o** (opinion) on the line by each sentence. The first one has been done for you.

- f 1. Hawaii is the only island state.
- o 2. The best fishing is in Michigan.
- o 3. It is easy to find a job in Wyoming.
- f 4. Trenton is the capital of New Jersey.
- f 5. Kentucky is nicknamed the Bluegrass State.
- o 6. The friendliest people in the United States live in Georgia.
- o 7. The cleanest beaches are in California.
- o 8. Summers are most beautiful in Arizona.
- f 9. Only one percent of North Dakota is forest or woodland.
- f 10. New Mexico produces almost half of the nation's uranium.
- f 11. The first shots of the Civil War were fired in South Carolina on April 12, 1861.
- f 12. The varied geographical features of Washington include mountains, deserts, a rainforest and a volcano.
- f 13. In 1959, Alaska and Hawaii became the 49th and 50th states admitted to the Union.
- f 14. Wyandotte Cave, one of the largest caves in the United States, is in Indiana.

Write one fact and one opinion about your own state.

Fact: _____

Opinion: _____

Answers will vary.

COMPLETE YEAR GRADE 5

162

Week 15 Practice

You Be The Judge

The lawyer is asking the witnesses many questions. Some of the answers are facts, some are opinions. The judge will only accept facts. Read each question and answer. Check fact or opinion next to each answer. If you checked fact, write a second answer that is an opinion. If you checked opinion, write a second answer that is a fact.

FACT   OPINION?

☑ fact ☐ opinion 1. **question:** Mr. Wallace, what was the stranger wearing?
answer: He was wearing a blue coat, red scarf, black slacks and black shoes.

☐ fact ☑ opinion 2. **question:** Mr. Henry, what did you hear from your window?
answer: I heard a sound that must have been the intruder breaking in.

☑ fact ☐ opinion 3. **question:** Ms. Harris, what time did you notice the broken lock?
answer: It was 10:15 p.m. when I arrived home.
Answer

☐ fact ☑ opinion 4. **question:** Mr. Patterson, do you know the owner of the stolen painting?
answer: He is the nicest boss I have ever worked for.

☑ fact ☐ opinion 5. **question:** Mr. Samuels, was the painting insured?
answer: Yes, the painting was insured for ten thousand dollars.

☐ fact ☑ opinion 6. **question:** Miss Ryan, did you see the defendant take the painting?
answer: Of course he took it! It had to be him.

COMPLETE YEAR GRADE 5

163

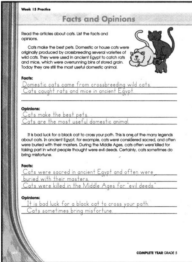

Week 15 Practice

Facts and Opinions

Read the articles about cats. List the facts and opinions.

Cats make the best pets. Domestic or house cats were originally produced by crossbreeding several varieties of wild cats. They were used in ancient Egypt to catch rats and mice, which were overrunning bins of stored grain. Today they are still the most useful domestic animal.

Facts:
Domestic cats come from crossbreeding wild cats.
Cats caught rats and mice in ancient Egypt.

Opinions:
Cats make the best pets.
Cats are the most useful domestic animal.

It is bad luck for a black cat to cross your path. This is one of the many legends about cats. In ancient Egypt, for example, cats were considered sacred, and often were buried with their masters. During the Middle Ages, cats often were killed for taking part in what people thought were evil deeds. Certainly, cats sometimes do bring misfortune.

Facts:
Cats were sacred in ancient Egypt and often were buried with their masters.
Cats were killed in the Middle Ages for "evil deeds."

Opinions:
It is bad luck for a black cat to cross your path.
Cats sometimes bring misfortune.

COMPLETE YEAR GRADE 5

164

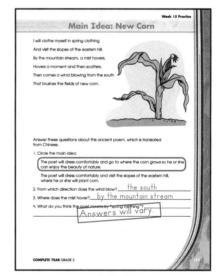

Week 15 Practice

Main Idea: New Corn

I will clothe myself in spring clothing
And visit the slopes of the eastern hill.
By the mountain stream, a mist hovers,
Hovers a moment and then scatters.
Then comes a wind blowing from the south
That brushes the fields of new corn.

Answer these questions about this ancient poem, which is translated from Chinese.

1. Circle the main idea:
   [The poet will dress comfortably and go to where the corn grows so he or she can enjoy the beauty of nature.]

   The poet will dress comfortably and visit the slopes of the eastern hill, where he or she will plant corn.

2. From which direction does the wind blow? the south
3. Where does the mist hover? by the mountain stream
4. What do you think the poet means by "spring clothing"?
   Answers will vary.

COMPLETE YEAR GRADE 5

165

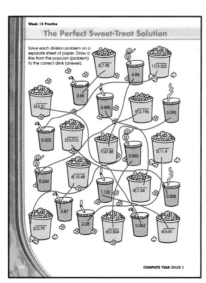

Week 15 Practice

The Perfect Sweet-Treat Solution

Solve each division problem on a separate sheet of paper. Draw a line from the popcorn (problem) to the correct drink (answer).

3) 7.95
11) 3.322
6.84
2.65
5) 0.31
0.905
9) 2.196
0.395
0.302
2) 0.016
7) 47.88
5) 11.4
0.063
0.244
4) 15.48
1.135
8) 7.24
0.008
2) 0.79
3.87
2.28
8) 0.504
0.062
6) 6.81

COMPLETE YEAR GRADE 5

166

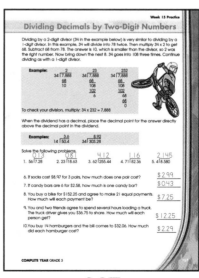

Week 15 Practice

Dividing Decimals by Two-Digit Numbers

Dividing by a 2-digit divisor (34 in the example below) is very similar to dividing by a 1-digit divisor. In this example, 34 will divide into 78 twice. Then multiply 34 x 2 to get 68. Subtract 68 from 78. The answer is 10, which is smaller than the divisor, so 2 was the right number. Now bring down the next 8. 34 goes into 108 three times. Continue dividing as with a 1-digit divisor.

Example:

2	23	232
34) 7,888	34) 7,888	34) 7,888
68	68	68
10	108	108
	102	102
	6	68
		68
		0

To check your division, multiply: 34 x 232 = 7,888

When the dividend has a decimal, place the decimal point for the answer directly above the decimal point in the dividend.

Examples:

3.6	8.92
14) 50.4	34) 303.28

Solve the following problems.

1. 0.13 56) 7.28
2. 0.81 23) 18.63
3. 4.12 62) 255.44
4. 1.16 47) 82.36
5. 2.145 4) 8.580

6. If socks cost $8.97 for 3 pairs, how much does one pair cost? $2.99
7. If candy bars are 6 for $2.58, how much is one candy bar? $0.43
8. You buy a bike for $152.25 and agree to make 21 equal payments. How much will each payment be? $7.25
9. You and two friends agree to spend several hours loading a truck. The truck driver gives you $36.75 to share. How much will each person get? $12.25
10. You buy 14 hamburgers and the bill comes to $32.06. How much did each hamburger cost? $2.29

COMPLETE YEAR GRADE 5

167

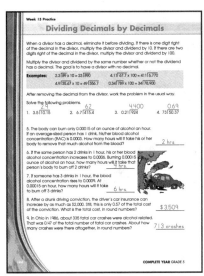

168

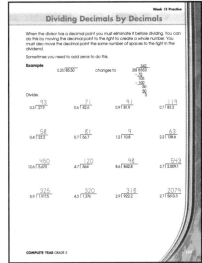

169

Dividing by Decimals (170)

What kind of problems will these decimal glasses help you solve? Solve the problems. Then, write them in descending order (from greatest to least) beneath the blanks at the bottom of the page. Write each matching letter above the number to solve the riddle.

S 2.1) 8.4 = 21.84   V 0.36) 1.872   O 1.24) 0.4712

    4   5.2   3.8

N 8) 1.12   D 0.3) 17.7   I 6) 126

  0.14   59   21

I .082) 0.3772   — 7.4) 103.6   I 5.5) 3.025

  4.6   14   0.55

D I - V I S I O N

170

How to Write a Book Report (172)

172

Book Report: A Book I Devoured (173)

Answers will vary.

173

Book Report: Comparing Two Books (174)

Answers will vary.

174

Page 175 — Working With Decimals

Week 16 Practice

1. Write 207.426 in words.
   two hundred seven and four hundred twenty-six thousandths
2. Write forty-seven and thirteen thousandths in numerals. 47.013
3. Use > or < to indicate which decimal fraction is greater.
   17.35 > 17.295

Fill in the blanks.
4. Round 12.836 to the nearest whole number. 13
5. Round 12.836 to the nearest tenth. 12.8
6. Round 12.836 to the nearest hundredth. 12.84
7. Write 0.36 as a fraction in lowest terms. $\frac{36}{100} = \frac{9}{25}$
8. Write 0.25 as a fraction in lowest terms. $\frac{25}{100} = \frac{1}{4}$
9. Write $\frac{3}{4}$ as a decimal number. 0.75

Solve.
10. 36.2 + 27.325 = 63.525
11. 87.36 - 84.95 = 2.41
12. 4.6 x 1.2 = 5.52
13. 3.46 x 10 = 34.6
14. 11.55 ÷ 7 = 1.65
15. 39 ÷ 12 = 3.25
16. 367.52 ÷ 10 = 36.752

COMPLETE YEAR GRADE 5

175

Page 176 — Decimal Test

Week 16 Practice

1. 0.45 + 0.96 + 0.52 = 1.93
2. 26.3 - 4.8 = 21.5
3. Use > or < to compare each pair of numbers.
   5.01 > 5.003   6.15 > 6.015   3.05 < 5.03
4. Write sixty-one hundredths in numeral form. 0.61
5. 35.1 + 475.11 + 0.54 + 0.3 + 15 = 526.05
6. 81 - 0.04 = 80.96
7. Round 27.553 to the nearest tenth. 27.6
8. Round 62.814 to the nearest hundredth. 62.81
9. Round 5.06921 to the nearest hundredth. 5.07
10. Write 0.07 in words. seven hundredths

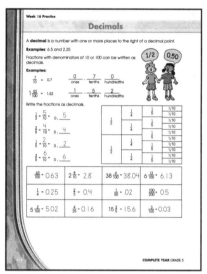

.001 + .01 + .1 =
364.01 + .0458 =
1.05 - .03 + 33.47 =

11. 16 x 0.18 = 2.88
12. 0.504 ÷ 12 = 0.042
13. 63 x 0.5 = 31.5
14. 90 - 10.50 = 79.5
15. 25.6 x 0.11 = 2.816
16. 22.1 ÷ 0.008 = 22.108
17. 3.65 + 20 = 0.1825
18. 2.64 ÷ 5 = 0.528

COMPLETE YEAR GRADE 5

176

Page 177 — Snails in a Pail

Week 16 Practice

Sly Me Slugg, world-famous French chef, has made his fast-food business, **Snails in a Pail**, the most popular restaurant in the whole area. This is his menu:

Slime Soup $.49
Slugburger $1.64
Chicken-Fried Snails $2.99
Slimy Slush $.89
Snailcream Shake $1.49
Snailbits Salad $1.09

Solve the problems on another sheet of paper.

	Answer space
1. Sly Me Slugg sold 60 Slimy Slushes and 40 Snailcream Shakes on Friday. How much did he make on drinks that day?	$113.00
2. A coach treated 15 of his team players to Slugburgers. How much change did he receive from $40.00?	$14.65
3. Your brother was so hungry that he ordered one of everything on the menu. How much change did he get from a $10.00 bill?	$1.36
4. Sly Me Slugg sold $43.61 in Slime Soup orders on Wednesday and $38.22 in soup orders on Thursday. How many orders of slime Soup did he sell in those 2 days?	167
5. You had a party at **Snails in a Pail** and bought 9 Slugburgers, 3 orders of Chicken-Fried Snails, 2 Snailbits Salads, 5 Snailcream Shakes and 10 Slimy Slushes. What was the total cost for the party?	$42.71
6. In one week, Sly Me Slugg sold 200 Slugburgers and 79 orders of Chicken-Fried Snails. How much money did he earn from these 2 items?	$574.21
7. You ordered 10 Slugburgers, 10 Snailcream Shakes and 10 Slimy Slushes. What was your total cost?	$40.70
8. On Friday, Sly Me earned $1,252. On Saturday, he earned $1,765. On Sunday, he earned $2,998. What was his average daily earnings for those 3 days?	$2005

COMPLETE YEAR GRADE 5

177

Page 178 — Decimals

Week 16 Practice

A **decimal** is a number with one or more places to the right of a decimal point.

Examples: 6.5 and 2.25

Fractions with denominators of 10 or 100 can be written as decimals.

Examples:
$\frac{7}{10} = 0.7$
$1\frac{52}{100} = 1.52$

Write the fractions as decimals.
$\frac{1}{2} = \frac{5}{10} = .5$
$2\frac{4}{10} = .4$
$\frac{1}{2} = \frac{2}{10} = .2$
$\frac{6}{10} = .6$

$\frac{63}{100} = 0.63$	$2\frac{8}{10} = 2.8$	$38\frac{4}{100} = 38.04$	$6\frac{13}{100} = 6.13$
$\frac{1}{4} = 0.25$	$\frac{2}{5} = 0.4$	$\frac{1}{50} = .02$	$\frac{100}{200} = 0.5$
$5\frac{2}{100} = 5.02$	$\frac{4}{25} = 0.16$	$15\frac{3}{5} = 15.6$	$\frac{3}{100} = 0.03$

COMPLETE YEAR GRADE 5

178

Page 179 — Comparing Decimals and Fractions

Week 16 Practice

The symbol > means greater than. The number on its left is greater than that on its right. The symbol < means less than. The number on its left is less than that on its right. An equal sign, =, shows the same value on each side.

Use the sign >, = or < to make each statement true.

1. 0.4 < $\frac{2}{3}$
2. 1.25 > $\frac{3}{4}$
3. 0.7 < $\frac{4}{5}$
4. 0.68 > $\frac{5}{7}$
5. 0.1 > $\frac{1}{12}$
6. 0.45 < $\frac{1}{2}$
7. 0.75 > $\frac{3}{8}$
8. 0.6 < $\frac{5}{8}$
9. 0.54 > $\frac{2}{5}$
10. 0.8 > $\frac{4}{6}$
11. 0.25 > $\frac{1}{7}$
12. 1.8 > $\frac{12}{7}$
13. 0.625 > $\frac{4}{8}$
14. 0.33 = $\frac{1}{3}$

15. Jenna looked carefully at the labels on two different types of cookies. The chocolate ones had $\frac{3}{4}$ pound in the package. The package of vanilla cookies claimed it had 0.67 pound of cookies inside. Were the chocolate cookies <, > or = to the vanilla cookies?
   $\frac{3}{4}$ > 0.67

COMPLETE YEAR GRADE 5

179

Page 180 — Decimals

Week 16 Practice

1. Write out 36.124 in words. thirty-six and one hundred twenty-four thousandths
2. Write two hundred thirty-seven and twenty-six hundredths in numerals. 237.26
3. Use > or < to indicate which decimal fraction is greater.
   3.147 < 3.205   3.06 > 3.059
4. Round 87.658 to the nearest whole number. 88
5. Round 87.658 to the nearest tenth. 87.7
6. Round 87.658 to the nearest hundredth. 87.66
7. Write 0.5 as a fraction in lowest terms. $\frac{5}{10} = \frac{1}{2}$
8. Write 0.69 as a fraction in lowest terms. $\frac{69}{100}$
9. Write 7.85 as a fraction in lowest terms. $7\frac{85}{100} = \frac{785}{100} = 7\frac{17}{25}$
10. Draw a model of 0.3.

COMPLETE YEAR GRADE 5

180

Answer Key

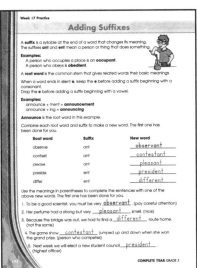

Adding Suffixes

A **suffix** is a syllable at the end of a word that changes its meaning. The suffixes **ant** and **ent** mean a person or thing that does something.

Examples:
A person who occupies a place is an **occupant**.
A person who obeys is **obedient**.

A **root word** is the common stem that gives related words their basic meanings.

When a word ends in silent **e**, keep the **e** before adding a suffix beginning with a consonant.
Drop the **e** before adding a suffix beginning with a vowel.

Examples:
announce + ment = **announcement**
announce + ing = **announcing**

Announce is the root word in this example.

Combine each root word and suffix to make a new word. The first one has been done for you.

Root word	Suffix	New word
observe	ant	observant
contest	ant	contestant
please	ant	pleasant
preside	ent	president
differ	ent	different

Use the meanings in parentheses to complete the sentences with one of the above new words. The first one has been done for you.

1. To be a good scientist, you must be very **observant**. (pay careful attention)
2. Her perfume had a strong but very **pleasant** smell. (nice)
3. Because the bridge was out, we had to find a **different** route home. (not the same)
4. The game show **contestant** jumped up and down when she won the grand prize. (person who competes)
5. Next week we will elect a new student council **president**. (highest officer)

182

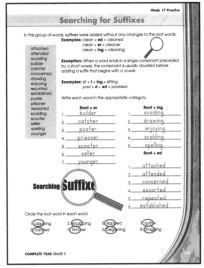

Searching for Suffixes

In this group of words, suffixes were added without any changes to the root words.

Examples: clean + ed = cleaned
clean + er = cleaner
clean + ing = cleaning

Exception: When a word ends in a single consonant preceded by a short vowel, the consonant is usually doubled before adding a suffix that begins with a vowel.

Examples: sit + t + ing = sitting
pad + d + ed = padded

Word box: attached, attended, avoiding, builder, catcher, concerned, drawing, enjoying, escorted, established, poster, prisoner, repeated, scalding, scooter, seller, spelling, younger

Write each word in the appropriate category.

Root + er
1. builder
2. catcher
3. poster
4. prisoner
5. scooter
6. seller
7. younger

Root + ing
1. avoiding
2. drawing
3. enjoying
4. scalding
5. spelling

Root + ed
1. attached
2. attended
3. concerned
4. escorted
5. repeated
6. established

Circle the root word in each word.
1. clapping 3. squabbling 5. slapped 7. quitter
2. carried 4. trimmer 6. beginning 8. dragging

183

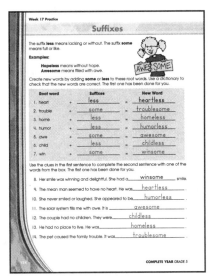

Suffixes

The suffix **less** means lacking or without. The suffix **some** means full or like.

Examples:
Hopeless means without hope.
Awesome means filled with awe.

Create new words by adding **some** or **less** to these root words. Use a dictionary to check that the new words are correct. The first one has been done for you.

Root word	Suffixes	New Word
1. heart	less	heartless
2. trouble	some	troublesome
3. home	less	homeless
4. humor	less	humorless
5. awe	some	awesome
6. child	less	childless
7. win	some	winsome

Use the clues in the first sentence to complete the second sentence with one of the words from the box. The first one has been done for you.

8. Her smile was winning and delightful. She had a **winsome** smile.
9. The mean man seemed to have no heart. He was **heartless**.
10. She never smiled or laughed. She appeared to be **humorless**.
11. The solar system fills me with awe. It is **awesome**.
12. The couple had no children. They were **childless**.
13. He had no place to live. He was **homeless**.
14. The pet caused the family trouble. It was **troublesome**.

184

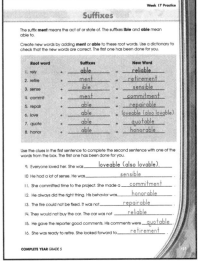

Suffixes

The suffix **ment** means the act of or state of. The suffixes **ible** and **able** mean able to.

Create new words by adding **ment** or **able** to these root words. Use a dictionary to check that the new words are correct. The first one has been done for you.

Root word	Suffixes	New Word
1. rely	able	reliable
2. retire	ment	retirement
3. sense	ible	sensible
4. commit	ment	commitment
5. repair	able	repairable
6. love	able	loveable (also lovable)
7. quote	able	quotable
8. honor	able	honorable

Use the clues in the first sentence to complete the second sentence with one of the words from the box. The first one has been done for you.

9. Everyone loved her. She was **loveable (also lovable)**.
10. He had a lot of sense. He was **sensible**.
11. She committed time to the project. She made a **commitment**.
12. He always did the right thing. His behavior was **honorable**.
13. The tire could not be fixed. It was not **repairable**.
14. They would not buy the car. The car was not **reliable**.
15. He gave the reporter good comments. His comments were **quotable**.
16. She was ready to retire. She looked forward to **retirement**.

185

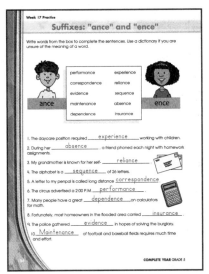

Suffixes: "ance" and "ence"

Write words from the box to complete the sentences. Use a dictionary if you are unsure of the meaning of a word.

Word box: performance, correspondence, evidence, maintenance, dependence, experience, reliance, sequence, absence, insurance

1. The daycare position required **experience** working with children.
2. During her **absence**, a friend phoned each night with homework assignments.
3. My grandmother is known for her self-**reliance**.
4. The alphabet is a **sequence** of 26 letters.
5. A letter to my penpal is called long distance **correspondence**.
6. The circus advertised a 2:00 P.M. **performance**.
7. Many people have a great **dependence** on calculators for math.
8. Fortunately, most homeowners in the flooded area carried **insurance**.
9. The police gathered **evidence** in hopes of solving the burglary.
10. **Maintenance** of football and baseball fields requires much time and effort.

186

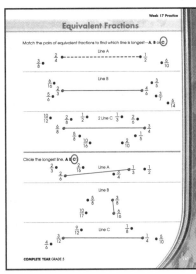

Equivalent Fractions

Match the pairs of equivalent fractions to find which line is longest—A, B or **C**.

Line A: $\frac{3}{8}$ — $\frac{1}{2}$ — $\frac{6}{10}$

Line B: $\frac{6}{16}$, $\frac{2}{3}$, $\frac{5}{6}$ — $\frac{3}{5}$, $\frac{4}{9}$, $\frac{3}{7}$, $\frac{6}{14}$

Line C: $\frac{10}{12}$, $\frac{2}{8}$, $\frac{1}{2}$ — $\frac{2}{3}$, $\frac{1}{4}$; $\frac{8}{8}$, $\frac{5}{16}$, $\frac{10}{16}$ — $\frac{1}{8}$, $\frac{2}{10}$

Circle the longest line. A **C** C

Line A: $\frac{2}{3}$, $\frac{6}{8}$ — $\frac{1}{3}$, $\frac{1}{2}$, $\frac{3}{4}$

Line B: $\frac{10}{17}$ — $\frac{3}{8}$, $\frac{1}{16}$

Line C: $\frac{9}{12}$, $\frac{4}{4}$ — $\frac{1}{8}$, $\frac{1}{4}$, $\frac{6}{10}$; $\frac{3}{12}$

187

419

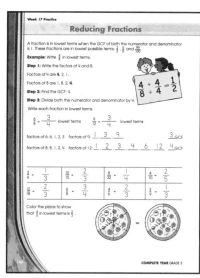

Week 17 Practice

Reducing Fractions

A fraction is in lowest terms when the GCF of both the numerator and denominator is 1. These fractions are in lowest possible terms: $\frac{2}{3}$, $\frac{4}{5}$, $\frac{99}{100}$

Example: Write $\frac{4}{8}$ in lowest terms.

Step 1: Write the factors of 4 and 8.

Factors of 4 are **4**, 2, 1.

Factors of 8 are 1, 8, 2, **4**.

Step 2: Find the GCF: 4.

Step 3: Divide both the numerator and denominator by 4.

$$\frac{4 \div 4}{8 \div 4} = \frac{1}{2}$$

Write each fraction in lowest terms.

$\frac{6}{8} = \frac{3}{4}$ lowest terms $\qquad \frac{9}{12} = \frac{3}{4}$ lowest terms

factors of 6: 6, 1, 2, 3 $\quad$ factors of 9: 1, 3, 9 $\qquad$ 3 GCF

factors of 8: 8, 1, 2, 4 $\quad$ factors of 12: 1, 2, 3, 4, 6, 12 $\quad$ 4 GCF

$\frac{2}{6} = \frac{1}{3}$	$\frac{10}{15} = \frac{2}{3}$	$\frac{8}{32} = \frac{1}{4}$	$\frac{4}{10} = \frac{2}{5}$
$\frac{12}{18} = \frac{2}{3}$	$\frac{6}{8} = \frac{3}{4}$	$\frac{4}{6} = \frac{2}{3}$	$\frac{3}{9} = \frac{1}{3}$

Color the pizzas to show that $\frac{2}{8}$ in lowest terms is $\frac{1}{4}$.

COMPLETE YEAR GRADE 5

188

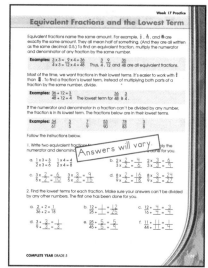

Week 17 Practice

Equivalent Fractions and the Lowest Term

Equivalent fractions name the same amount. For example, $\frac{1}{2}$, $\frac{4}{8}$, and $\frac{16}{32}$ are exactly the same amount. They all mean half of something. (And they are all written as the same decimal: 0.5.) To find an equivalent fraction, multiply the numerator and denominator of any fraction by the same number.

Examples: $\frac{3 \times 3}{4 \times 3} = \frac{9}{12} \quad \frac{4 \times 4}{12 \times 4} = \frac{36}{48}$ Thus, $\frac{3}{4}$, $\frac{9}{12}$ and $\frac{36}{48}$ are all equivalent fractions.

Most of the time, we want fractions in their lowest terms. It's easier to work with $\frac{1}{2}$ than $\frac{36}{72}$. To find a fraction's lowest term, instead of multiplying both parts of a fraction by the same number, divide.

Examples: $\frac{36 \div 12}{48 \div 12} = \frac{3}{4}$ The lowest term for $\frac{36}{48}$ is $\frac{3}{4}$.

If the numerator and denominator in a fraction can't be divided by any number, the fraction is in its lowest term. The fractions below are in their lowest terms.

Examples: $\frac{34}{61} \quad \frac{3}{7} \quad \frac{7}{90} \quad \frac{53}{83} \quad \frac{78}{83} \quad \frac{3}{8}$

Follow the instructions below.

1. Write two equivalent fractions. *Answers will vary.*

a. $\frac{1 \times 3}{2 \times 3} = \frac{3}{6} \quad \frac{1 \times 4}{2 \times 4} = \frac{4}{8}$

b. $\frac{2 \times 3}{3 \times 3} = \frac{6}{9} \quad \frac{2 \times 4}{3 \times 4} = \frac{8}{12}$

c. $\frac{3 \times 2}{5 \times 2} = \frac{6}{10} \quad \frac{3 \times 3}{5 \times 3} = \frac{9}{15}$

d. $\frac{8 \times 2}{9 \times 2} = \frac{16}{18} \quad \frac{8 \times 3}{9 \times 3} = \frac{24}{27}$

2. Find the lowest terms for each fraction. Make sure your answers can't be divided by any other numbers. The first one has been done for you.

a. $\frac{2 \div 2}{36 \div 2} = \frac{1}{18}$ $\quad$ b. $\frac{12 \div}{25 \div} = \frac{12}{25}$ $\quad$ c. $\frac{12 \div 4}{16 \div 4} = \frac{3}{4}$

d. $\frac{3 \div 3}{9 \div 3} = \frac{1}{3}$ $\quad$ e. $\frac{25 \div 5}{45 \div 5} = \frac{5}{9}$ $\quad$ f. $\frac{11 \div}{44 \div} = \frac{1}{4}$

COMPLETE YEAR GRADE 5

189

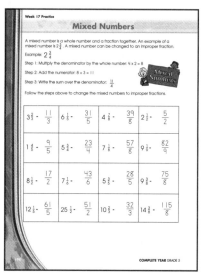

Week 17 Practice

Mixed Numbers

A mixed number is a whole number and a fraction together. An example of a mixed number is $2\frac{3}{4}$. A mixed number can be changed to an improper fraction.

Example: $2\frac{3}{4}$

Step 1: Multiply the denominator by the whole number: $4 \times 2 = 8$

Step 2: Add the numerator: $8 + 3 = 11$

Step 3: Write the sum over the denominator: $\frac{11}{4}$

Follow the steps above to change the mixed numbers to improper fractions.

$3\frac{2}{3} = \frac{11}{3}$	$6\frac{1}{5} = \frac{31}{5}$	$4\frac{7}{8} = \frac{39}{8}$	$2\frac{1}{2} = \frac{5}{2}$
$1\frac{4}{5} = \frac{9}{5}$	$5\frac{3}{4} = \frac{23}{4}$	$7\frac{1}{8} = \frac{57}{8}$	$9\frac{1}{9} = \frac{82}{9}$
$8\frac{1}{2} = \frac{17}{2}$	$7\frac{1}{6} = \frac{43}{6}$	$5\frac{3}{5} = \frac{28}{5}$	$9\frac{3}{8} = \frac{75}{8}$
$12\frac{1}{5} = \frac{61}{5}$	$25\frac{1}{2} = \frac{51}{2}$	$10\frac{2}{3} = \frac{32}{3}$	$14\frac{3}{8} = \frac{115}{8}$

COMPLETE YEAR GRADE 5

190

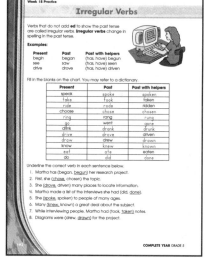

Week 18 Practice

Irregular Verbs

Verbs that do not add **ed** to show the past tense are called irregular verbs. **Irregular verbs** change in spelling in the past tense.

Examples:

Present	Past	Past with helpers
begin	began	(has, have) begun
see	saw	(has, have) seen
drive	drove	(has, have) driven

Fill in the blanks on the chart. You may refer to a dictionary.

Present	Past	Past with helpers
speak	spoke	spoken
take	took	taken
ride	rode	ridden
choose	chose	chosen
ring	rang	rung
go	went	gone
drink	drank	drunk
drive	drove	driven
draw	drew	drawn
know	knew	known
eat	ate	eaten
do	did	done

Underline the correct verb in each sentence below.

1. Martha has (began, <u>begun</u>) her research project.
2. First, she (<u>chose</u>, chosen) the topic.
3. She (<u>drove</u>, driven) many places to locate information.
4. Martha made a list of the interviews she had (did, <u>done</u>).
5. She (<u>spoke</u>, spoken) to people of many ages.
6. Many (<u>knew</u>, known) a great deal about the subject.
7. While interviewing people, Martha had (took, <u>taken</u>) notes.
8. Diagrams were (drew, <u>drawn</u>) for the project.

COMPLETE YEAR GRADE 5

192

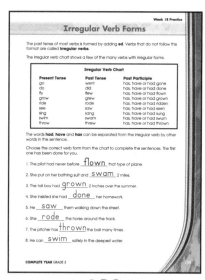

Week 18 Practice

Irregular Verb Forms

The past tense of most verbs is formed by adding **ed**. Verbs that do not follow this format are called **irregular verbs**.

The irregular verb chart shows a few of the many verbs with irregular forms.

Irregular Verb Chart

Present Tense	Past Tense	Past Participle
go	went	has, have or had gone
do	did	has, have or had done
fly	flew	has, have or had flown
grow	grew	has, have or had grown
ride	rode	has, have or had ridden
see	saw	has, have or had seen
sing	sang	has, have or had sung
swim	swam	has, have or had swum
throw	threw	has, have or had thrown

The words **had**, **have** and **has** can be separated from the irregular verb by other words in the sentence.

Choose the correct verb form from the chart to complete the sentences. The first one has been done for you.

1. The pilot had never before _flown_ that type of plane.
2. She put on her bathing suit and _swam_ 2 miles.
3. The tall boy had _grown_ 2 inches over the summer.
4. She insisted she had _done_ her homework.
5. He _saw_ them walking down the street.
6. She _rode_ the horse around the track.
7. The pitcher has _thrown_ the ball many times.
8. He can _swim_ safely in the deepest water.

COMPLETE YEAR GRADE 5

193

Week 18 Practice

Irregular Verb Forms

Use the irregular verb chart on the previous page. Write the correct verb form to complete each sentence.

1. Has she ever _grown_ carrots in her garden?
2. She was so angry she _threw_ a tantrum.
3. The bird had sometimes _flown_ from its cage.
4. The cowboy has never _ridden_ that horse before.
5. Will you _go_ to the store with me?
6. He said he had often _seen_ her walking on his street.
7. She insisted she has not _grown_ taller this year.
8. He _swam_ briskly across the pool.
9. Have the insects _flown_ away?
10. Has anyone _seen_ my sister lately?
11. He hasn't _done_ the dishes once this week!
12. Has she been _thrown_ out of the game for cheating?
13. I haven't _seen_ her yet today.
14. The airplane _flew_ slowly by the airport.
15. Have you _ridden_ your bike yet this week?

COMPLETE YEAR GRADE 5

194

Answer Key

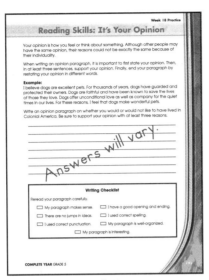

195

196

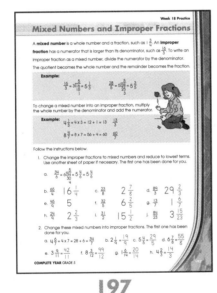

197

198

199

200

Answer Key

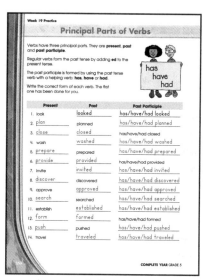

206

Principal Parts of Verbs

Week 19 Practice

Verbs have three principal parts. They are **present**, **past** and **past participle**.

Regular verbs form the past tense by adding **ed** to the present tense.

The past participle is formed by using the past tense verb with a helping verb: **has, have** or **had**.

Write the correct form of each verb. The first one has been done for you.

has have had

	Present	Past	Past Participle
1.	look	looked	has/have/had looked
2.	plan	planned	has/have/had planned
3.	close	closed	has/have/had closed
4.	wash	washed	has/have/had washed
5.	prepare	prepared	has/have/had prepared
6.	provide	provided	has/have/had provided
7.	invite	invited	has/have/had invited
8.	discover	discovered	has/have/had discovered
9.	approve	approved	has/have/had approved
10.	search	searched	has/have/had searched
11.	establish	established	has/have/had established
12.	form	formed	has/have/had formed
13.	push	pushed	has/have/had pushed
14.	travel	traveled	has/have/had traveled

COMPLETE YEAR GRADE 5

207

Writing: Future-Tense Verbs

Week 19 Practice

Future-tense verbs tell about things that will happen in the future. To form future-tense verbs, use **will** before the verb.

Example: Tomorrow I **will walk** to school.

When you use **will**, you may also have to add a helping verb and the ending **ing**.

Example: Tomorrow I **will be walking** to school.

Imagine what the world will be like 100 years from now. Maybe you think robots will be doing our work for us, or that people will be living on the moon. What will our houses look like? What will school be like? Write a paragraph describing what you imagine. Be sure to use future-tense verbs.

Paragraphs will vary.

COMPLETE YEAR GRADE 5

208

Verb Tense

Write a sentence using the present tense of each verb.

1. walk
2. dream
3. achieve

Write a sentence using the past tense of each verb.

1. dance
2. study
3. hike

Answers will vary.

Write a sentence using the future tense of each verb.

1. bake
2. write
3. talk

COMPLETE YEAR GRADE 5

209

Writing: Subjects and Verbs

Make each group of words below into a sentence by adding a subject, a verb, or a subject and a verb. Then write **S** over each subject and **V** over each verb.

Example: the dishes in the sink

    S   V
The dishes in the sink were dirty.

1. a leash for your pet
2. dented the table
3. a bowl of punch for the party
4. rinsed the soap out
5. a lack of chairs
6. bragging about his sister
7. the stock on the shelf
8. with a flip of the wrist

Answers will vary.

COMPLETE YEAR GRADE 5

210

Subject/Verb Agreement

Week 19 Practice

Singular subjects require singular verbs. **Plural subjects** require plural verbs. The subject and verb must agree in a sentence.

Example:
Singular: My dog runs across the field.
Plural: My dogs run across the field.

Circle the correct verb in each sentence.

1. Maria (talk/**talks**) to me each day at lunch.
2. Mom, Dad and I (**is**/are) going to the park to play catch.
3. Mr. and Mrs. Ramirez (**dance**/dances) well together.
4. Astronauts (**hope**/hopes) for a successful mission.
5. Trees (**prevent**/prevents) erosion.
6. The student (**is**/are) late.
7. She (**asks**/ask) for directions to the senior high gym.
8. The elephants (**plod**/plods) across the grassland to the watering hole.
9. My friend's name (**is**/are) Rebecca.
10. Many people (**enjoy**/enjoys) orchestra concerts.
11. The pencils (is/**are**) sharpened.
12. My backpack (hold/**holds**) a lot of things.
13. The wind (**blows**/blow) to the south.
14. Sam (collect/**collects**) butterflies.
15. They (**love**/loves) cotton candy.

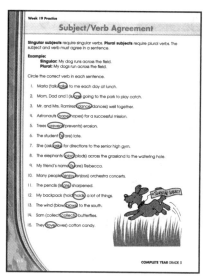

COMPLETE YEAR GRADE 5

211

Egyptian Math

Week 19 Practice

Help build the pyramid by adding the fractions.
Reduce each to its lowest term.
Use the following rule:

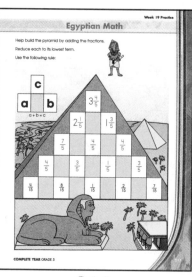

COMPLETE YEAR GRADE 5

Page 212

Adding Unlike Fractions

Solve the problems. Shade in your answers on the pizzas below to show which pieces have been eaten.

$\frac{1}{10} + \frac{4}{10} = \frac{5}{10}$ $\frac{1}{12} + \frac{4}{12} = \frac{5}{12}$ $\frac{1}{2} + \frac{1}{3} = \frac{5}{6}$ $\frac{1}{4} + \frac{3}{5} = \frac{19}{20}$ $\frac{1}{3} + \frac{1}{5} = \frac{8}{15}$

$\frac{2}{4} + \frac{1}{3} = \frac{11}{12}$ $\frac{2}{6} + \frac{1}{4} = \frac{7}{12}$ $\frac{2}{4} + \frac{1}{5} = \frac{17}{20}$ $\frac{1}{3} + \frac{1}{6} = \frac{5}{9}$ $\frac{3}{5} + \frac{1}{10} = \frac{7}{10}$

$\frac{1}{10} + \frac{1}{5} = \frac{3}{10}$ $\frac{1}{5} + \frac{1}{3} = \frac{13}{15}$ $\frac{2}{3} + \frac{1}{8} = \frac{23}{24}$ $\frac{2}{8} + \frac{1}{5} = \frac{23}{40}$ $\frac{1}{9} + \frac{1}{5} = \frac{14}{45}$

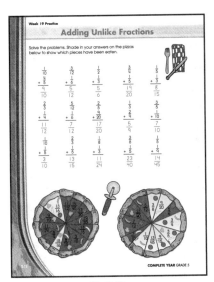

Page 213

Adding Unlike Fractions

Example: $\frac{4}{5} + \frac{1}{4}$

$$\frac{4}{5} + \frac{1}{4} = \frac{4(4)}{5(4)} + \frac{1(5)}{4(5)} = \frac{16}{20} \xrightarrow{add} \frac{5}{20} = \frac{21}{20} = 1\frac{1}{20}$$

5, 10, 15, ㉒
4, 8, 12, 16, ㉒

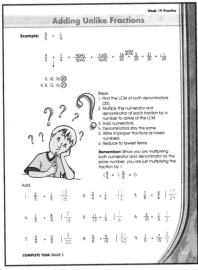

Steps:
1. Find the LCM of both denominators (20).
2. Multiply the numerator and denominator of each fraction by a number to arrive at the LCM.
3. Add numerators.
4. Denominators stay the same.
5. Write improper fractions as mixed numbers.
6. Reduce to lowest terms.

Remember: Since you are multiplying both numerator and denominator by the same number, you are just multiplying the fraction by 1. $(\frac{4}{4} = 1, \frac{5}{5} = 1)$.

Add.

1. $\frac{2}{3} + \frac{1}{5}$ $\frac{13}{15}$ 2. $\frac{3}{4} + \frac{1}{6}$ $\frac{11}{12}$ 3. $\frac{7}{8} + \frac{5}{6}$ $1\frac{17}{24}$

4. $\frac{1}{2} + \frac{5}{9}$ $1\frac{7}{18}$ 5. $\frac{1}{12} + \frac{1}{4}$ $\frac{1}{6}$ 6. $\frac{3}{10} + \frac{1}{5}$ $\frac{1}{2}$

7. $\frac{3}{4} + \frac{5}{6}$ $1\frac{7}{20}$ 8. $\frac{9}{10} + \frac{1}{4}$ $1\frac{21}{40}$ 9. $\frac{1}{3} + \frac{7}{15}$ $\frac{4}{5}$

Page 214

Adding Unlike Numbers

To add mixed numbers, first find the least common denominator. Always reduce the answer to lowest terms.

Example: $5\frac{3}{4}$ → $5\frac{3}{12}$
$+6\frac{1}{3}$ → $+6\frac{4}{12}$
$11\frac{7}{12}$

Add. Reduce the answers to lowest terms.

$8\frac{1}{2} + 7\frac{1}{4} = 15\frac{3}{4}$ $5\frac{1}{4} + 2\frac{3}{8} = 7\frac{5}{8}$ $9\frac{3}{10} + 7\frac{1}{5} = 16\frac{1}{2}$ $8\frac{1}{4} + 6\frac{1}{10} = 14\frac{9}{10}$

$4\frac{4}{5} + 3\frac{3}{10} = 8\frac{1}{10}$ $3\frac{1}{2} + 7\frac{1}{4} = 10\frac{3}{4}$ $4\frac{1}{2} + 1\frac{1}{3} = 5\frac{5}{6}$ $6\frac{1}{2} + 3\frac{1}{4} = 9\frac{5}{6}$

$5\frac{1}{3} + 2\frac{3}{8} = 7\frac{2}{3}$ $6\frac{1}{3} + 2\frac{2}{8} = 8\frac{11}{15}$ $2\frac{2}{7} + 4\frac{1}{14} = 6\frac{5}{14}$ $3\frac{1}{2} + 3\frac{1}{4} = 6\frac{3}{4}$

The boys picked $3\frac{1}{2}$ baskets of apples. The girls picked $5\frac{1}{2}$ baskets. How many baskets of apples did the boys and girls pick in all? _____ 9

Page 216

Matching Subjects and Verbs

If the subject of a sentence is singular, the verb must be singular. If the subject is plural, the verb must be plural.

Example:
The **dog** with floppy ears **is eating**.
The **dogs** in the yard **are eating**.

Write the singular or plural form of the subject in each sentence to match the verb.

1. The (yolk) __yolk__ in this egg is bright yellow.
2. The (child) __children__ are putting numbers in columns.
3. Both (coach) __coaches__ are resigning at the end of the year.
4. Those three (class) __classes__ were assigned to the gym.
5. The (lunch) __lunches__ for the children are ready.
6. (Spaghetti) __Spaghetti__ with meatballs is delicious.
7. Where are the (box) __boxes__ of chalk?
8. The (man) __men__ in the truck were collecting broken tree limbs.
9. The (rhythm) __rhythm__ of that music is exactly right for dancing.
10. Sliced (tomato) __tomatoes__ on lettuce are good with salmon.
11. The (announcer) __announcer__ on TV was condemning the dictator.
12. Two (woman) __women__ are campaigning for mayor of our town.
13. The (group) __group__ of travelers was on its way to three foreign countries.
14. The (choir) __choir__ of thirty children is singing hymns.
15. In spite of the parade, the (hero) __heroes__ were solemn.

Page 217

Agreement of Subject and Verb

A **singular subject** takes a singular verb.
Example: Bill washes the dishes.

A **plural subject** takes a plural verb.
Example: They watch television.

A **compound subject** connected by **and** takes a plural verb.
Example: Mary and Bill read books.

For a **compound subject** connected by **either/or** or **neither/nor**, the verb agrees with the subject closer to it.

Examples: Either my aunt or my uncle takes us.
Neither my grandfather nor my grandmothers are over 85.

A **singular indefinite pronoun** as the subject takes a singular verb (anybody, anyone, everybody, everyone, no one, somebody, someone, something).
Example: Everyone enjoys games.

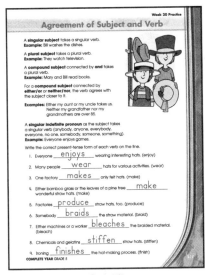

Write the correct present-tense form of each verb on the line.

1. Everyone __enjoys__ wearing interesting hats. (enjoy)
2. Many people __wear__ hats for various activities. (wear)
3. One factory __makes__ only felt hats. (make)
4. Either bamboo grass or the leaves of a pine tree __make__ wonderful straw hats. (make)
5. Factories __produce__ straw hats, too. (produce)
6. Somebody __braids__ the straw material. (braid)
7. Either machines or a worker __bleaches__ the braided material. (bleach)
8. Chemicals and gelatins __stiffen__ straw hats. (stiffen)
9. Ironing __finishes__ the hat-making process. (finish)

Page 218

Commas

Commas are used to separate items in a series.

Example:
The fruit bowl contains oranges, peaches, pears, and apples.

Commas are also used to separate geographical names and dates.

Example:
Today's date is January 13, 2000.
My grandfather lives in Tallahassee, Florida.
I would like to visit Paris, France.

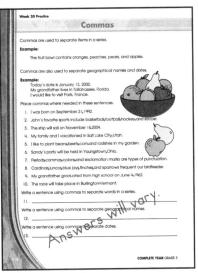

Place commas where needed in these sentences.

1. I was born on September 21, 1992.
2. John's favorite sports include basketball, football, hockey, and soccer.
3. The ship will sail on November 16, 2004.
4. My family and I vacationed in Salt Lake City, Utah.
5. I like to plant beans, beets, corn, and radishes in my garden.
6. Sandy's party will be held in Youngstown, Ohio.
7. Periods, commas, colons, and exclamation marks are types of punctuation.
8. Cardinals, juncos, blue jays, finches, and sparrows frequent our birdfeeder.
9. My grandfather graduated from high school on June 4, 1962.
10. The race will take place in Burlington, Vermont.

Write a sentence using commas to separate words in a series.

11. _____

Write a sentence using commas to separate geographical names.

12. _____

Write a sentence using commas to separate dates.

13. _____

Answers will vary.

Answer Key

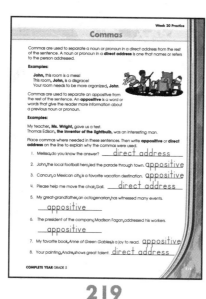

219

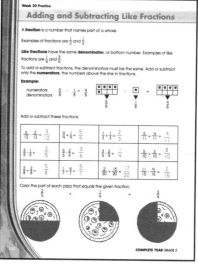

220

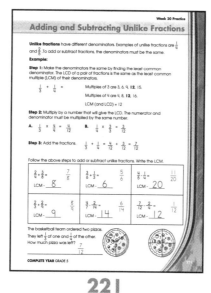

221

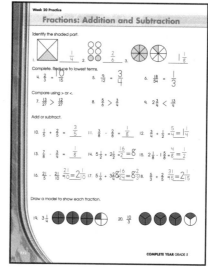

222

223

224

Answer Key

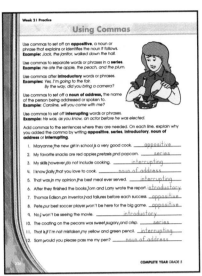

226

227

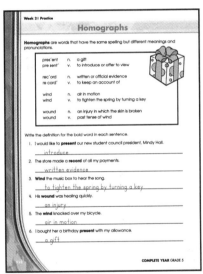

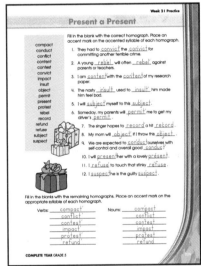

228

229

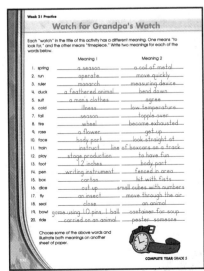

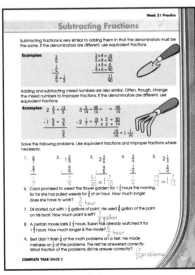

230

231

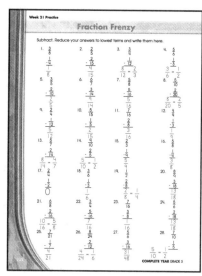

Week 21 Practice

Fraction Frenzy

Subtract. Reduce your answers to lowest terms and write them here.

232

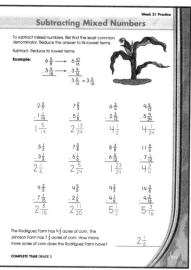

Week 21 Practice

Subtracting Mixed Numbers

To subtract mixed numbers, first find the least common denominator. Reduce the answer to its lowest terms.

Subtract. Reduce to lowest terms.

The Rodriguez Farm has $9\frac{1}{2}$ acres of corn. The Johnson Farm has $7\frac{1}{3}$ acres of corn. How many more acres of corn does the Rodriguez Farm have? $2\frac{1}{6}$

COMPLETE YEAR GRADE 5

233

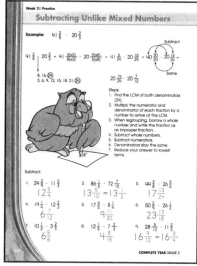

Week 21 Practice

Subtracting Unlike Mixed Numbers

Example: $41\frac{2}{8} - 20\frac{2}{3}$

234

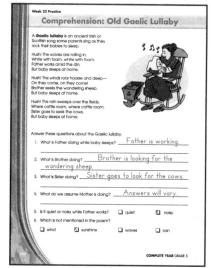

Week 22 Practice

Comprehension: Old Gaelic Lullaby

A **Gaelic lullaby** is an ancient Irish or Scottish song some parents sing as they rock their babies to sleep.

Hush! The waves are rolling in,
White with foam, white with foam,
Father works amid the din,
But baby sleeps at home.

Hush! The winds roar hoarse and deep—
On they come, on they come!
Brother seeks the wandering sheep,
But baby sleeps at home.

Hush! The rain sweeps over the fields,
Where cattle roam, where cattle roam.
Sister goes to seek the cows,
But baby sleeps at home.

Answer these questions about the Gaelic lullaby.

1. What is Father doing while baby sleeps? Father is working.
2. What is Brother doing? Brother is looking for the wandering sheep.
3. What is Sister doing? Sister goes to look for the cows.
4. What do we assume Mother is doing? Answers will vary.
5. Is it quiet or noisy while Father works? ☐ quiet ☒ noisy
6. Which is not mentioned in the poem? ☐ wind ☒ sunshine ☐ waves ☐ rain

COMPLETE YEAR GRADE 5

236

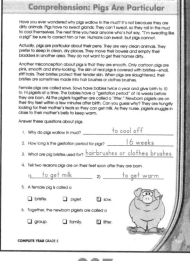

Week 22 Practice

Comprehension: Pigs Are Particular

Have you ever wondered why pigs wallow in the mud? It's not because they are dirty animals. Pigs have no sweat glands. They can't sweat, so they roll in the mud to cool themselves. The next time you hear anyone who's hot say, "I'm sweating like a pig!" be sure to correct him or her. Humans can sweat, but pigs cannot.

Actually, pigs are particular about their pens. They are very clean animals. They prefer to sleep in clean, dry places. They move their bowels and empty their bladders in another area. They do not want to get their homes dirty.

Another misconception about pigs is that they are smooth. Only cartoon pigs are pink, smooth and shiny-looking. The skin of real pigs is covered with bristles—small, stiff hairs. Their bristles protect their tender skin. When pigs are slaughtered, their bristles are sometimes made into hair brushes or clothes brushes.

Female pigs are called sows. Sows have babies twice a year and give birth to 10 to 14 piglets at a time. The babies have a "gestation period" of 16 weeks before they are born. All the piglets together are called a "litter." Newborn piglets are on their tiny feet within a few minutes after birth. Can you guess why? They are hungrily looking for their mother's teats so they can get milk. As they nurse, piglets snuggle in close to their mother's belly to keep warm.

Answer these questions about pigs.

1. Why do pigs wallow in mud? to cool off
2. How long is the gestation period for pigs? 16 weeks
3. What are pig bristles used for? hairbrushes or clothes brushes
4. Tell two reasons pigs are on their feet soon after they are born.
   1) to get milk   2) to get warm
5. A female pig is called a
   ☐ bristle.   ☐ piglet.   ☒ sow.
6. Together, the newborn piglets are called a
   ☐ group.   ☐ family.   ☒ litter.

COMPLETE YEAR GRADE 5

237

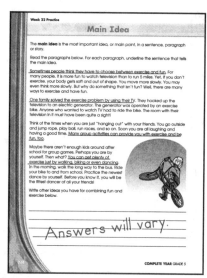

Week 22 Practice

Main Idea

The **main idea** is the most important idea, or main point, in a sentence, paragraph or story.

Read the paragraphs below. For each paragraph, underline the sentence that tells the main idea.

Sometimes people think they have to choose between exercise and fun. For many people, it is more fun to watch television than to run 5 miles. Yet, if you don't exercise, your body gets soft and out of shape. You move more slowly. You may even think more slowly. But why do something that isn't fun? Well, there are many ways to exercise and have fun.

One family solved the exercise problem by using their TV. They hooked up the television to an electric generator. The generator was operated by an exercise bike. Anyone who wanted to watch TV had to ride the bike. The room with their television in it must have been quite a sight!

Think of the times when you are just "hanging out" with your friends. You go outside and jump rope, play ball, run races, and so on. Soon you are all laughing and having a good time. Many group activities can provide you with exercise and be fun, too.

Maybe there aren't enough kids around after school for group games. Perhaps you are by yourself. Then what? You can get plenty of exercise just by walking, biking or even dancing. In the morning, walk the long way to the bus. Ride your bike to and from school. Practice the newest dance by yourself. Before you know it, you will be the fittest dancer of all your friends!

Write other ideas you have for combining fun and exercise below.

Answers will vary.

COMPLETE YEAR GRADE 5

238

Answer Key

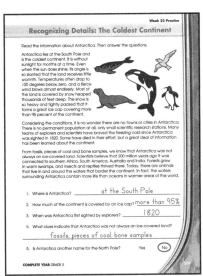

Recognizing Details: The Coldest Continent

Read the information about Antarctica. Then answer the questions.

Antarctica lies at the South Pole and is the coldest continent. It is without sunlight for months at a time. Even when the sun does shine, its angle is so slanted that the land receives little warmth. Temperatures often drop to 100 degrees below zero, and a fierce wind blows almost endlessly. Most of the land is covered by snow heaped thousands of feet deep. The snow is so heavy and tightly packed that it forms a great ice cap covering more than 95 percent of the continent.

Considering the conditions, it is no wonder there are no towns or cities in Antarctica. There is no permanent population at all, only small scientific research stations. Many teams of explorers and scientists have braved the freezing cold since Antarctica was sighted in 1820. Some have died in their effort, but a great deal of information has been learned about the continent.

From fossils, pieces of coal and bone samples, we know that Antarctica was not always an ice-covered land. Scientists believe that 200 million years ago it was connected to southern Africa, South America, Australia and India. Forests grew in warm swamps, and insects and reptiles thrived there. Today, there are animals that live in and around the waters that border the continent. In fact, the waters surrounding Antarctica contain more life than oceans in warmer areas of the world.

1. Where is Antarctica? __at the South Pole__

2. How much of the continent is covered by an ice cap? __more than 95%__

3. When was Antarctica first sighted by explorers? __1820__

4. What clues indicate that Antarctica was not always an ice-covered land?
__fossils, pieces of coal, bone samples__

5. Is Antarctica another name for the North Pole?   Yes   (No)

COMPLETE YEAR GRADE 5

239

Main Idea: Penguins

Read the information about penguins.

People are amused by the funny, duck-like waddle of penguins and by their appearance because they seem to be wearing little tuxedos. Penguins are among the best-liked animals on Earth, but are also a most misunderstood animal. People may have more wrong ideas about penguins than any other animal.

For example, many people are surprised to learn that penguins are really birds, not mammals. Penguins do not fly, but they do have feathers, and only birds have feathers. Also, like other birds, penguins build nests and their young hatch from eggs. Because of their unusual looks, though, you would never confuse them with any other bird!

Penguins are also thought of as symbols of the polar regions, but penguins do not live north of the equator, so you would not find a penguin on the North Pole. Penguins don't live at the South Pole, either. Only two of the seventeen **species** of penguins spend all of their lives on the frozen continent of Antarctica. You would be just as likely to see a penguin living on an island in a warm climate as in a cold area.

Draw an **X** on the blank for the correct answer.

1. The main idea is:

___ Penguins are among the best-liked animals on earth.

_X_ The penguin is a much misunderstood animal.

2. Penguins live

___ only at the North Pole.

___ only at the South Pole.

_X_ only south of the equator.

3. Based on the other words in the sentence, what is the correct definition of the word **species**?

___ number

___ bird

_X_ a distinct kind

4. List three ways penguins are like other birds.
__have feathers, lay eggs, build nests__

COMPLETE YEAR GRADE 5

240

Fun Facts

Some skyscrapers are so large that they have their own...

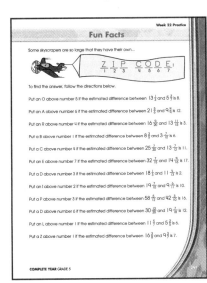

$$\underset{1\ \ 2\ \ 3}{\text{Z I P}} \ \ \underset{4\ \ 5\ \ 6\ \ 7}{\text{C O D E}}$$

To find the answer, follow the directions below.

Put an O above number 5 if the estimated difference between $13\frac{1}{2}$ and $5\frac{3}{5}$ is 8.

Put an A above number 6 if the estimated difference between $21\frac{5}{8}$ and $9\frac{3}{4}$ is 12.

Put an R above number 4 if the estimated difference between $16\frac{5}{8}$ and $13\frac{1}{11}$ is 3.

Put a B above number 1 if the estimated difference between $8\frac{2}{3}$ and $3\frac{1}{12}$ is 6.

Put a C above number 4 if the estimated difference between $25\frac{1}{4}$ and $13\frac{7}{12}$ is 11.

Put an E above number 7 if the estimated difference between $32\frac{1}{3}$ and $14\frac{5}{6}$ is 17.

Put a D above number 3 if the estimated difference between $18\frac{1}{4}$ and $11\frac{5}{8}$ is 2.

Put an I above number 2 if the estimated difference between $19\frac{1}{10}$ and $9\frac{3}{4}$ is 10.

Put a P above number 3 if the estimated difference between $58\frac{9}{10}$ and $42\frac{8}{10}$ is 16.

Put a D above number 6 if the estimated difference between $30\frac{10}{11}$ and $19\frac{1}{18}$ is 12.

Put an L above number 1 if the estimated difference between $11\frac{1}{5}$ and $5\frac{2}{9}$ is 6.

Put a Z above number 1 if the estimated difference between $16\frac{3}{8}$ and $9\frac{3}{7}$ is 7.

COMPLETE YEAR GRADE 5

241

Fractions

Subtract. Reduce your answers to lowest terms and write them here. The first one has been done for you.

1. 5
$-\ 4\frac{4}{4}$
$4\frac{1}{8}$

2. 8
$-\ \frac{7}{8}$
$7\frac{1}{8}$

3. 4
$3\frac{3}{6} = 3\frac{1}{2}$

4. 10
$-\ \frac{1}{8}$
$9\frac{7}{8}$

5. 14
$13\frac{3}{5}$

6. 11
$10\frac{7}{9}$

7. 4
$3\frac{5}{8}$

8. 7
$6\frac{5}{6}$

9. 6
$5\frac{2}{4} = 5\frac{1}{2}$

10. 12
$11\frac{3}{8} = 11\frac{3}{8}$

11. 9
$8\frac{3}{4}$

12. 3
$2\frac{7}{10} = 2\frac{2}{5}$

13. 7
$6\frac{4}{11}$

14. 40
$39\frac{3}{7}$

15. 5
$4\frac{5}{6}$

16. 8
$7\frac{3}{4}$

17. 11
$10\frac{6}{12} = 10\frac{1}{2}$

18. 4
$3\frac{3}{10}$

19. 6
$5\frac{3}{8}$

20. 9
$8\frac{3}{4}$

21. 12
$11\frac{4}{9}$

22. 4
$3\frac{6}{11}$

23. 7
$6\frac{5}{10} = 6\frac{1}{2}$

24. 32
$31\frac{3}{8}$

25. $24\frac{1}{4}$

$19\frac{3}{8}$

$4\frac{3}{8} = 4\frac{1}{2}$

$7\frac{3}{8}$

COMPLETE YEAR GRADE 5

242

A Trip to the Ocean

Maria's girls' club earned enough money from their cookie sale to go on a camping trip by the ocean. Read about their trip. Write your answers in complete sentences.

1. The bus started with $6\frac{1}{2}$ gallons of gasoline. When the driver added $9\frac{1}{2}$ more gallons of gasoline, how much gasoline did the bus have in it?
__There were 16 gallons of gas in the bus.__

2. The girls and their leaders stopped for a picnic after driving $58\frac{1}{4}$ miles. After the picnic, they drove another $43\frac{3}{4}$ miles before reaching the ocean. How far were they from home?
__They were 102 miles from home.__

3. Before leaving home, the girls made sandwiches for their lunch. They had $7\frac{1}{2}$ tuna sandwiches, $4\frac{1}{4}$ cheese sandwiches, $2\frac{3}{4}$ peanut butter sandwiches and $5\frac{1}{2}$ beef sandwiches. How many total sandwiches did they bring?
__They brought 20 sandwiches.__

4. The leader cut a watermelon into 16 slices for lunch. The girls ate 8 of the slices. What fraction of the watermelon did they eat? $\frac{8}{16}$
__They ate $\frac{8}{16}$ or $\frac{1}{2}$ of the melon.__

5. When they arrived, they took $1\frac{1}{4}$ hours to set up the tents. They spent another $\frac{3}{4}$ hour getting their bedrolls ready. How long did they work before they could play in the ocean?
__They worked 2 hours.__

6. The girls swam and played in the water for $1\frac{3}{4}$ hours. Then, they sat in the sun for $\frac{3}{4}$ hour. How many hours did they play and sunbathe? $2\frac{1}{2}$
__They played and sunbathed for $2\frac{1}{2}$ hours.__

7. After dinner, they had a campfire. First, they sang for $1\frac{1}{4}$ hours. Then, they told ghost stories for $\frac{3}{4}$ hour. If they put out the fire and went to sleep at 10:30 P.M., what time did they begin the campfire?
__They began the campfire at 8:30 P.M.__

8. The next morning, $\frac{3}{8}$ of the girls went fishing. The rest of the girls hunted for shells. If there were 8 girls altogether, how many hunted for shells?
__Five hunted for shells.__
How many went fishing? __Three went fishing.__

COMPLETE YEAR GRADE 5

243

Research Time

Mr. Write-A-Lot assigned research papers to his class. He divided the class into two groups. One person from each group was responsible for each part of the research process.

1. Marisha and John each found several books on their subjects. It took Marisha $2\frac{1}{2}$ hours to skim through her stack of books, and it took John $1\frac{3}{4}$ hours to look through his. How much longer did it take Marisha? $\frac{3}{4}$ hour longer

2. Neal and Geraldo were working on note cards. Neal was able to complete his in $48\frac{3}{4}$ minutes, and it took Geraldo $51\frac{5}{6}$ minutes to finish his. How much longer did Geraldo take? $2\frac{17}{24}$ minutes longer

3. Bobby and Gordon found it difficult to write outlines. It took Bobby $38\frac{2}{3}$ minutes and Gordon $36\frac{5}{6}$ minutes. How many more minutes did it take Bobby?
$1\frac{11}{12}$ more minutes

4. Anita finished the first draft of her report in 48 minutes, and it took Pablo $51\frac{3}{8}$ minutes to write his. How much longer did it take Pablo?
$3\frac{3}{8}$ minutes longer

5. The final draft of their reports went smoothly for Katie and Laura. Katie zipped hers off in $18\frac{3}{4}$ minutes, and Laura's took $21\frac{1}{8}$ minutes. How much longer did Laura's final draft take? $2\frac{3}{8}$ minutes longer

Extension: Subtract $2\frac{7}{8}$ from ...

a. 4 $1\frac{1}{8}$
b. $5\frac{1}{8}$ $2\frac{1}{4}$
c. $8\frac{7}{8}$ 6

d. $6\frac{3}{8}$ $3\frac{1}{2}$
e. $7\frac{5}{8}$ $4\frac{3}{4}$
f. $9\frac{3}{4}$ $6\frac{7}{8}$

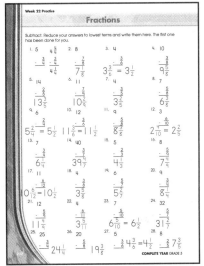

COMPLETE YEAR GRADE 5

244

Answer Key

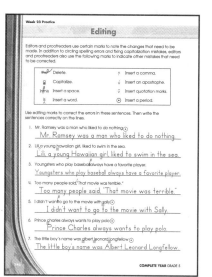

246

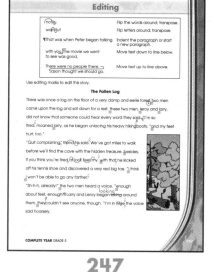

247

248

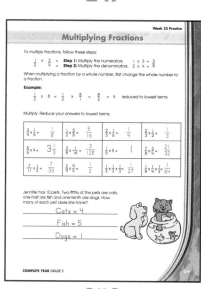

249

250

251

Answer Key

Multiplying Mixed Numbers

Multiply mixed numbers by first changing them to improper fractions. Always reduce your answers to lowest terms.

Example:

$2\frac{1}{3} \times 1\frac{1}{8} = \frac{7}{3} \times \frac{9}{8} = \frac{63}{24} = 2\frac{15}{24} = 2\frac{5}{8}$

Multiply. Reduce to lowest terms.

$4\frac{1}{4} \times 2\frac{1}{5} = 9\frac{7}{20}$	$1\frac{1}{3} \times 3\frac{1}{4} = 4\frac{1}{3}$	$1\frac{1}{4} \times 3\frac{3}{5} = 4$
$1\frac{9}{5} \times 4\frac{1}{2} = 8\frac{5}{14}$	$2\frac{3}{4} \times 2\frac{5}{8} = 7\frac{3}{20}$	$4\frac{2}{3} \times 3\frac{1}{7} = 14\frac{2}{3}$
$6\frac{2}{3} \times 2\frac{1}{8} = 13\frac{3}{5}$	$3\frac{1}{7} \times 4\frac{5}{8} = 14\frac{15}{28}$	$7\frac{3}{4} \times 2\frac{1}{4} = 15\frac{41}{72}$

Sunnyside Farm has two barns with 25 stalls in each barn. Cows use $\frac{3}{5}$ of the stalls, and horses use the rest.

How many stalls are for cows? ___30___

How many are for horses? ___20___

(Hint: First, find how many total stalls are in the two barns.)

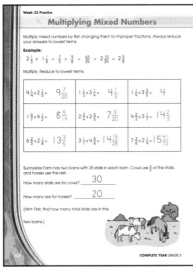

COMPLETE YEAR GRADE 5

252

Multiplication With Mixed Numbers

When multiplying by a mixed number, change the mixed number to an improper fraction. Cancel if possible. Multiply the numerators, then the denominators. Write the improper fractions as mixed numbers.

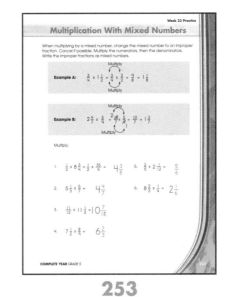

Example A: $\frac{3}{4} \times 1\frac{1}{2} = \frac{3}{4} \times \frac{3}{2} = 1\frac{1}{8}$

Example B: $2\frac{4}{7} \times \frac{5}{8} = \frac{18}{7} \times \frac{5}{8} = \frac{10}{7} = 1\frac{3}{7}$

Multiply.

1. $\frac{1}{2} \times 8\frac{3}{4} = \frac{1}{2} \times \frac{35}{4} = 4\frac{3}{8}$ 5. $\frac{2}{5} \times 2\frac{1}{12} = \frac{5}{6}$

2. $5\frac{1}{3} \times \frac{6}{7} = 4\frac{4}{7}$ 6. $8\frac{2}{3} \times 1\frac{1}{4} = 2\frac{1}{6}$

3. $\frac{11}{12} \times 11\frac{1}{3} = 10\frac{7}{18}$

4. $7\frac{1}{2} \times \frac{8}{9} = 6\frac{2}{3}$

COMPLETE YEAR GRADE 5

253

Invert and Multiply

Solve the problems. Reduce your answers to lowest terms.

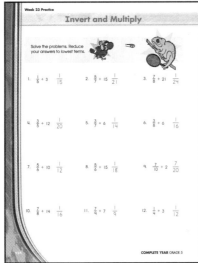

1. $\frac{1}{5} \div 3 = \frac{1}{15}$ 2. $\frac{5}{7} \div 15 = \frac{1}{21}$ 3. $\frac{7}{8} \div 21 = \frac{1}{24}$

4. $\frac{3}{5} \div 12 = \frac{1}{20}$ 5. $\frac{3}{7} \div 6 = \frac{1}{14}$ 6. $\frac{3}{8} \div 6 = \frac{1}{16}$

7. $\frac{5}{6} \div 10 = \frac{1}{12}$ 8. $\frac{5}{6} \div 15 = \frac{1}{18}$ 9. $\frac{7}{10} \div 2 = \frac{7}{20}$

10. $\frac{7}{8} \div 14 = \frac{1}{16}$ 11. $\frac{7}{4} \div 7 = \frac{1}{9}$ 12. $\frac{1}{4} \div 3 = \frac{1}{12}$

COMPLETE YEAR GRADE 5

254

Author's Purpose

Authors write to fulfill one of three purposes: to **inform**, to **entertain** or to **persuade**.

Authors who write to inform are providing facts for the reader in an informational context.

Examples: Encyclopedia entries and newspaper articles

Authors who write to entertain are hoping to provide enjoyment for the reader.

Examples: Funny stories and comics

Authors who write to persuade are trying to convince the reader to believe as they believe.

Examples: Editorials and opinion essays

Read each paragraph. Write **inform**, **entertain** or **persuade** on the line to show the author's purpose.

1. The whooping crane is a migratory bird. At one time, this endangered bird was almost extinct. These large white cranes are characterized by red faces and trumpeting calls. Through protection of both the birds and their habitats, the whooping crane is slowly increasing in number.

   ___inform___

2. It is extremely important that all citizens place bird feeders in their yards and keep them full for the winter. Birds that spend the winter in this area are in danger of starving due to lack of food. It is every citizen's responsibility to ensure the survival of the birds.

   ___persuade___

3. Imagine being able to hibernate like a bear each winter! Wouldn't it be great to eat to your heart's content all fall? Then, sometime in late November, inform your teacher that you will not be attending school for the next few months because you'll be resting and living off your fat? Now, that would be the life!

   ___entertain___

4. Bears, woodchucks and chipmunks are not the only animals that hibernate. The queen bumblebee also hibernates in winter. All the other bees die before winter arrives. The queen hibernates under leaves in a small hole. She is cold-blooded and therefore is able to survive slightly frozen.

   ___inform___

COMPLETE YEAR GRADE 5

256

Author's Purpose

Write a paragraph of your own for each purpose. The paragraph can be about any topic.

1. to inform

_____

_____

2. to persuade

Answers will vary.

_____

3. to entertain

_____

_____

Reread your paragraphs. Do they make sense? Check for grammar, spelling and punctuation errors and make corrections where needed.

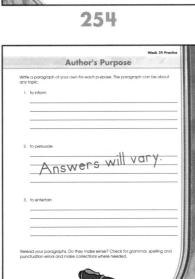

COMPLETE YEAR GRADE 5

257

Persuasive Writing

When trying to persuade someone, it helps to look at both sides of the issue. If you can understand both sides, you will have a better idea how to convince someone of your point of view.

Follow these steps to write two persuasive paragraphs about which form of transportation is better: airplanes or cars.

1. On another sheet of paper, list three or four reasons why planes are better and three or four reasons why cars are better.
2. Put each list of reasons in order. Often, persuasive writing is strongest when the best reason is placed last. Readers tend to remember the last reason best.
3. Write topic sentences for each paragraph.
4. Read each paragraph and make any necessary changes so one sentence leads smoothly to the next.
5. Write your paragraphs below.

Airplanes Are Better Transportation Than Cars _____

Paragraphs will vary.

_____

Cars Are Better Transportation Than Planes _____

_____

_____

_____

6. Write two more paragraphs on another sheet of paper. Select any topic. Write from both points of view.

COMPLETE YEAR GRADE 5

258

Answer Key

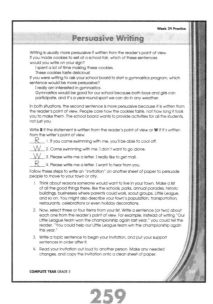

Week 24 Practice

Persuasive Writing

Writing is usually more persuasive if written from the reader's point of view. If you made cookies to sell at a school fair, which of these sentences would you write on your sign?
I spent a lot of time making these cookies.
These cookies taste delicious!
If you were writing to ask your school board to start a gymnastics program, which sentence would be more persuasive?
I really am interested in gymnastics.
Gymnastics would be good for our school because both boys and girls can participate, and it's a year-round sport we can do in any weather.

In both situations, the second sentence is more persuasive because it is written from the reader's point of view. People care how the cookies taste, not how long it took you to make them. The school board wants to provide activities for all the students, not just you.

Write **R** if the statement is written from the reader's point of view or **W** if it's written from the writer's point of view.

  R   1. If you come swimming with me, you'll be able to cool off.

  W   2. Come swimming with me. I don't want to go alone.

  W   3. Please write me a letter. I really like to get mail.

  R   4. Please write me a letter. I want to hear from you.

Follow these steps to write an "invitation" on another sheet of paper to persuade people to move to your town or city.

1. Think about reasons someone would want to live in your town. Make a list of all the good things there, like the schools, parks, annual parades, historic buildings, businesses where parents could work, scout groups, Little League, and so on. You might also describe your town's population, transportation, restaurants, celebrations or even holiday decorations.

2. Now, select three or four items from your list. Write a sentence (or two) about each one from the reader's point of view. For example, instead of writing "Our Little League team won the championship again last year," you could tell the reader, "You could help our Little League team win the championship again this year."

3. Write a topic sentence to begin your invitation, and put your support sentences in order after it.

4. Read your invitation out loud to another person. Make any needed changes, and copy the invitation onto a clean sheet of paper.

COMPLETE YEAR GRADE 5

259

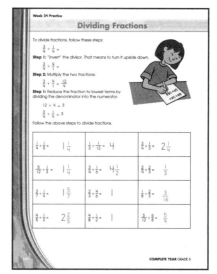

Week 24 Practice

Dividing Fractions

To divide fractions, follow these steps:

$$\frac{3}{4} \div \frac{1}{4} =$$

Step 1: "Invert" the divisor. That means to turn it upside down.

$$\frac{3}{4} \div \frac{4}{1}$$

Step 2: Multiply the two fractions:

$$\frac{3}{4} \times \frac{4}{1} = \frac{12}{4}$$

Step 3: Reduce the fraction to lowest terms by dividing the denominator into the numerator.

$$12 \div 4 = 3$$
$$\frac{3}{4} \div \frac{1}{4} = 3$$

Follow the above steps to divide fractions.

$\frac{1}{4} \div \frac{1}{5} = 1\frac{1}{4}$	$\frac{1}{3} \div \frac{1}{12} = 4$	$\frac{3}{4} \div \frac{1}{3} = 2\frac{1}{4}$
$\frac{5}{12} \div \frac{1}{3} = 1\frac{1}{4}$	$\frac{3}{4} \div \frac{1}{6} = 4\frac{1}{2}$	$\frac{2}{9} \div \frac{2}{3} = \frac{1}{3}$
$\frac{3}{7} \div \frac{1}{4} = 1\frac{5}{7}$	$\frac{2}{3} \div \frac{4}{6} = 1$	$\frac{1}{8} \div \frac{2}{3} = \frac{3}{16}$
$\frac{4}{5} \div \frac{1}{3} = 2\frac{2}{5}$	$\frac{3}{4} \div \frac{1}{2} = 1$	$\frac{5}{8} \div \frac{1}{2} = \frac{5}{4}$

COMPLETE YEAR GRADE 5

260

Week 24 Practice

Dividing Fractions

When dividing fractions, change the problem to multiplication. Invert the divisor. Cancel if possible. Multiply the numerators, then the denominators. Write improper fractions as mixed numbers.

Example A: $\frac{3}{10} \div \frac{3}{5} = \frac{3}{10} \times \frac{5}{3} = \frac{1}{2}$

Example B: $\frac{5}{12} \div \frac{3}{8} = \frac{5}{12} \times \frac{8}{3} = \frac{10}{9} = 1\frac{1}{9}$

Divide.

1. $\frac{1}{2} \div \frac{3}{4} = \frac{1}{2} \times \frac{4}{3} = \frac{2}{3}$

5. $\frac{1}{10} \div \frac{2}{5} = \frac{1}{4}$

2. $\frac{3}{8} \div \frac{1}{4} = 1\frac{1}{2}$

6. $\frac{5}{6} \div \frac{11}{12} = \frac{10}{11}$

3. $\frac{4}{9} \div \frac{2}{3} = \frac{2}{3}$

7. $\frac{14}{15} \div \frac{2}{3} = 1\frac{2}{5}$

4. $\frac{3}{8} \div \frac{5}{12} = \frac{9}{10}$

8. $\frac{4}{5} \div \frac{3}{10} = 2\frac{2}{3}$

COMPLETE YEAR GRADE 5

261

Week 24 Practice

Dividing Fractions

Reciprocals are two fractions that, when multiplied together, make 1. To divide a fraction by a fraction, turn one of the fractions upside down and multiply. The upside-down fraction is a reciprocal of its original fraction. If you multiply a fraction by its reciprocal, you always get 1.

Examples of reciprocals: $\frac{2}{3} \times \frac{3}{2} = 1$ $\frac{11}{9} \times \frac{9}{11} = \frac{99}{99} = 1$

Example of dividing by fractions: $\frac{2}{5} \div \frac{2}{9} = \frac{2}{5} \times \frac{9}{2} = 1\frac{9}{10} = 1\frac{4}{5}$

To divide a whole number by a fraction, first write the whole number as a fraction (with a denominator of 1). (Write a mixed number as an improper fraction.) Then finish the problem as explained above.

Examples: $4 \div \frac{2}{6} = \frac{4}{1} \times \frac{6}{2} = \frac{24}{2} = 12$ $3\frac{1}{2} \div \frac{2}{5} = \frac{7}{2} \times \frac{5}{2} = \frac{35}{4} = 8\frac{3}{4}$

Solve the following problems, writing answers in their lowest terms. Change any improper fractions to mixed numbers.

1. $\frac{1}{3} \div \frac{2}{5} = \frac{5}{6}$ 2. $\frac{6}{7} \div \frac{1}{3} = 2\frac{4}{7}$ 3. $3 \div \frac{3}{4} = 4$ 4. $\frac{1}{4} \div \frac{2}{3} = \frac{3}{8}$

5. Judy has 8 candy bars. She wants to give $\frac{1}{3}$ of a candy bar to everyone in her class. Does she have enough for all 24 students?   **Yes**

6. A big jar of glue holds $3\frac{1}{2}$ cups. How many little containers that hold $\frac{1}{4}$ cup each can you fill?   **14 containers**

7. A container holds 27 ounces of ice cream. How many $4\frac{1}{2}$-ounce servings is that?   **6 servings**

8. It takes $2\frac{1}{2}$ teaspoons of powdered mix to make 1 cup of hot chocolate. How many cups can you make with 45 teaspoons of mix?   **18 cups**

9. Each cup of hot chocolate also takes $\frac{2}{3}$ cup of milk. How many cups of hot chocolate can you make with 12 cups of milk?   **18 cups**

COMPLETE YEAR GRADE 5

262

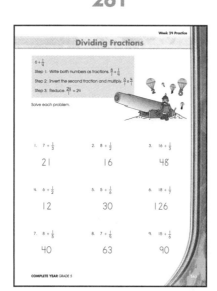

Week 24 Practice

Dividing Fractions

$$6 \div \frac{1}{4} =$$

Step 1: Write both numbers as fractions. $\frac{6}{1} \div \frac{1}{4}$

Step 2: Invert the second fraction and multiply. $\frac{6}{1} \times \frac{4}{1}$

Step 3: Reduce. $\frac{24}{1} = 24$

Solve each problem.

1. $7 \div \frac{1}{3}$ 2. $8 \div \frac{1}{2}$ 3. $16 \div \frac{1}{3}$
     21   **16**   **48**

4. $6 \div \frac{1}{2}$ 5. $5 \div \frac{1}{6}$ 6. $18 \div \frac{1}{7}$
     12   **30**   **126**

7. $8 \div \frac{1}{5}$ 8. $7 \div \frac{1}{9}$ 9. $15 \div \frac{1}{6}$
     40   **63**   **90**

COMPLETE YEAR GRADE 5

263

Week 24 Practice

Dividing Whole Numbers by Fractions

Follow these steps to divide a whole number by a fraction:

$$8 \div \frac{1}{4} =$$

Step 1: Write the whole number as a fraction:

$$\frac{8}{1} \div \frac{1}{4} =$$

Step 2: Invert the divisor.

$$\frac{8}{1} \times \frac{4}{1} =$$

Step 3: Multiply the two fractions:

$$\frac{8}{1} \times \frac{4}{1} = \frac{32}{1}$$

Step 4: Reduce the fraction to lowest terms by dividing the denominator into the numerator: $32 \div 1 = 32$

Follow the above steps to divide a whole number by a fraction.

$6 \div \frac{1}{3} =$ **18**	$4 \div \frac{1}{2} =$ **8**	$21 \div \frac{1}{3} =$ **63**
$8 \div \frac{1}{2} =$ **16**	$3 \div \frac{1}{6} =$ **18**	$15 \div \frac{1}{7} =$ **105**
$9 \div \frac{1}{5} =$ **45**	$4 \div \frac{1}{9} =$ **36**	$12 \div \frac{1}{6} =$ **72**

Three-fourths of a bag of popcorn fits into one bowl. How many bowls do you need if you have six bags of popcorn?   **8**

COMPLETE YEAR GRADE 5

264

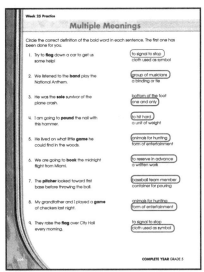

Week 25 Practice

Multiple Meanings

Circle the correct definition of the bold word in each sentence. The first one has been done for you.

1. Try to **flag** down a car to get us some help! — (to signal to stop) / cloth used as symbol
2. We listened to the **band** play the National Anthem. — (group of musicians) / a binding or tie
3. He was the **sole** survivor of the plane crash. — bottom of the foot / (one and only)
4. I am going to **pound** the nail with this hammer. — (to hit hard) / a unit of weight
5. He lived on what little **game** he could find in the woods. — (animals for hunting) / form of entertainment
6. We are going to **book** the midnight flight from Miami. — (to reserve in advance) / a written work
7. The **pitcher** looked toward first base before throwing the ball. — (baseball team member) / container for pouring
8. My grandfather and I played a **game** of checkers last night. — animals for hunting / (form of entertainment)
9. They raise the **flag** over City Hall every morning. — to signal to stop / (cloth used as symbol)

COMPLETE YEAR GRADE 5

266

Week 25 Practice

Learning New Words

Write a word from the box to complete each sentence. Use a dictionary to look up words you are unsure of.

bouquet	unconscious	inspire	disability
inherit	hovering	assault	enclosure
commotion	criticize		

1. He was knocked ___unconscious___ by the blow to his head.
2. Megan never let her ___disability___ stand in the way of accomplishing what she wanted.
3. The teacher burst into the noisy room and demanded to know what all the ___commotion___ was about.
4. He offered her a ___bouquet___ of flowers as a truce after their argument.
5. The zoo was in the process of building a new ___enclosure___ for the elephants.
6. The mother was ___hovering___ over her sick child.
7. The movie was meant to ___inspire___ people to do good deeds.
8. My friend will eventually ___inherit___ a fortune from his grandmother.
9. Not many people enjoy having someone ___criticize___ their work.
10. The female leopard led the ___assault___ on the herd of zebras.

COMPLETE YEAR GRADE 5

267

Week 25 Practice

Using the Dictionary

Guide words are the words that appear at the top of dictionary pages. They show the first and last words on each page.

Read the guide words on each dictionary page below. Then look around for objects whose names come between the guide words. Write the names of the objects, and then number them in alphabetical order.

babble	buzz		magic	myself
cabin	cycle			
dairy	dwarf		scar	sword
feast	future		tack	truth

Answers will vary.

COMPLETE YEAR GRADE 5

268

Week 25 Practice

Using the Dictionary

Read about dictionaries. Then answer the questions.

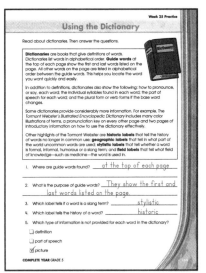

Dictionaries are books that give definitions of words. Dictionaries list words in alphabetical order. **Guide words** at the top of each page show the first and last words listed on the page. All other words on the page are listed in alphabetical order between the guide words. This helps you locate the word you want quickly and easily.

In addition to definitions, dictionaries also show the following: how to pronounce, or say, each word; the individual syllables found in each word; the part of speech for each word; and the plural form or verb forms if the base word changes.

Some dictionaries provide considerably more information. For example, The *Torrent Webster's Illustrated Encyclopedic Dictionary* includes many color illustrations of terms, a pronunciation key on every other page and two pages of introductory information on how to use the dictionary effectively.

Other highlights of the Torrent Webster are **historic labels** that tell the history of words no longer in common use; **geographic labels** that tell in what part of the world uncommon words are used; **stylistic labels** that tell whether a word is formal, informal, humorous or a slang term; and **field labels** that tell what field of knowledge—such as medicine—the word is used in.

1. Where are guide words found? ___at the top of each page___
2. What is the purpose of guide words? ___They show the first and last words listed on the page.___
3. Which label tells if a word is a slang term? ___stylistic___
4. Which label tells the history of a word? ___historic___
5. Which type of information is not provided for each word in the dictionary?
   - ☐ definition
   - ☐ part of speech
   - ☑ picture

COMPLETE YEAR GRADE 5

269

Week 25 Practice

Using a Dictionary

Use the dictionary entry below to answer the questions.

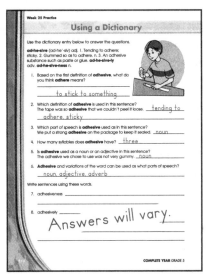

ad-he-sive (ad-he´-siv) adj. 1. Tending to adhere; sticky. 2. Gummed so as to adhere. n. 3. An adhesive substance such as paste or glue. **ad-he-sive-ly** adv. **ad-he-sive-ness** n.

1. Based on the first definition of **adhesive**, what do you think **adhere** means?
   ___to stick to something___
2. Which definition of **adhesive** is used in this sentence? The tape was so **adhesive** that we couldn't peel it loose. ___tending to adhere, sticky___
3. Which part of speech is **adhesive** used as in this sentence? We put a strong **adhesive** on the package to keep it sealed. ___noun___
4. How many syllables does **adhesive** have? ___three___
5. Is **adhesive** used as a noun or an adjective in this sentence? The adhesive we chose to use was not very gummy. ___noun___
6. **Adhesive** and variations of the word can be used as what parts of speech? ___noun, adjective, adverb___

Write sentences using these words.

7. adhesiveness _____
8. adhesively ___Answers will vary.___

COMPLETE YEAR GRADE 5

270

Week 25 Practice

Fractions: Multiplication and Division

Solve.

1. $\frac{7}{9} \times \frac{1}{4} = \frac{7}{36}$
2. $\frac{5}{6} \times \frac{1}{10} = \frac{5}{60} = \frac{1}{12}$
3. $\frac{9}{10} \times \frac{2}{3} = \frac{18}{30} = \frac{3}{5}$

4. $8 \times \frac{1}{4} = \frac{8}{4} = 2$
5. $\frac{1}{3} \times 15 = \frac{15}{3} = 5$

6. Jaime sat in his chair for $\frac{5}{6}$ of an hour. For $\frac{1}{3}$ of this time, he worked on this assignment. What fraction of an hour did he work on this assignment?
   $\frac{1}{3} \times \frac{5}{6} = \frac{5}{18}$

7. $\frac{1}{2} \div \frac{1}{5} = \frac{5}{2} = 2\frac{1}{2}$
8. $\frac{1}{5} \div \frac{1}{2} = \frac{2}{5}$

9. $\frac{3}{4} \div \frac{3}{8} = \frac{4}{2} = 2$
10. $\frac{7}{16} \div \frac{4}{7} = \frac{49}{64}$

COMPLETE YEAR GRADE 5

271

Answer Key

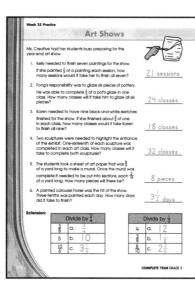

272

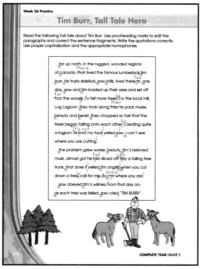

273

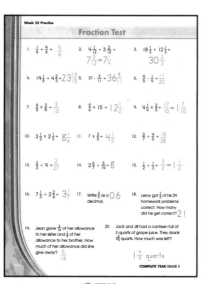

274

276

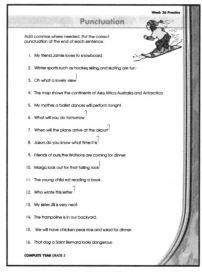

277

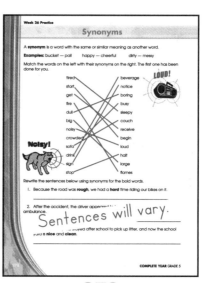

278

Answer Key

Page 279

Finding Synonyms

Circle a word, or group of words, in each sentence that is a synonym for a word in the box. Write the synonym on the line.

| statue | imagination | jealous | future | arrangements |
| furniture | stranger | project | justice | capture |

Example: She will (lend) me her book. loan — loan

1. He tried to (catch) the butterfly. — capture
2. No one knows what will happen in the (time to come.) — future
3. They are loading the (chairs and tables and beds) into the moving van. — furniture
4. We almost finished our team (assignment.) — project
5. They made (plans) to have a class party. — arrangements
6. Penny made a (model) of a horse. — statue
7. The accused man asked the judge for (fairness.) — justice

Write your own sentences for these words: **stranger, imagination, jealous.** Then choose one other word from the box and use it in a sentence. Make each sentence at least ten words long. The sentences should show that you know what the word means.

1. _____
2. _____

Sentences will vary.

Page 280

This Is So Fine

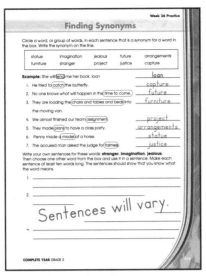

Rewrite each sentence below, replacing the word **fine** with one of the synonyms given. Since the synonyms have slight differences in meaning, be careful to choose the correct one.

Fine: clear, delicate, elegant, small, sharp, subtle

1. The queen wore a **fine** gown encrusted with jewels.
   The queen wore an elegant gown encrusted with jewels.
2. I wash this blouse by hand because of its **fine** lace collar.
   I wash this blouse by hand because of its delicate lace collar.
3. The sand in an hourglass must be very **fine** to trickle as it does.
   The sand in an hourglass must be very small to trickle as it does.
4. We need **fine** weather for sailing.
   We need clear weather for sailing.
5. Dad used a whetstone to put a **fine** edge on the knife.
   Dad used a whetstone to put a sharp edge on the knife.
6. Sometimes there is a **fine** line between innocence and guilt.
   Sometimes there is a subtle line between innocence and guilt.

Page 281

Length in Customary Units

The **customary system** of measurement is the most widely used in the United States. It measures length in inches, feet, yards and miles.

Examples:
12 inches (in.) = 1 foot (ft.)
3 ft. (36 in.) = 1 yard (yd.)
5,280 ft. (1,760 yds.) = 1 mile (mi.)

To change to a larger unit, divide. To change to a smaller unit, multiply.

Examples:
To change inches to feet, divide by 12.   24 in. = 2 ft.   27 in. = 2 ft. 3 in.
To change feet to inches, multiply by 12.   3 ft. = 36 in.   4 ft. = 48 in.
To change inches to yards, divide by 36.   108 in. = 3 yd.   80 in. = 2 yd. 8 in.
To change feet to yards, divide by 3.   12 ft. = 4 yd.   11 ft. = 3 yd. 2 ft.

Sometimes in subtraction you have to borrow units.

Examples:
3 ft. 4 in. = 2 ft. 16 in.   3 yd. = 2 yd. 3 ft.
− 1 ft. 11 in.   − 1 ft. 11 in.   − 1 yd. 2 ft.   − 1 yd. 2 ft.
                 1 ft. 5 in.   1 yd. 1 ft.

Solve the following problems.

1. 108 in. = __9__ ft.
2. 68 in. = __5__ ft. __8__ in.
3. 8 ft. = __2__ yd. __2__ ft.
4. 3,520 yd. = __2__ mi.
5. What form of measurement (inches, feet, yards or miles) would you use for each item below?
   a. pencil __inches__   b. vacation trip __miles__
   c. playground __yards or feet__   d. wall __feet or yards__
6. One side of a square box is 2 ft. 4 in. What is the perimeter of the box? — 9 ft. 4 in.
7. Jason is 54 in. tall. Kent is 5 ft. 1 in. tall. Who is taller and by how much? — Kent, 2 in.
8. Karen bought a doll 2 ft. 8 in. tall for her little sister. She found a box that is 29 in. long. Will the doll fit in that box? — No
9. Dan's dog likes to go out in the backyard, which is 85 ft. wide. The dog's chain is 17 ft. 6 in. long. If Dan attaches one end of the chain to a pole in the middle of the yard, will his dog be able to leave the yard? — No

Page 282

Length in Metric Units

The **metric system** measures length in meters, centimeters, millimeters, and kilometers.

Examples:
A **meter (m)** is about 40 inches or 3.3 feet.
A **centimeter (cm)** is 1/100 of a meter or 0.4 inches.
A **millimeter (mm)** is 1/1000 of a meter or 0.04 inches.
A **kilometer (km)** is 1,000 meters or 0.6 miles.

As before, to find a larger unit divide and multiply to find a smaller unit.

Examples:
To change cm to mm, multiply by 10.
To change cm to meters, divide by 100.
To change mm to meters, divide by 1,000.
To change km to meters, multiply by 1,000.

Solve the following problems.

1. 600 cm = __6__ m   2. 12 cm = __120__ mm   3. 47 m = __700__ cm
4. In the sentences below, write the missing unit: m, cm, mm or km.
   a. A fingernail is about 1 __mm__ thick.
   b. An average car is about 5 __m__ long.
   c. Someone could walk 1 __km__ in 10 minutes.
   d. A finger is about 7 __cm__ long.
   e. A street could be 3 __km__ long.
   f. The Earth is about 40,000 __km__ around at the equator.
   g. A pencil is about 17 __cm__ long.
   h. A noodle is about 4 __mm__ wide.
   i. A teacher's desk is about 1 __m__ wide.
5. A nickel is about 1 mm thick. How many nickels would be in a stack 1 cm high? — 10
6. Is something 25 cm long closer to 10 inches or 10 feet? — 10 inches
7. Is something 18 mm wide closer to 0.7 inch or 7 inches? — 0.7 inch
8. Would you get more exercise running 4 km or 500 m? — 4 km

Page 283

Weight in Customary Units

Here are the main ways to measure weight in customary units:

16 ounces (oz.) = 1 pound (lb.)
2,000 lb. = 1 ton (tn.)
To change ounces to pounds, divide by 16.
To change pounds to ounces, multiply by 16.

BRIDGE UNSAFE FOR TRUCKS OVER 2 TONS

As with measurements of length, you may have to borrow units in subtraction.

Examples:
4 lb. 5 oz. = 3 lb. 21 oz.
− 2 lb. 10 oz.   − 2 lb. 10 oz.
                 1 lb. 11 oz.

Solve the following problems.

1. 48 oz. = __3__ lb.   2. 39 oz. = 2.44 lb.   3. 4 lb. = __64__ oz.
4. What form of measurement would you use for each of these: ounces, pounds or tons?
   a. pencil __ounces__   b. elephant __tons__   c. person __pounds__
5. Which is heavier, 0.25 ton or 750 pounds? — 750 lbs.
6. Twenty-two people, each weighing an average of 150 lb., want to get on an elevator that can carry up to 1.5 tons. How many of them should wait for the next elevator? — 2 people
7. A one-ton truck is carrying 14 boxes that weigh 125 lb. each. It comes to a small bridge with a sign that says, "Bridge unsafe for trucks over 2 tons." Is it safe for the truck and the boxes to cross the bridge? — Yes
8. A large box of Oat Boats contains 2 lb. 3 oz. of cereal, while a box of Honey Hunks contains 1 lb. 14 oz. How many more ounces are in the box of Oat Boats? — 5 oz.
9. A can of Peter's Powdered Drink Mix weighs 2 lb. 5 oz. A can of Petunia's Powdered Drink Mix weighs 40 oz. Which one is heavier? — Petunia's
10. A can of Peter's Drink Mix is 12 cents an ounce. How much does it cost? — $4.44

Page 284

Weight in Metric Units

A **gram (g)** is about 0.035 oz.
A **milligram (mg)** is 1/1000 g or about 0.000035 oz.
A **kilogram (kg)** is 1,000 g or about 2.2 lb.
A **metric ton (t)** is 1,000 kg or about 1.1 lb.

To change g to mg, multiply by 1,000.
To change g to kg, divide by 1,000.
To change kg to g, multiply by 1,000.
To change t to kg, multiply by 1,000.

Solve the following problems.

1. 3 kg = 3,000 g   2. 2 g = 2,000 mg   3. 145 g = 0.145 kg
4. 3,000 kg = __3__ t   5. 0.450 g = 450 mg   6. 3.5 t = 3,500 kg
7. Write the missing units below: g, mg, kg or t.
   a. A sunflower seed weighs less than 1 __g__.
   b. A serving of cereal contains 14 __g__ of sugar.
   c. The same serving of cereal has 250 __mg__ of salt.
   d. A bowling ball weighs about 7 __kg__.
   e. A whale weighs about 90 __t__.
   f. A math textbook weighs about 1 __kg__.
   g. A safety pin weighs about 1 __g__.
   h. An average car weighs about 1 __t__.
8. Is 200 g closer to 7 oz. or 70 oz.? — 7 oz.
9. Is 3 kg closer to 7 lb. or 70 lb.? — 7 lbs.
10. Does a metric ton weigh more or less than a ton measured by the customary system? — more
11. How is a kilogram different from a kilometer? — A kilogram measures weight, a kilometer measures length.
12. Which is heavier, 300 g or 1 kg? — 1 kg

286

Week 27 Practice

Multiple Meanings

Use context clues to determine the meaning of each bold word. The first one has been done for you.

1. My grandfather always has his **spectacles** perched on his nose.

Meaning: _lenses worn in front of the eyes to aid vision_

2. The Fourth of July fireworks display was an amazing **spectacle**.

Meaning: _dramatic public display_

3. We enjoy a rugged vacation, staying in a hunting **lodge** rather than a hotel.

Meaning: _large rustic cabin for vacationers_

4. Don't let the baby have hard candy because it could **lodge** in his throat.

Meaning: _get stuck_

5. Termites will **bore** through the rotten wood in our basement if we don't have it replaced.

Meaning: _to make a hole by digging_

6. That television show could **bore** even a small child!

Meaning: _to weary by being dull_

7. Don't **resort** to lies just to get what you want!

Meaning: _to turn to for help_

8. The **resort** is packed with tourists from May to September each year.

Meaning: _place providing recreation and entertainment_

COMPLETE YEAR GRADE 5

287

Week 27 Practice

Antonyms

An **antonym** is a word with the opposite meaning of another word.

Examples: hot — cold
up — down
start — stop

Match the words on the left with their antonyms on the right. The first one has been done for you.

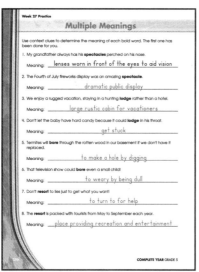

asleep — sloppy
stiff — shut
excited — full
north — awake
wild — tame
hairy — stand
open — bored
quick — bald
neat — south
hungry — slow

In the sentences below, replace each bold word with a synonym or an antonym so that the sentence makes sense. Write the word on the line. Then, write either **synonym** or **antonym** to show its relationship to the given word. The first one has been done for you.

1. If the weather stays warm, all the plants will **perish**. _live-antonym_

2. Last night, mom made my favorite meal, and it was **delicious**.

3. The test was **difficult**, and everyone in the class passed it. _Answers will vary_

4. The music from the concert was so **loud** we could hear it in the parking lot.

5. The bunks at camp were **comfortable**, and I didn't sleep very well.

COMPLETE YEAR GRADE 5

288

Week 27 Practice

Finding Antonyms

Write a word that is an antonym for each bold word in the sentences below.

1. Jared made his way **quickly** through the crowd.

2. My friends and I arrived **late** to the party.

3. My sister loves to watch airplanes.

4. The teacher seem... ...morning.

5. When ... ...your project?

Antonyms will vary.

Write an... ...the following words on the lines. Then write a short paragraph... ...ing all the words you wrote.

dirty _____ whisper _____
old _____ carefully _____
down _____
s... _____

Paragraphs and answers will vary.

COMPLETE YEAR GRADE 5

289

Week 27 Practice

Synonym or Antonym?

Draw a green circle around each word that is a synonym of the first word.
Draw an orange box around each word that is its antonym. Use a dictionary to look up any words you do not know.

forfeit	choose	generous	gain	lose
adjacent	sudden	nearby	clean	remote
pompous	modest	festive	noisy	proud
nosegay	unhappy	bouquet	puncture	weeds
exquisite	careful	beyond	hideous	delightful
impeccable	flawed	perfect	scarce	painful
wary	alert	brittle	unguarded	tired
harry	furry	attract	annoy	soothe
despondent	happily	elegantly	crazily	unhappily
interrogate	cross-examine	dislike	persecute	hush
cull	answer	charge	select	scatter
elude	confront	scold	avoid	frighten

COMPLETE YEAR GRADE 5

290

Week 27 Practice

Capacity in Customary Units

Here are the main ways to measure capacity (how much something will hold) in customary units:

8 fluid ounces (fl. oz.) = 1 cup (c.)
2 c. = 1 pint (pt.)
2 pt. = 1 quart (qt.)
4 qt. = 1 gallon (gal.)

To change ounces to cups, divide by 8.
To change cups to ounces, multiply by 8.
To change cups to pints or quarts, divide by 2.

As with measurements of length and weight, you may have to borrow units in subtraction.

Example: 3 gal. 2 qt. = 2 gal. 6 qt.
  − 1 gal. 3 qt.   − 1 gal. 3 qt.
       1 gal. 3 qt.

Solve the following problems.

1. 32 fl. oz. = _2_ pt. 2. 4 gal. = _32_ pt. 3. _3_ c. = 24 fl. oz.

4. 5 pt. = _2½_ qt. 5. 16 pt. = _2_ gal. 6. 3 pt. = _48_ fl. oz.

7. A large can of soup contains 19 fl. oz. A serving is about 8 oz. How many cans should you buy if you want to serve 7 people? _4_

8. A container of strawberry ice cream holds 36 fl. oz. A container of chocolate ice cream holds 2 pt. Which one has more ice cream? How much more? _strawberry 4 fl. oz._

9. A day-care worker wants to give 15 children each 6 fl. oz. of milk. How many quarts of milk does she need? _3 qt._

10. This morning, the day-care supervisor bought 3 gal. of milk. The kids drank 2 gal. 3 c. How much milk is left for tomorrow? _13 cups_

11. Harriet bought 3 gal. 2 qt. of paint for her living room. She used 3 gal. 3 qt. How much paint is left over? _3 qt._

12. Jason's favorite punch takes a pint of raspberry sherbet. If he wants to make 1½ times the recipe, how many fl. oz. of sherbet does he need? _24 fl. oz._

COMPLETE YEAR GRADE 5

291

Week 27 Practice

Capacity in Metric Units

A **liter** (L) is a little over 1 quart.
A **milliliter** (mL) is 1/1000 of a liter or about 0.03 oz.
A **kiloliter** (kL) is 1,000 liters or about 250 gallons.

Solve the following problems.

1. 5,000 mL = _5_ L

2. 2,000 L = _2_ kL

3. 3 L = _3,000_ mL

4. Write the missing unit: L, mL, or kL.

a. A swimming pool holds about 100 _kL_ of water.

b. An eyedropper is marked for 1 and 2 _mL_ of medicine.

c. A pitcher could hold 1 or 2 _L_ of juice.

d. A teaspoon holds about 5 _mL_ of medicine.

e. A birdbath might hold 5 _L_ of water.

f. A tablespoon holds about 15 _mL_ of salt.

g. A bowl holds about 250 _mL_ of soup.

h. We drank about 4 _L_ of punch at the party.

5. Which is more, 3 L or a gallon? _gallon_

6. Which is more, 400 mL or 40 oz.? _40 oz._

7. Which is more, 1 kL or 500 L? _1 kL_

8. Is 4 L closer to a quart or a gallon? _gallon_

9. Is 480 mL closer to 2 cups or 2 pints? _2 cups_

10. Is a mL closer to 4 drops or 4 teaspoonful? _4 drops_

11. How many glasses of juice containing 250 mL each could you pour from a 1-L jug? _4 glasses_

12. How much water would you need to water an average-sized lawn, 1 kL or 1 L? _1 kL_

COMPLETE YEAR GRADE 5

Answer Key

292

Week 27 Practice

Capacity

The **fluid ounce, cup, pint, quart** and **gallon** are used to measure capacity in the United States.

I cup | I pint | I quart | I half gallon | I gallon

8 fluid ounces (fl. oz.) = I cup (c.)
2 cups = I pint (pt.)
2 pints = I quart (qt.)
2 quarts = I half gallon (½ gal.)
4 quarts = I gallon (gal.)

Convert the units of capacity.

13 gal. = **52** qt.   10 pt. = **20** c.   12 c. = **6** pt.

4 gal. = **16** qt.   16 qt. = **4** gal.   5 c. = **2½** pt.

36 pt. = **4½** gal.   12 qt. = **24** pt.   6 gal. = **48** pt.

16 c. = **4** qt.   32 oz. = **4** c.   16 oz. = **1** pt.

COMPLETE YEAR GRADE 5

293

Week 27 Practice

Units of Capacity

Complete each equation so that it equals I gallon.

1. 3 qt. + **1** qt. = I gal.
2. 4 c. + 2 pt. + **2** = I gal.
3. 2 c. + I pt. + **3** = I gal.
4. 3 qt. + 2 c. + **2** c. = I gal.

I pt. = 2 c.   I qt. = 2 pt.   I gal. = 4 qt.

5. 2 pt. + **2** qt. + I qt. = I gal.
6. 6 c. + **2** c. + 2 qt. = I gal.

Match each equivalent capacity.

Which unit would best measure each example below?
1. Amount of water used to take a shower **gallons**
2. Amount of flour to make bread **cups**
3. Amount of water to fill your pool **gallons**
4. A single serving of yogurt **cups**
5. A container of motor oil **quarts**

gallons
cups
pints
quarts

COMPLETE YEAR GRADE 5

294

Week 27 Practice

Weight and Capacity

Weight
I pound (lb.) = 16 ounces (oz.)
I ton (T.) = 2,000 pounds

Capacity
I cup (c.) = 8 fluid ounces (fl. oz.)
I pint (pt.) = 2 cups
I quart (qt.) = 2 pints
I gallon (gal.) = 4 quarts

Example I
To change from a larger unit to a smaller unit, multiply.
5 T. = _____ lb.
I T. = 2,000 lb.
5 x 2,000 = 10,000
5 T. = 10,000 lb.

Example 2
To change from a smaller unit to a larger unit, divide.
176 fl. oz. = _____ c.
8 fl. oz. = I c.
176 ÷ 8 = 22
176 fl. oz. = 22 c.

Example 3
Express remainders in terms of the original unit.
25 c. = 12 pt. I c.
25 c. = _____ pt.
2 c. = I pt.
25 ÷ 2 = 12 R I

Complete.
1. 16 pt. = **8** qt.   2. 12 gal. = **48** qt.   3. 5 lb. = **80** oz.
4. 150 oz. = **9** lb. **6** oz.   5. 5 gal. 3 qt. = **23** qt.   6. 2 lb. 3 oz. = **35** oz.

Compare using >, <, =.
7. I gal. **<** 6 qt.   8. 560 oz. **=** 35 lb.   9. 15 pt. **>** 25 c.

COMPLETE YEAR GRADE 5

300

Week 28 Practice

Spelling: Syllables

A **syllable** is a part of a word with only one vowel sound. Some words have only one syllable, like **eat**, **leaf** and **ship**. Some words have two or more syllables. **Be-lief** and **trac-tor** have two syllables. **to-geth-er** and **ex-cel-lent** have three syllables and **con-ver-sa-tion** has four syllables. Some words can have six or more syllables! The word **ex-tra-ter-res-tri-al**, for example, has six syllables.

Be lief

Follow the instructions below.

1. Count the syllables in each word below, and write the number of syllables on the line.
   a. badger **2**   f. grease **1**
   b. location **3**   g. relationship **4**
   c. award **2**   h. communication **5**
   d. national **3**   i. government **3**
   e. necessary **4**   j. Braille **1**

2. Write four words with four syllables each in the blanks.
   a. _____ Answers will vary. _____
   b. _____

3. Write one word with five syllables and one with six syllables. If you need help, use a dictionary.
   Five syllables: _____ Answers will vary. _____
   Six syllables: _____

COMPLETE YEAR GRADE 5

301

Week 28 Practice

Y Says "I"

Match each word from the list to its proper pronunciation. Refer to a dictionary, if necessary.

bylaw
cycle
cyclone
dynamic
dynamite
dynasty
gyrate
hydrant
hydraulic
hydrogen
hygiene
hyphen
hypothesis
lyre
python
typhoon
typist
tyrant

hyphen   **hī′ fen**
hygiene   **hī′ jēn**
gyrate   **jī′ rāt**
bylaw   **bī′ lô**
typhoon   **tī foon′**
hydrant   **hī′ drent**
hydraulic   **hī drô′ lik**

dynamic   **dī năm′ ik**
typist   **tī′ pist**
cycle   **sī′ kel**
dynamite   **dī′ ne mīt**
python   **pī′ thŏn**
dynasty   **dī′ ne stē**
hypothesis   **hī pŏth′ ĭ sis**

cyclone   **sī′ klōn**   tyrant   **tī′ rent**
hydrogen   **hī′ dre jen**   lyre   **fr**

Write a metaphor using the words. A metaphor is a direct comparison that does not use **like** or **as** to compare one thing to another. **Example:** The typhoon was an enraged monster destroying the small oceanside town.

_____ Answers will vary. _____

COMPLETE YEAR GRADE 5

302

Week 28 Practice

Spelling: Finding Mistakes

Circle the four spelling mistakes in each paragraph. Then write the words correctly on the lines below.

Last nite our family went to a nice restaurant. As we were lookeing at the menus, a waiter walked in from the kichen carrying a large tray of food. As he walked by us, he triped and the tray went flying! The food flew all over our table and all over us, too!

night   **looking**
tripped   **kitchen**

Last week, while my dad was washing the car, our dog Jack dicided to help. He stuck his nose in the pale of soapy water, and it tiped over and soaked him! As he shook himself off, the water from his fur went all over the car. "Look!" Dad offed. "Jack is doing his part!"

decided   **pail**
tipped   **laughed**

For our next feld trip, my class is going to the zoo. We have been studying about animals in sceince class. I'm very exsited to see the elephants, but my friend Karen really wants to see the monkeys. She has been to the zoo before, and she says the monkeys are the most fun to watch.

field   **science**
excited   **friend**

It seems the rain will never stop! It has been raining for seven days now, and the sky is always dark and cloudy. Everyone at school is in a bad mood, because we have to stay inside during reses. Will we ever see the son again?

raining   **cloudy**
recess   **sun**

COMPLETE YEAR GRADE 5

Answer Key

Spelling: Proofreading Practice

Week 28 Practice

Circle the six spelling and pronoun mistakes in each paragraph. Write the words correctly on the lines below.

Jenna always braged about being ready to meet any chalenge or reach any gole. When it was time for our class to elekt it's new officers, Jenna said we should voat for her to be president.

bragged	challenge	goal
elect	its	vote

Simon wanted to be our president, too. He tried to coaks everyone to vote for his. He even lowned kids money to get their votes! Well, Jenna may have too much pryde in herself, but I like her in spit of that. At least she didn't try to buy our votes!

our	coax	him
loaned	pride	spite

Its true that Jenna tried other ways to get us to vote for hers. She scrubed the chalkboards even though it was my dayly job for that week. One day, I saw her rinseing out the paintbrushes when it was Peter's turn to do it. Then she made sure we knew about her good deeds so we would praize her.

It's	her	scrubbed
daily	rinsing	praise

We held the election, but I was shalked when the teacher releesed the results. Simon won! I wondered if he cheeted somehow. I feel like our class was robed. Now Simon is the one who's braging about how great he is. I wish he knew the tite of president doesn't mean anything if no one wants to be around you!

shocked	released	cheated
robbed	bragging	title

COMPLETE YEAR GRADE 5

303

Summer Daze

Week 28 Practice

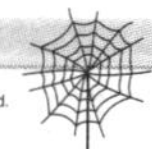

Write the number of the definition that applies to each **bold** word.

3 1. When Mr. Wong works, he never **putters** around.

2 2. Mabel would **cop** the prize as the best stickball player in the sixth grade.

2 3. The two small girls will **stalk** the tiger swallowtail very carefully.

3 4. The **cop** smiled as Shirley humbly scurried by.

1 5. I would wear gloves if I wished to climb that **spruce** in the forest.

2 6. Shirley imagined spiders **stalking** her in the furnace room.

1 7. She never considered that she might **cop** fruit from the market.

3 8. Will the students **spruce** up the playground before they leave for the summer?

2 9. The **putter** missed the ninth hole by a mile.

1 10. Shirley discovered that she liked celery **stalks** very much.

Glossary

stalk 1) a plant stem 2) to stealthily pursue one's prey 3) to walk with a slow, stiff stride

putter 1) a golf club used on the green 2) a golfer who putts 3) to work slowly

cop 1) to steal 2) to capture 3) a police officer

spruce 1) an evergreen tree 2) the wood from this tree 3) to make neat

COMPLETE YEAR GRADE 5

304

Temperature

Week 28 Practice

The customary system measures temperature in Fahrenheit (F°) degrees.

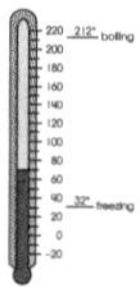

The metric system uses Celsius (C°) degrees.

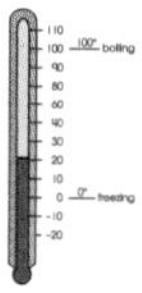

Study the thermometers and answer these questions.

1. Write in the temperature from both systems:

	Fahrenheit	Celsius
a. freezing	32°	0°
b. boiling	212°	100°
c. comfortable room temperature	Answers	will vary.
d. normal body temperature	98.6°	37°

2. Underline the most appropriate temperature for both systems.

a. a reasonably hot day	34°	54°	(84°)	10°	20°	(35°)
b. a cup of hot chocolate	(95°)	120°	190°	(60°)	90°	120°
c. comfortable water to swim in	55°	(75°)	95°	10°	25°	(40°)

3. If the temperature is 35°C is it summer or winter? Summer
4. Would ice cream stay frozen at 35°F? No
5. Which is colder, -10°C or -10°F? -10°F
6. Which is warmer, 60°C or 60°F? 60°C

COMPLETE YEAR GRADE 5

305

Comparing Measurements

Week 28 Practice

Use the symbols greater than (>), less than (<) or equal to (=) to complete each statement.

10 inches	>	10 centimeters
40 feet	<	120 yards
25 grams	<	25 kilograms
16 quarts	=	4 gallons
2 liters	>	2 milliliters
16 yards	>	6 meters
3 miles	>	3 kilometers
20 centimeters	<	20 meters
85 kilograms	>	8 grams
2 liters	<	1 gallon

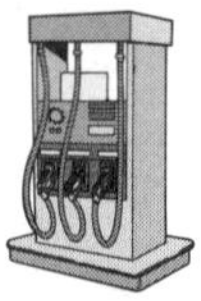

COMPLETE YEAR GRADE 5

306

Conversion

Week 28 Practice

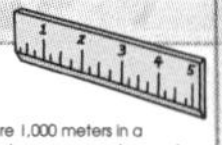

Find the number of units in each fraction described.

1. If there are 12 eggs in a dozen, how many eggs are in . . .
   - $\frac{1}{2}$ dozen? 6
   - $\frac{1}{4}$ dozen? 3
   - $\frac{1}{3}$ dozen? 4
2. If there are 100 centimeters (cm) in a meter, how many cm are in . . .
   - $\frac{1}{2}$ meter? 50
   - $\frac{1}{4}$ meter? 25
   - $\frac{1}{10}$ meter? 10
3. If there are 16 ounces in a pound, how many ounces are in . . .
   - $\frac{1}{2}$ pound? 8
   - $\frac{1}{4}$ pound? 4
   - $\frac{3}{8}$ pound? 6
4. If there are 4 quarts in a gallon, how many quarts are in . . .
   - $\frac{1}{2}$ gallon? 2
   - $\frac{1}{4}$ gallon? 1
   - $\frac{3}{4}$ gallon? 3
5. If there are 60 seconds in a minute, how many seconds are in . . .
   - $\frac{1}{2}$ minute? 30
   - $\frac{1}{4}$ minute? 15
   - $\frac{3}{4}$ minute? 45
6. If there are 1,000 meters in a kilometer, how many meters are in . . .
   - $\frac{1}{10}$ kilometer? 100
   - $\frac{1}{2}$ kilometer? 500
   - $\frac{1}{4}$ kilometer? 250
7. If there are 30 days in most months, how many days are in . . .
   - $\frac{1}{3}$ month? 10
   - $\frac{1}{6}$ month? 5
   - $\frac{1}{10}$ month? 3
8. If there are 24 hours in a day, how many hours are in . . .
   - $\frac{1}{3}$ day? 8
   - $\frac{2}{3}$ day? 16
   - $\frac{1}{4}$ day? 6
9. If there are 36 inches in a yard, how many inches are in . . .
   - $\frac{2}{3}$ yard? 24
   - $\frac{1}{4}$ yard? 9
   - $\frac{1}{2}$ yard? 18
10. If there are 2,000 pounds in a ton, how many pounds are in . . .
    - $\frac{1}{2}$ ton? 1,000
    - $\frac{1}{4}$ ton? 500
    - $\frac{1}{20}$ ton? 100

COMPLETE YEAR GRADE 5

307

Adding Inches and Feet

Week 28 Practice

When adding inches, regroup 1 foot for every 12 inches.

Examples:

a. 1 ft. 8 in. + 1 ft. 8 in. = 16 in.
16 in. = 1 ft. 4 in.

b. 1 ft. 8 in. + 1 ft. 8 in. = 4 in. (regroup 1)

c. 1 ft. 8 in. + 1 ft. 8 in. = 3 ft. 4 in. (regroup 1)

1. 2 ft. 4 in. + 1 ft. 9 in. = 4 ft. 1 in.
2. 12 ft. 10 in. + 1 ft. 5 in. = 14 ft. 3 in.
3. 12 ft. 7 in. + 8 ft. 8 in. = 21 ft. 3 in.
4. 1 ft. 5 in. + 3 ft. 6 in. = 4 ft. 11 in.
5. 1 ft. 6 in. + 1 ft. 6 in. = 3 ft. 0 in.
6. 7 ft. 4 in. + 5 ft. 5 in. = 12 ft. 9 in.
7. 28 ft. 8 in. + 4 ft. 9 in. = 33 ft. 5 in.
8. 8 ft. 9 in. + 7 in. = 9 ft. 4 in.
9. 3 ft. 3 in. + 6 ft. 7 in. = 9 ft. 10 in.

COMPLETE YEAR GRADE 5

308

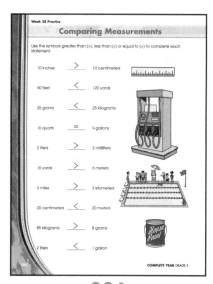

Page 310

Subjects and Predicates

The **subject** tells who or what a sentence is about. The **predicate** tells what the subject does, did or is doing. All complete sentences must have a subject and a predicate.

Examples:

Subject	Predicate
Hamsters	are common pets.
Pets	need special care.

Circle the subjects and underline the predicates.

1. Many children keep hamsters as pets.
2. Mice are good pets, too.
3. Hamsters collect food in their cheeks.
4. My sister sneezes around furry animals.
5. My brother wants a dog instead of a hamster.

Write subjects to complete these sentences.

6. _____ has two pet hamsters.
7. _____ got a new pet last week.
8. _____ to feed his goldfish.

Write predicates to com~~plete~~   *Answers will vary.*

9. Baby hamsts _____
10. Pet mice _____
11. If _____

Write **S** if the group of words is a sentence or **NS** if the group of words is not a sentence.

12. NS   A new cage for our hamster.
13. NS   Picked the cutest one.
14. S   We started out with two.
15. NS   Liking every one in the store.

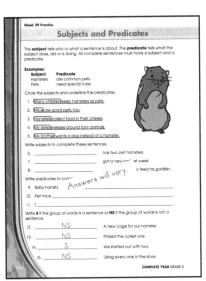

COMPLETE YEAR GRADE 5

Page 311

Combining Subjects

Too many short sentences make writing sound choppy. Often, we can combine sentences with different subjects and the same predicate to make one sentence with a compound subject.

Example:

Lisa tried out for the play. Todd tried out for the play.
Compound subject: Lisa and Todd tried out for the play.

When sentences have different subjects and different predicates, we cannot combine them this way. Each subject and predicate must stay together. Two short sentences can be combined with a conjunction.

Examples:

Lisa got a part in the play. Todd will help make scenery.
Lisa got a part in the play, and Todd will help make scenery.

If a pair of sentences share the same predicate, combine them with compound subjects. If the sentences have different subjects and predicates, combine them using **and**.

1. Rachel read a book about explorers. Eric read the same book about explorers.
   Rachel and Eric read a book about explorers.
2. Rachel really liked the book. Eric agreed with her.
   Rachel really liked the book, and Eric agreed with her.
3. Vicki went to the basketball game last night. Dan went to the basketball game, too.
   Vicki and Dan went to the basketball game last night.
4. Vicki lost her coat. Dan missed his ride home.
   Vicki lost her coat, and Dan missed his ride home.
5. My uncle planted corn in the garden. My mother planted corn in the garden.
   My uncle and my mother planted corn in the garden.
6. Isaac helped with the food drive last week. Amy helped with the food drive, too.
   Isaac and Amy helped with the food drive last week.

COMPLETE YEAR GRADE 5

Page 312

Combining Predicates

If short sentences have the same subject and different predicates, we can combine them into one sentence with a compound predicate.

Example:

Andy got up late this morning.
He nearly missed the school bus.
Compound predicate: Andy got up late this morning and nearly missed the school bus.

The pronoun **he** takes the place of Andy in the second sentence, so the subjects are the same and can be combined.

When two sentences have different subjects and different predicates, we cannot combine them this way. Two short sentences can be combined with a conjunction.

Examples:

Andy got up late this morning. Cindy woke up early.
Andy got up late this morning, but Cindy woke up early.

If the pair of sentences share the same subject, combine them with compound predicates. If the sentences have different subjects and predicates, combine them using **and** or **but**.

1. Kyle practiced pitching all winter. Kyle became the pitcher for his team.
   Kyle practiced pitching all winter and became the pitcher for his team.
2. Kisha studied two hours for her history test. Angela watched TV.
   Kisha studied two hours for her history test, but Angela watched TV.
3. Jeff had an earache. He took medicine four times a day.
   Jeff had an earache and took medicine four times a day.
4. Nikki found a new hairstyle. Melissa didn't like that style.
   Nikki found a new hairstyle, but Melissa didn't like that style.
5. Kirby buys his lunch every day. Sean brings his lunch from home.
   Kirby buys his lunch every day, but Sean brings his lunch from home.

COMPLETE YEAR GRADE 5

Page 313

Compound Subjects and Predicates

A compound subject has two or more nouns or pronouns joined by a conjunction. Compound subjects share the same predicate.

Examples:

Suki and Spot walked to the park in the rain.
Cars, buses and trucks splashed water on them.
He and I were glad we had our umbrella.

A compound predicate has two or more verbs joined by a conjunction. Compound predicates share the same subject.

Examples:

Suki **went** in the restroom **and wiped** off her shoes.
Paula **followed** Suki **and waited** for her.

A sentence can have a compound subject and a compound predicate.

Example: **Tina and Maria went** to the mall **and shopped** for an hour.
Circle the compound subjects. Underline the compound predicates.

1. Steve and Jerry went to the store and bought some gum.
2. Police and firefighters worked together and put out the fire.
3. Karen and Marsha did their homework and checked it twice.
4. In preschool, the boys and girls drew pictures and colored them.

Write compound subjects to go with these predicates.

5. _____ ate peanut butter sandwiches.
6. _____ left early.
7. _____ don't make good pets. *Answers will vary.*
8. _____ found their way home.
9. _____ are moving to Denver.

Write compound predicates to go with these subjects.

10. A scary book _____
11. My friend's sister _____
12. The shadow _____
13. The wind _____   *Answers will vary.*
14. The runaway car _____

COMPLETE YEAR GRADE 5

Page 314

Joining Sentences

Conjunctions are words that join sentences, words or ideas. When two sentences are joined with **and**, they are more or less equal.

Example: Julio is coming, **and** he is bringing cookies.

When two sentences are joined with **but**, the second sentence contradicts the first one.

Example: Julio is coming, **but** he will be late.

When two sentences are joined with **or**, they name a choice.

Example: Julio might bring cookies, **or** he might bring a cake.

When two sentences are joined with **because**, the second one names the reason for the first one.

Example: I'll bring cookies, too, **because** Julio might forget his.

When two sentences are joined with **so**, the second one names a result of the first one.

Example: Julio is bringing cookies, **so** we will have a snack.

Complete each sentence. The first one has been done for you.

1. We could watch TV, or we could play a game.
2. I wanted to seize the opportunity, but _____
3. You had better not deceive me, because _____
4. My neighbor was on vacation, so _____
5. Veins take blood _____   *Sentences will vary.*
6. You _____ your impulses, because _____
7. I know _____ is your belief, but _____
8. It could be reindeer on the roof, or _____
9. Brent was determined to achieve his goal, so _____
10. Brittany was proud of her height, because _____

COMPLETE YEAR GRADE 5

Page 315

Subtracting Different Units

Subtract the units. Regroup the feet and inches.

Example:

```
    3 ft.  5 in.
  - 1 ft.  8 in.
```
Cannot take 8 from 5, so regroup 1 foot.
```
    2   12 in.
    3 ft.  5 in.
  - 1 ft.  8 in.
```
```
    2   17 in.
    3 ft.  5 in.
  - 1 ft.  8 in.
    1 ft.  9 in.
```

1.
```
    5 ft.  8 in.
  - 3 ft.  9 in.
    1 ft. 11 in.
```
2.
```
   17 ft.  3 in.
  -       5 in.
   16 ft. 10 in.
```
3.
```
   11 ft.  5 in.
  - 8 ft.  6 in.
    2 ft. 11 in.
```
4.
```
   20 ft.  4 in.
  - 6 ft.  8 in.
   13 ft.  8 in.
```
5.
```
   17 ft.  0 in.
  - 1 ft.  6 in.
   15 ft.  6 in.
```
6.
```
   115 ft.
  -  7 ft.  8 in.
   107 ft.  4 in.
```

7. The carpenter's board was 8 ft. 8 in. long. She cut off 1 ft. 10 in. to use on a bench. How much of the board was left?
   6 ft. 10 in.

Subtract the units. Regroup the days and weeks.

Example:

```
   3 weeks  1 day
  - 1 week   5 days
```
Cannot take 5 from 1, so regroup 1 week.
```
   2    + 7 days
   3 weeks  1 day
  - 1 week   5 days
```
```
   2    8 days
   3 weeks  1 day
  - 1 week   5 days
   1 week   3 days
```

8.
```
   4 weeks  2 days
  - 2 weeks  5 days
   1 week   4 days
```
9.
```
   3 weeks  5 days
  - 1 week   2 days
   2 week   3 days
```
10.
```
   11 weeks  4 days
  -  7 weeks  4 days
   4 week   0 days
```

COMPLETE YEAR GRADE 5

Page 316

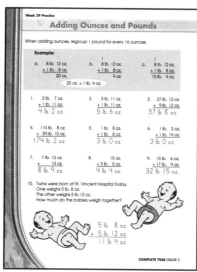

Week 29 Practice

Adding Ounces and Pounds

When adding ounces, regroup 1 pound for every 16 ounces.

Example:

a. 8 lb. 12 oz.
  + 1 lb. 8 oz.
  20 oz.
  20 oz. = 1 lb. 4 oz.

b. 8 lb. 12 oz.
  + 1 lb. 8 oz.
  4 oz.

c. 8 lb. 12 oz.
  + 1 lb. 8 oz.
  10 lb. 4 oz.

1. 2 lb. 7 oz. + 1 lb. 11 oz. = **4 lb. 2 oz.**
2. 3 lb. 11 oz. + 1 lb. 11 oz. = **5 lb. 6 oz.**
3. 27 lb. 12 oz. + 9 lb. 12 oz. = **37 lb. 8 oz.**
4. 114 lb. 8 oz. + 59 lb. 10 oz. = **174 lb. 2 oz.**
5. 1 lb. 8 oz. + 1 lb. 8 oz. = **3 lb. 0 oz.**
6. 1 lb. 2 oz. + 1 lb. 14 oz. = **3 lb. 0 oz.**
7. 7 lb. 12 oz. + 13 oz. = **8 lb. 9 oz.**
8. 15 oz. + 3 lb. 8 oz. = **4 lb. 4 oz.**
9. 15 lb. 6 oz. + 17 lb. 9 oz. = **32 lb. 15 oz.**

10. Twins were born at St. Vincent Hospital today. One weighs 5 lb. 8 oz. The other weighs 5 lb. 12 oz. How much do the babies weigh together?

5 lb. 8 oz. + 5 lb. 12 oz. = **11 lb. 4 oz.**

COMPLETE YEAR GRADE 5

316

Page 317

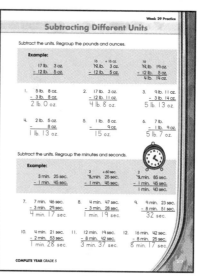

Week 29 Practice

Subtracting Different Units

Subtract the units. Regroup the pounds and ounces.

Example:

17 lb. 3 oz. − 12 lb. 5 oz.

16 (+16 oz.) lb. 3 oz. − 12 lb. 5 oz.

16 lb. 19 oz. − 12 lb. 5 oz.
4 lb. 14 oz.

1. 5 lb. 8 oz. − 3 lb. 8 oz. = **2 lb. 0 oz.**
2. 17 lb. 3 oz. − 12 lb. 11 oz. = **4 lb. 8 oz.**
3. 9 lb. 11 oz. − 3 lb. 14 oz. = **5 lb. 13 oz.**
4. 2 lb. 5 oz. − 8 oz. = **1 lb. 13 oz.**
5. 1 lb. 8 oz. − 9 oz. = **15 oz.**
6. 7 lb. − 1 lb. 9 oz. = **5 lb. 7 oz.**

Subtract the units. Regroup the minutes and seconds.

Example:

3 min. 25 sec. − 1 min. 45 sec.

2 (+60 sec.) min. 25 sec. − 1 min. 45 sec.

2 min. 85 sec. − 1 min. 45 sec.
1 min. 40 sec.

7. 7 min. 46 sec. − 3 min. 29 sec. = **4 min. 17 sec.**
8. 4 min. 47 sec. − 3 min. 28 sec. = **1 min. 19 sec.**
9. 9 min. 23 sec. − 8 min. 51 sec. = **32 sec.**
10. 4 min. 21 sec. − 2 min. 53 sec. = **1 min. 28 sec.**
11. 12 min. 19 sec. − 8 min. 42 sec. = **3 min. 37 sec.**
12. 16 min. 42 sec. − 8 min. 25 sec. = **8 min. 17 sec.**

COMPLETE YEAR GRADE 5

317

Page 318

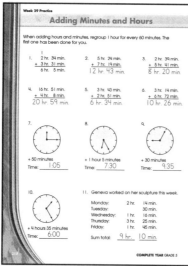

Week 29 Practice

Adding Minutes and Hours

When adding hours and minutes, regroup 1 hour for every 60 minutes. The first one has been done for you.

1. 2 hr. 34 min. + 3 hr. 31 min. = **6 hr. 5 min.**
2. 5 hr. 24 min. + 7 hr. 19 min. = **12 hr. 43 min.**
3. 2 hr. 39 min. + 5 hr. 41 min. = **8 hr. 20 min.**
4. 16 hr. 51 min. + 4 hr. 8 min. = **20 hr. 59 min.**
5. 3 hr. 43 min. + 2 hr. 51 min. = **6 hr. 34 min.**
6. 3 hr. 14 min. + 6 hr. 72 min. = **10 hr. 26 min.**

7. + 50 minutes   Time: **1:05**
8. + 1 hour 5 minutes   Time: **7:30**
9. + 30 minutes   Time: **9:35**

10. + 4 hours 35 minutes   Time: **6:00**

11. Geneva worked on her sculpture this week.

Monday:	2 hr. 14 min.
Tuesday:	30 min.
Wednesday:	1 hr. 16 min.
Thursday:	3 hr. 25 min.
Friday:	1 hr. 45 min.

Sum total: **9 hr. 10 min.**

COMPLETE YEAR GRADE 5

318

Page 320

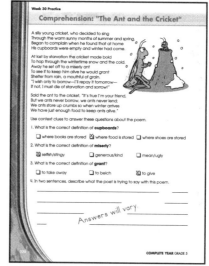

Week 30 Practice

Comprehension: "The Ant and the Cricket"

A silly young cricket, who decided to sing
Through the warm sunny months of summer and spring,
Began to complain when he found that at home
His cupboards were empty and winter had come.

At last by starvation the cricket made bold
To hop through the wintertime snow and the cold.
Away he set off to a miserly ant
To see if to keep him alive he would grant
Shelter from rain, a mouthful of grain.
"I wish only to borrow—I'll repay it tomorrow—
If not, I must die of starvation and sorrow!"

Said the ant to the cricket, "It's true I'm your friend,
But we ants never borrow, we ants never lend;
We ants store up crumbs so when winter arrives
We have just enough food to keep ants alive."

Use context clues to answer these questions about the poem.

1. What is the correct definition of **cupboards**?
☐ where books are stored ☒ where food is stored ☐ where shoes are stored

2. What is the correct definition of **miserly**?
☒ selfish/stingy ☐ generous/kind ☐ mean/ugly

3. What is the correct definition of **grant**?
☐ to take away ☐ to belch ☒ to give

4. In two sentences, describe what the poet is trying to say with this poem.

Answers will vary.

COMPLETE YEAR GRADE 5

320

Page 321

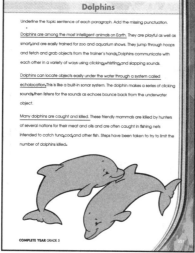

Week 30 Practice

Dolphins

Underline the topic sentence of each paragraph. Add the missing punctuation.

__Dolphins are among the most intelligent animals on Earth.__ They are playful as well as smart, and easily trained for zoo and aquarium shows. They jump through hoops and fetch and grab objects from the trainer's hands. Dolphins communicate with each other in a variety of ways using clicking, whistling, and slapping sounds.

__Dolphins can locate objects easily under the water through a system called echolocation.__ This is like a built-in sonar system. The dolphin makes a series of clicking sounds, then listens for the sounds as echoes bounce back from the underwater object.

Many dolphins are caught and killed. These friendly mammals are killed by hunters of several nations for their meat and oils and are often caught in fishing nets intended to catch tuna, cod, and other fish. Steps have been taken to try to limit the number of dolphins killed.

COMPLETE YEAR GRADE 5

321

Page 323

Week 30 Practice

Understanding Rembrandt

Answer the questions below from your reading of page 322.

True or False

Rembrandt . . .
_T_ was one of the greatest artists of all time.
_F_ was born on July 15, 1606, in Florence, Italy.
_T_ began to paint at an early age.
_F_ traveled to Amsterdam at the age of fifteen to study architecture.

Check and write:

Rembrandt used ☐ soft ☒ bright colors and _glossy_ paints.

Underline:

In 1634, Rembrandt married . . .
__a wealthy and educated girl named Saskia.__
a poor girl from Amsterdam named Saskia.

Check and write:

Although Rembrandt was successful as an artist,
☒ tragedy ☐ good fortune began to strike his family.

Three of his _4_ children died at a very early age.

In 1642, ☐ Rembrandt's father died. ☒ Rembrandt's wife died.

Rembrandt's sadness caused him to use ☒ darker ☐ lighter colors.

Check, circle and write:

Rembrandt died on October 4, ☒ 1669. ☐ 1700.

Rembrandt's most famous painting was called _The Night Watch_.

Rembrandt's works included:
☒ paintings ☒ drawings ☒ etchings ☒ self-portraits

COMPLETE YEAR GRADE 5

323

Answer Key

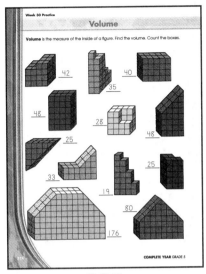

324

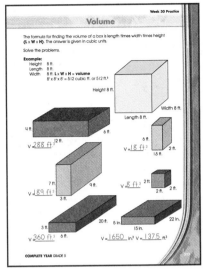

325

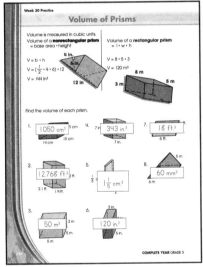

326

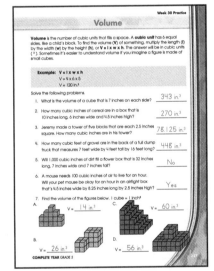

327

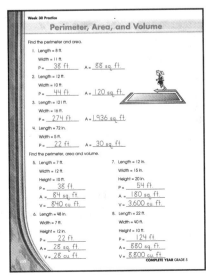

328

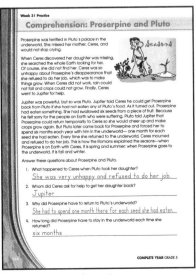

330

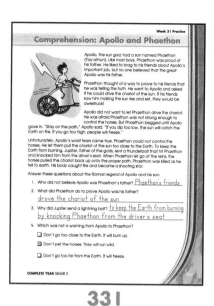

331

Proofreading

Proofreading or "proofing" means to carefully look over what has been written, checking for spelling, grammar, punctuation and other errors. At a newspaper, this is the job of a copyeditor. All good writers carefully proofread and correct their own work before turning it in to a copyeditor—or a teacher.

Here are three common proofreading marks:

Correct spelling ~~der~~ dog

Replace with lowercase letter ✗

Replace with uppercase letter a

Carefully read the following paragraphs. Use proofreading marks to mark errors in the second paragraph. Correct all errors. The first sentence has been done for you.

alarm
A six ~~alarm~~ fire at 2121 Windsor Terrace on the northeast

Eleven building
side awoke apartment ✗esidents at 3 A.M. yesterday

blaze
morning. ~~Eleven~~ people were in the ~~blabing~~. No one was

hurt in the ~~blaze~~ which caused $200,000 of property

damage. Property alarm
~~Property~~ manager Jim smith credits a perfectly ✗unctioning smoke-~~alarm~~ system

sprinkler was
for waking residents so they could get out safely. A ~~springler~~ system ~~were~~ also

place panic Everyone
in ~~place~~. "There was ~~no panic~~," Smith said proudly. "~~Everone~~ was calm and

✗rderly."

332

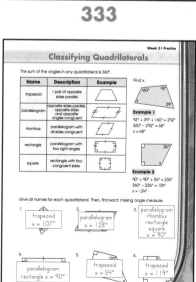

333

Types of Quadrilaterals

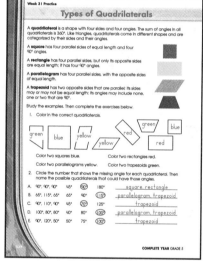

334

Classifying Quadrilaterals

The sum of the angles in any quadrilateral is 360°.

Name	Description	Example
trapezoid	1 pair of opposite sides parallel	
parallelogram	opposite sides parallel, opposite sides and opposite angles congruent	
rhombus	parallelogram with all sides congruent	
rectangle	parallelogram with four right angles	
square	rectangle with four congruent sides	

Find x.

Example 1
93° + 39° + 160° = 292°
360° − 292° = 68°
x = 68°

Example 2
90° + 90° + 56° = 236°
360° − 236° = 124°
x = 124°

Give all names for each quadrilateral. Then, find each missing angle measure.

1. trapezoid
   x = 107°

2. parallelogram
   x = 128°

3. parallelogram
   rhombus
   rectangle
   square
   x = 90°

4. parallelogram
   rectangle x = 90°

5. trapezoid
   x = 54°

6. trapezoid
   x = 119°

337

Shapes in Hiding

Shade triangles to make each shape.

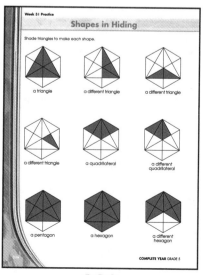

a triangle · a different triangle · a different triangle

a different triangle · a quadrilateral · a different quadrilateral

a pentagon · a hexagon · a different hexagon

338

Answer Key

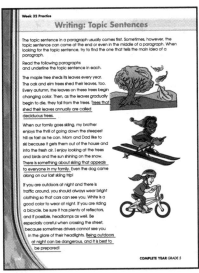

340

Writing: Topic Sentences

The topic sentence in a paragraph usually comes first. Sometimes, however, the topic sentence can come at the end or even in the middle of a paragraph. When looking for the topic sentence, try to find the one that tells the main idea of a paragraph.

Read the following paragraphs and underline the topic sentence in each.

The maple tree sheds its leaves every year. The oak and elm trees shed their leaves, too. Every autumn, the leaves on these trees begin changing color. Then, as the leaves gradually begin to die, they fall from the trees. Trees that shed their leaves annually are called deciduous trees.

When our family goes skiing, my brother enjoys the thrill of going down the steepest hill as fast as he can. Mom and Dad like to ski because it gets them out of the house and into the fresh air. I enjoy looking at the trees and birds and the sun shining on the snow. There is something about skiing that appeals to everyone in my family. Even the dog came along on our last skiing trip!

If you are outdoors at night and there is traffic around, you should always wear bright clothing so that cars can see you. White is a good color to wear at night. If you are riding a bicycle, be sure it has plenty of reflectors, and if possible, headlamps as well. Be especially careful when crossing the street, because sometimes drivers cannot see you in the glare of their headlights. Being outdoors at night can be dangerous, and it is best to be prepared!

COMPLETE YEAR GRADE 5

341

Writing: Supporting Sentences

A **paragraph** is a group of sentences that tell about one topic. The **topic sentence** in a paragraph usually comes first and tells the main idea of the paragraph. **Supporting sentences** follow the topic sentence and provide details about the topic.

Write at least three supporting sentences for each topic sentence below.

Example: Topic Sentence: Carly had an accident on her bike. **Supporting Sentences:** She was on her way to the store to buy some bread. A car came weaving down the road and scared her. She rode her bike off the road so the car wouldn't hit her. Now, her knee is scraped, but she's all right.

1. I've been thinking of ways I could make some more money after school.

2. In my opinion, cats (dogs, fish, etc.) make the best pets.

3. My life wa... Answers will vary. ...ger brother, older sist...

4. I'd like to live next door to a (swimming pool, video store, movie theater, etc.).

COMPLETE YEAR GRADE 5

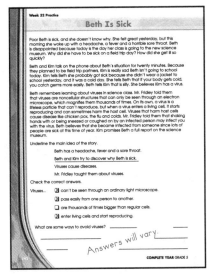

342

Beth Is Sick

Poor Beth is sick, and she doesn't know why. She felt great yesterday, but this morning she woke up with a headache, a fever and a horrible sore throat. Beth is disappointed because today is the day her class is going to the new science museum. Why did she have to be sick on a field trip day? How did she get it so quickly?

Beth and Kim talk on the phone about Beth's situation for twenty minutes. Because they planned to be field trip partners, Kim is really sad Beth isn't going to school today. Kim tells Beth she probably got sick because she didn't wear a jacket to school yesterday, and it was a cold day. She tells Beth that if your body gets cold, you catch germs more easily. Beth tells Kim that is silly. She believes Kim has a virus.

Beth remembers learning about viruses in science class. Mr. Fridley told them that viruses are noncellular structures that can only be seen through an electron microscope, which magnifies them thousands of times. On its own, a virus is a lifeless particle that can't reproduce, but when a virus enters a living cell, it starts reproducing and can sometimes harm the host cell. Viruses that harm host cells cause disease like chicken pox, the flu and colds. Mr. Fridley told them that shaking hands with or being sneezed or coughed on by an infected person may infect you with the virus. Beth believes that she became infected from someone since lots of people are sick at this time of year. Kim promises Beth a full report on the science museum.

Underline the main idea of the story.

Beth has a headache, fever and a sore throat.

<u>Beth and Kim try to discover why Beth is sick.</u>

Viruses cause diseases.

Mr. Fridley taught them about viruses.

Check the correct answers.

Viruses...
- ☒ can't be seen through an ordinary light microscope.
- ☒ pass easily from one person to another.
- ☐ are thousands of times bigger than regular cells.
- ☒ enter living cells and start reproducing.

What are some ways to avoid viruses?
Answers will vary.

COMPLETE YEAR GRADE 5

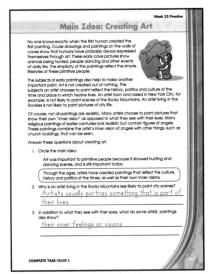

343

Main Idea: Creating Art

No one knows exactly when the first human created the first painting. Crude drawings and paintings on the walls of caves show that humans have probably always expressed themselves through art. These early cave pictures show animals being hunted, people dancing and other events of daily life. The simplicity of the paintings reflect the simple lifestyles of these primitive people.

The subjects of early paintings also help to make another important point. Art is not created out of nothing. The subjects an artist chooses to paint reflect the history, politics and culture of the time and place in which he/she lives. An artist born and raised in New York City, for example, is not likely to paint scenes of the Rocky Mountains. An artist living in the Rockies is not likely to paint pictures of city life.

Of course, not all paintings are realistic. Many artists choose to paint pictures that show their own "inner vision" as opposed to what they see with their eyes. Many religious paintings of earlier centuries look realistic but contain figures of angels. These paintings combine the artist's inner vision of angels with other things, such as church buildings, that can be seen.

Answer these questions about creating art.

1. Circle the main idea:

   Art was important to primitive people because it showed hunting and dancing scenes, and is still important today.

   (Through the ages, artists have created paintings that reflect the culture, history and politics of the times, as well as their own inner vision.)

2. Why is an artist living in the Rocky Mountains less likely to paint city scenes?
   Artists usually portray something that is part of their lives.

3. In addition to what they see with their eyes, what do some artists' paintings also show?
   their inner feelings or visions

COMPLETE YEAR GRADE 5

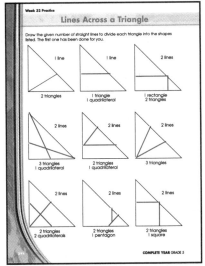

344

Lines Across a Triangle

Draw the given number of straight lines to divide each triangle into the shapes listed. The first one has been done for you.

1 line / 1 line / 2 lines
2 triangles / 1 triangle 1 quadrilateral / 1 rectangle 2 triangles

2 lines / 2 lines / 2 lines
3 triangles 1 quadrilateral / 2 triangles 1 quadrilateral / 3 triangles

2 lines / 2 lines / 2 lines
2 triangles 2 quadrilaterals / 2 triangles 1 pentagon / 2 triangles 1 square

COMPLETE YEAR GRADE 5

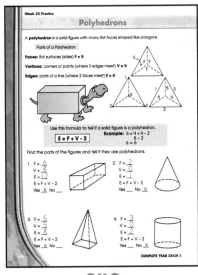

348

Polyhedrons

A **polyhedron** is a solid figure with many flat faces shaped like polygons.

Parts of a Polyhedron

Faces: flat surfaces (sides) F = 4

Vertices: corners or points (where 3 edges meet) V = 4

Edges: parts of a line (where 2 faces meet) E = 6

Use this formula to tell if a solid figure is a polyhedron.
$$E = F + V - 2$$
Example: 6 = 4 + 4 − 2
6 = 8 − 2
6 = 6

Find the parts of the figures and tell if they are polyhedrons.

1. F = 6
   V = 8
   E = 12
   E = F + V − 2
   Yes _X_ No ___

2. F = 2
   V = 1
   E = 1
   E = F + V − 2
   Yes ___ No _X_

3. F = 5
   V = 5
   E = 8
   E = F + V − 2
   Yes _X_ No ___

4. F = 3
   V = 2
   E = 2
   E = F + V − 2
   Yes ___ No _X_

COMPLETE YEAR GRADE 5

Week 33 Practice

Comprehension: "The Eagle"

Personification is a figure of speech in which human characteristics are given to an animal or object.

Example: The trees danced in the wind.

Trees do not dance; therefore, the trees are being personified.

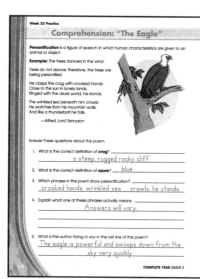

He clasps the crag with crooked hands;
Close to the sun in lonely lands,
Ringed with the azure world, he stands.

The wrinkled sea beneath him crawls;
He watches from his mountain walls,
And like a thunderbolt he falls.

—Alfred, Lord Tennyson

Answer these questions about the poem.

1. What is the correct definition of **crag**?
   a steep, rugged rocky cliff

2. What is the correct definition of **azure**? _blue_

3. Which phrases in the poem show personification?
   crooked hands, wrinkled sea . . . crawls, he stands

4. Explain what one of these phrases actually means.
   Answers will vary.

5. What is the author trying to say in the last line of the poem?
   The eagle is powerful and swoops down from the sky very quickly.

COMPLETE YEAR GRADE 5

350

Week 33 Practice

Comprehension: Epitaphs

Epitaphs are verses written on tombstones and were very popular in the past. The following epitaphs were written by unknown authors.

On a Man Named Merideth

Here lies one blown out of breath
Who lived a merry life and died a Merideth.

On a Dentist

Stranger, approach this spot with gravity;
John Brown is filling his last cavity.

On Leslie Moore

Here lies what's left
Of Leslie Moore
No Les
No more

Answer these questions about the epitaphs.

1. What does the phrase "blown out of breath" mean?
   dead—no longer breathing

2. What does the author mean when he says "and died a Merideth"?
   This is a play on words—the person's name and "merry death."

3. What cavity is John Brown filling? _the grave_

4. Write an epitaph of your own.
   Answers will vary.

COMPLETE YEAR GRADE 5

351

Week 33 Practice

Get the Facts, Max

Read the paragraphs to answer the questions below.

The islands of Aruba, Bonaire and Curaçao, sometimes known as the ABC islands, are part of the Netherlands Antilles. They lie 50 miles north off the coast of Venezuela. Three more islands, St. Eustatius, Saba and St. Martin (the northern half of which belongs to France), are approximately 500 miles northeast of the ABC islands.

Until 1949, the islands were known as the Dutch West Indies or Curaçao Territory. In 1986, Aruba separated to become a self-governing part of the Netherlands Realm.

On the island of Curaçao, most food is imported. Because it is so rocky, little farming is possible. The island is the largest and most heavily populated of the Netherlands Antilles. Its oil refineries, among the largest in the world, give its people a relatively high standard of living. Today, most people of Curaçao work in the shipping, refining or tourist industry.

Netherlands Antilles—other Facts

Area:		Capital: Willemstad
Aruba	75 square miles	
Bonaire	111 square miles	**Major languages:** Dutch,
Curaçao	171 square miles	Papiamento (a mixture of
Saba	5 square miles	Spanish, Dutch,
St. Eustatius	11 square miles	Portuguese, Carib and
St. Martin	13 square miles	English), English, Spanish

1. Name the capital of the Netherlands Antilles. _Willemstad_
2. What industry gives the people a high standard of living? _oil refinery_
3. Name the ABC islands. _Aruba, Bonaire and Curaçao_
4. What is Papiamento? _a mixture of languages_
5. Why must food be imported to Curaçao? _land is too rocky for farming_
6. Which island is smallest? _Saba_
7. Which two islands are the largest? _Bonaire and Curaçao_
8. Which island belongs in part to France? _St. Martin_
9. In what year did Aruba become self-governing? _1986_

COMPLETE YEAR GRADE 5

352

Week 33 Practice

Advantages and Disadvantages

As in the comparison/contrast essay, it is easiest to put all of the advantages in one paragraph and the disadvantages in another paragraph.

Write an essay in response to the prompt.

Writing Prompt: Think about what a society would be like if all people had the same skin tone, hair color, eye color, height and weight. What would the benefits of living in such a society be? Would there be any disadvantages? What would they be?

Answers will vary.

When you finish writing, reread your essay. Use this checklist to help make corrections.

☐ My essay makes sense.
☐ I used correct spelling, grammar and punctuation.
☐ I answered the writing prompt.
☐ I have varied sentence length.

COMPLETE YEAR GRADE 5

353

Week 33 Practice

Tables

Organizing data into tables makes it easier to compare numbers. As evident in the example, putting many numbers in a paragraph is confusing. When the same numbers are organized in a table, you can compare numbers at a glance. Tables can be arranged several ways and still be easy to read and understand.

Example: Money spent on groceries:
Family A: week 1 — $68.50; week 2 — $72.25; week 3 — $67.00; week 4 — $74.50.
Family B: week 1 — $42.25; week 2 — $47.50; week 3 — $50.25; week 4 — $53.50.

	Week 1	Week 2	Week 3	Week 4
Family A	$68.50	$72.25	$67.00	$74.50
Family B	$42.25	$47.50	$50.25	$53.50

Complete the following exercises.

1. Finish the table below. Then answer the questions. Data: Steve weighs 230 lb. and is 6 ft. 2 in. tall. George weighs 218 lb. and is 6 ft. 3 in. tall. Chuck weighs 225 lb. and is 6 ft. 1 in. tall. Henry weighs 205 lb. and is 6 ft. tall.

	Henry	George	Chuck	Steve
Weight	205 lbs.	218 lbs.	225 lbs.	230 lbs.
Height	6 ft.	6 ft. 3 in.	6 ft. 1 in.	6 ft. 2 in.

a. Who is tallest? _George_   b. Who weighs the least? _Henry_

2. On another sheet of paper, prepare 2 tables comparing the amount of money made by 3 booths at the school carnival this year and last year. In the first table, write the names of the games in the left-hand column (like **Family A** and **Family B** in the example). In the second table (using the same data), write the years in the left-hand column. Here is the data: fish pond—this year $15.60, last year $13.50; bean-bag toss—this year $13.45, last year $10.25; ring toss—this year $23.80, last year $18.80. After you complete both tables, answer the following questions.

a. Which booth made the most money this year?
   ring toss

b. Which booth made the biggest improvement from last year to this year?
   ring toss

COMPLETE YEAR GRADE 5

354

Week 33 Practice

Charting the Weather

For four months, the students in Ms. Forecaster's class charted the sunny, partly sunny and cloudy days. The following chart shows their findings to the nearest tenth.

MONTH	SUNNY	PARTLY SUNNY	CLOUDY
October	13.4	12.8	4.8
November	7	13.1	9.9
December	6.3	11	13.7
January	8.4	16.7	5.9

1. How many more sunny days did January have than December? _2.1 days_

2. In November, how many more cloudy days were there than sunny days? _2.9 days_

3. How many more partly sunny days were there than sunny days in January? _8.3 days_

4. What is the difference in days between the month with the most cloudy days and the month that had the fewest cloudy days? _8.9 days_

5. Which month had the most sunny days? How many more sunny days did it have than the month with the second most? Which came in second? _October/5 days January_

6. Which month had the most cloudy days? Which month had the fewest cloudy days? How many total cloudy days were there in these four months? _December/October 34.3 days_

Extension: Find the total number of sunny, partly sunny and cloudy days in these four months. Then, find the average number of days for each type of weather.

Sunny: 35.1 days
Partly Sunny: 53.6 days
Cloudy: 34.3 days

Averages
Sunny: 8.8 days
Partly Sunny: 13.4 days
Cloudy: 8.6 days

COMPLETE YEAR GRADE 5

355

Answer Key

Bar Graphs

Another way to organize information is a **bar graph**. The bar graph in the example compares the number of students in 4 elementary schools. Each bar stands for 1 school. You can easily see that School A has the most students and School C has the least. The numbers along the left show how many students attend each school.

Example:

Complete the following exercises.

1. This bar graph will show how many calories are in 1 serving of 4 kinds of cereal. Draw the bars the correct height and label each with the name of the cereal. After completing the bar graph, answer the questions. Data: Korn Kernals—150 calories; Oat Floats—160 calories; Rite Rice—110 calories; Sugar Shapes—200 calories.

   A. Which cereal is the best to eat if you're trying to lose weight? __Rite Rice__

   B. Which cereal has nearly the same number of calories as Oat Floats?
   __Korn Kernals__

2. On another sheet of paper, draw your own graph, showing the number of TV commercials in 1 week for each of the 4 cereals in the graph above. After completing the graph, answer the questions. Data: Oat Floats—27 commercials; Rite Rice—15; Sugar Shapes—35; Korn Kernals—28.

   A. Which cereal is most heavily advertised? __Sugar Shapes__

   B. What similarities do you notice between the graph of calories and the graph of TV commercials? __Sugar Shapes is highest in sugar and advertisements.__

COMPLETE YEAR GRADE 5

356

Dog and Jog Graphs

Answer the questions using the graphs indicated.

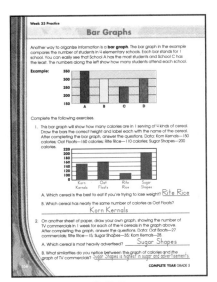

Dog Owners at Lincoln Elementary School

1. How many students own Great Danes at Lincoln Elementary School?
   __70__

2. Which breed of dog is owned by the fewest students?
   __Toy Poodle__

3. Which breed is owned by the most students?
   __Golden Retriever__

4. How many students own Doberman pinschers?
   __80__

5. How many more students own German shepherds than collies?
   __50__

1. What class jogged the most during a one-week period?
   __Ms. Lee's__

2. Which class jogged the most miles during this four-week period? What was the difference between classes?
   __Mr. Halverson's, 11__

3. Which week had the greatest range between the two classes?
   __2__

4. Which week had the smallest range?
   __4__

5. What was the range for Mr. Halverson's class during these four weeks?
   __5.5 to 8.5__

Distance Jogged During P.E.

COMPLETE YEAR GRADE 5

357

Graphs

Complete the graph using the information in the table.

Student	Books read in February
Sue	20
Joe	8
Peter	12
Cindy	16
Dean	15
Carol	8

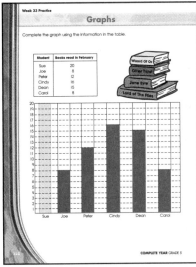

COMPLETE YEAR GRADE 5

358

"Who" Clauses

A **clause** is a group of words with a subject and a verb. When the subject of two sentences is the same person or people, the sentences can sometimes be combined with a "who" clause.

Examples:

Mindy likes animals. Mindy feeds the squirrels.
Mindy, **who likes animals**, feeds the squirrels.

A "who" clause is set off from the rest of the sentence with commas. Combine the pairs of sentences, using "who" clauses.

1. Teddy was late to school. Teddy was sorry later.
   __Teddy, who was late to school, was sorry later.__

2. Our principal is retiring. Our principal will be 65 this year.
   __Our principal, who will be 65 this year, is retiring.__

3. Michael won the contest. Michael will receive an award.
   __Michael, who won the contest, will receive an award.__

4. Charlene lives next door. Charlene has three cats.
   __Charlene, who lives next door, has three cats.__

5. Burt drew that picture. Burt takes art lessons.
   __Burt, who drew that picture, takes art lessons.__

6. Marta was elected class president. Marta gave a speech.
   __Marta, who was elected class president, gave a speech.__

7. Amy broke her arm. Amy has to wear a cast for 6 weeks.
   __Amy, who broke her arm, has to wear a cast for 6 weeks.__

8. Dr. Bank fixed my tooth. He said it would feel better soon.
   __Dr. Bank, who fixed my tooth, said it would feel better soon.__

COMPLETE YEAR GRADE 5

360

"Which" Clauses

When the subject of two sentences is the same thing or things, the sentences can sometimes be combined with a "which" clause.

Examples:

The guppy was first called "the millions fish." The guppy was later named after Reverend Robert Guppy in 1866.
The guppy, which was first called "the millions fish," was later named after Reverend Robert Guppy in 1866.

A "which" clause is set off from the rest of the sentence with commas. Combine the pairs of sentences using "which" clauses.

1. __Guppies, which also used to be called rainbow fish, were brought to Germany in 1908.__

2. __The male guppy, which is about 1 inch long, is smaller than the female.__

3. __The guppies' colors, which range from red to violet, are brighter in the males.__

4. __Baby guppies, which hatch from eggs inside the mothers bodies, are born alive.__

5. __The young, which are usually born at night, are called "fry."__

6. __Female guppies, which have 2 to 50 fry at one time, sometimes try to eat their fry!__

7. __These fish, which have been studied by scientists, actually like dirty water.__

8. __Wild guppies, which eat mosquito eggs, help control the mosquito population.__

COMPLETE YEAR GRADE 5

361

"That" Clauses

When the subject of two sentences is the same thing or things, the sentences can sometimes be combined with a "that" clause. We use **that** instead of **which** when the clause is very important in the sentence.

Examples:

The store is near our house. The store was closed.
The store **that is near our house** was closed.

The words **that is near our house** are very important in the combined sentence. They tell the reader which store was closed. A "that" clause is not set off from the rest of the sentence with commas.

Examples:

Pete's store is near our house. Pete's store was closed.
Pete's store, which is near our house, was closed.

The words **which is near our house** are not important to the meaning of the combined sentence. The words **Pete's store** already told us which store was closed.

Combine the pairs of sentences using "that" clauses.

1. The dog lives next door. The dog chased me.
   __The dog that lives next door chased me.__

2. The bus was taking us to the game. The bus had a flat tire.
   __The bus that was taking us to the game had a flat tire.__

3. The fence is around the school. The fence is painted yellow.
   __The fence that is around the school is painted yellow.__

4. The notebook had my homework in it. The notebook is lost.
   __The notebook that had my homework in it is lost.__

5. A letter came today. The letter was from Mary.
   __A letter that was from Mary came today.__

6. The lamp was fixed yesterday. The lamp doesn't work today.
   __The lamp that was fixed yesterday doesn't work today.__

7. The lake is by our cabin. The lake is filled with fish.
   __The lake that is by our cabin is filled with fish.__

COMPLETE YEAR GRADE 5

362

Answer Key

363

Combining Sentences

Not every pair of sentences can be combined with "who," "which" or "that" clauses. These sentences can be combined in other ways, either with a conjunction or by renaming the subject.

Examples:

Tim couldn't go to sleep. Todd was sleeping soundly.
Tim couldn't go to sleep, **but** Todd was sleeping soundly.

The zoo keeper fed the baby ape. A crowd gathered to watch.
When the zoo keeper fed the baby ape, a crowd gathered to watch.

Combine each pair of sentences using "who," "which" or "that" clauses, by using a conjunction or by renaming the subject.

1. The box slipped off the truck. The box was filled with bottles.
   The box that was filled with bottles slipped off the truck.

2. Carolyn is our scout leader. Carolyn taught us a new game.
   Carolyn, who is our scout leader, taught us a new game.

3. The girl is 8 years old. The girl called the emergency number when her grandmother fell.
   The girl, who is 8 years old, called the emergency number when her grandmother fell.

4. The meatloaf is ready to eat. The salad isn't made yet.
   The meatloaf is ready to eat, but the salad isn't made yet.

5. The rain poured down. The rain canceled our picnic.
   The rain poured down and canceled our picnic.

6. The sixth grade class went on a field trip. The school was much quieter.
   When the sixth grade class went on a field trip, the school was much quieter.

COMPLETE YEAR GRADE 5

364

Parallel Structure

Parts of a sentence are parallel when they "match" grammatically and structurally.

Faulty parallelism occurs when the parts of a sentence do not match grammatically and structurally.

For sentences to be parallel, all parts of a sentence—including the verbs, nouns and phrases—must match. This means that, in most cases, verbs should be in the same tense.

Examples:

Correct: She liked running, jumping and swinging outdoors.

Incorrect: She liked running, jumping and to swing outdoors.

In the correct sentence, all three of the actions the girl liked to do end in **ing**. In the incorrect sentence, they do not.

Rewrite the sentences so all elements are parallel.
The first one has been done for you.

1. Politicians like making speeches and also to shake hands.
   Politicians like making speeches and shaking hands.

2. He liked singing, acting and to perform in general.
   He liked singing, acting and performing in general.

3. The cake had icing, sprinkles and also has small candy hearts.
   The cake had icing, sprinkles and small candy hearts.

4. The drink was cold, frosty and also is a thirst-quencher.
   The drink was cold, frosty and a thirst-quencher.

5. She was asking when we would arrive, and I told her.
   She asked when we would arrive, and I told her.

6. Liz felt like shouting, singing and to jump.
   Liz felt like shouting, singing and jumping.

COMPLETE YEAR GRADE 5

365

Sentences

A simple sentence has a complete subject and predicate.
Example: The little brown rabbit hopped all around the yard.

A compound sentence has two or more simple sentences joined together.
Example: Patrick tried to pick the rabbit up, but it quickly hopped away.

A complex sentence contains one independent clause and one or more dependent clauses.
Example: After several tries, Patrick finally caught the frightened rabbit.

Label the sentences below as simple, compound or complex.

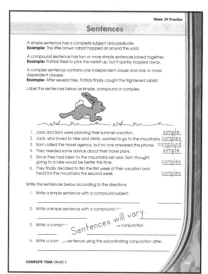

1. Jack and Sam were planning their summer vacation. *simple*
2. Jack, who loved to hike and climb, wanted to go to the mountains. *complex*
3. Sam called the travel agency, but no one answered the phone. *compound*
4. They needed some advice about their travel plans. *simple*
5. Since they had been to the mountains last year, Sam thought going to a lake would be better this time. *complex*
6. They finally decided to fish the first week of their vacation and head for the mountains the second week. *complex*

Write the sentences below according to the directions.

1. Write a simple sentence with a compound subject.

2. Write a simple sentence with a compound _____
   Sentences will vary.

3. Write a compound _____ conjunction.

4. Write a complex sentence using the subordinating conjunction after.

COMPLETE YEAR GRADE 5

366

Picture Graphs

Newspapers and textbooks often use pictures in graphs instead of bars. Each picture stands for a certain number of objects. Half a picture means half the number. The picture graph in the example indicates the number of games each team won. The Astros won 7 games, so they have $3\frac{1}{2}$ balls.

Example:

Games Won				
Astros	⚾	⚾	⚾	◗
Orioles	⚾	⚾		
Bluebirds	⚾	⚾	⚾	⚾
Sluggers	◗			

(1 ball = 2 games)

Complete the following exercises.

Finish this picture graph, showing the number of students who have dogs in 4 sixth-grade classes. Draw simple dots in the graph, letting each drawing stand for 2 dogs. Data: Class 1—12 dogs; Class 2—16 dogs; Class 3—22 dogs; Class 4—12 dogs. After completing the graph, answer the questions.

Dogs Owned by Students	
Class 1	●●●●●●
Class 2	●●●●●●●●
Class 3	●●●●●●●●●●●
Class 4	●●●●●●

(One dog drawing = 2 students' dogs)

1. Why do you think newspapers use picture graphs? *Answers will vary.*
   It simplifies information and is easier to read.

2. Would picture graphs be appropriate to show exact number of dogs living in America? Why or why not?
   No; there are too many!

COMPLETE YEAR GRADE 5

367

Circle Graphs

Circle graphs are useful in showing how something is divided into parts. The circle graph in the example shows how Carly spent her $10 allowance. Each section is a fraction of her whole allowance. For example, the movie tickets section is $\frac{1}{2}$ of the circle, showing that she spent $\frac{1}{2}$ of her allowance, $5, on movie tickets.

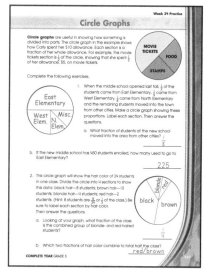

Complete the following exercises.

1. When the middle school opened last fall, $\frac{1}{2}$ of the students came from East Elementary, $\frac{1}{4}$ came from West Elementary, $\frac{1}{8}$ came from North Elementary and the remaining students moved into the town from other cities. Make a circle graph showing these proportions. Label each section. Then answer the questions.

   a. What fraction of students at the new school moved into the area from other cities? $\frac{1}{8}$

   b. If the new middle school has 450 students enrolled, how many used to go to East Elementary? *225*

2. This circle graph will show the hair color of 24 students in one class. Divide the circle into 4 sections to show this data: black hair—8 students; brown hair—10 students; blonde hair—4 students; red hair—2 students. (Hint: 8 students are $\frac{8}{24}$ or $\frac{1}{3}$ of the class.) Be sure to label each section by hair color. Then answer the questions.

   a. Looking at your graph, what fraction of the class is the combined group of blonde- and red-haired students? $\frac{1}{4}$

   b. Which two fractions of hair color combine to total half the class? *red/brown*

COMPLETE YEAR GRADE 5

368

Circle Graph

Ned earns an allowance of $10.00 each week. He created this circle graph on his computer to show his parents how he spends the money. Refer to the graph to answer each question below.

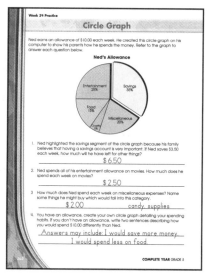

Ned's Allowance

1. Ned highlighted the savings segment of the circle graph because his family believes that having a savings account is very important. If Ned saves $3.50 each week, how much will he have left for other things? *$6.50*

2. Ned spends all of his entertainment allowance on movies. How much does he spend each week on movies? *$2.50*

3. How much does Ned spend each week on miscellaneous expenses? Name some things he might buy which would fall into this category. *$2.00 candy, supplies*

4. You have an allowance, create your own circle graph detailing your spending habits. If you don't have an allowance, write two sentences describing how you would spend $10.00 differently than Ned.
   Answers may include: I would save more money.
   I would spend less on food.

COMPLETE YEAR GRADE 5

444

Answer Key

370

Week 35 Practice

Using a Thesaurus

A **thesaurus** is a type of reference book that lists words in alphabetical order followed by their synonyms and antonyms. **Synonyms** are words that mean the same. **Antonyms** are words that mean the opposite.

A thesaurus is an excellent tool for finding "just the right word." It is also a valuable resource for finding a variety of synonyms and/or antonyms to make your writing livelier.

Each main entry in a thesaurus consists of a word followed by the word's part of speech, its definition, an example, a list of related words and other information.

Here is a typical entry in a thesaurus, with an explanation of terms below:

SLOW

ADJ **SYN** deliberate, dilatory, laggard, leisurely, unhasty, unhurried **REL** lateness, limited, measured, slowish, steady, unhurrying, slowfooted, plodding, pokey, straggling, snail-like **IDIOM** as slow as molasses in January; as slow as a turtle **CON** blitz, quick, rapid, swift **ANT** fast

ADJ means adjective
CON means contrasted words
SYN means synonym
ANT means antonym
REL means related words
idiom means a common phrase that is not literal

Use the thesaurus entry to answer the questions.
1. What is the antonym listed for **slow**? _fast_
2. How many contrasting words are listed for **slow**? _4_
3. How many synonyms are listed for **slow**? _6_
4. What is **slow** compared to in the two idioms listed? _molasses, turtle_
5. What is the last related word listed for **slow**? _snail-like_

COMPLETE YEAR GRADE 5

371

Week 35 Practice

Using a Thesaurus to Find Synonyms

A thesaurus can help you find synonyms.

Example: Sample Answers:
FIND:
VERB **SYN** locate, discover, detect, uncover, see, etc.
Use a thesaurus. Replace each word in bold with a synonym.

1. My father does not like our **artificial** Christmas tree.
fake
2. The **fabulous** home sat on a large hill overlooking a wooded ravine.
terrific
3. My dog is allowed to be **loose** if someone is home.
free
4. A **peaceful** rally was held to bring attention to the needs of the homeless.
nonviolent
5. The artist completed his **sketch** of the girl.
drawing
6. The **timid** boy could not bring himself to speak to the man at the counter.
shy
7. My family is cutting down the **timber** at the back of our property.
trees
8. Her necklace was very **attractive**.
pretty
9. The girl looked hopelessly at her **clothes** and moaned that she had nothing to wear.
apparel
10. The team's **feat** of winning 20 games in a row was amazing.
accomplishment

COMPLETE YEAR GRADE 5

372

Week 35 Practice

Using a Thesaurus to Find Antonyms

Antonyms are words that mean the opposite. Antonyms can also be found in a thesaurus. They are identified by the abbreviation **ANT**.

Examples: Sample Answers:
FOUND:
VERB **ANT** misplaced, gone, lost, missing, mislaid, etc.
RIDDLE:
NOUN **ANT** key, solution, answer, etc.
ANCIENT:
ADJECTIVE **ANT** new, recent, current, etc.

Use a thesaurus to replace each word in bold with an antonym.

dry 1. Today's weather will undoubtedly be very **humid**.
take 2. Can you **give** my sister a napkin?
complimented 3. The man **insulted** me by laughing at my artwork.
strict 4. I thought the rules for the classroom were too **lax**.
painless 5. The broken leg was quite **painful**.
delay 6. We made great **progress** last night on the parade float.
penalty 7. The girl received a **reward** for returning the lost wallet.
combine 8. The teacher asked us to **separate** the types of art brushes.
extravagant 9. The home was decorated in a **simple** manner.
relaxed 10. They became very **tense** during the earthquake.
yesterday 11. Mr. Kurtzman gave us a math test **today**.
valleys 12. My father loves hiking in the **hills**.
old 13. Stephen ran over my **new** red bike.

COMPLETE YEAR GRADE 5

373

Week 35 Practice

The Right Stuff

Circle the resource book you would use to find . . .

1. A recipe for baking homemade bread.
encyclopedia (cookbook) The Life of a Beaver
2. A description of how beavers make dams.
almanac (The Life of a Beaver) The Guinness Book of World Records
3. A map of the United Kingdom.
thesaurus (world atlas) The Guinness Book of World Records
4. The ingredients for Turkish delight.
The Life of a Beaver   world atlas   (cookbook)
5. Information about the author, C. S. Lewis.
almanac (encyclopedia) Guidebook for Art Instructors
6. The name of the world's most massive dam.
(The Guinness Book of World Records) dictionary thesaurus
7. The oldest words in the English language.
almanac   atlas (The Guinness Book of World Records)
8. Another word for "trouble."
(thesaurus) atlas cookbook
9. Why a beaver slaps its tail.
dictionary (The Life of a Beaver) atlas
10. The pronunciation of "courtier."
The Hobbit (dictionary) almanac
11. What camphor is used for.
(dictionary) The Life of a Beaver   thesaurus

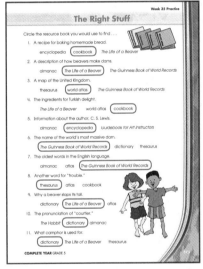

COMPLETE YEAR GRADE 5

374

Week 35 Practice

Making Inferences: Encyclopedias

Read each question. Then check the answer for where you would find the information in an encyclopedia.

1. If you wanted to grow avocado pits on a windowsill, under which topic should you look?
☐ window ☒ avocado ☐ food
2. To find information about the Cuban revolution of 1969, which topic should you look up?
☒ Cuba ☐ revolution ☐ 1969
3. Information about Rudolph Diesel, the inventor of the Diesel engine, would be found under which topic?
☐ engine ☒ Diesel ☐ inventor
4. If you wanted to find out if the giant panda of China was really a bear or a raccoon, what should you look up?
☐ bear ☐ China ☒ panda
5. Under which topic should you look for information on how to plant a vegetable garden?
☐ plant ☐ vegetable ☒ gardening
6. If you wanted to write a report on both wild and pet gerbils, under which topic should you look for information?
☐ animal ☒ gerbil ☐ pet
7. To find out if World War I was fought only on European soil, which topic should you look up?
☐ Europe ☒ World War I ☐ war
8. Under which topic should you look for information on how bats guide themselves in the dark?
☐ guide ☐ flying ☒ bat
9. The distance of all the planets from the sun might be found under which topic?
☒ planets ☐ sky ☐ distance

COMPLETE YEAR GRADE 5

375

Week 35 Practice

Double Trouble

Fill in the blanks with the correct definition number for each underlined word.

Example: _3_ I was covered with <u>pitch</u> after climbing the pine tree.

winding	1. having bends or curves
	2. the act of turning something around a central core
wolf	1. to gulp down
	2. a large carnivorous member of the dog family
pitch	1. to sell or persuade
	2. to throw a ball from the mound to the batter
	3. a resin that comes from the sap of pine trees

_1_ 1. Do girls' clubs <u>pitch</u> cookies?
_2_ 2. We are <u>winding</u> the top's string tightly.
_2_ 3. The adult <u>wolf</u> returned to her lair.
_2_ 4. Red didn't <u>pitch</u> after the fourth inning.
_1_ 5. The Mather family had a <u>winding</u> driveway.
_1_ 6. The young ball player <u>wolfed</u> down his lunch and left.

choke	1. to strangle
	2. to bring the hands up on the bat
hitch	1. obstacle
	2. to fasten or tie temporarily
windup	1. the swing of the pitcher's arm just before the pitch
	2. a concluding part

_2_ 1. We <u>hitched</u> the mule to the cart.
_2_ 2. Tip would not <u>choke</u> up on his bat.
_1_ 3. Paul wished to play, but there was just one <u>hitch</u>.
_2_ 4. The program's <u>windup</u> was filled with more of Joe's record hits.
_1_ 5. Mom was afraid the dog would <u>choke</u> itself on its leash.
_1_ 6. He has a great <u>windup</u> and curve ball.

COMPLETE YEAR GRADE 5

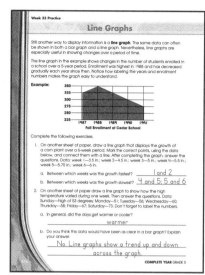

Week 35 Practice

Line Graphs

Still another way to display information is a **line graph**. The same data can often be shown in both a bar graph and a line graph. Nevertheless, line graphs are especially useful in showing changes over a period of time.

The line graph in the example shows changes in the number of students enrolled in a school over a 5-year period. Enrollment was highest in 1988 and has decreased gradually each year since then. Notice how labeling the years and enrollment numbers makes the graph easy to understand.

Example:

Fall Enrollment at Cedar School

Complete the following exercises.

1. On another sheet of paper, draw a line graph that displays the growth of a corn plant over a 6-week period. Mark the correct points, using the data below, and connect them with a line. After completing the graph, answer the questions. Data: week 1—3.5 in.; week 2—4.5 in.; week 3—5 in.; week 4—5.5 in.; week 5—5.75 in.; week 6—6 in.

   a. Between which weeks was the growth fastest? **1 and 2**

   b. Between which weeks was the growth slowest? **4 and 5; 5 and 6**

2. On another sheet of paper draw a line graph to show how the high temperature varied during one week. Then answer the questions. Data: Sunday—high of 53 degrees; Monday—51; Tuesday—56; Wednesday—60; Thursday—58; Friday—67; Saturday—73. Don't forget to label the numbers.

   a. In general, did the days get warmer or cooler? **warmer**

   b. Do you think this data would have been as clear in a bar graph? Explain your answer. **No. Line graphs show a trend up and down across the graph.**

COMPLETE YEAR GRADE 5

376

Week 35 Practice

Graphs

Graphs have a vertical axis and a horizontal axis. The axes are labeled to show what is being compared.

Average Number of Rainy Days in Miami, Florida

Use the data plotted on the graph to answer the following questions.

1. What is the title of the graph? **Average Number of Rainy Days in Miami, Florida**

2. How is the vertical axis labeled? **Rainy Days**

3. What is contained in the horizontal axis? **Months of the year**

4. Which month had the greatest number of rainy days? **September**

5. Which two-month period shows the greatest change in the number of rainy days? **October to November**

6. Which month was the driest? **February**

Use the graph to fill in the blanks below.

7. range: **20** 8. mean: **12.16** 9. median: **8.75** 10. mode: **7.5**

COMPLETE YEAR GRADE 5

377

Week 35 Practice

Graphing Data

Complete the following exercises.

1. Use the following information to create a bar graph.

Cities	Population (in 1,000's)
Dover	20
Newton Falls	12
Springdale	25
Hampton	10
Riverside	5

2. Study the data and create a line graph showing the number of baskets Jonah scored during the season.

Game 1—10
Game 2—7
Game 3—11
Game 4—10
Game 5—9
Game 6—5
Game 7—9

Fill in the blanks.
a. High game: **3**
b. Low game: **6**
c. Average baskets per game: **8.7**

3. Study the graph, then answer the questions.

   a. Which flavor is the most popular? **chocolate**

   b. Which flavor sold the least? **Blue Moon**

   c. What decimal represents the two highest sellers? **0.75**

   d. Which flavor had 1/10 of the sales? **vanilla**

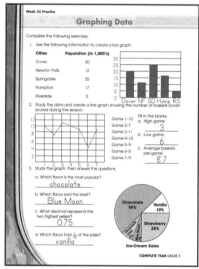

Ice-Cream Sales

COMPLETE YEAR GRADE 5

378

Week 36 Practice

Comprehension: "The Lark and the Wren"

"Goodnight, Sir Wren!" said the little lark.
"The daylight fades; it will soon be dark.
I've sung my hymn to the parting day.
So now I fly to my quiet glen
In yonder meadow—Goodnight, Wren!"

"Goodnight, poor Lark," said the haughty wren,
With a flick of his wing toward his happy friend.
"I also go to my rest profound
But not to sleep on the cold, damp ground.
The fittest place for a bird like me
Is the topmost bough of a tall pine tree."

Use context clues for these definitions.

1. What is the correct definition of **hymn**?
   ☐ whisper   ☒ song   ☐ opposite of her

2. What is the correct definition of **yonder**?
   ☒ distant   ☐ mountaintop   ☐ seaside

3. What is the correct definition of **haughty**?
   ☐ happy   ☐ friendly   ☒ pompous

4. What is the correct definition of **profound**?
   ☐ restless   ☒ deep   ☐ uncomfortable

5. What is the correct definition of **bough**?
   ☐ to bend over   ☐ tree roots   ☒ tree branch

6. Write another verse of the poem. **Answers will vary.**

COMPLETE YEAR GRADE 5

380

Week 36 Practice

Comprehension: Proverbs

Proverbs are bits of advice for daily life. The following proverbs were written by Benjamin Franklin in 1732. They were published in *Poor Richard's Almanack*.

1. Keep conscience clear,
   Then never fear.

2. Little strokes
   Fell great oaks.

3. From a slip of foot you may soon recover,
   But a slip of the tongue you may never get over.

4. Doing an injury puts you below your enemy;
   Revenging one makes you but even with him;
   Forgiving it sets you above him.

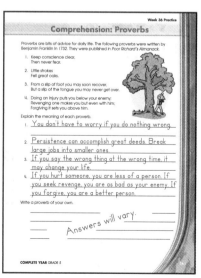

Explain the meaning of each proverb.

1. **You don't have to worry if you do nothing wrong.**

2. **Persistence can accomplish great deeds. Break large jobs into smaller ones.**

3. **If you say the wrong thing at the wrong time, it may change your life.**

4. **If you hurt someone, you are less of a person. If you seek revenge, you are as bad as your enemy. If you forgive, you are a better person.**

Write a proverb of your own.

Answers will vary.

COMPLETE YEAR GRADE 5

381

Week 36 Practice

The Sign of the Beaver

Read the following sentences. Based on context, write a definition for each bold word. Then, look up the definitions and circle yes if you were correct. If you were not correct, change your answer.

1. ". . . when his rage died down, that he felt a **prickle** of fear."
   Prickle means _____ yes

2. ". . . he saw the sunlight glinted through the **chinks** on the roof."
   Chinks means _____ yes

3. ". . . but he thought he'd rather have the **pesky** insects himself."
   Pesky means _____ yes

4. "Matt sat **pondering** the strange idea."
   Pondering means _____ yes

5. "He strutted and pran..."
   Contorts... _____ yes

6. "Now **wa**...good to pay for gun."
   Wampum means _____ yes

7. "**Warily**, he made his way through the brush."
   Warily means _____ yes

8. "The brown eyes looked up at the Indian boy with **admiration**."
   Admiration means _____ yes

9. ". . . they **wielded** their bats with no need to each other's heads. . ."
   Wielded means _____ yes

10. "Matt forced himself to eat **sparingly** of these things."
    Sparingly means _____ yes

Answers will vary.

COMPLETE YEAR GRADE 5

382

Answer Key

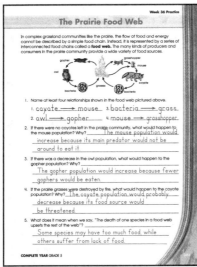

383

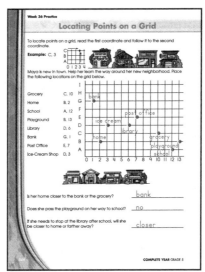

384

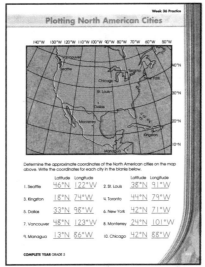

385

Answer Key

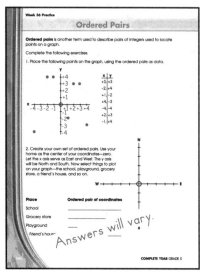

386

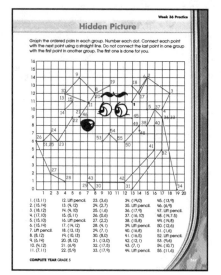

387

Plotting Graphs

A graph with horizontal and vertical number lines can show the location of certain points. The horizontal number line is called the **x axis**, and the vertical number line is called the **y axis**. Two numbers, called the **x coordinate** and the **y coordinate**, show where a point is on the graph.

The first coordinate, x, tells how many units to the right or left of 0 the point is located. On the example graph, point A is +2, two units to the right of 0.

The second coordinate, y, tells how many units above or below 0 the point is located. On the example, point A is –3, three units below 0.

Thus, the coordinates of A are +2, –3. The coordinates of B are –3, +2. (Notice the order of the coordinates.) The coordinates of C are +3, +1; and D, –2, –2.

Study the example. Then answer these questions about the graph below.

1. What towns are at these coordinates?

+1, +3   Patterson
+1, –3   Harlow
–4, +1   Stewart
–2, –3   Clinton
–3, –2   Weston
–3, +3   Hillsville

2. What are the coordinates of these towns?

Hampton   –2, +1
Wooster   +3, +2
Beachwood   +2, –4
Middletown   +1, –1
Kirby   –4, –1
Arbor   +3, –2

COMPLETE YEAR GRADE 5

388